Origins and History of Jats and Other Allied Nomadic Tribes of India

900 B.C.—1947 A.D.

B.S. Nijjar

ATLANTIC

PUBLISHERS & DISTRIBUTORS (P) LTD

Published by
ATLANTIC
PUBLISHERS & DISTRIBUTORS (P) LTD
7/22, Ansari Road, Darya Ganj, New Delhi-110002
Phones : +91-11-40775252, 40775214, 23273880, 23275880
Fax: +91-11-23285873
Web: www.atlanticbooks.com
E-mail: orders@atlanticbooks.com

Printed & bound in India by Atlantic Print Services

Preface

This book deals with the origin and history of Jats and other allied nomadic tribes of the Panjab from 900 B.C. to 1947 A.D. Jats, Rajputs, Ahirs, Gujjars, Baloches and Pathans are the descendants of these foreign nomadic tribes such as Scythians, Abhiras, Huns, Yueh-Ches, Kushans, and Turks respectively, who invaded India, one after the other, for many centuries, beginning the 7th century B.C. All of these nomadic tribes were inhabitants of Siberia, Eastern Europe and Western China. They entered India as invaders but ultimately, they assimilated into the Indian civilisation, embraced its religions and peacefully settled in India. Today, they are an inseparable part of Indian society which is called the melting pot of several cultures, communities, races and religions.

I am certainly at a loss to understand why, almost all the anthropologists, who tried their pens to write dynastic histories of the people of the Panjab (900 B.C. to 1947 A.D.), did not include the accounts of the Scheduled Classes (Dalits), namely Harijans, Chamars, etc. who are truly the descendants of these invading hordes like other people of India? All of them have the same characteristics of the so-called privileged classes. Since 1947, after the achievement of India's independence, they got an opportunity of equal rights in every sphere of Indian life, with the result that some of them have gone ahead of their fellows, in the political field, science, technology, army, medicine, engineering, agriculture, executive, judiciary, sports, and have produced top personalities, like Baba Saheb Ambedkar, K. R. Narayanan, Sardar Boota Singh, Sardar Beant Singh, and Sardar Kehar Singh the martyrs and many more. They have the same ferocity, abilities, enterprising capabilities, and hence should not be addressed with derogatory epithets like, Harijans, Scheduled Classes or Dalits, etc.

Primarily endogamous communities calling themselves or known as Jatt, Jat, Getae or Zutt, lived predominantly in large parts of northern and north-western India and in southern and eastern area, now in Pakistan, as sedentary farmers or nomadic pastoralists. In certain areas they tend to call themselves Jats, Ahirs, Gujjars, Rajputs, Baloches and Pathans. Most of these tribes are integrated as castes into the locally prevalent caste systems.

The book brings forth various facets of origins and history of all the above classes. References have been painstakingly collected from various authentic sources. It will be highly useful for students, teachers, researchers and historians, etc. Common readers interested in knowing about the origins and history of Jats and other nomadic tribes of India will also find it interesting and informative.

B.S. Nijjar

Contents

Contents

Origin and History of Scythians and Other Allied Nomadic Tribes of India

(Jats, Ahirs, Gujars, Rajputs, Baloches and Pathans)

1

THE SCYTHIANS, FIERCE HORSEMEN OF THE STEPPES[1]

"Among the mounted nomads of the Russian Plains and shadowy tribe rode supreme for a time: The Scythians. Barbarous even by the standards of their own epoch, they strangled scores of their own people in grim rituals. For centuries, they were Europe's chief guard against the Mongol hordes of the East. In, the end, these brutal warriors rode out of history as they had entered it, without a word. For they had no writing. All they left were footnotes in Greek history and some of the finest gold art in the world"[2].

DERIVATION

Scythian (derivation unknown) has been known variously:

A nomad tribe inhabiting the steppes north of the Black Sea from about the 7th to the 1st century B.C.[3] This tribe comprises the various peoples in and around the steppes that it had subjugated and any barbarous, especially a nomad, from the north-east quadrant of the world. Later geographers, *e.g.* Ptolemy[4], unwilling to drop the name, found a place far it in north Asia, but common usage still connected it with the Black Sea.

The Byzantines[5] called new invaders the Goths[6] and Russians by the classical name of Scythians[7].

ETHNIC ORIGIN OF THE SCYTHS

The Scythians and Sarmatians[8] used to be regarded as the ancestors of the Slavs; these are rather to be found among the north-west neighbours, the Neuri[9], the northern tribes adjoining being probably Finns. Niebhr, and after him Neumann, struck by the many detailed resemblances in custom, took the Scyths to be Mongols or Turko-Tatars. Millenhoff declared them, on the basis of the few names and words preserved, to be Iranians. No doubt Iranians formed the great bulk of the steppe population before the great migrations; this is proven by the foreign names in Greek inscriptions from Olbia[10] and Tanais[11], most of which can be explained from the Iranian language of the Ossetes, a people now confined to the Central Caucasus, but undoubtedly a remnant of the Sarmatians[12]. But it looks as, if in the true Scyth dominant caste, there was an element similar to the Huns, early Turks and the like; this type is suggested by Hippocrates[13] by 5th century B.C. Greek terracottas of Sacae from Memphis, showing that the Mongoloid type was already not confined to the extreme north-east of Asia, and by certain representations of natives found in Solokha[14]. These all have beards, but this feature is quickly introduced by any crossing with Iranian blood. If the rulers were non-Aryans, it would explain why many words, *e.g.* the god names do not lend themselves to Iranian interpretation, though indeed no suggestions are very convincing. Similar customs too are mostly the product of similar physical conditions. Still the balance of the evidence inclines to the view that, while the steppe population, *e.g.* the Cimmerians and agricultural Scythians were predominantly Iranian, the actual name Scyth belongs to a horde akin to the Turko-Tatars, which made great inroads in the 7th century B.C., was decadent by the 5th century B.C., and gave way in the 3rd century B.C. to the Sarmatians with Iranian views of religion of kingship, and of the free position of women natural among nomads. The substitution of the Sarmatians was a change of name rather than of population or general mode of life, and the "Scythic" tombs belong at least as much to Sarmatians as to Scyths.

ORIGINS OF THE SCYTHS

Herodotus[15] gives two mutually irreconcilable descriptions of Scythia, capital of the Scythian Empire[16]. The general meaning is that Scythia extended from the Danube to the Don and inland to the edge of the forest, a line running east-north and east from the Bukovia[17]to about Samara[18]. In the western half were Tyritae on the Dnester[19] and south to north, from the Olbia[20] at the mouth of the Bug[21] to the government of the Kiev[22], stretched tribes called Callipidae[23], Alazones Scythae Georgi, Scythae Aroteres, all probably representing an older, partly agricultural population and subject to the royal or nomad Scyths. These ranged over the eastern half between the Dnieper[24], the Sea of Azov[25], and the Don[26], and over the northern part of the Crimea, the southern part of which was held by the non-Scythian Tauri[27]. Round the borders of Scythia so defined dwelt Gatae[28] in south of the Danube[29], Agathyrsi[30] in

Transylvania[31], Neuri[32] in Volhynia[33] and the government of Kiev, Androphagi[34], north of the Charnigov[35], Melanchlaeni[36] north of Tamboy[37], Budini[38] with a trading settlement, Gelonus[39] on the middle Volga[40] above Samara[41], east of the Don, and Maeotae[42] east of the Sea of Azov[43].

SCYTHIA (SI-THEE-YUH)

Scythia is an ancient region of Eurasia, extending from the Danube River on the west to the borders of China on the east. The Scythians flourished from the 8th to the 4th century B.C. They spoke an Indo-Iranian language but had no system of writing. They were nomadic conquerors and skilled horsemen. They seemed to be related to the Saka, another nomadic tribe that roamed the steppes of Central Asia at about the same time. The so-called royal Scythians established a kingdom in the east Crimea before the 9th century B.C. They seem to have maintained themselves as a ruling class while others (probably native inhabitants worked in the grain fields). The Scythians are traditionally associated with the area between the Danube and the Don rivers, but modern excavations in Altai Mountain, particularly at the site of Pazyryk, suggest that their origins were in the west Siberia before they moved east into Russia in the early first millennium B.C.[44]

ANOTHER VIEW

Ancient region of south Europe was inhabited by the Scythians. Its extent varied with power of the Scythians, but heart of the region was on north shore of the Black Sea, on lower courses of the Don and the Dnieper, and in the Crimea. A Scythian kingdom was established long before the end of 9th century B.C. After 7th century B.C. the Scythians, the barbarians, par excellence to the Greeks, traded grain and their services as mercenaries for Greek wine, Greek ornaments, and other luxury items. They successfully invaded the Assyrian[45] Empire and late in the 7th century held Palestine. They also pushed down into the Balkan Peninsula. In 3rd century B.C., the Scythians were replaced by the related Sarmatians, and part of their shadowy empire became Sarmatia[46].

The tradition of very early Scythian empire in Asia, if it has any foundation, goes back to the Hittite[47] rule. The real historian of the Scyths is Herodotus. He gives three legends as to their origin: the first to variations to the same tale, represents them as autochthonous and seem really to belong to a settled tribe, not to nomads; perhaps, as says Aristeas, quoted by Herodotus themselves impelled by Issedones[48] and Arimaspi[49] farther east, drove the Scyths out of Asia across the Araxes[50] (Volga?) into Europe against the Cimmerians[51] in Southern Russia. These were cut in two, part driven west to join the Thracians[52], part forced through the Causasus[53].

The Scyths pursued these and missing their way, found themselves in Media[54], which they ruled for 28 years. Then the Medes[55] (q.v.) expelled them by the rising power, after being commemorated at the feast called Sacaea, and they returned to their own Southern Russia. This story finds confirmation in Assurian records. Asarhaddon's[56] inscription (680 B.C.) tells of Gimirrai[57], north of Urartu[58] (Ararat), attacked from the north by As-gu-zu-ai[59] and thus forced to invade the vassal state and incur the enmity of Assyria. The latter made friends with the Asquzaai and used them not only to drive the Gimirri[60] west, but in the next generation against the Medes and apparently against Egypt, that parties of the plundered Ascalon[61] and held Bethshan, hence called Scythopolis.

So the Scyths returned from Media to Southern Russia and reestablished their lordship over the Slavs, whom they had left behind. We know nothing of their history for over a century but the fate of Anacharsis (c. 530 B.C.) who was so attracted by the life of Greeks then established colonies along the Euxine coasts that he actually journeyed to Greece, but on his return was slain by his kin-folk for being untrue to their ancestral customs.

EARLY HISTORY OF THE SCYTHIANS

Between 750 and 700 B.C., according to the evidence of Greek historians supplemented by Assyrian chronology, the Cimmerians were dispossessed of the steppes of southern Russia by the Scythians, who came from Turkestan and western Siberia. The peoples known to the Greeks by the name of Scyths (Skythai) are those whom the Assyrians called Ashkuz and to whom Persians and Indians gave the name of Saka[62]. As may be deduced from the nomenclature, the Scythians belonged to the Iranian race[63]. They were Iranians of the north who had remained nomads in "the original Iranian country" in the steppes of present-day Russian Turkestan, and who had thus to a large extent escaped the influence of the material civilisation of Assur and Babylon: the civilisation which so strongly affected their sedentary brothers—the Medes and Persians—who had settled farther south on the plateau of Iran. The Scythians, like their kindred, the Sarmatians, were to remain strangers also to historical Mazdeism and to the Zoroastrian reforms which shortly afterward would progressively transform the Medo-Persian beliefs.

THEIR VIVID PORTRAITS

Vivid portraits of these Scythians have been left on the Greco-Scythian vases of Kul Oba and Voronezh. They were bearded, and wore, like their Saka brothers in the bas-reliefs of Persepolis, the pointed cap that protected the ears against the bitter winds of the plains, and the roomy garments— tunic and wide trousers— common to the Saka and to their Median and Persian cousins. The horse—the splendid horse of the steppe, reproduced on the silver amphora of the Chertomlyk tumulus— was their inseparable companion, and their favourite weapon was the bow[64]. These mounted archers "had no city" save what one may call "traveling cities", that is to say, the wagon trains that accompanied them on their seasonal migrations, as was still the custom, nineteen hundred years later, in the thirteenth century—the days of Piano Carpini and William of Rubruck— when similar convoys followed the Jenghiz-Khanite Mongols across these same Russian steppes. On these wagons, they piled their women and their wealth: gold ornaments, plaques for harness and equipment, and no doubt carpets too, all wares for which the demand was to bring Scythian art to birth and determine its form and general orientation. Such as they then were, they remained lords of the Russian steppe from the seventh to the third century B.C.

OPINIONS OF THE MODERN LINGUISTS

Modern linguists believe that the Scythians should be classified as Iranian people, an Indo-European family, of the Indo-Iranian or Aryan group. As was just noted, however, their way of life was very similar to that of the Hunnic tribes of Turko-Mongol stock which, at about the same time, became active at the other end of the steppe, on the borders of China. Indeed, nomadic living conditions on the steppe, whether north of the Black Sea and, Caspian Sea or in Mongolia, were much alike, although in the latter region they were markedly more severe. No wonder then if—physical type and language apart— the Scythians, described by Greek historians and portrayed on Greco-Scythian vases are reminiscent, so far as culture and general way of life are concerned, of the Hsiung-nu, T'u-chüeh, and Mongols described or painted by Chinese annalists and artists. A certain number of customs common to both groups is found, either because their similar ways of life compelled them to arrive at solutions (as, for example, the use by both Scythia and Hun mounted archers of trousers and boots instead of the robe of the Mediterranean peoples or of the early Chinese, and the use also of the stirrup[65], or because actual geographical contact between Scythian and Hunnic peoples at the same cultural stage gave rise to the same practices. (An example of this is shown by the funerary immolations which continued to a very late period among both Scythians and Turko-Mongols, whereas in western Asia and China they had long since disappeared, ever since the burials of Ur and Anyang[66].) They gash their faces with a knife so that one may see blood flow with their tears.

THEIR MOVEMENTS

Thus between 750 and 700 B.C., the Scythians (or rather a part of the Scytho-Saka peoples, for the majority of the Sakas remained round the vicinity of T'ien Shan, near Fergana and in Kashgaria) moved from the Turgai region and the Ural River into southern Russia, whence they drove out the Cimmerians[67]. Some of the Cimmerians, it seems, had to take refuge in Hungary, which was probably already inhabited by other peoples of Thracian affinities; and it is these fugitives who are believed to have buried the "treasures" of Mihaeni near Szilagyi and of Fokuru near Heves, and also that of Mikhailovka in Galicia. The rest of the Cimmerians fled via Thrace, says Strabo, or, according to Herodotus, via Colchis, into Asia Minor, where they wandered in Phrygia (ca. 720), then in Cappadocia and Ciljcia (ca. 650), and finally in Pontis (ca. 630). Some of the Scythians set off in pursuit (720-700), but Herodotus says they took the wrong route, crossed the Caucasus through the Derbent Gateway, and came into contact with the Assyrian Empire, which their king Ishkapai attacked, though without success (ca. 678). Bartatua, another petty Scythian king, was more astute; he made friendly advances to the Assyrians, with whom he had a common enemy: the Cimmerians, who were threatening the Assyrian frontier in the region of Cilicia and Cappadocia. A Scythian army, acting in conformity with Assyrian policy, entered Pontis to crush the last of the Cimmerians (ca. 638). About ten years later, Bartatua's son, referred to by Herodotus as Madyes, came at the request of Assyria, which had been overrun by the Medes, and himself invaded and subjugated Media (ca. 628). The

Medes soon rebelled, however, their king Cyaxares[68] massacred the Scythian leaders, and the remainder of the Scythians turned back via the Caucasus to southern Russia. These are just a few but most noteworthy of the episodes of the Scythian invasions, which frightened western Asia for nearly seventy years. Throughout this period, the great Indo-European barbarians were the terror of the Old World. Their cavalry galloped in search of plunder from Cappadocia to Media, from the Caucasus to Syria. This great stirring of peoples, of which an echo can be detected even among the prophets of Israel, represents the first irruption in historical times of the nomads of the northern steppe[69] into the old civilisations of the south: a movement that will be repeated through some twenty centuries.

WARS WITH IRAN

When the Persians replaced the Assyrians, Babylonians, and Medes as masters of western Asia, they set to work to render sedentary Iran secure from fresh invasions from outer Iran. According to Herodotus, it was against the Massagetae that Cyrus led his last campaign, that is to say, against the Scythians of the region, east of Khiva (ca. 529). Darius launched his first great expedition against the Scythians of Europe (ca. 514-512). By way of Thrace and present-day Bessarabia he penetrated the steppe, where, following the usual nomad tactics, the Scythians, instead of accepting battle, retreated before him, luring him ever farther into the wilderness. He was wise enough to withdraw in time. Herodotus is inclined to regard this “Russian campaign” as the folly of a despot, yet in fact, the Achaemenid monarch intended by this to implement a quite natural policy, the Persianisation of outer Iran, or Pan-Iranian union. The enterprise having failed, the Scythians escaped Persian influence and remained in peaceful possession of southern Russia for another three centuries. Darius’ expedition did at least result in securing permanent protection for western Asia against the incursions of the nomads[70].

SETTLED IN UKRAINE

Discoveries of Scythian art offers a glimpse, with Tallgren, of the progress of Scythian occupation in Russia[71]. At first, from approximately 700 B.C. to 550 B.C., the center of Scythian culture remained in the southeast, in the Kuban region and the Taman Peninsula. The Scythians were doubtless already dominant in the south of the Ukraine at this time, between the lower Dnieper and the lower Bug, as is proved by the finds at Martonocha and Melgunov, though apparently in a more sporadic manner. It was not until between approximately 550 B.C. and 450 B.C., according to Tallgren, that Scythian culture sprang vigorously into being in the Ukraine of today, to reach its peak from about 350 B.C. to 250 B.C., as may be seen from the great royal Kurgans of the lower Dnieper, at Chertomlyk, Alexandropol, Solokha, Denev, and others. The most northerly area in the west to be reached by the Scythian expansion ran along the northern border of the forest steppes, a little to the south of Kiev and in the Voronezh region. Northeastward, the expansion moved up the Volga to Saratov, where important discoveries have been made and where Tallgren places the Scythian or quasi-Scythian people—Iranian in either case— the Sarmatians.

It is possible that the Scythians of southern Russia were never more than an aristocracy superimposed on a Cimmerian, that is, a Thraco-Phrygian, substratum. Benveniste points out that in *Herodotus* (IV, 5-10) information alleged to be of Scythian origin reveals a purely Iranian nomenclature, whereas other information about these same Scythians, stated to originate in Greece, reveals a nomenclature still Thraco-Phrygian[72]. Linguistic survivals have been corroborated by archaeological remains. "The Hallstatt culture of the Cimmerian bronze period," says Tallgren, "lived on in the Ukraine as a peasant culture even while Scythism and Hellenism were becoming established".[73]

Finally, north of the Scythian zone, with its more or less Cimmerian substratum, dwelt non-Scythian barbarians whom Herodotus calls Androphagi, Melankhlenes, and Issedones, and who may have been of Finno-Ugrian stock. Tallgren suggests that the Androphagi should be placed north of Chernigov and the Melankhlenes north of Voronezh. It is known that these two peoples joined with the Scythians to repel Darius' invasion. As for the Issedones, Benveniste seeks them in the Ural region, near Ekaterinburg. Also, Tallgren attributes to the Androphagi and the Melankhlenes, that is to say the Finno-Ugrian neighbours of the Scythians, the so-called Mordvian culture, of which traces have been found in the excavations of the Desna and the Oka, and which is characterized by a rather inferior geometric ornamentation entirely lacking in the animal style of the Scythians[74].

INVASION OF PERSIA

According to Herodotus, Darius, the king of Persia about 512 century B.C. marched through Macedonia and Thrace, crossed the Danube, leaving the Ionians[75] with orders to guard his bridge for 60 days, and invaded Scythia. Enticed by the Scyths as far as the river Oarus[76] (Volga) he attacked eight forts but leaving them unfinished turned west again and was led round the edges of the country through the lands of the border nations who had refused to help against the invader. Meanwhile the Scyths had tried to get the Ionians[77] to desert and destroy the bridge, but they kept it in being even beyond the date promised. Finally Darius, unable to catch up with the Scyths and running short of provisions, abandoned his wounded and baggage and returned hastily to the bridge. Ctesias[78] and Strabo[79] make much less of expeditions, which was probably more or less unsuccessful demonstration meant to protect the new Persian conquests and magnified to exhibit the poor spirit of the Ionians and the advantages of nomad warfare.

SCYTHS RETALIATED

In revenge the Scyths made a raid that reached the Thracian Chersonese[80], drove out Miltiades and even proposed to Cleomenes[81] of Sparta[82], a joint invasion of Asia. During the 5th century B.C., Scythian archers were employed as policemen in Athens[83]. They were often represented on painted vessels, but it is hard to distinguish their equipment from that of Persians, Amazons[84], and the like.

THE FEROCIOUS WARRIORS

"What men! They are real Scythians!" Napoleon[85] is said to have exclaimed at the sight of thundering charge by cossack[86] cavalry, as his tattered forces fought endless rearguard action on the wintery, retreat from Moscow. Thus nearly 2,000 years after their barbaric domination of Central Russia had been ended, the magnificent Scythian warriors of the Pontic Steppes[87] lived on as a byword for ferocity and daring. Looming on horseback eight feet above the ground, screaming maniacally, capable of unleashing repetitive and deadly flights of triple-edged arrows, Scythians must have seemed the very embodiment of horror to those who had to stand and fight them. Nor were such fears unwarranted, for Scythian warriors regularly beheaded their enemies and sometimes even skinned them whole. If an enemy were known personally, his skull might receive special treatment; sewn through below the eyes, it would be cleaned and painstakingly fashioned into a richly painted drinking vessel. Not surprisingly, Scythian ceremonies, especially royal funerals, were drenched in blood and were among the grisliest inhuman history."[88]

EFFECTS OF HORSE RIDING

Hippocrates[89], discussing the effect of climate upon human physique, describes the peculiarities of the Scythians, who he finds as little like other men as are the Egyptians. The special points are a close mutual resemblance, a reddish complexion, fatness, slackness, and excess of humours, a look as of eunuchs, and in certain cases a sexual indifference that amounts to actual impotence. This disease was well known. Herodotus says that it was incurred through the sack of the temple of Derceto at Ascalon, but Hippocrates declares it to be a disease just like any other disease and it was due to excessive riding. Men thus afflicted took their place absolutely, among the women and were called 'Enarees' (Impotents). He adds that all this applied only to the most noble and rich among the Scyths. The women, he says, always sit in wagons, whereas among the Sauromatae, they ride astride and took their share even in war.

SCYTHIANS, GREAT ARTSMEN

These thundering, rapacious, illiterate horsemen were capable of remarkable accomplishments as well as of stunning military strategy and, even more mysteriously of the creation of dazzling array of exquisitely formed golden objects. Combs, breastplates, chalices, scabbards, helmets, rings—all either executed by Scythian metalsmiths or commissioned from Greek craftsmen—have been found in glittering profusion amid the carnage of royal gravesites.

THEIR CHARACTERISTICS

Blood and gold, bestiality and beauty, myth and fact, these were the strands that bring the curious paradox of the Scythians. Where did they come from? Scholars ask, and what was their life 2,500 years ago? Why had they no coins, no written language? And at the heart of the mystery this question: what forces conspired to infuse these barbarous nomads with a deep and clearly delightful appreciation of beautifully crafted gold?

THEIR CUSTOMS

Herodotus, the Greek historian, gives a full account of Scythian customs; almost always he had in view the normal Scyths, but some details seem to contradict their general scheme of life and were more probably true of the agricultural Scythians near Olbia[90], whence Herodotus seems to have obtained his information. The life of the nomad Scyths was conditioned by the necessity of tending their beasts: chief of these was the horse, used for riding and also to supply meat and mare's milk kumys', cheese, butter and butter milk, while the oxen drew the great wagons in which the women lived. They also ate sheep and goat but eschewed the pig. They used some vegetable food grain, onions, garlic and wild bulbs: when they could get it they drank wine and unlike the Greeks they drank it neat. For cooking, they used great cauldrons and they cooked animal in its own skin, skin burning the bones at the same time. Of their dress, he tells us only that they wore belts and trousers and pointed caps. Their great weapon was the bow, with arrows and quiver, used from horseback; accordingly it was not a simple self-bow but a rather short bow with a complicated curve compared to that of the north coast of the Euxine[91]. They also used darts, short swords or daggers and axes. For defence, they had shields and scale armour.

THEIR FUNERAL CUSTOMS

In the case of the kings, funeral customs were very magnificent and cruel; the burials took place in the land of the Gerrhi, near the great bend of the Dnepr (Dnieper) and to this region the king was brought whenever he may have died. The body was embalmed and put on a wagon. Its attendants disfigured themselves and all whom they met, as they brought it from tribe to tribe to the appointed place, where it was laid in a great square pit under a roof of wicker-work. They strangled and lay in the vacant space one of the dead man's concubines, his cup-bearer, cook, groom, and messenger, also horses, set by him his cups of gold (they made no use of silver or bronze) and firstlings mound. After a year, they slay 50 of his favourite servants, free Scyths all, and 50 horses stuffed them and set them in a circle round the mound. An ordinary Scyth when dead was carried about on a wagon to visit his friends, who feasted the dead man and his attendants until, after 40 days, he was laid in his grave.

OTHER CUSTOMS

One or two other customs may be worth mention; that by which a Scyth who had slain an enemy in war drank his blood and scalped him, the scalp being a voucher in the distribution of booty, and the making into cups of the skulls of private adversaries vanquished in combat before the king showed an extreme of barbarism[92]. Herodotus seems to describe three separate customs under one—a ceremonial purification from the taint of a corpse, the usual vapour-bath still popular in Russia, and a custom of intoxication with the vapour of hemp; he adds that the women whitened their skin with a paste of pounded cypress, cedar, and frankincense, which suggest considerable luxury and wide commercial connections.

WITCHCRAFT

Witchcraft played a great part in Scythian life. The wizards divined with bundles of sticks, and the Enarees by plaiting fast. If the king fell sick, it was because someone had sworn by the royal hearth and had broken his oath, thus bringing down upon the king the deity's vengeance. Accordingly the wizards were called in to name the perjurer, and he escaped with his life only if he could adduce two sets of wizards to declare him innocent. If wizards were judged to have brought a false accusation, then they were burnt on a pyre set on a cart.

The ceremony for taking oaths and swearing blood- brotherhood was widely prevalent; the parties mixed their blood with wine in great cups, put there in a sword, an arrow, an axe, and a dart, and after praying long over it, drank it together[93].

This picture of Scythian life is supplemented, and on the whole confirmed, by the result of excavations made in southern Russia during the past hundred years. Though no tomb can be said exactly to correspond to the ritual described by Herodotus, nearly every point can be paralleled from some burial or other. From Podolia[94] and the southern part of the Kiev and Poltava[95] governments, south of the Euxine and the neighbourhood of the Greek cities of the Crimea and east across the Dnieper and the Doon to the valley of the Kuban along the northern slope of the Caucasus, are found groups of barrows of every size up to the 70 ft. high and 400 ft. across. The best was mostly about the bend of the Dnieper, just where we should seek the land of Gerrhus. The oldest contained skeletons coloured red and a few pots, but the rich contents of the greater number showed them to be tombs of nomad people in touch with Assyrian, Iranian and Greek civilization and dating from about the 7th century B.C. to the period of the great migrations. Most of them have been plundered, either just after their construction or by successive generations of tomb-robbers, but a few have kept their treasures, at any rate in part to reward scientific investigation.

We may take as an example the latest great find, made by N.I. Veselovski in 1912-13.

THE SCYTHIAN TOMBS

The tumulus Solokha is 15 miles south of Nicopolis[96] in the middle of the Gerrhus group. In the centre had been the tomb of a woman arrayed in all her finery and supplied with drinking vessels, a cauldron, and a gridiron, and nearby two heroes with gold trapping. In the south-east part of the mound, approached by a deep shaft and a covered way, was a larger chamber containing the body of a king or chief, by him his sword-bearer, and another servant near the entrance. A little to the west was a second pit with the skeletons of five horses and a groom by them. Clearly the queen had died first, and the king had later been put into the same barrow. Other examples show that, if the king had died, his wife would have immediately followed him into the grave. The king's grave-goods were wonderfully rich: he wore a great line-ended torque and five gold bracelets, some 300 gold plaques with repousse designs, flowers, beasts and human figures were sewn on to his pall; above his head lay a bone-handled knife, a rusted sword, a coat of mail (armour for the body), a pair of greaves, a wooden cup to which gold plate had been knotted, by his shoulder lay a bronze Greek helmet; by his right are two iron lances and copper mace; by his leg a leather gorytus (combination quiver and bow case); by his right hip two iron swords, one of them with a gold hilt and a peculiar sheath. Not far from his right shoulder was wonderful golden comb of the finest Greek work, adorned with figures of three warriors; nearby stood seven silver cups with men or animals in relief. In niches in the wall of the chamber, among other things, were ten Greek wine-jars, three great cauldrons with beef and mutton bones, and another amphare, a colander, and silver mounted drinking-horn; a special hiding-place held a garytus of repousse silver, bearing a wonderful representation of Scythians in combat and containing 180 arrow-heads, and a great golden saucer with a central boss, animals in repousse, all round and obliterated Greek inscription. The whole may be dated c. 300 B.C.

INVENTORY OF SCYTHIAN TOMBS

The general inventory of the other great tombs is much the same and dictated by the same ideas as the funeral rites described by Herodotus, illustrating them in such details as the presence of wooden tabernacles over the body, the remains of the funeral car and the funeral feast, etc. Discrepancies are the presence of silver and bronze and the rarity of any kind of axe. As to their style, the objects found are:

1. A few Assyrian and perhaps Iranian.
2. Archaic Ionian.
3. Native Scythic.
4. 'Finest' and Hellenistic Greek.

Some of the latest are of extreme beauty, and they are important as being easily dated and as presenting detailed representations of Scythians.

Women's wear and things of general use are mostly of this class, weapons (except the goryti) and horse-trapping are usually of the other three. The native craftsman, though utterly failing to imitate the finest Greek work, succeeded better with the Ionian style, but imported into it a grotesque element recalling upper Asia and Siberia, sometimes even China; he was very fond of animals, especially reindeer, and beasts and birds of prey, so foreshadowing the best style of the great migration period. The most interesting types (both known also in Siberia) were the cauldron and the short sword with a heart-shaped guard; its sheath had a side projection and separate tip necessary for a special way of suspending it from the belt; just such are shown upon bas-reliefs at Persepolis[97].

POLITICAL ORGANISATION

The political organisation of the Scythians consisted of an over-king, under-kings, nobles, freemen and slaves. The women of the Scyths themselves rode in the wagons and had apparently much less freedom than those of the other nomad peoples of queens Tomyris[98], Zarinaia[99], Amage[100], and Tirgatae[101]. The kings were polygamous and married foreign women. On his father's death the son took over his wives, excepting, of course, his own mother. Their warlike tactics were proverbial—retiring before an invader, wasting the country, cutting off his supplies, harassing his rear, enticing him by feigned flight, and gradually exhausting him, while the nomads carry their supplies with them and were perfectly mobile. When they attacked other countries, they left no forces to guard their own, being quite independent of their base and so able to concentrate all their strength upon point. But, when Thueydides[102] says, that as the most numerous people of the world, they could, unite and vanquish any other nation. He exaggerated both their number and their power.

THE BARBARIAN ASPECTS OF SCYTHIAN LIFE

It was nearly 2,700 years ago, in the middle of the 5th century B.C. that Herodotus, gathering information for his monumental *History of the Greeco-Persian Wars*, journeyed to the frontier trading city of Olbia on the Black Sea. To the east of this burgeoning Greek outpost lay the Don River, to the west of the Carpathian Mountains and the Danube river, to the north the broad sweeping girth of the Pontic steppes, terminated only hundreds of miles away by rough forest and intractable marshes. In the months that followed, Herodotus appears to have learned as much about the Scythians as the battles he came to chronicle. For as revealed in Book IV of his *Persian Wars*, the barbarian aspects of Scythian life held a great fascination for Herodotus, and he took a great pleasure in describing them, knowing that he would make his readers tremble even in the 5th century B.C.

TREATMENT WITH ENEMIES

Having beheaded and skinned an enemy, for example, Herodotus reports that the Scythians sometimes made coats, caps and cushions out of the skins. It is unclear whether Herodotus actually saw or perhaps even touched such grisly artifacts, but he does describe them as being white and glossy. In their use of human skulls, Scythian warriors, if they were rich, might not only cut and clean but also bring skulls exterior with rough cowhide and gild its interior for use as a drinking cup. Entertaining a guest, the warrior might then courteously offer his visitor a drink served in one of those skulls and provide as well as chillingly detailed explanation of the crime that had merited the punishment. Sometimes the victim might be relative, perhaps one as close as a father or brother, who had been foolish enough to start a quarrel.

BLOOD THIRSTY

In battle, Scythian warriors not only performed in a bloodthirsty manner, but they were also, drinking the blood of the enemy they killed. Each year, in fact, as the tribes gathered, it was considered a great disgrace not to have killed anyone since the previous festival. On the battlefield, Scythians also believed in obtaining proof of their viciousness; they took scalps, that Herodotus described in vivid detail. "The Scythian soldier" he wrote, "scraps the scalp clean of flesh and, softening it by rubbing it between the hands, uses it thenceforth as a napkin. The Scyth is proud of these scalps and hangs them from his bridle-rein; the greater the number of such napkins that a man can show the more highly is he esteemed among them. Many make themselves cloaks by sewing a quantity of these scalps together...."

TREATMENT WITH THE PRISONERS

All prisoners were not scalped. In honour of their god of war, Scythian warriors also performed sacrifices. One of each hundred prisoners was ceremoniously offered up. This the Scythians did by killing the prisoner, then slicing off his right hand and arm and tossing the severed limb into the air. Then the other victims are slain. Herodotus wrote, "Those who have offered the sacrifice depart, leaving the hands and arms where they may chance to have fallen, and the bodies, as well separate." Blood also bathed Scythian agreements and alliances, with the participants joining in the creation of a mixture of blood and wine. They might then dip arrows or javelins or swords in the potion and finish by drinking it down.

STANDARD OF LIVING

Despite his obvious fascination with Scythian barbarism, Herodotus provided a more mundane and perhaps more important view of the mysterious Scythian world. His portrait is hardly flattering, for it tells of people with wild, covetous eyes, long and undoubtedly filthy hair and weathered, leathery skin. It tells of men who rarely, if ever, bathed and women who used a kind of mashed herb paste to do so. It tells of hard cruel men who had numerous wives, who relished strong, undiluted wine and the smoke of hashish. These men lived constantly in the saddle and were as wedded to the steppes as the horses they rode. 'Level, well-watered and abounding in pasture' is the way Herodotus described their domain.

EXTENT OF PERSIAN EMPIRE
(Wars with Persia)

This was the race that Darius[103] the Great of Persia prepared to crush, and Herodotus has left us a remarkably graphic account of the Scythians' cunning scorched-earth triumph over Darius' powerful armies by the end of the 6th century B.C. Darius' empire was truly vast. To the west, it spread to the Balkans in Europe; to the south it bordered Libya, Tunisia and the sunbaked wastes of Ethiopia and the Sudan. To the east, the empire covered the whole of southern Asia as far as the Panjab and the Indus Valley, ending at the Indian Ocean and the Arabian desert.

Darius' northern frontier, however, consisted of seas, icy mountains and deserts, the Caspian and Aral, Caucasus, the Gobi. And it was this stretch of broken terrain that most worried Darius. Far behind, it roamed the shadowy but terrible Ashguzai horsemen, the Scythians. They had suddenly appeared from nowhere three or four generations earlier sweeping down astride their tireless horses like an avalanche from the passes of the eastern Caucasus. They had ridden all over upper Asia, spreading terror, pillaging and slaughtering everyone who resisted until king Cyaxares of Media took advantage of drinking about and massacred their chiefs. But this did not put an end to the Scythian threat on the Persian frontier.

In the spring of 514 B.C., Darius, hoping to end the Scythian menace and conquer the steppes from the west, crossed the Bosphorus at the head of a vast army and moved up through Thrace into Scythian territory. It would take a month or two to suppress these upstart horsemen, Darius reckoned.

THE WAR STRATEGIES

What happened in fact was that the 7,00,000 men of Persian force was very nearly consumed by the Scythians in what must be considered one of the most remarkable examples of tactical wizardry in military history. According to Herodotus, writing almost half a century later, "Darius and his troops simply could not find the enemy's army. Nonetheless, crops were burned and wells filled in as the Persian probing actions were teasing forever forward in pursuit of an enemy who always vanished just over the horizon. And thus for months did the Scythians, helped by neighbouring tribes, toy with Darius, leading him in all directions between the Danube and the Volga without ever letting him take them or their herds by surprise. Finally, Darius challenged the courage of phantoms, he sought to destroy by sending on ahead a message in which he commanded the Scythians to fight or surrender. The succinct reply was: 'Go weep'. In the end, troops exhausted, supply lines perilously thin, the struggle to find food as torturous as fighting itself, Darius withdrew, leaving the Scythians in total command of steppes."

PIONEERS OF GUERRILLA WARFARE

However, this story of a scorched-earth guerrilla war is not the only interesting point in Herodotus' account. A man of great curiosity, he was the first person to make a proper study of the customs of different races. To use his own words, he was the first man to study about the different races. He was not content with simply 'ensuring that the great deeds of men are not effaced by time. He wanted to see the countries that had been the scenes of these great deeds and to observe the daily life of their inhabitants.

In one memorable passage of his *Persian Wars*, he comes perhaps closest to capturing the essence of the Scythians, "Having neither cities nor forts," he wrote, "and carrying their dwelling, wherever they go; accustomed moreover, one and all, to shoot from horseback; and living not by crops but from their cattle, their wagons, the only horses they possess, how can they fail of being unconquerable and unassailable?"

Jat-Sikhs and Rajputs, descendants of Scythians, fought against Nadir Shah (1739 A.D.) and Ahmed Shah Abdali (1739-69 A.D.), invaders from Iran, with the same technique of guerrilla warfare. During the invasions of Nadir Shah, the Jat-Sikhs collected in small bands and plundered both the stragglers of the Persian army and wealthy inhabitants who fled towards the hills on the first appearance of the conqueror, or when the massacre at Delhi became known.

Not long afterwards another famous Greek, Hippocrates[104], the father of medicine, corroborated and expanded Herodotus' account with these words, "The smallest of these of wagons of Scyths have four wheels, but some have six; they are covered in with filth, and they are constructed in the manner of houses, some having but a single apartment, and some three; they are proof against rain, snow and winds. The wagons are drawn by yokes of oxen."

A GIFT OF GOLD

The Scythians became and remained for more than 200 years uncertain figures in a world of myth and legend. In 1715, the spell was broken by a gift of gold, from the owner of Siberian mines to Tsar Peter of Russia. Thus, began the modern effort to explain the blood-and-gold paradox of the Scythians.

After that first shipment of Scythians gold, some 20 exquisite pieces in all, other discoveries followed, and other treasures reached Peter. Finally, when it became clear that dozens of graves or 'Kurgans', had been robbed in the search of gold, Peter ordered such looting stopped and commanded that all Scythians' treasures be delivered to the crown. Nonetheless, the opening continued, especially after Peter's death in 1725; and with each, scholars came closer to a very exciting conclusion.

SCYTHIAN ART

The consequences of the great Scythian invasions of the Caucasus, Asia Minor, Armenia, Media, and the Assyrian Empire in the 7th century extend beyond the field of political history. The initial contact of the Scythians with the Assyrian world, of which they were allies and confederates, that close contact which lasted for nearly a century, is a fact of paramount importance to any student of steppe art. First, it is very probable that it was during their wanderings across western Asia in the 7th century that the Scythians completed their transition from the bronze to the iron age.?

The beginnings of Scythian art were not uninfluenced by the Hallstatt iron technique, in the Celto-Danubian region (Hallstatt between 1000 or 900 and 500 or 450, Scythian between 700 and 200)[105]. But it was, above all, the Caucasus and the Median country, in this case Luristan, which the tumult of peoples in the 7th century brought into such close relations with the Scythians. Franz Hancar, in agreement with his colleague of Vienna, F.W. Konig, holds that it is indeed to the 7th century that must be attributed a large proportion of the Koban bronzes in the Caucasus, as well as some of those of Luristan, on the southwest side of old Media. In Hancar's view, the Koban bronzes and even those of Luristan were partly due to the Cimmerians[106]. What is evident is the connection between both of these and the beginnings of Scythian art at this time, when squadrons of Scythian and Cimmerian invaders were eddying over the same regions.

There is irrefutable evidence of the direct influence exerted by Assyro-Babylonia Mesopotamia on the first Scythian works of art: the iron and gold axe of Kelermes in Kuban[107] (dating from about the 6th century). This axe displays the old Assyro-Babylonian and Luristanian theme of two ibexes standing about the tree of life, together with some fine deer. The animals are depicted in a realistic manner, and the art form is clearly inspired by Assyrian animal art. However, it is specifically Scythian in the decorative use to which it is put.

From the starting point we behold the rise of all Scythian animal art, which may be defined as turning Assyrian (or Greek) naturalism to a decorative purpose. This art appears in its definitive form with the golden deer of the Kostromskaya tomb, whose antlers are stylized in spirals. Almost certainly in the 6th century, it also appears in Kuban.

In this manner, the aesthetics of the steppe took up their centuries-long abode in southern Russia, with those clearly defined tendencies of which we shall follow the eastward development as far as Mongolia and China. From the beginning, a dual stream is noted: the naturalist current, doubtless, periodically renewed from Assyro-Achaemenid sources, on the one hand, and from Hellenic ones, on the other, and the decorative stream which, as has been stated, bends, twists and diverts that current to purely ornamental purposes[108]. In the end, the realism of the animal style, never lost sight of by these horse breakers and hunters, became merely the peg and the pretext for stylised decorations.

Such a tendency is explained by the nomadic way of life, whether of the Scytho-Sarmatians in the west or of the Huns in the east. Possessing neither stable settlements nor landed property, they remained strangers to statuary, bas-relief and painting, which alone require realism. Their luxuries were confined to richness of dress and personal adornment, and to ornamentation of equipment, harness, and so on. Objects of this sort—hooks and plaques for belts, harness plates, sword-belt buckles, wagon panels, all sorts of handles and hilts, to say nothing of carpets, as at Noin Ula—seemed designed for stylised, even heraldic, treatment.

As has been said, the northern nomads—whether of Iranian stock like the Scythian or of Turko-Mongol like the Huns— lived their steppe life on horseback, engaged in chasing herds of deer or wild assess and watching wolves hunt antelope over the boundless plains. Both their way of life and the peculiar character of their wealth made it natural that, of the Assyro-Babylonian influences they had received, they should have retained only heraldic themes and stylized representations of fighting animals. Lastly, as Anderson points out, it appears that these animal portrayals had a specifically magical purpose, like the frescoes and bone carvings of the Magdalenians[109].

Except for Greco-Scythian examples of goldsmiths' work, Scythian only in subject, and executed by Greek artists working either for the Hellenic colonies of the Crimea or directly for the kings of the steppe, in almost all Scythian art the figures of animals are fashioned in a formal, geometrical style with a view solely to ornamental effect. There are examples at Kostromskaya, dating, according to Schefold, from the 5th century B.C.; at Elizavetovskaya, from the same period; at Kul Oba in the Crimea, between 450 B.C. and 350 B.C.; in the treasure of Peter the Great, originating in western Siberia in the Sarmatian period (the first century of this era); and at Verkhneudinsk in Transbaikalia, in Hunnic art dating from approximately the beginning of this era. In all these are found deer antlers, horses' manes, and even the claws of felines proliferating in curls and spirals which at times double the height of the animal. The upper lip of the horse is coiled like a snail shell. In the Scytho-Sarmatian art of western Siberia, as also in the identically inspired art elaborated by the Hsiung-nu of the Ordos, the stylisation of animal forms is at times so complete, they entwine and interlace with one another in such complexity, and branch in such unexpected profusion, that despite the sustained realism in the treatment of deers' and horses' heads, or in those of bears and tigers, it is only with difficulty that beast can be distinguished from ornamentation. Horns and tails of animals terminate in foliage or blossom out in the shape of birds. Animal realism ends by submerging and losing itself in the ornamentation that sprang from it[110].

Steppe art is thus in direct contrast to that of neighbouring sedentary peoples—Scythian versus Assyro-Achaemenid, Hunnic versus Chinese—and in the very field where they have most in common: scenes of hunting and of fighting animals. Nothing could be more different from the animal classicism—all swiftness and spare delineation—of the Assyrians or the Achaemenids on the one hand, the Hun on the other, than the contortions, convolutions, and obscurities of steppe art. Assyrians and Achaemenids, like the China of the Hun, show prowling beasts, pursuing or defying each other within a simple, airy setting. Steppe artists, whether Scythians or Huns, show scuffles, often as entangled as a thicket of lianas, between animals locked in a death struggle. Theirs is a dramatic art of crushed limbs, of horses or deer seized by leopards, bears, birds of prey, or griffins, the bodies of the victims being often wrenched completely round. No swiftness here, no flight; instead, a patient and methodical tearing of throats in which, as has been said, the victim appears to drag the slayer to his death. Yet there is an inner dynamic which, despite this "slowness," might have attained to tragic heights were it not for the luxuriant stylisation by which the forms are interwoven and elaborated, and which usually removes all realism from the killings.

The varied elements and tendencies of steppe art are unevenly distributed over the huge area extending from Odessa to Manchuria and the Yellow River. The Scythian art of the steppe, spreading toward the forest region of the upper Volga, influenced the Ananino culture near Kazan (ca. 600-200 B.C.), which was doubtlessly a Finno-Ugrian civilization. A rich burial ground discovered there has yielded, in addition to the usual bronze spiked axes and daggers, some animal motifs in which the animals' bodies are curled up. These have Scythian affinities, though executed here in a somewhat meager and simplified form. Nevertheless, according to Tallgren's observations, the Scythian animal style was only partially adopted at Ananino, and the decoration continued to be based on geometric patterns[111].

At Minusinsk, in central Siberia, the situation was not entirely the same. During the most flourishing period of the bronze age (sixth to third centuries B.C.), this important metal working centre of the Altai went on producing socketed axes decorated with purely geometric designs (*e.g.*, the "angled" decoration of Krasnoyarsk). Yet from the same period the site yields animal bronzes of a sober, simplified stylisation, in contrast to the intricate elaboration of other provinces. It is here, therefore, that Borovka is inclined to seek the origin, both topographical and chronological, of steppe art.

The importance of the question is evident. Was it at Minusinsk, the geographical centre of this art, situated halfway between the Black Sea and the Gulf of Chihli, that the ancient smiths of the Altai hammered out the first animal designs? And were these designs, still elementary and weak, to become enriched both by the Assyro-Achaemenid contributions of the Scythians in the south-west and the Chinese borrowings of the Hsiung-nu in the south-east? Or is the poverty of the Minusinsk animal designs explained, as Rostovtzeff believes, by the decline of Scythian art as it spread to the Siberian forests, as happened at Ananino to the art which was to spread to the forest region of Perm? If this is true, Ananino and Minusinsk represent no more than a faint echo of the Russian steppe.

It should be noted also that in southern Russia itself, at the beginning, that is, from the 7th and 6th centuries B.C., only somewhat austere examples of animal stylisation which are found, as in the bronzes of the Seven Brothers tumuli, of Kelermes, Ulski, and Kostromskaya in the Kuban, of Chigirin near Kiev, of Kerch and Kul Oba (these being dated as early as the 5th and 4th centuries) in the Crimea, for example. In the 5th and 4th centuries, the stylisation apparently became more complex, as at Solokha near Melitopol on the Sea of Azov. There, alongside a fine piece of Greek goldsmith's work, based on Scythian themes, are contorted animal figures, with characteristic branching's and elaboration. The same holds true at Elizavetovskaya near Azov, where floral and ramifying motifs pierced in bronze are wrought for their own sake.

THE KURGANS (THE GRAVES)

Herodotus had been remarkably accurate in his descriptions of Scythians funerals. He wrote in one account, "When a king dies, they dig a great square pit, and, when it is ready, they take up the corpse, which has been previously slit open, cleaned out and filled with various aromatic substances, crushed galingale (an aromatic plant) parsley seed, and anise; it is then sown up again and the whole body is coated over with wax. Then the king's body was carried in a wagon from tribe to tribe until the funeral's cortege reached the land of the Gerrhi, the most isolated of the Scythian tribes."

DISPOSAL OF THE CORPSE

In his description about the disposal of the corpse, Herodotus wrote, "The corpse was laid in the tomb on a mattress, with spears fixed in the ground on either side to support a roof of brush laid on wooden poles, while in other parts of the great square pit, various members, of king's household are buried beside him; one of his concubines, his butler, his cook, his groom, his steward, and his chamberlain, all of them strangled. Horses are buried too, and gold cups (the Scythians do not use silver or bronze), and a selection of his other treasures.... This ceremony over, everybody with great enthusiasm sets about raising a mound of earth, each competing to make it as big as possible."

In 1898, N.I. Veselovsky excavated 'Kurgan' (the grave site) at Ulski Aul, in the Lrasmpdpe district north-east of the Black Sea. Under the 49-ft. high earthwork of one he found a wooden structure. "All around," he wrote, "wooden pickets had been planted, near which lay the skeletons of horses." Two oxen and more than 360 horses were buried next to the 'Kurgan'. During the 20th century, the discoveries continued, especially after the Second World War. And in 1971, near Ordzhonikidze, on the Dnieper, a Russian archaeologist, named B.N. Mozoloevskii found another variant of the scene, described by Herodotus: the servants seemed to be leading their horses.

Comparing reports of 'Kurgan' excavation with the Greek historian's accounts, it seems that Herodotus may have been writing about the 'Ideal Kurgan' if such a word may be used to describe what happened on the first anniversary of the burial. "When a year is gone by," Herodotus wrote, "further ceremonies take place. Fifty of the late king's attendants are taken...and are strangled with fifty of the most beautiful horses."

"When they are dead, their bowels are taken out, and the cavity cleaned, filled full of chaff, and straightway sewn up again. This done, a number of posts are set into the ground, in sets of two pairs each; atop every pair of stakes half the rim of a wheel is placed to form an arch. Then strong stakes are run lengthwise through the bodies of the horses from tail to neck, and they are set on top of the rims so that the arch supports the shoulders of the horse, while the one behind holds up the belly and quarters, the legs dangling in mid-air. Each horse is given a bridle, which is stretched out in front of the horses and fastened to a peg."

The fifty strangled youths are then mounted on the fifty horses. To affect this, a stake is passed through their bodies along the course of the spine to the neck, the lower end of which projects from the body and is fixed into a socket made in the stake that runs lengthwise down the horse. The fifty riders are thus hanged in a circle round the tomb and so left.

The grisly remains of such a scene, created perhaps by the Scythians to protect their king after death or perhaps to frighten away potential grave robbers, may be unearthed one day as more 'Kurgans' were opened. Yet even without such proof, scholars no longer doubt Herodotus—at least in his reporting of funeral customs.

THE SHAMAN (RELIGION)

The Scythians, for example, believed in the 'Shaman' who formed an important part of Scythian life. This unusual, significant figure, who has appeared in many cultures, was a unique sort of amalgam for the Scythian part medicine man, part magician, part soothsayer and, perhaps most importantly, part animal. In his healing and predicting rites, he used a variety of instruments—drums, sticks, bark strips, rattles, willow wands. And he also used drugs, as did all Scythian males, and probably relied on self-induced seizures and trances as well. Thus it is at least possible to speculate that the Scythian 'Shaman' might have served as a kind of artistic touchstone, or prime source, from the animal themes that so dominate Scythian art.

REASONS

There are two perfectly good reasons for this; firstly the Scythians, like many early and primitive people, viewed their world in animistic terms. Surrounded by living things and natural phenomena that they could not comprehend, they quite naturally assigned special power to them, especially the animals. Aspects of this transfer show up in the golden animal figures the Scythians created. Often such creatures are represented only in part by a claw or a head, or in a dead or contracted position, most probably this was an attempt by the Scythians to control or extract their powers. Secondly, the 'Shaman' shared his prestigious position in society with only one the metalsmith. Both had unique power, both worked with fire, and both were participants in the special rituals and myths that made gold a sacred part of Scythians' life. Though it came to the Scythians from distinctly earthly sources the Caucasus, Ural and distant Altai ranges the metal was very nearly worshipped by them. "The Royal Scythians guard the sacred gold with the most special care", Herodotus wrote, "and year by year offer great sacrifices in its honour."

SHAMANISM

Shamanism is the name given to the native religion of the Ural[112] Altaic people from Baring Straits to the borders of Scandinavia. Weakened through the progress of Buddhism, Islam, and Christianity, it still exists even among tribes professing these faiths. On the whole, it is in a more or less moribund condition; and although its nature was everywhere much the same, its development varied in different tribes. Analogous phenomena are found among the Eskimos, and also among many American Indian tribes, whose medicine-men are often called shamans by investigators. How far it exists elsewhere either as a system of religion or with its various aspects more or less reproduced, is discussed below.

ITS DERIVATION

The word 'Shaman' appears to be derived from the native Tungus Evenk, also called Evenki, for merely Tungus, the most numerous and widely scattered of the many small nationalities of northern Siberia, name for the priest or medicine-man, saman used also with other names among the Buriats[113] and Yakuts[114]. Saman has been thought to be an adaptation of the Pali samana (Skr. Sramana), a Buddhist monk or medicant, through the Chinese shaman, but evidence is lacking. Still less likely is the derivation from Persian shaman, an idol or temple. Other native names are: Oyun fern, Udayan; Buriat, Bo, Fern odeyon, Utyyan; Altaian, Kam; Ostyak, Senin, Fern, Senim; 'Samoyed, tadibei; Lapp, noid.

THE SHAMAN (SCYTHIAN PRIEST)

He is a mediator between gods and spirits on the one hand and men on the other. He knows the secrets of gods and spirits, often malevolent, and the well-being of all depends on his power to cajole or overcome them by various actions, rites and their sacrifices. By these he can enlist the services of spirits. Among the Yakuts a shaman has ani-emekhet, or guardian-spirits, a divinity or the spirit of a dead shaman, who aids and advises him. In other cases, he may have many spirits in his control, and the more of these he has the more powerful he is.

THE OFFICE OF SHAMAN

In some tribes (Samoyeds[115] Ostyaks[116]) the office is hereditary, in others a predisposition to it suffices. The youth show signs of a childhood, which are thought to prove that he has been chosen by the spirits (Tunguses, Yakuts, Altai tribes). Among the Buriats, while anyone may become a shaman or be chosen by the gods, the office is usually hereditary. Both systems are also found among the Lapps[117]. Yet whether hereditary or selected, the youth generally show a predisposition to the office. He is nervous, moody, irritable, dreamy, given to hallucinations and trances, or he is epileptic. The Tungus youth declares that a dead shaman has chosen him in a dream as his successor, but he also shows himself crazy, timorous, and stupefied. Similarly among the Yakuts he gabbles like a maniac takes to the woods, jumps into river or water, injures himself with weapons. Among the Dstyaks, the shaman, chooses one of his sons according to his fitness, but the youth then spend his time in practices that irritate the nervous system and excite the imagination. The Buriat hereditary shaman shows special signs as a child; he is subject to fits and trances, is fond of solitude and it is then thought that his soul is with the spirits, being trained by them.

HIS FUNCTIONS

On the whole, the shaman is abnormal, neurotic, and epileptic; his functions are based on his abnormal qualities and aggravate these in turn. But in any case, a period is devoted to training and austerities. The youth may live for a time in the woods in a half-crazy state, practising austerities or shamanist exercises. In addition, he is usually taught for a longer or shorter period by an old shaman regarding the different kinds of spirits and the manner of summoning them. Thus the whole preliminary period is given to methods which augment the abnormal state and still more separate the postulant from other men. These methods including aggravation of the nervous systems, trances or fits, austerities, communion with spirits, visits to the spirit-world in trance, acquisition of knowledge from the spirits, are reproduced in the rites of the shaman, once he is consecrated to his office[118].

The shaman assumes an exceptional position, takes vows upon himself, becomes the propriety of spirits who. though subject to his summons, have yet full power over him[119].

Among the Yakuts an old shaman takes him to a hill or an open field, clothes him in shaman's dress and gives him the tambourine and drumstick and setting him between nine chaste youths and nine maidens, makes him promise that he will be faithful to the spirit who will fulfil his prayer. He tells him where the spirits dwell, what diseases they cause, and how they may be appeased. Then having killed a sacrificial animal, he sprinkles the candidate's dress with the blood. The spectators finally feast on the flesh. Among the Buriats the ceremony is much more elaborate[120].

FUNCTIONS OF THE SHAMAN

The shaman may be regarded as one whose priestly, prophetic, and magical-medical functions have not been differentiated. As to his priestly functions, while he acts occasionally as sacrificer, his presence as priest and sacrificer is of secondary importance to his other functions. He performs sacrifices from time to time and at these carries on dialogues with gods, but there are many sacrifices at which his presence is not essential, and which are offered, *e.g.* by the elder of a tribe or head of a household. As far as the shaman is concerned, his connection with sacrifice is mainly the fact that he knows what sacrifices will be pleasing to the gods on any particular occasion and the right means of appeasing them, since they are most particular about the form of sacrifice and prayer. Sacrifice is an important part of the shamanistic rites of healing and divination, but the shaman merely directs the nature and method of offering from his knowledge of the gods and spirits.

In healing, after the magical ceremonies, aids by the presence of spirits, it is indispensable to please gods who have relieved the patient, and the shaman decides what offerings are to be made to them.

The priestly functions of the shaman, and their connection with magic, may be seen from his actions at the great sacrifice to the god Bai-Yulgan among the Altai[121].

PROCEDURE FOR SELECTION OF THE SACRIFICIAL ANIMAL

On the first evening a yurt[122] is prepared in a place selected by him, and a young birch tree, with the lower branches lopped, is set up in it. A cattle pen is made outside, and a horse is chosen, which is held by a man called the holder of the head. The shaman waves a birch twig over it, thus driving its soul to gods, accompanied by the holder's soul. Then he assembles the spirits in his tambourine, sits on the image of a god, and is supposed to be pursuing the soul of the horse upon it. Having captured the soul, he blesses it, and with the aid of assistants slays the horse. The bones and skin form the offering; the flesh is eaten by the shaman and the company. Next evening, having fed the spirits in the tambourine he cleanses the soul of all present by certain rites, and prepares the head of the household to understand the prophecies which he is about to utter. In a state of ecstasy, he describes how he is mounting the heavens on the soul of the victim or on the goose.

SHAMAN, IN ECSTASY

He describes what he sees in the heavens, prophesies and utters secrets learned there, and finally, having reached the ninth or even the tenth or twelfth heaven, he invokes Bari Yulgan, learns whether he accepts the sacrifice, and obtains information regarding the comment whether, the harvest, etc. as well as the sacrifices which will then be required. He now falls exhausted. Frequently a third day is devoted to feasting and libations to the gods. The number of heavens scaled by the shaman depends upon his powers.

In this rite, the prophetic powers of the shaman are seen, and these, as well as his healing powers, distinguish him from a regular priest. While divination may be practised by means of a shoulder blade, a stick covered with runes[123], or the flight of arrows, the method of foretelling the future, supplying information regarding the winning of success or averting of misfortune, or explaining the perplexities of inquirers is the Seance, or what is locally known as Kamlanie.

SPIRITS REVEAL DIVINE INFORMATION

In this the shaman, his assistants, and the spectators are collected in a darkened hut. The dress necessary to the occasion is donned. The shaman beats his tambourine, summoning the spirits and collects them in it. He sings, dances, cries out, converses with the spirits, and by these means proves his inspired state. He rushes round till he falls fainting and produces delirium. While he is in this state, the spirits reveal their will to him or give him the desired information[124]. He foretells the future and declares the will of the gods. When he awakens, he remembers nothing of what has passed. During the performance voices and noises of various kinds are heard, and these are believed to be produced by spirits. Or, again, the shaman will allege that he is rising through the heavens, pushing aside the stars, and he describes his experiences, rhythmic songs, prayers and adorations are used by the Shaman Kamlanie.

The healing powers of the shaman, are partially medical, and mainly connected with the belief that diseases are caused by spirits which have lodged themselves in the sufferer. Hence the purpose of the ceremonies is to placate them or drive them out.

But are myths and shamans enough to explain remarkable art of the Scythians and their barbarity? Or is it possible that some further piece of evidence exists, a more complete account of life among the Scythians, perhaps one lost for thousands of years?

ERLIK'S REALM

Erlik is a king of the dead and master of death, who assumes the role of a fraudulent and unfortunate collator with supreme being. In stories about the origin of the universe, he appears as an aquatic bird in charge (under the supreme being) of fishing a kuttle earth from the bottom of the primordial sea—a theme also well-known in the East European folklore. In other myths, a similar being spirits on human beings as the time passes. They are created by God or breathes his bad spirit into man or woman *(Encyclopaedia of Britannica,* Vol. 26, p. 558).

The shaman may take over the spirits causing the disease into himself, and indicate necessary sacrifice, into which he now conveys it; or he may decide that the patient's soul has left his body or been carried off to Erlik's realm[125]. It is during the course of the performance he pursues it, even to its prison with Erlik, who may release it for certain sacrifices or may demand another soul in its stead. This soul is ensnared by the shaman and takes to Erlik, and its owner then dies. Such a performance is lengthy and expensive. Or, again, after much smoking, tambourine-playing, noise-producing, and singing (by which the shaman brings down his guardian-spirit), he dances and sings, and having discovered the cause of the illness, is assured of the help of powerful spirits. Still dancing and beating he sucks it out and drives it away. Finally, sacrifice is offered to propitiate the gods who have relieved the sufferer. Among the Samoyeds [126], if it is thought that the supreme deity Num[127], has sent the illness, the shaman refuses to oppose the divine will, but in other cases, he will persuade a tadebtsi (spirit) to go and implore Num to lend his aid[128].

A GREAT SHOW

At all such trances the spectators are much impressed by the whirling, dancing, singing, screaming tambourine-playing, and ecstatic behaviour of the shaman, and believe that spirits are present. Equally they believe in all that he is asserting—his flight through the air or into the heavens and his visits to distant regions. They are terror-struck, and their nerves are much affected. Frequently the shaman proves his power by conjuring tricks, or by being bound and then released by the spirits whom he has summoned, or by thrusting knives into his body. But this does not exclude the possibility of a profound conviction on the part of the shamans that they are chosen by the spirits, have intercourse with them, and possess a mysterious power over the forces of nature[129].

In the south of Siberia mystery plays in which the shamans are the actors are common. Among the Altaians the shaman's supposed journey to Erlik's realm is acted in the most dramatic fashion. This dramatization is also found among the Buriats, the shaman acting the part of the deity and other personages[130]. At the trances the dialogues carried on by the shaman with the spirits—their voices being produced by himself—are also of a highly dramatic character. Here we approach what is fully developed among many American-Indian tribes—the dramatization of the life of the gods by members of a mystery- cult who represent the various divinities.

THE SHAMAN'S DRESS AND ACCESSORIES

At his ceremonies the shaman wears a special dress, a coat hung with iron, rattles, rings, and representations of mythical animals, or with twisted handkerchiefs representing snakes, a mask, a breastplate, a hat, and embroidered stocking. All these havc a definite meaning and purpose, and often a mystic character. Among the accessories are a tambourine and drumstick. The tambourine has a crossbar hung with rattles and is decorated with figure of a symbolic kind, connected with shamanistic beliefs and mysteries. The spirits give this tambourine to the shaman and spirits are called up by it and collected in it, while on it he is carried through the air. Horse- staves of wood or iron, specially prepared and decorated, are also used in the rites, and on them the shaman flies to heaven[131].

THE SCYTHIANS, SAKAS AND THE PARTHIANS IN INDIA

The Scythians (also known as Sakas) who brought an end to the Greek rule first in Bactria and then in India, were originally Scythians of present Ukraine in Russia. Persians named them Sakas, who onwards began to be called Sakas, in India.

Herodotus expressly states that the term 'Sakas' was used by the Persians to denote Scythians generally; and this statement is certainly in accordance with the use of the word in the inscriptions of Darius, the king of Iran. In one of these, it occurs together with descriptions which show that it denotes certain Scythians in Europe as well as two branches of Scythians in Asia. These, we have reason to believe, are specimens merely of the innumerable swarms of nomads which had been finding their way during untold centuries from that great hive of humanity, China, to Western Asia and to Europe.

The settlements of Sakas which affected the history of India at this period were two in number. One of these occupied the country of the Jazartes to the north of Bactria and Sigdiana, and had for ages past been regarded as a great danger to Persian and Hellenic civilization in Central Asia; while the other inhabited the province of Drangiana, (Seistan) which lay between Persia and India and which subsequently bore the name of Sakasthana, 'the abode of the Sakas' (the later Sijistan and the modern Seistan). It is probable that both of these bodies of Sakas were stirred into activity in the middle of the second century B.C. by the same cause and the impact of further swarms of nomads who are known as the Yue-chi. The result of this impact was twofold.

On the one hand, the Hellenic kingdom of Bactria was submerged in a flood of barbarian invasion, and, on the other, the Parthian kings had occupied during two reigns (Phraates II, 138-128 B.C. and Artabanus II, 128-123 B.C.) in endeavours to stem the tide which had extended to Seistan, and were only completely successful in the following reign (Mithradates II the Great, 123-88 B.C.). The effect of the Saka invasion on the Parthian kingdom, was thus to increase the power of the Sakas (Scythian) settlement which was already established in the Parthian province of Seistan, and the result of the struggles between the Sakas and the Parthians in this region was the creation of a kingdom, probably more or less dependent on kingdom of Parthiana in which the two people were associated[132].

SCYTHIANS IN INDIA

They were forced to migrate out of their country by the hostility of neighbouring tribes. Soon after their infiltration into India, the lower Indus Valley came to be named as Scythia after them. Inscriptions and coins attest to the rule of a line of four Saka rulers, *viz.* Maues, Azes I, Azilizes, and Azes II. The nationality of these rulers is often questioned, some claiming the three as Parthian (Indian Pahlava). The Parthian traits may be due to the racial admixture which the Sakas certainly underwent during their long stay in eastern Iran, before their penetration into India, with the result that the members of the same family bear Scythian, Parthian, and also Persian names. In truth, the political career of the Scythians in India is so much mixed up with that of the Parthians that it is not always possible to differentiate between them. The Sakas and Pahlavas are mentioned side by side in Indian literature.

The rule of Azes II was supplanted in the first quarter of the first century A.D. by that of Gondophernes, unanimously acclaimed as Parthian. The Ubdi-Parthian supremacy was ephemeral, to be shattered by the mote vigorous and extensive rule of the Kushans who, however, retained the services of the Saka Satraps under their nominal allegiance.

REFERENCES

1. One of the Great Plains of Southern Europe and Asia, having few trees.
2. *The World's Last Mysteries,* Michael Ainsworth, p. 221.
3. Encyclopaedia of Religion and Ethics. **Vol. 11. p. 693.**
4. Claudius Ptolemaeus, commonly known as Ptolemy, was the last and the most famous of the Greek astronomers of antiquity. He worked at Alexandria laboratory from 127 to 151 A.D.
5. The people of Byzantine, on the present site of Instanbul, Turkey.
6. *Encyclopaedia of Britannica*, Vol. 5. p. 382.
7. *Encyclopaedia of Britannica*, Vol. 10. pp. 576-73.
8. *Encyclopaedia of Britannica,* Vol. 10. pp. 455-56.
9. Probably, the Finns.
10. A town north-east of Sardinia, Italy.
11. A Russian river.
12. The people of ancient district near the Don River occupied by the Sarmatians from 3rd century B.C. to 2nd century A.D., who spoke Indo-Iranian language, and were nomadic relatives of the Scythians *(The Concise Columbia Encyclopaedia,* p. 750).
13. Greek physician, c. 460 B.C.–370. B.C.
14. A river in Russia.
15. The historian and geographer (485 B.C.–425 B.C.), an Asian Greek, born at Halicarnassus.
16. An ancient region in south-eastern Europe Asia, in the Ukraine, Russia.
17. Rum, Bucovian, region, East Europe, in north-east Romania.
18. A river in south-east European Russia SFRS, rises from Obshchi Syrt foothills of the south Urals.
19. A river in Russia.
20. A river in west European USSR, rises north-west of Turkey, in Carpathian Mountains, flows 876 miles *(World Gazetteer,* p. 519).
21. A town in Sassari province, north-east Sardinia, part of Gulf of Terranova *(World Gazetteer,* p. 1374).
22. A river, Ukrainian SSR and Poland *(World Gazetteer,* p. 286).
23. Capital of Ukraine, Russia.
24. Dnieper River, USSR *(World Gazetteer,* p. 519).
25. Russian SFSR, fishing port in the southern part of the Don River delta mouth near the Sea of Azov *(World Gazetteer,* p. 133).
26. One of the streams, 1222 miles of Europe, in south-central European -Russian SFSR *(World Gazetteer*, p. 526).

27. Peninsula and Oblast of south European-Russian SFSR, on the Black Sea *(World Gazetteer*, p. 464).
28. A river in Germany.
29. A river in Germany.
30. A historic province of Rumania.
31. A historic province of central Rumania-chief city (*World Gazetteer*; p. 1939).
32. World Gazetteer, **p. 1303.**
33. A historic region in north-west Ukrainian SSR, name derived from extinct city of Volyn on the Bug River.
34. North of Chernijov.
35. City port in Ukrainian SSR, port of high right bank of Desna River *(World Gazetteer* p. 385).
36. Situated north of Tambov city.
37. City, SFSR, on Tana River (Head of navigation and 200 miles Southeast of Moscow).
38. Situated near city of Tambov.
39. One of the trades centers.
40. A city, Russian SFSR, popularly known as Kuibyshev *(World Gazetteer,* p. 1657).
41. A river in south-east European-Russian SFSR.
42. *Columbia Gazetteer of the World,* 3 Vols. Columbia University, New York, p. 2850.
43. Azob, City 31° 44' N 16°15' W Eur. Russia, a port on the Don River, delta, on Taganrog Bay of the seat of Azob, 25 miles southwest of Rostov-nadonu RR junction.
44. Columbia Gazetteer of the World, **3 Vol. p. 2850.**
45. An ancient empire in western Asia, in the region of the upper Tigris River: Capital, Nineveh, in the 7th Century B.C.
46. *Encyclopaedia of Religion and Ethics,* Vol. 9. p. 1723. The ancient district hear the Don River occupied by the Sarmatians from 3rd century B.C. to 2nd century A.D. They spoke Indo-Iranian language and were nomadic relatives of the Scythians. The term Samartia is also used for the land along the Danube and over the Carpathians, where the Sarmatians were later driven by the Huns *(The Concise Columbia Encylopaedia*, p. 750).
47. A member of ancient people who lived in Asia Minor and Syria from 2000 B.C. to about 700 B.C.
48. *Strabo,* Vol. II. p. 4.
49. *Herodotus,* Vol. I. p. 105.

50. The Aras River, Russian Araks, Persian Rude-E-Aras, Turkish Aras, Nehri Greek Araxes, river rising south of Eraurum in Bingol Daglori (mountains) of Turkish Armenia. *(Encyclopaedia of Britannica,* Vol. I. p. 518).
51. A member of an ancient people living north of Caucasus and the Sea of Azov, driven by the Scythians out of southern Russia *(Encyclopaedia of Britannica,* Vol. 3. p. 321).
52. Modern Greek Thraki, Latin Thracia.
53. Russian Kavkaz region and mountain system lying between the Black Sea and the Azov Sea. *(Encyclopaedia of Britannica,* Vol 2. p. 966).
54. *Strabo,* Vol. XI. VII-4, *Herodotus,* Vol. p. 105, *Josephus Ant.* XII- VIII-5. Ancient country of north-western Iran, generally corresponding to the modern regions of Azerbaijan, Kurdistan and parts of Rmansheh *(Encyclopaedia of Britannica,* Vol. 7. p. 999). Its Inhabitants were the Medes, an Indo-European, people who extended their rule over the Persia in the reign of Sargon. (d. 705 B.C.) and captured Nineveh in 612. B. C. Their capital was Ecbatana. Media was forcibly annexed (C. 550 B.C.) to Persia by Cyrus the Great.
55. Country of west Asia occupying generally what is now west and south Azerbaijan *(The Columbia Gazetteer,* Vol. 2. p. 1938).
56. 56° 12" N 14° 50" 50' E.
57. Located in the Caucasus Mountains.
58. Ancient kingdom of Armenia centered about L. Van in present day east of Turkey *(Columbia Gazetteer,* Vol. 3. p. 3286).
59. Popularly known as IS-KU-ZA-AI Mountain.
60. Ginir, a town called Gimir.
61. A city in west Palestine.
62. Persian Achaemenid nomenclature distinguished between (a) The Saka Hau Mavarka, corresponding to our Sakas in the strict sense, who must have inhabited Fergana and the neighbourhood of Kashgar, (b) The Saka Tigrakhanda of the Aral region on the lower Syr Darya and (c) The Saka Taradrava, that is "from overseas," in southern Russia, these being the historical Scythians.
63. *Die Sprache der Ossenten,* Vol. 1. W. Miller, p. 114.
64. *Scythians and Greeks.* (1913), E.H. Minns, p. 165.
65. "Sur Papparition de Fetrier chez les Scyths" *ESA,* Vol. IX (1934). p. 208.
66. *Documents Sur les Tou-Kiniue,* Ja (1864). p. 332.
67. Ancient and little known people who were driven in 8th century B.C. from the Crimea to the Lake Van region, modern eastern Turkey.

68. Died 585 B.C., King of Media (C. 625-585 B.C.). He made the kingdom of the Medes a major power in the Middle-East. In 612 B.C., Cyaxares took Ninveh and completely defeated the Assyrians by 605 B.C.
69. *Herodotus*, Vol. IV, p. 13.
70. *Sud-Russland in Alterthum$_3$* p. 162, (Leipzig 1921) Max Elliert.
71. "Sur Torigine des Antiquites dits mordviennes" *ESA*, Vol. XI (1937), p. 123.
72. *Statement to the Societe*. April 7, (1938), Emile Bennveni.
73. *ESA*, Vol. XI (1937), Tallgren, p. 128.
74. *ESA*, Vol. XI (1937), Tallgren, p. 138.
75. Region of Asia Minor.
76. Volga, in Russia.
77. Ancient Greek region of Asia Minor on the east Mediterranean in present day Turkey.
78. A Greek writer.
79. Greek historian.
80. A river in Hungary.
81. Ruler of Greece.
82. A city in Greece.
83. The political, economic and cultural centre of Greece.
84. Asia Minor.
85. Napoleon: Originally Napoleon Bonaparte (1769-1821), called "the Little Corporal", emperor of France, (1804-1814).

    A brilliant military strategist, he deposed French Directory (1799) and proclaimed himself first Consul and, later Emperor (1804).
86. A number of people of southern Russia, famous as horsemen.
87. One of the great plains of southern Europe and Asia having few trees.
88. The World's Last Mysteries, Michael Ainsworth.
89. Of Chios (ff 460 B.C.–360 B.C.), Greek physician recognised as the father of medicine.
90. Historic region, south-west of Ukraine, Russia.
91. Central Ukraine 49° 30" N 34° 00" E, in Dnieper lowland.
92. Encyclopaedia of Religion and Ethics, **Vol. 4. pp. 73-75.**
93. *History of Greco-Persian Wars*. Book IV, Herodotus, pp. 67-69.
94. Region in south-west Ukraine, Russia.
95. A city in Ukraine, SSR. Russia.
96. A city in Greece.
97. Ancient city of Persia.

98. The Queen of the Massagetai or Scythian Queen. *Encyclopaedia of Religion and Ethics,* Vol. XI. p. 277.
99. The Scythian Queen, *Encyclopaedia of Religion and Ethics,* Vol. XI. p. 88.
100. Queen of Sharmanism, Encyclopaedia of Religion and Ethics, Vol. XI. p. 277.
101. Qr. Tirgated, the Scythian Queen, *Encyclopaedia of Religion and Ethics,* Vol. XI. p. 277.
102. A Greek historian, 460 B.C.—400 B.C.
103. Darius the Great (Shahan-e-Shah of Iran), (549 B.C.—486 B.C.), the emperor of Persia and successor to Cambyses-II, after defeating a false claimant, Magian Gomates. Darius, a member of Achaemenid (q.v.) dynasty, proved a great ruler. He extended the Persian Empire into northern India and Europe, and in the battle against Scythians, he invaded Macedonia and Thrace in 515 B.C.
104. The ancient Greek physician (C-460 B.C.—377 B.C.), the father of medicine, put a definitive stamp on the whole character of Greek medicine *(Encyclopaedia of World Biography,* Vol. 7. pp. 408-410).
105. *Ibid.* p. 146.
106. *Scythian Art* (New York-1925) G.I. Borovka. p. 123.
107. A river C. 570 miles long S. East Russia, rising in the Greater Caucasus Mountains on west slopes of Mt. Elbrus *(Columbia Gazetteer of World,* Vol. II, p. 1624).
108. *Scythian Art* (New York-1925) G.I. Borovka. p. 222.
109. *Hunting Magic in the Animal Style.* BMFEA-No.4 (1932), J.G. Anderson, p. 259.
110. Cf. Josef "D'er Tierzauher" *AA* Vol. (1935), p. 202.
111. "Sur Forigine des antiquites mordvienes," *ESA* Vol. XI (1937), p. 133.
112. The Ural River, the traditional border between Europe and Asia and separating the Russian plain from the west Siberian lowland.
113. Also Buryat, northernmost land of the major Mongol people, living south and east of Lake Barkal by the Treaty of Nerchink (1689). Their land was ceded by China to the Russian Empire.
114. Yakut or Sakha, one of the major peoples of eastern Siberia, numbering some 380,000 in the late 20th century.
115. Also called Nenets or Nentsy or Yurat, autonomous Okrug (district) Arkhangelsk province, north-western Russia.
116. Khanty, Mansujsk, formerly, until 1940 Ostyako-Vogulsk, city and administrative centre of Khanty, Mansi, autonomous Okrug (district), a part of Tyumen province, Russia, also called Ostyaks.

117. Or Laplanders who constitute the indigenous population occupying north Norway, where they are called Samme or Fins, number less than 40,000.
118. A Van Gennep-Les-Ritesde passage, Paris 1909. p. 158.
119. V. M. Milk-Railov ski-i-shamanism is Siberia and European Russia Tr. O. Wordrop 1895. p. 90.
120. See Art Buriats, p. 30.
121. South-west Siberia, Russia, in the basin of the upper Ob River. Rolling plains and the foothills of the Altai Mountains.
122. A circular, domed tent used by the nomadic Mongols of Siberia. Turkish yurt, home.
123. A secret mystery, runic character; readopted in 17th century.
124. V. V. Bedlov Aus Vol. II. 20 ff.
125. A buriated deity.
126. Nomadic ancient tribe of west Siberia and Russia.
127. Num knows and sees all that happen upon the earth. *Encyclopaedia of Religion and Ethics*, Vol. II. p. 121b.
128. M. A. Castren.
129. Mikhailovskii, p. 143. Leipaig (1863), p. 114 f.
130. Ct. Buriats F. 27.
131. For details please see Buriat's *Encyclopaedia of Religion and Ethics* Vol. III. p. 16.
132. *Ancient India*, E. J. Rapson, pp. 135-37.

BIBLIOGRAPHY

Blunt, E.A.H. *The Caste System of Northern India.*

Dallon. *Descriptive Ethonology,* Bengal.

Darling, Nelson. The Panjab Peasant in Prosperity and Debt, 4th ed.

H.A. Rose. *A Glossary of the Tribes and Castes of the Panjab North-West Frontier Province*, Vols. I, II, III.

Hastings, James (Ed). *Encyclopaedia of Religion and Ethics*, Vols. II, I, XI, (1909). M.A.D.D.

Risley, Sir Herbert. *Tribes and Castes in the Panjab*, Vol. I.

The Columbia Lippinoott Gazetteer of the World.

The New Encyclopaedia of Britannica, Vol. 6. 2003.

The Jats
(Descendants of Scythians)

2

ORIGIN

The Jats are the descendants of Scythians, whose kingdom's capital was Scythia, in the present Ukraine (Ukrainian), Soviet Social Republic, is the constituent Republic of the European USSR (Population 49,757,000) in 1947. Now Ukraine's capital is Kiev, the third leading city in Russia. Before the invasion of the golden herd, 13th century B.C. Scythian, ancient kingdom of indeterminate boundaries, centered in the area north of the Black Sea. "The Scythians were nomadic horsemen who made periodic incursions into the area to the south. They flourished from 9th century B.C. to the 2nd century B.C., when they were conquered by the Sarmatians."[1] Sufficient details have been mentioned about the origin of the Scythians, in the first chapter of this book. However a summary of the background of the Jats is given hereunder for more information:

THE ORIGIN OF THE JAT

Perhaps no question connected with the ethnology of peoples of the Panjab has been so much discussed as the origin of the Jat race. It is not the intention here to reproduce any of the arguments adduced. They will be found in the *Archaeological Survey Reports*, Vol. II, pages 51-61; in Tod's *Rajasthan*, Vol. I, pages 52-75 and 96-101 (Madras Reprint, 1880); in Elphinstone's *History of India*, pages 250-253; and in Elliot's *Races of the N.W.F.R*, Vol. I, pages 130-137 and suffice it to say that both General Cunningham and Major Tod agree in considering the Jats to be of Indo-Scythian stock. The former identifies them with the Zanthii of Strabo[2] and the Jatii of Pliny and Ptolemy; and holds that they probably entered the Panjab from their home on the Oxus very shortly after the Meds or Mands, who also were Indo-Scythians, and who moved into the Panjab about a century before Christ. The Jats seem to have first occupied the Indus Valley as far down as Sindh, whither the Meds followed them about the beginning of the present era. But before the earliest Muslim invasion the Jats had spread into the Panjab proper where they were firmly established in the beginning of the 11th century A.D. By the time of Babar the Jats of the Salt-range Tract had been subdued by the Gakkhars, Awans, and Janjuas, while as early as the 7th century the Jats and Meds of Sindh were ruled over by a Brahman dynasty. Major Tod classes the Jats as one of the great Rajput tribes and extends his identification with the Getae to both races; but here General Cunningham differs, holding the Rajputs to belong to the original Aryan stock, and the Jats too belong to a later wave of immigrants from the north-west of Scythian race.

JATS AND RAJPUTS

It may be that the original Rajput and the original Jat entered India at different periods in its history, though the term 'Rajput' is an occupational rather than an ethnological expression. But if they do originally represent two separate waves of immigration, it is at least exceedingly probable, both from their almost identical physique and facial character and from the close communion which has always existed between them, that they belong to one and the same ethnic stock; while whether this be so or not, it is almost certain that they have been for many centuries and still are so intermingled and so blended into one people that it is practically impossible to distinguish them as separate wholes. It is indeed more than probable that the process of fusion has not ended here, and the Rajput, if these two ever were distinct, is by no means free from foreign elements. How the Pathan people have assimilated Saiyads, Turks, and Mughals, and how it was sufficient for a Jat tribe to retain its political independence and organisation in order to be admitted into the Baloch nation. How a character for sanctity and social exclusiveness combined in a few generations make a Qureish or a Saiyad; and it is almost certain that the joint Jat-Rajput stock contains not a few tribes of aboriginal descent, though it is probably in the main Aryo- Scythian, if Scythian be not Aryan. The Jat and the Rajput belonged to the one and the same race. There is a mention of the pedigrees of these two races and the writer has concluded: "I think they (the pedigrees) may be retried on in so far as they show that most of the Rajputs and Jats of these parts belong to one and the same race, originally[3]. The Man, Her, and Bhular Jats

(Section 435) are known as ASL or original Jats because they claim no Rajput ancestry, but are supposed to be descended from the hair (Jat) of the aboriginal god Shiva; the Jats of the south-eastern districts divide themselves into two sections, SHIVGOTRI of the family of Shiva, and KASABGOTRI who claim connection with the Rajputs; and the names of the ancestor Bar of the Shivgotris and of his son Barbara are the very words which the ancient Brahmans give them as the marks of the barbarian aborigines. Many of the Jat tribes of the Panjab have customs which apparently point to non-Aryan origin, and a rich and almost virgin field for investigation is here open to the ethnologist."

ARE THE JATS AND RAJPUTS DISTINCT?

But whether Jats and Rajputs were or were not originally distinct, and whatever aboriginal elements may have affiliated to their society, the two now form a common stock, the distinction between the Jat and the Rajput being social rather than ethnic. It is believed that those families of that common stock whom the tide of fortune has raised to political importance have become Rajputs almost by mere virtue of their rise; and that their descendants have retained the title and their privileges on the condition, strictly enforced, of observing the rules by which the higher are distinguished from the lower castes in the Hindu scale of precedence; of preserving their purity of blood by refusing to marry with families of inferior social rank, of rigidly abstaining from widow marriage, and of refraining from degrading occupations. Those who transgressed these rules have fallen from their high position and ceased to be Rajputs, while such families as, attaining a dominant position in their territory, began to affect social exclusiveness and to observe the rules, have become not only Rajas, but also Rajputs or "sons of Rajas". For the last seven centuries the process of elevation at least has been almost at a standstill. Under the Delhi emperors king-making was practically impossible. Under the Sikh, the Rajput was overshadowed by the Jat, who resented his assumption of superiority and his refusal to join him on equal terms in the ranks of the Khalsa, deliberately persecuted him wherever and whenever he had the power and preferred his title of Jat Sikh to that of the proudest Rajput. On the frontier, the dominance of Pathans and Baloches and the general prevalence of Mohammedan feelings and ideas placed recent Indian origin at a discount, and led the leading families who belonged to neither of these two races to claim connection, not with the Kshatriyas of the Sanskrit classics, but with the Mughal conquerors of India or the Qureshi cousins of the Prophet; insomuch that even admittedly Rajput tribes of famous ancestry, such as the Khokhar, have begun to follow the example. But in the hills, where Rajput dynasties with genealogies perhaps more ancient and unbroken than can be shown by any other royal families in the world retained their independence till yesterday, and where many of them still enjoy as great social authority as ever, the twin processes of degradation from and elevation to Rajput rank are still to be seen in operation. The Raja is there the fountain not only of honour but also of caste, which is the same thing in India. Writes a scholar:

"Till lately the limits of caste do not seem to have been so immutably fixed in the hills as in the plains. The Raja was the fountain of honour and could do much as he liked. I have heard old men quote instances within their memory in which a Raja promoted a Girth to be a Rathi, and a Thakar to be a Rajput, for service done or money given; and at the present day the power of admitting back into caste fellowship persons put under a ban for some grave act of defilement, is a source of income to the Jagirdar Rajas."

"I believe that Mr. Campbell, the present Lieutenant Governor of Bengal, has asserted that there is no such thing as a distinct Rajput stock; that in former times before caste distinctions had become crystallized, any tribe or family whose ancestor or head rose to royal rank became in time Rajput. This is certainly the conclusion to which many facts point with regard to the Rajputs of these hills. Two of the old royal and now essentially Rajput families of this district, *viz.* Kotlehr and Bangahal, are said to be Brahmin by original stock. Mr. Barnes says that in Kangra the son of a Rajput by a low-caste woman takes place as a Rathi; in Seoraj and other places in the interior of the (Shivalik) hills I have met families calling themselves Rajputs, and growing into general acceptance as Rajputs, in their own country at least, whose only claim to the title was that their father or grandfather was the offspring of a Kanetui by a foreign Brahmin. On the border line in the Himalayas, between Tibet and India proper, anyone can observe caste growing before his eyes; the noble is changing into a Rajput, the priest into a Brahmin, the peasant into a Jat and so on down to the bottom of the scale. The same process was, I believe, more or less in force in Kangra proper down to a period not very remote from today".

PROCESS OF DEGRADATION

The reverse process of degradation from Rajput to lower rank is too common to require proof of its existence, which will be found, if needed, together with further instances of elevation, in the section which treats the Rajputs and kindred castes. In the eastern districts of the province, where Brahmanism is stronger than in any other part of the Panjab and Delhi to allow of families rising to political independence, it is probable that no elevation to the rank of Rajput has taken place within recent times. But many Rajput families have ceased to be Rajputs. Setting aside the general tradition of the Panjab Jats to the effect that their ancestors were Rajputs who married Jats or began to practise widow marriage, we have the Gaurwa Rajputs of Gurgaon and Delhi, who have indeed retained the title of Rajputs because they grow vegetables like the Arain; in Karnal, we have Rajputs who within the living generation have ceased to be Rajputs and become Sheikhs, because poverty and loss of land forced them to weaving as an occupation; while the Delhi Chauhan, within the shadow of the city where their ancestors once ruled and led the Indian armies in their last struggle with the Mussalman invaders, have lost their caste by yielding to the temptations of Karewa[4]. In the Sikh tract, as has been said, the Jat is content to be a Jat and has never since the rise of Sikh power wished to be anything else. In the western plains the freedom of marriage allowed by Islam has superseded caste restrictions, and social rank is measured by the tribe rather than by the larger unit of caste. But even their families which were a few generations ago reputed Jats have now risen by social exclusiveness to be recognised as Rajputs, and families which were lately known as Rajputs have sunk till they are now classed with Jats; while the great ruling tribes, the Sial, the Gondal, the Tiwana in Pakistan are commonly spoken of as Rajputs, and their smaller brethren as Jats. The same tribe even is Rajput in one district and Jat in another, according to its position among the local tribes. In the Salt-range Tract, Pakistan, the dominant tribes, the Janjua, Manhas found in both the Panjabs and the like, are Rajputs when they are not Mughals or Arabs: while all agricultural tribes of Indian origin which cannot establish their title to Rajput rank are Jats. Finally, on the frontier the Pathan and the Baloch have overshadowed Jat and Rajput alike; and Bhatti, Punwar, Tunwar, all the proudest tribe of Rajputana are included in the name and have sunk to the level of Jat, for there can be no Rajputs where there are no Rajas or traditions of Rajas. It is well known that the views herein set forth will be held heretical and profane by many, and that they ought to be supported by a greater wealth of instance than have been produced in the following pages.

THE POSITION OF JAT IN THE PANJAB

The Jat is, in every respect, the most important of the Panjab peoples. In point of numbers, he surpasses the Rajput who comes next to him in the proportion of nearly three to one; while the two together constitute 27 per cent of the whole population of the Province. Politically, he ruled the Panjab till the Khalsa yielded to the British arms. Ethnologically, he is the peculiar and most prominent product of the plains of the five rivers. And from an economical and administrative point of view, he is the husbandman, the peasant, the revenue-payer *par excellence* of the province. His manners do not bear the impress of generations of wild freedom which marks the races of our frontier mountains. But he is more honest, more industrious, sturdier and no less manly than they. Sturdy independence, indeed, and patient vigorous labour are his strongest characteristics. The Jat is of all Panjab races the most impatient of tribal or communal control, and the one which asserts the freedom of the individual most strongly. In tracts where, as in Rohtak, the Jat tribes have the field to themselves, and are compelled, in default of rival castes as enemies, to fall back upon each other for somebody to quarrel with, the tribal ties are strong. But as a rule a Jat is a man who does what seems right in his own eyes and sometimes what seems wrong also and will not be said by any man. However, he is turbulent; as a rule he is very far from being so. He is independent and he is self-willed; but he is reasonable, peaceably inclined, if left alone, and not difficult to manage. He is usually content to cultivate his fields and pay his revenue in peace and quietness, if people will let him do so; though when he does go wrong he "takes to anything from gambling to murder, with perhaps a preference for stealing other people's wives and cattle". As usual the proverbial wisdom of the villages describes him very fairly, though perhaps somewhat too severely: "The soil, fodder, clothes, hemp, grass fibre, and silk these six are best beaten; and the seventh is the Jat". "A Jat, a Bhat, a caterpillar, and a widow woman; these four are best hungry. If they eat to their fill they do harm." "The Jat, like a wound, is better when bound." In agriculture, the Jat is pre-eminent. The market-gardening castes; the Arian, the Mali, the Saini, are perhaps more skillful cultivators on a small scale; but they cannot rival the Jat as landowners and yeoman cultivators. The Jat calls himself zamindar or "husbandman" as often as Jat, and his women and children alike work with him in the fields: "The Jat and his women and baby have a plough handle for a plaything". "The Jat stood on his corn heap and said to the king's elephant-drivers— 'Will you sell those little donkeys?'"

SOCIAL POSITION

Socially, the Jat occupies a better position, which is shared by the Ror, the Gujjar, and the Ahir, all four eating and smoking together. He is of course far below the Rajput, from the simple fact that he practises widow marriage. The Jat father is made to say, in the rhyming proverbs of the countryside, "Come my daughter and be married; if this husband dies there are plenty more." But among the widow-marrying castes, he stands first. The Banya, with his sacred thread, his strict Hinduism, and his twice-born standing, looks down on the Jat as a Sudra. But the Jat looks down upon the Banya as a cowardly spiritless money-grubber, and society in general agrees with the Jat. The Khatri, who is far superior to the Banya in manliness and vigour, probably takes precedence of the Jat. But among the races or tribes of purely Hindu origin, the Jat stands next after the Brahman, the Rajput, and the Khatri.

THE SIKH JATS

The Jat of the Sikh tracts is of course the typical Jat of the Panjab. The Jat of the south-eastern districts differs little from him save in religion; though on the Bikaner border the puny Bagri Jat, immigrant from his rainless prairies where he has been held in bondage for centuries, and ignorant of cultivation save in its rudest form, contrasts strongly with the stalwart and independent husbandman of the Malwa. On the lower Indus the word 'Jat' is applied generically to a congeries of tribes Jat proper, Rajputs, lower castes, and mongrels, who have no points in common save their Muslim religion, their agricultural occupation, and their subordinate position. In the great western grazing grounds it is impossible to draw any sure line between Jat and Rajput, the latter term being commonly applied to those tribes who have attained political supremacy, while the people who attained dispossession of their territory to live a semi-nomad life in the central steppes are more often classed as Jats; and the state of things in the Salt-range tract, Pakistan, is very similar. Indeed the word 'Jat' is the

Panjabi term for a grazier or herdsman; though Mr. O'Brien says that in Jatki, Jat, the cultivator, is spelt with a hard 't', and Jat, the herdsman or camel-grazier, with a soft 't'. Thus the word 'Jat:' in Rohtak or Amritsar districts means a great deal; in Muzaffargarh or Bannu, Pakistan, it means nothing at all, or rather perhaps it means a great deal more than any single word can afford to mean if it is to be of any practical use; and the two classes respectively indicated by the term in these two parts of the province must not be too readily confounded.

DISTRIBUTION OF THE JATS

It may be concluded that the Jats of the Panjab became Sikhs on the persuation of Guru Gobind Singh and became the rulers with his blessings, whereas the Rajputs did not agree to embrace Sikhism only because of the caste superiority complex in them. If they had taken Pauhal as the Guru advised at Rawalsar, they could have expanded their kingdom. During the rule of the Sikh Misls, the Jats started considering themselves to be the rulers, while the Rajputs became their subjects. During the rule of Maharaja Ranjit Singh (1799-1839) the Jat showed this superiority over the Rajputs of the Panjab in every field of life and this position still exists probably due to their numerical strength. Jats are in majority in the Panjab, while they are in minority in Rajasthan".[5] Beyond the Panjab, Jats are chiefly found in Sindh where they form the mass of the population, in Bikaner, Jaisalmer, and Marwar, where they probably equal in numbers all the Rajput races put together, and along the upper valleys of the Ganges and Jamna from Bareilly, Farrukhabad, and Gwalior upwards. They are especially numerous in the central Sikh districts and in the Panjab state in the southeastern districts, and in the Derajat. Under and among the hills and in the Rawalpindi division Pakistan, Rajputs take their place, while on the frontier both upper and lower, they are almost wholly confined to the cis-Indus, tracts and the immediate Indus riverine on both sides of the stream. The Jats of the Indus are probably still in the country which they had occupied ever since their first B.C. entry into India, though they have been driven back from the foot of the Suleman's on to the river by the advance of the Pathan and the Baloch. The Jats of the western plains have almost without exception come up the river valleys from Sindh or western Rajputana. The Jats of the western and central sub-montane have also in part come by the same route; but some of them retain a traditional connection with

Ghazni, which perhaps refers to the ancient Ghaznipur, the side of the modern Rawalpindi, while many of them trace their origin from the Jammu Hills.

The Jats of the Central and Eastern Panjab have also in many cases come up the Satluj valley; but many of them have moved from Bikaner straight into the Malwa, while the great central plains of the Malwa itself are probably the original home of many of the Jat tribes of the Sikh tract. The Jats of the south-eastern districts and the Jamna zone have for the most part worked up the Jamna valley from the direction of Bharatpur, with which some of them still retain a traditional connections, though some few have moved in eastwards from Bikaner and the Malwa. The Bharatpur Jats are themselves said to be immigrants who left the banks of the Indus in the time of Aurangzeb. Whether the Jats of the Great plains are really as late immigrants as they represent, or whether their story is merely founded upon a wish to show recent connection with the country of the Rajputs.

VIEWS ON THE ORIGIN OF JATS

According to Saiyad Muhammad Latif, author of *History of the Panjab* (1891), "When the Median King Cyaxares checked the advance of the Scythian hordes, in the mid-7th century B.C. from overrunning his Indus domain, the routed Scythians fled to Panjab where a portion of these settlers' descendants of Massagetae[6], were called the Getaes from whom spring the modern Jats."[7] J.D. Cunningham informs us that, "The plains of upper India, in which the Brahmans and Kshatriyas had developed a peculiar civilization, have been overrun by Persian and Scythic tribes, from the age of Darius and Alexander (and that there has been) along antecedent emigration of hordes of Jats from the plains of upper Asia."

He believes that the Hindu civilisation "absorbed (these) barbarous invaders, and that in the lapse of centuries the Jats became essentially Brahmanical in language and beliefs."[8]. Major A.E. Barstow observes that, "Meanwhile the Medii, Xanthii[9], Jatti, Getae and other Scythian races, were gradually working their way from the banks of the Oxus into southern Afghanistan and the pastoral highland about Quetta whence they forced their way by the Bolan Pass, through the Sulaiman Mountains into India, settling in the Panjab about the beginning of the first century B.C. It is from these Scythian immigrants that most of the Jat tribes are at any rate partly descended[10]. J.W. McCrindle wrote "that mention is made by Arrian of nomads in the Swat and Indus Valley, Pakistan." Diodoros refers to them as Siboi, people claiming descent from the soldiers of Herakles. The Siboi had occupied lands between the Indus River and the Jhelum River, Pakistan, additionally. Traces of their habitation are also to be found in Siwistan (modern Sind[11]). Buddha Parkash informs that, "These people are known in the Indian texts as Subis and their modern descendants seem to be Chibs."[12]

Dr. Dhillon confirms that Sibs "mentioned in a Shorkot (Pakistan) inscription" are the modern Siboi who belong to a Jat clan[13]. Major General A. Cunningham in his *Archaeological Report* (1863-64), identifies Jat "with the Xzanthii of Strabo (born 64 B.C.), and the Jatii of Pliny (born 23 A.D.) and Ptolemy that their parent country must have been on the banks of the Oxus, between Bactria, Byrkania and Khorasmia...they may have been known in early times by the general name of their horde, as Abars, instead of their tribal name as Jats."[14] According to this view, the main body of the Jatii would have occupied the district of Abiria and the towns of Paradabathra in Sindh, Pakistan; or southern Indo-Scythia, while the Panjab or northern Indo-Scythia was chiefly colonized by their brethren the Medes[15]. Identical postulates have been advanced by Sir Denzil Ibbetson, in his Census Report titled *A Glossary of the Tribes and Castes of the Panjab and North-West Frontier Province,* and according to him similar assertions will be found in Lt. Col. Tod's *Annals and Antiquities of Rajasthan*, M. Elphinstone's *The History of India,* Sir H.M. Elliot's *Races of the North-West Province.*

In his overtly, lengthy and stretched out explanation regarding the origin of Jats in his *Jats, Origin, Antiquity and Migrations*, Hukam Singh Pawar's coral dimension rests on, as he puts it, "First we hold that Aryans and Scythians are identical entities; secondly, that Jats are of Aryan/Scythian ancestry, and thirdly, that the original home of the Aryans/Scythians (Jats) was in Sapta Sindhu. Fourthly, we believe that there was a religious schism, and this became one of the compelling motive forces of migrations as well as of denunciation of certain Aryan/ Scythian tribes by the Aryans of another religious dispensation. Fifthly, we hold that during the earliest Aryan/Vedic period the present United Province and Bihar consisted of a vast sea.... Sixthly, it is our contention that the Jats were the most prominent among the westward waves of migration of Aryans and that is why there are so many variations of the word "Jat" spread all over many lands, and their gotras, such as Mann, Gill, Dhillon, Virk (and so on) are to be found prevalent in the countries of the west."[16]

Among the early Indian monarchs, Akbar the Great (1605 A.D.) took steps, at the initiative of his efficient minister Todar Mal in 1572 A.D. to develop the state revenue department. Todar Mal, a Khatri of Lahore, with the joint efforts of his energetic minister, Abul Fazl, the land of some of the provinces of India was for the first time measured and given to the owners.

Bhupinder Singh Mahal writes, "The next mention about Jats is to be found in the records of *Ain-i-Akbari*, compiled about 1595, which includes a catalogue of governance all the way down to the village level. Soon after his accession (February 1556), Akbar the Great, was to place a high priority in streamlining the administrative functions of his empire, in particular the system of tax collection. He was to partition his realm into administrative units consisting of provinces which were divided into districts which in turn were subdivided into parganas. The Karkun (record-keeper) of the pargana, the lowest fiscal unit, was to keep records of arable land, cultivator, crop raised and collection of taxes. According to Prof. Irfan Habib, "*The Ain* lists Zamindar castes (landowners) against each pargana. These lists show that the Jats were now concentrated in a region extending from the Jech and Upper Rechna Doab, across the upper and central Bari Doab, to the cis-Sutlej territories of Sirhind and Hisar Firoza. There were two other blocks, rating into Rohilkhand; and, the other consisting of Delhi to south of Chambal. This by and large accord with the present settlements of the Jatt (Jat) castes, except that towards the southeast a modern map would show a more extensive area, thanks to the expansion of Jat Zamindari during the 18th century Jat kingdom of Suraj Mal."[17]

To further quote Bhupinder Singh Mahal in his 1971 Presidential address titled "Jats of Panjab and Sindh" said that Prof. Irfan Habib of Aligarh University informs us that Hiuen Tsang, the founder of the 7th century A.D. Kingdom of Tsekkia (Arabic Takia), bounded by the rivers Beas to the Indus, describes the people he met in Sindh as follows: "By the side of the river Sindh, along the flat marshy lowlands for some thousand lie, there are several hundreds of thousands (a very great many) families settled....They give themselves to tending cattle and from this derive their livelihood....They have no masters, and whether men or women, have neither rich nor poor....They claimed to be Buddhists, but they were of an unfeeling temper and hasty disposition." He further continues to state, quoting Prof. Irfan Habib that "This large pastoral population, left unnamed by Hiuen Tsang, is described in practically identical terms by the *Cbachanama*, the celebrated account of the Arab conquest of Sindh (710-14 A.D.). The important addition is that these people are given the name of Jat....They are designated Dashti, *i.e.* belonging to the steppe or wastes. There were no small or great among them.... Besides pastoralism, the only other occupations, they pursued were those of soldiers and boatmen."

According to Prof. Habib the presence of Jats in Panjab is first witnessed in the 11th century A.D. when "we suddenly have the appearance in strength of Jats of Multan and Bhatiya, (by) the banks of Sihun (Indus)", who with their 4,000 or 8,000 boats engaged the forces of Mahmud Ghazni. The Jat's presence in the Panjab is also attested by the statement of another Ghaznid historian that these 'Seditious Hindus' had supported Sultan Masud's officers against the rebel Yenaltigin.... A northward migration of the Jats into the southern Panjab from Sindh Pakistan must have taken place by the eleventh century A.D. One can see how these fits in with the philological evidence which attests to the considerable influence of the language akin to Sindhi in the Multan area, a situation one would naturally expect to have followed the migration of the Jats into the region".

EXPLANATION

Jat (Fe, Jatni; Panjab Jat, Fe, Jatti)

The Jats are found all over north-west of India, in Panjab, Sindh, Uttar Pradesh and the northern parts of Rajasthan, especially Bharatpur, but hardly in Kashmir or Himachal Pradesh. In west of the Indus, Pakistan, they are found in the Northwest Frontier Province, especially in its southern districts, but not in Afghanistan or in Balochistan, though they appear to have once occupied the latter territory. The Balochi term for a Jat is Jagdal or Jaghdal, and one of the Baloch tribes traces its descent from a Jat, a Jaghal, a nobody, who on account of a woman, *i.e.* by marrying a Baloch bride, became a Baloch. The Jotoi tribe of the Baloch is also of the Jat origin.

Herodotus, father of history, a Greek and a contemporary historian, wrote:

"These are the historical data. Scanty as they are, they serve to establish the fact that during a long period of time swarms of nomadic people, whose outlandish names are conveniently summed up in the generic term Scythian, poured into India, conquered and governed." Their coins are now the sole memorial of their rule, but their inroads probably began many centuries before coins were struck or annals compiled. Of the people themselves all traces seem to have vanished, and the student who enquires what has become of them, finds nothing more tangible than the mere conjecture that they are represented by the Jats and the Rajputs. But the grounds for this opinion are of the flimsiest description and consist mainly of the questionable assumption that the people, who are called Jats of the present day must have something to do with the people who were known to Herodotus as Getae. Now apart from the fact that resemblances of names are mostly misleading—witness the Roman identification of these very Getae with the Goths—we have good historical reasons for believing that the Scythian invaders of, India came from a region occupied exclusively by broad-headed races and must themselves have belonged to that type. They were, by all accounts, nations or hordes of horsemen, with broad faces and high cheekbones, short and sturdy of stature, and skilled in the use of the bow. In their original homes on the Central Asian steppes their manner of life was that of pastoral nomads; and their instincts were of the predatory order. It seems, therefore, *prima facia* unlikely that their descendants are to be looked for among tribes who are essentially of the long-headed type, tall, heavy men, without any natural aptitude for horsemanship, settled agriculturists with no traditions of a nomadic and marauding past.

GETAE (JAT)

An elaboration of Getae is given hereunder:

"Getae were ancient people of Thracian origin, inhabiting the banks of the lower Danube region and nearby plains. First appearing in the 6th century B.C., the Getae were subjected to Scythian influence and were known as expert mounted archers and devotees of the deity Zalmoxis[18]. Although the daughter of their king became the wife of Philip II of Macedon in 342 B.C. The Macedonians under Philip IPs son, Alexander, crossed the Danube and the Getae capital seven years later. Getae technology was influenced by that of the invading Celts in the 4th and 3rd centuries B.C. under Burelistas (first century B.C.). The Getae and nearby Dacians formed a powerful but short-lived state. By the middle of the following century, when the Romans had gained control over the lower Danube region, thousands of Getae (Jats) were displaced from history. Later writers wrongly gave the name Getae to the Goths. "The Getae and Dacians were closely related. Their culture is sometimes called Getae Dacian."[19]

THE CONFLICTING VIEWS

Writers such as Greek, Ibbetson, Risley and Baden-Powell have discussed some of the ethnological and sociological problems connected with the Jats, notably their origin and various theories concerning it, their ethnic affiliation with Rajputs, Gujjars, Ahirs, Baloches and the Pathans, their customs of widow marriage, polyandry and taking wives from other castes, the custom of the Bhaichara (brotherhood) and its bearing on the clan fraternities, and their tribal political organizations. These writings of sixty or eighty years ago have facilitated the investigation of such problem as they present themselves today and have helped in analysis of social change within the Jat community. Here some of these problems have been discussed briefly in order to show their sociological importance for the present study of the Jats.

There are conflicting views on the origin of the Jats. For example, Ibbetson, Cunningham and Tod consider them to be of Indo-Scythian stock and hold that they entered Panjab from their home on the Oxus about a century before Christ. Tod classes the Jats one of the greatest Rajput tribes, but Cunningham differs in holding the Rajputs to belong to original Aryan stock and the Jats to a later wave of immigrations from the North-West[20], Badan-Powell thinks that this controversy whether the Jats are pre-Macedonian or belong to invasions closer to the commencement of the Christian era should be left open[21].

Others consider the Jats to be of Aryan stock. According to Nesfield's theory, the word 'Jat' is nothing more than the modern Hindu pronunciation of Yadu or Jady, which is now represented by the modern Jodon Rajputs[22]. Similarly, Miller thinks that much ingenuity has been spent on the attempt to prove them to be Scythians; but if physiognomy counts for anything, no one could doubt their Aryan origin[23].

This controversy about the Aryan status of the Jats is of sociological importance because the Jats of Meerut Division consider themselves to be pure Aryans. For them it is highly charged emotional issue. A popular book on the history of the Jat community published in recent years by a Jat author in the vernacular[24] takes great pains to quote various English and Indian writers and historians proving that the Jats are true Aryans and that they belong to the same ethnic stock as the Rajputs. The Jats of Meerut Division believe that the Rajputs and the Jats are one race, and to support this argument, they cite the names of various gotras (clan names) which are common to all these castes.

There seems to be no doubt as to the racial affinity of the Jats with Rajputs, Gujjars and Ahirs. But if the Jats are not Aryans, it probably means that they are trying to raise their caste status in the ritual hierarchy of the Hindu caste system. Nevertheless, it is wrong to apply the term 'Aryan' as if it were a racial term and not a linguistic one.

THE JITS

Jats are also spelt as Jits. Tod had given a very graphic account of Jits or Jitts or Jats.

In all the ancient catalogues of the thirty-six royal races (36 Agani-Kul-Rajputs) of India the Jit has a place, though by none is he ever styled 'Rajpoot'; nor there is any instance of a Rajpoot's intermarriage with Jit. It is a name widely disseminated over India, though it does not now occupy a very elevated place amongst the inhabitants, belonging chiefly to the agricultural classes.

In the Panjab, they still retain their ancient name of Jit. On the Jamna and Ganges region they are styled Jats of whom the chief of Bharatpur is the most conspicuous. On the Indus and in Saurashtra, they are termed Juts. The greater portion of the husbandmen in Rajasthan are Jits; and there are numerous tribes beyond the Indus, Pakistan, now proselytise to the Mahomedan religion, who derive their origin from this class.

Of its ancient history sufficient has been already said. It will merely be added that the kingdom of the great Goths, whose capital was on the Jaxartes, preserved its integrity and name from the period of Cyrus[25] to the 14th century, when it was converted from idolatry to the faith of Islam. The ancient Persian empire, based largely in these areas, was technologically, economically, and culturally on a par with China and India. It was founded in 550

B.C. by Cyrus the Great, who extended his conquests westwards to the Mediterranean and Asia Minor, now Turkey and eastward into Afghanistan and north-west India, where his successor Darius I (552 B.C.- 486 B.C.) added parts of the Panjab.

Herodotus informs us that the Getae were theists and held the tenet of soul's immortality; and De Guignes, from Chinese authorities, asserts that at very early period they had embraced the religion of Fo or Buddha.

The traditions of the Jits claim the regions west of the Indus as the cradle of the race and make them of Urdu extraction thus corroborating the annals of the Yadus, which state their migration from Zabulistan, and almost inducing with the descent of this tribe.

MAHMUD OF GHAZNI ATTACKED

That the Jits continued as a powerful community on the east bank of the Indus and in the Panjab, full five centuries after the period our inscription and their annals illustrate, we have the most interesting records in the history of Mahmud, the conqueror of India, whose progress they checked in a manner unprecedented in the annals of continental warfare. It was in 416 of Muslim era (A.D. 1026) that Mahmud marched with an army against the Jits, who had harassed and insulted him on the return from his last expedition against Saurashtra. The interest of the account of authorities is being given from the original[26] sources:

"The Jits (Jatts) inhabited the country on the borders of Multan, Pakistan, along the river that runs by the mountains of Joud[27] when Mahmud reached Multan; fighting the Jit country defended by great rivers, he built fifteen hundred boats[28], each armed with six iron spikes projecting from their prows, to prevent their being boarded by the enemy expert in this kind of warfare. In each boat, he placed twenty archers, and some with fire-balls of naphtha to burn the Jit fleet. The monarch having determined on their extirpation, awaited the result at Multan. The Jits sent their wives, children, and effects to Sindh Sagur[29], and launched four thousand, or as others, say, eight thousand boats, well-armed to meet the Ghaznians. A terrible conflict ensued, but the projecting spikes sunk the Jit boats while others were set on fire. Few escaped from this scene of terror; and those who did met with the more severe fate of captivity."

Many dauntless did escape; and is most probably that the Jit communities, on whose overthrow the state of Bikaner was founded, were remnants of this very warfare.

No longer after this event the original empire of the Getae Jatts was overturned, when many fugitives found a refuge in India. In 1360, Togultash[30] Timoor was the great Khan of the Getae nation; idolaters even to this period. He had conquered Khurassaii, invaded Transoxiana (whose prince fled, but whose nephew, Ameer Timoor, averted its subjugation), gained the friendship of Togultash, and commanded a hundred thousand Getae warriors. In 1369, when the Getae Getic Khan died, such was the ascendancy obtained by Timoor over his subjects, that Couraltai, or general assembly, transferred the title of Grand Khan from the Getic to the Chagtai Timoor. In 1370, he married a Getic princess, and added Kogend and Samarkand to his patrimony, Transoxiana. Rebellions and massacres almost depopulated this nursery of mankind, ere the Getaes abandoned their independence; nor was it till 1388, after six invasions, in which he burnt their towns, brought away their wealth, and almost annihilated the nation, that he felt himself secure.

In his expedition into India, having overrun great part of Europe, "taken bow, and slain the soldiers of the barbarous Ooroos," he encountered his old foes the Getaes, who inhabited the plains of Toheem, where he put two thousand to the sword, pursuing them into the desert and slaughtering many more near the Ghaggar[31].

Still the Jitt (Jat) maintained himself in the Panjab, and the most powerful and independent prince of India at this day was the Jitt prince of Lahore, holding dominion over the identical regions where the Yuchi colonised in the 5th century, and where the Yadus, driven from Ghazni, established themselves on the ruins of the Taks. The Jitt cavalier retained a portion of his Scythic manners, and preserved the use of the Chukra or discuss, the weapon of the Yadu Crishna in the remote age of the Bharat.

HUNS OR HOONS

Amongst the Scythic tribes who have secured for themselves a niche with the thirty-six races of India, is the Hun. At what period this race, so well-known by its ravages and settlement in Europe, invaded India, we know nothing about this. Doubtless, it was in the society of many others yet found in the peninsula of Saurashtra, as the Catti, the Balia, the Macwahana, etc. It is, however, confined to the genealogies of that peninsula; for although we have mention of the Hun in the chronicles and inscriptions of India at a very early period, he failed to obtain a place in the catalogue of the northern bards.

The earliest notice of the tribe is in an inscription[32] recording the power of a prince of Behar, who, amidst his other conquests, "Humbled the pride of the Huns". In the annals of the early history of Mewar, in the catalogue of princes who made common cause with the chief of all the Rajputs, when Chetore was assailed in the first eruption of the Mahomedans, was Ungutsi, lord of the Huns, who led his quota on this occasion. De Guigness[33] describes Ungut as being the name of a considerable horde of Huns or Mogols; and Abulgazi says that the Tartar tribe who guarded the great wall of China were termed Ungutti, who had a distinct prince with high pay and honour. The countries inhabited by the Hiong-nou and the Ouhuon[34], the Turks and Moghuls, called 'Tatar' from Tatan, the name of the country from the banks of the Irtish along the mountains of Altai to the shores of the Yellow Sea, whom and other original sources, the historians of the Fall of Rome have given great interest to his narrative of their march into Europe. But those who are desirous to learn all that relates to the past-history and manners of these people, must consult that monument of erudition and research, *The Geography of Malte Brun*[35]. Crishna, and to pronounce it an important colony of the Yuchi. Yuti, or Jitts. Of the first migration from Central Asia of this race within the Indus, it might have been simultaneous with the Takshae, from the wars of Cyrus[36] or his ancestors.

It is to be said, that the Jitt divided with the Takshae the claim of being the parent's name of the various tribes called Scythic invaders of India; and there is now before the author an inscription of the 5th century applying both epithets to the same prince[37], who is insisted more over with the Scythic quality of worshipping the sun. It states, likewise, that the mother of this Jitt prince was of Yadu race; strengthening their claims to a niche amongst the thirty-six Rajputs, as well as their Yadu descent.

INSCRIPTION

The 5th century of the Christian era, to which this inscription belongs, is a period of interest in Jitt history. De Guigness, from original authorities, states the Yuchi, or Jitts, to have established themselves in the Panjab in the 5th and 6th century, and the inscription now quoted, applies to a prince whose capital is styled Salindrapoora in these regions; and doubtless the Sali-Indrapoor[38] where the Yadu Bhattis[39] established themselves on the expulsion of the Tak.

How much earlier than this the Jitt penetrated into Rajasthan must be left to more ancient inscriptions to determine, suffice it, that in A.D. 440 we find him in power.

When the Yadu was expelled from Salivahanpoora, and forced to seek refuges across the Sutledge among the Dahia[40] and Johya[41] Rajputs of the Indian desert, where they founded their capital Derrasul, many from compulsion embraced the Mohammedan faith; on which occassion, they assumed the name of Jatt[42] of which at least twenty different offsets are enumerated in the Yadu chronicles.

IBN KHURDADBA

The earliest mention of the Jats in History occurs in Ibn Khurdadba, before A.D. 912. He describes the Zats (Jats) as keeping watch over the country between Kirman[43] and Mansura[44]. *The Mujnil-ut-Tawarikh* observes that by the Arabs the Hindus are called Jats; they and the Meds[45], a Sindh tribe, are descendants of Ham. The Arabs appear to have found Jats at Ghazni as well as in Sindh, but the Muslims who later invaded the Panjab cannot be said with certainty to have found them in that Province, and it is not until Timor's invasion, in 1398, that we have any indubitable reference to Jats as settled to the north of Delhi. While then, it is credible that there was a Scythic element in the Jats, it is impossible to regard them as identifiable with 'wintry Getae' the Massagetai, of the Goths[46].

JATS TOTEMISTIC ORIGIN

The tribes of Jats probably number more than a thousand, and among the Hindus and Sikhs, they are spoken of as Gots, a corruption of the Sanskrit Gotra.

Some of these tribes bear names which suggest a totemistic origin. Such are the Jun ('louse') Goraya ('blue-cow'), Roja, or Raja (same meaning), Karir ('the wild caper,' 'Capparis aphylla'), Waihri ('heifer'), Bandar ('monkey'), Gidar ('jackal'), Pipla from pipal, (Ficus religiosa), Jandia (from Jand, prosopic spicigera), Mor ('peacock'), Kohar ('hatchet'), and Gandasia (from gandasa, 'axe'). But no reverence is paid to any of these things. The Pankhal tribe is so-called because a Jat girl married to a Rajput, fell out with him, and so he massacred all its members save those who had placed 'peacock's feathers' on their heads. The Mor ancestor was protected by a peacock from a snake. The Joria (from Jora, 'twins') is said to have five branches, or apparently subsepts, all named after parts of the Ber tree (Zizyphus Jujuba), *viz.* Rangi (from Rang, 'bark'), Jaria (from Jar, 'root'), Beria (from the plum or fruit), Jhari ('seedling') and Khichar ('bud'). It is also very common to find a tribe named from some event at an ancestor's birth. Thus the Garewal is so-called because its ancestress was suddenly confined near a 'haystack,' and the Sibi or Siwi tribe derives its name from Siwa, a funeral pile, because its ancestress gave birth to a son when about to commit Sati. But such tales are told of countless tribes which are not Jats, and folk etymology is probably responsible for most of them.

DEVOTEES OF THE JAT TRIBAL CULT

Though nominally adherents to the great orthodox religions, the Jats are often devotees of some sect, or devotees of a tribal or personal cult, as well. Thus in Hissar, a district in Haryana, large numbers are Bishnois[47], a Vaisnavite sect while in Karnal, a district in Haryana, many of them are Sadhs or 'Pure' saints, belonging to a sect, founded about 280 years ago, which effects great personal cleanliness, forbids smoking, and addresses only the one God under the title of Sat, or the 'True One'. Other Jats, do not eat or marry with them. Another cult, very popular among the Jats, is that of the 'generous' Sakhi Sarwar. The Sultan, the 'giver of Lakhs' (Lakhdata), of Nigaha (Nigahia), the earth-god, probably Siva taken over by Islam and transformed into the cult of Muhammaden saint (and his descendants) with Paphian elements. Fertility which is the object of worship naturally appeals to a landed peasantry.

JATHERAS AND BAKHUAS

Thus a Jat may be by birth and by education a Hindu, a Sikh or a Muslim, by choice or by conviction a Sikh, a Sultani, or a sectary who has thrown in his lot with one of the countless sects old and new to be found in India. He can even become a Christian. But under or alongside of his religion and his sect is a mass of usage partly social, partly religious, and wholly based on custom, not on belief to which he clings with a tenacity all the greater, because it is international. In the northern and central districts of the Panjab, these usages centre round the worship of forefathers (Jatheras), but in the south-west of that province they cluster round the godling of the village (Khera) rather than the tribal ancestor. This change in the religious system is congruous with the evolution from the tribal system of the tracts towards the north-west frontier to the village community organization of the long civilised territories round Delhi. Tk: Jathera is usually styled Bawa ('master') or Siddh ('perfect') and bears some conventional name which shows that his real name has been forgotten. His tomb is sometimes called Bakhuhan *(pl.)*, and consists of three or four pits, with pillars formed of earth dug out of them. He is usually worshipped at marriage.

THE JAT WEDDING

A typical Jat wedding according to the rites in vogue in the sub-montane districts which lie under the Himalayas in the north Panjab is thus described:

"About five days before the wedding a lump of coarse sugar is given to the barber (in his capacity of villages go- between (Vichola)) and he brings in return a twig of the Jand[48]. This twig is placed in a heap of wheat weighing about 42 sers (84 lb), and by it are put 21 sers of coarse sugar. A lamp is lit and placed on the ground; to it all the females of the family and the bridegroom do obeisance. The bridegroom cuts the twig with a knife or sword; and half to the mirasi (geneologist). The latter then brings a ram (chatra, whence the name of the rite itself), cuts its ear, and with his thumb imprints a mark (Tika) of its blood on the youth's forehead, and on those of all present. He gets the ram and a rupee as his vail. The youth then bathes, and boiled wheat (Baklian) is distributed. He is oiled and a red tape (gana) is tied round his forehead. Thence forward he must keep a knife or sword in his hand till the wedding day. On that day he bathes again, breaks earthen vessels, and dons' new cloths. His kinsmen offer their presents, and the menials get their dues. The bride is then brought home and the newly-wedded pair, with all the females of the family, go to the temple of Baba-Manga (Mange-di-Mari), the progenitor of the tribe, offer him a double cloth and a cake (the priest's perquisite), and bow their heads in worship. This completes the wedding ceremony among the Bajba Jats, an important Jat tribe. Bajba Manga's shrine is at Pasrur[49], a town of some antiquity, in Sialkot, Pakistan."

DIFFERENT WEDDING CEREMONIES

With some modification similar rites are observed by other Jat tribes.

In one tribe the Dhariwal Jats, the pair circumambulate the Siddh's temple seven times. The Randhawa tribe employs a

Brahman to fetch the twig, the ram's blood is smeared only on the foreheads of bachelors, and after the wedding, when the Sidh's temple is visited, the bride and other females take clay out of an adjacent pond (Jathera-pond). Very often, the boy cuts a twig from the Jand tree himself, and a few tribes, *e.g.* the Ghamman, cut it from a Bar, or Ber tree (Zizyphus Jujuba), and that tribe offers two lumps of sugar, one to the saint Lakhdata, the other to his priest the drummer (Bharai), who is styled Shaikh, and appear to ignore its Jathera Siddh Dulchi. The ram is frequently replaced by a he-goat and often sacrificed. Its flesh being distributed in various ways. The Virk Jats assemble— men and women—at a Ber tree, wash the ram, and if it shakes its head, regard this as a token that their ancestor is pleased. The Samrai perform the Chatra on the first Monday of the lunar month before the wedding. This rite is, however, unknown in the south-west of the Panjab, as it involves animal sacrifice, and in the central districts the ram is never killed, though its ear may be cut[50].

FOUNDING NEW VILLAGE

In the south-east, when a new village was founded before any house built, a mound of earth was raised near the site proposed for the village and a Jand tree planted on it. Houses may then be built, and first man to die in the village, whatever his caste may be, was burned or buried in this mound and on it was built a masonry shrine named after him. He was thus deified as the Bhumia, or Earthed. Whatever ills befall, his shrine was the first place to which the Jats resort in time of trouble. But a tribe may have a tribal Siddh as well as a Bhumia in each village. The Bhumia too was often called Khera, and some tribes even styled their Jathera, Khera-Bhumia possibly the custom of deifying the first man to die in a new village was akin to the custom of killing a man and building him in when a new structure was raised, (ef. Foundation). He then became its Dwarapala, or Gatekeeper. The Jathera, however, did not appear to be thus chosen or regarded. He was often a martyr, or Shahid, who fell fighting with dacoits or in an affray with a neighbouring village. But he may be, it would seem, a Jogi, a Gosain, a Bairagi, or a Naga, though in such a case the priest regarded as the Jathera would appear to be a dim-embodiment of God Shiva or Vishnu. No Sati-worship was found among the Jats, for the very obvious reason that they allow widow remarriage, but the Dhindsa Jats affect a Sati's shrine called the Khangah, or monastery.

JATS, A DOMINANT TRIBE

In sheer numbers and power the Jats are the dominant caste of much of northern India. They are predominantly found in the Panjab plain, 'the land of the five rivers'.

Their dominant position as landowners enables the Jats to employ non-Jat labour for some essential services such as building.

They are spread into adjacent areas between the Jamuna and the Ganges rivers. East of the Ganges in Uttar Pradesh, they are far fewer, but they nevertheless form a sizeable proportion of the population. In the 1931 census of India, the last time when caste populations were enumerated separately, a figure of 8,000,000 was returned for the Jats, but today their total population far exceeds this.

MAINLY CULTIVATORS

Jats generally earn their livelihood as peasant cultivators but simply performing this type of work does not make a man a Jat. In order to be a Jat, a man must be born of Jat parents. The Jats are generally endogamous, but in cases where a man is physically disabled or has such a bad reputation that no respectable Jat family is willing to give him their daughter in marriage. It is not unknown for a Jat to marry a woman of low caste parentage such as the daughter of sweeper or tanner. No Jat, however, would ever allow his daughter to marry a man of another caste whether he be higher or lower than himself, because this would be an affront against his sense of honour.

JATS, A LIBERAL TRIBE

The fact that Jat men sometimes take low caste women as wives, is generally indicative of the fact that they are less rigid about caste purity than the Brahmans or the Rajputs.

Unlike high caste Indians, Jat women are allowed to remarry, if they have been widowed and they are less strict in their observation of Purdah, the practice common amongst high caste families, of secluding and veiling their women. Part of this lack of modesty on the part of Jat woman is necessitated by the nature of her work. She is often out in the fields, collecting fodder, feeding and caring for the animals and carrying meals to their husbands. Jat women, therefore, have a greater degree of independence and perform tasks vital to the village economy, whereas high caste Indian women are prohibited from working.

JAT'S DRESS

The Jats generally wear simple, functional clothing, in keeping with their works as farmers. The men wear a Kurta, a loose-fitting blouse, a Tamba, a wide cloth which they gird at the waist so that it has a skirt-like appearance and on their heads, a lightly-coloured turban which reflects the sun in summer and helps keep them warm in winter. Jat women also dress simple, preferring a Kamiz, or simple blouse, to the elegant Sari of their high caste counterparts and cotton trousers, or Salwar, over which married women traditionally wore a Ghagra, an ankle-length pleated skirt. Both sexes wear a thickly-woven cotton blanket to keep out the cold on winter mornings and evenings.

JAT WOMEN

Jat women are wonderfully adept in the use of the Charkha, the Indian spinning wheel. The cloth they produce is of high quality and extremely durable. Traditionally, Jat women had this handloomed cloth dyed black or dark red and embroidered the most beautiful flower designs on it in brightly coloured silk thread. These embroidered fabrics, called Phulkaris (flower-work), are now becoming increasingly rare. The introduction of cheap cotton prints such as those manufactured in the textile mills of the Panjab, has had an unfortunate effect on the traditional skills of spinning, weaving and embroidery.

JAT'S DIET

Despite his love of meat-eating, the Jat's staple diet consists of Roti, a type of unleavened bread made from wheat or sorghum flour. With this he generally eats curried Dal, a word which covers a wide variety of lentils and pulses. But in season, Jats also eat various vegetable curries made from potatoes, carrots, cabbage, turnips or cauliflower. It is true, however, that Jats seldom eat vegetables, they have not grown themselves. They prefer to eat their Roti with curd or pickle rather than to buy vegetables from someone else. A favourite winter dish is one prepared from spinach and served with thick sorghum Roti.

THE CROPS THEY GROW

The Jats do not grow rice (their own major crop being wheat and sorghum), since they consider it a food which, if eaten in excess, leaves the body weak and open to illness. But with the introduction of tube wells and other machinery, rice has become the bumper crop of the Jats. According to Jat belief, the essential ingredient of a healthy diet is Ghee, clarified butter which they consume in large amounts, both in curries and on Roti. They also have a great liking for milk, buttermilk and curds, all of which they consider to be extremely nutritious. Cows and buffaloes are kept for milk whereas he-buffalo and oxen are used as draught animals in the fields. The Hindu and Sikh Jats of India revere the cow as a goddess (known as Mother Cow), and they neither eat its meat nor use it for farm labour. Favourite meats among the Jats are goat and chicken and *less* commonly, pork. It is only since the Partition of India in 1947, and the elimination of the Muslim population that pigs have begun to be widely kept as farm animals. The Muslim Jats of Pakistan enjoy beef but consider eating of pork an abomination.

THEIR VILLAGE LIFE

A Jat village is generally inhabited by the members of a single clan, the patrilineal descendants of a common male ancestor. Amongst Hindu and Sikh Jats the village and clan is exogamous; the daughters of the men of the village must marry into another clan and go to live in their husbands' villages after marriage. Amongst Muslim Jats, on the other hand, the village and clan is an endogamous unit; women find their husbands amongst the men of their own village and relatives.

Most villages consist of a number of tightly-clustered houses interconnected by a series of narrow alleyways. Within the village, there are wells, a small shop, often a temple and nowadays usually a school. The houses are flat-roofed so that the inhabitants can sleep on them in the stifling heat of the summer months. Although houses were traditionally built of mud, more substantial brick structures are increasingly being erected, often two or three storeys high.

Every Jat village is surrounded by the fields which are largely owned by the Jat inhabitants and situated throughout are wells called Khu. The Khu is a form of artesian well, powered by the continual rotation of wooden shaft by an ox. This drives the cogs so that a chain of metal cups scoops up water and bring it to the surface. A number of close kinsmen share watering rights in each Khu. The land surrounding each well being divided between families which work from their father to sons and is divided into as many equal shares as a man has sons. Daughters, however, are excluded from the inheritance.

Although the land is generally owned and worked by the Jats, no village population is composed entirely of Jats. A number of other castes perform particular services for the Jat landowners; Brahmans act as their family priests; carpenters maintain their ploughs; water-carriers deliver water twice daily from the village wells to Jat households; barbers repair nails and cut hair, and act as messengers and servants at weddings and funerals. In some villages, there are also tailors, dyers, weavers, goldsmiths and Khatri shopkeepers. At the bottom of the caste hierarchy, the tanners remove dead cattle and tan the skins, and sweepers keep the streets and gutters clean.

MODE OF PAYMENTS

None of these castes is paid in cash by the Jats for their services but by the traditional system of Jajmani. At harvest time, the various members of service castes who have worked for each Jat family, are assembled and a proportion of the harvest is paid to each of them. The carpenter, for example, would receive his allotted share of two sheafs for every 100, the water-carrier would receive one, and so on. In this way, the economy functioned not on a day-to-day cash basis but on a once or twice yearly reckoning of payment in kind.

The Jats are generally feared and despised by the other castes because of their dominant position as landowners in the village. The Jat virtues such as thrift and industry are regarded as defects and they are ridiculed as being miserly, dirty and slow-witted.

A great deal of this hatred stems from physical fear of the Jats. They are tall, strong people, noted for their fearlessness in the battle. These qualities were immediately exploited by the British; the Jats were recruited in large numbers into the regiments of the British Army and they fought with distinction in the two World Wars.

Their superior physique, their ability to fight and their control over the livelihood of the other villagers would deter any non-Jat from quarrelling with a Jat. The Jats, moreover, are extremely proud and consider themselves not only the owners of the land but of the village itself. Fear and hatred of the Jats is, therefore, justified to a certain extent, and the Jats enjoy and profit from the fear they evoke in others.

RELIGION

The religion of the Jats is relatively simple as compared with that of the Brahmans or Rajputs. All Jats, like many peoples throughout India, were originally Hindus. However, during the wars which raged over northern India for hundreds of years many Jats were forced to become Muslims—often at the point of a sword. As a result of persistent Muslim persecution of Hindus during the Mughal Empires, there arose in the Panjab a new religious leader, Guru Nanak, the founder of Sikhism. His message was that God is one and that there is neither a Hindu nor a Muslim. Unfortunately, in time this message became so diluted that the Sikhs became as fanatically anti-Muslim as the Muslims had been anti-Hindus. Under the 10th Guru, Guru Gobind Singh, the Sikhs were organized as an army in opposition to the Muslim Emperors, the bulwark of which were the Jats, the first converts.

Today the Jats of the Panjab are almost 100 per cent Sikhs. Sikhism is a religion well suited to these simple farmers, resting as it does on faith in the Gurus, and in the Book, the *Adi Granth*, which contains their writings. Their ritual observances consist generally of prayers and hymn singing, and there is no elaborate ritual system which might interfere with the everyday routine of framework. In almost every village, there is a Gurudwara, a Sikh temple, and a Granthi, a priest, who performs the life cycle rites of marriage and death.

JATS ADVANCING AGRICULTURISTS

The Jats of north-west India and, particularly, the Jat Sikhs of Panjab, have welcomed modernisation and economic development. Increasingly, Jat farmers are sending their children on to further education in the colleges of the cities and there is a growing rate of literacy among the total population. Emigrants returning from Britain and, more recently, from Canada, the U.S.A., Australia and other countries of the world have introduced world-wide values into village life. On formal occasions many Jats now wear European-style clothing and enjoy the use of radios, TVs, record players and other manufactured electrical goods.

As towns have grown in importance they have set up commercial services, traditionally only available in the villages. The towns have also provided a much needed source of employment and many villagers, including an increasing number of Jats, now commute daily to work in the offices and factories of the towns. The old Jajmani system is gradually breaking down, and payment for labour is now increasingly made in cash.

The Jats have welcomed innovations in agriculture. The old wells are now being replaced by tube wells powered by electricity or diesel engines. New strains of wheat have been introduced which give better yields and are less susceptible to damage by high winds; chemical fertilisers are being used to increase the fertility of the soil.

An increasing number of tractors and other types of farm machinery are being bought by the Jats, thus dispensing with the need for unskilled agricultural labour. By the mid-1960s, the 'Green Revolution' was underway in northern India, especially in the Panjab, Himachal Pradesh and Haryana, and it appeared that for the first time, India was on the road to self-sufficiency in food production.

At the end of the 1960s, monsoons failed for several years. This meant a failure of the hydroelectric plants and a shortage of electricity, so that both agriculture and industry suffered. In 1971, the Indo-Pakistan conflict greatly dislocated both the Indian and Pakistan economies.

During 1974 and 1975, the situation still remained grim as it became apparent that hydroelectric plants were still not producing sufficient electricity for the developing economy. Moreover, diesel oil became scarce and expensive so that it could not readily be used as an alternative to electricity to power the new tube wells. Fertiliser also became scarce and the new varieties, which require such intensive care, had to give in. The result was that the Panjab, for example, was just producing enough to feed itself and there was no surplus to export or to feed the rest of India. The 'Green Revolution' had become anything but green.

The soil of northern India and especially of the Panjab, however, is good, and the Jats who work at it are people so industrious that if an abundance of grain can be produced, it is they who will produce it. The fate of India is very much in their hands.

Today Sikh Jats are very prominent in India. Therefore, it looks plausible that their brief account may also be given here. They are the most leading people at home and abroad, who are conspicuously found in every country of the world.

SIKH JATS

The approximately 18,000,000 Sikhs who reside in the Panjab and in scattered communities across the world share a reverence for "the ten Gurus" (from Guru Nanak to Guru Gobind Singh) and the teachings of their scripture, the *Adi Granth* or the *Guru Granth Sahib*. Worship is central for all devotees of Sikhism, India's youngest monotheistic religion, either in the form of daily observances at home or in corporate worship at the Gurudwara, a building, designated for congregational ceremonies and social events such as common kitchens (Langar) providing free food. Many Sikhs also observe a code of conduct and discipline that includes males wearing recognizable marks of orthodoxy (unshorn hair, a comb, a dagger, a steel bangle, and a pair of breeches, a ban on tobacco, and the use of common titles for male and female converts (Singh, "lion", and Kaur, "Princess", respectively). This orthodox group, which has gradually grown to dominate the public life of the community, consists of Amritdhari Sikhs (those who have undergone baptism). Other Sikhs in the community do not participate fully in the code of conduct but are accepted as Sikhs because of their devotion, participation in worship, and respect for the Gurus.

THE SIKH HOMELAND

The Panjab was and now remains the homeland for the Sikhs. The Sikhism evolved, incorporating various tribes and castes, including a preponderance of Jats, rural agriculturists, who along with others have shown great courage in times of persecution and political turmoil. The first Guru and founder of the faith was Guru Nanak (A.D. 1469-1539). By early 17th century the following had grown to such an extent in the Panjab area that it was seen as a threat to the Moghul rulers. Within a century the last of the ten Gurus had died (by 1708), and open rebellion had broken out. By the middle of the 18th century bands of Sikh guerrillas were hastening the collapse of the Moghul administration in their area, while keeping Afghan invaders at bay (1739-1769). These military struggles continued, but by the end of that century, Ranjit Singh had emerged as leader of the Sikhs and became Maharaja of the Panjab, a position, he retained until his death in 1839. This continuing military activity had greatly encouraged a tradition of constant military readiness in the community, and it largely explains the role of Sikh men in the modern armies of Great Britain, India and Pakistan.

THE SIKH SHRINES

The numerous shrines and holy spots associated with major events in Sikh history, most notably the Golden Temple at Amritsar, are primarily found in districts now in Pakistan or the Indian Panjab. In the 19th century, Jat Sikhs began migrating to southeast Asia, Africa, Europe, and North America, and nowadays large and often very affluent and highly educated Jat Sikh communities can be found in those areas. A new group of western Sikh converts, the Gora or "white" Sikhs led by Harbhajan Singh Jogi, are associated with many gurudwaras (house of worship) in North America and also have their own organisations. Although the centrality of the Panjabi language and culture within the daily lives of Sikhs sometimes divides those with roots in the Panjab from recent converts, common worship, beliefs, and a shared code of discipline tend to overcome the divisions aroused by ethnicity.

Sikh identity and institutions have been strengthened and at times modified by experiences over the last century. Organising themselves into Singh Sabhas in the late 1860s, Sikhs have emphasised their separateness from Hindus in areas such as theology, ritual, social practice, and politics. These efforts culminated in the dramatic, non-violent campaign (1920-1925) to wrest Sikh gurudwaras from the hands of British supported managers, often Hindu, and to place responsibility for all shrines in the hands of the community. Since 1925 the Sikh Gurudwaras Protection Committee (a Central Management Committee) has supervised the shrines and also played an important role in Sikh politics. The frustrations of their minority status, coupled with economic problems helped foster growing Sikh militancy in the 1970 culminating in the demands for a separate Sikh Nation, "Khalistan". The resulting government attack on armed militants in the Golden Temple (1984) led to a period of continuing political chaos in the Panjab, sparked dramatic episodes such as the assassination of Prime Minister Indira Gandhi and the resulting massacre of many Sikhs, and fostered debate among Sikhs about ideology and strategy. Despite this turbulence, Sikhs still maintain a positive outlook and continue to provide leadership in public institutions and professions wherever they reside.

DISTRICT-WISE, BRIEF ACCOUNT OF THE JATS OF THE PANJAB

On the basis of the Panjab (United Panjab, *I.e.* the Indian Panjab, Haryana, Himachal Pradesh and the Pakistani Panjab) *Government Revenue Records* district-wise brief account of the Jats is given here. This is mainly based on the *District Gazetteers, District Manuals*, and also the local traditions. The facts mentioned therein, will throw light up to the partition of India, in 1947 A.D. Lahore was the capital of the United Panjab. Therefore, while giving brief accounts, it is being started from the district of Lahore.

LAHORE

In physique, intelligence, and general strength of character without doubt for the finest specimens of the Jat tribe are to be found in Manjha, and among the Manjha (the districts of Lahore, Amritsar, Gurdaspur) Jats, the Sandhus, in all respects rank first. It was from these that most of Maharaja Ranjit Singh's military leaders were drawn; and indications of the wealth and power to which they then rose are to be found in the large masonry houses belonging to ancient Sikh Sardar families, which still stand in many of the Manjha villages though for the most part in bad condition. Before and during the Sikh rule all the Jats of the Lahore Manjha formed an important contribution to the British Army, but after the general disbandment that followed the extension of British rule over the Panjab, they appear to have returned to their villages and taken kindly to an independent rustic life, supporting themselves partly by means of carrying trade which brought in considerable profits before the expansion of British railway system and partly by the precarious fruits of cultivation, which was then almost entirely dependent on an uncertain rainfall, canal irrigation not yet having been extended to the Bari Doab tract. Of late years, the attraction of farming rendered easy by the new resource of canal water and general abundance of land had proved superior to the prospects held forth in Government service whether military or police, so far as the Manjha Jats are generally concerned. This was the more remarkable as in the adjoining district of Amritsar, the Sandhus had taken largely to service in the army and in the police. In the Lahore district, the sons seeing their fathers for the most part preferring an agricultural life, had followed suit and stayed at home.

MANJHA JATS

As an agriculturist, the Manjha Jat was only moderately good. Hitherto, their farming had been conducted on broad and tough principles; they have had large areas to deal with, which until within the last few years were dependent mainly on dry cultivation, and this was dependent for its success far more on the season than on any special efforts on the cultivator's part. The canal extension even had hitherto made little difference in the character of the farming. The Manjha Jats still had plenty of land, which under irrigation gave excellent produce in return for every little trouble on the cultivator's part.

MOST IMPORTANT TRIBE

The Jats are not only numerically the strongest tribe, but in many respects the most important also. In the early 20th century, they numbered 162,778, the distribution by religion being Hindus 3,916, Jats 98,241, Mohammedans 60,621. The Sikh Jats are a far more important section of the tribe than their mere numbers would lead one to think. Though the rules of conduct as laid down by Guru Gobind Singh are not observed so strictly as formerly, Sikhism still retains in part the prestige of the military organisation which made it the power it was in the Panjab in the time of Maharaja Ranjit Singh. The marauding instincts instilled into the minds of his followers by Guru Har Gobind, the fighting habits fostered in the race by the sword rule of Maharaja Ranjit Singh, and the constant fraction broils that prevailed between the separate units of the Maharaja's military, following when not engaged against a common foe, reveal themselves continually in the everyday life of the Sikh Jat of the present day, in his grasping rapacity and in his readiness to take up arms in defence of what he considers his rights. From an agricultural point of view, the distinction of religion is important, because the rules of conduct at present observed by the Jat Sikhs were much better adapted to the necessities of a cultivating life than the habits of Mohammedans at least, if not of Hindus. Chief among these is the rule prohibiting smoking; the Mohammedan and to a less extent the Hindu wastes his time, dulls his faculties, and to some extent predisposes himself to luxuriousness and indolence by excessive smoking. The immunity of the true Jat Sikh from this habit undoubtedly makes him a more efficient agriculturist as a rule than his brother Jat of any other religion. Similarly, being somewhat lax in his religious observance he has much more liberty as regards times for going to and stopping at his work in the fields than the Mohammedan Jat, who, though he may not carry out strictly the prescribed ritual prayers five times a day (Namaz), must conform more or less to the custom of his co-religionists. On the other hand, the Mohammedan and Hindu Jats are much less addicted, openly at least, to the vice of drinking, and which incapacitates many a Jat Sikh tract, on the north for instance, towards the Amritsar border, where population is beginning to press on the soil and the land in places shows signs of exhaustion, the people are coming to understand that to make their land yield continuously something more is required than a sowing preceded by two or three ploughings (tehar) and followed by copious canal irrigation.

Socially, the Manjha Jat's character is often open to reproach. The majority of them drink, and many of them drink to great excess. A considerable number of Manjha Jat villages have obtained an unenviable notoriety for the numerous bad characters, thieves and highway robbers, they shelter. Murders and murderous assault in the Manjha occupy far too prominent a place in the criminal records and appear to be increasing steadily as the Jats grow rich and riotous on the proceeds of their newly-irrigated lands. They are generally reputed to be deficient in chastity. It is not often that the village life is disturbed by any serious scandal of immorality. The fact that a Jat who has a woman of his own section outside his family to live with him incurs the general opprobrium of the brotherhood, and also the custom whereby a Jat usually takes as wife the widow of his deceased brother by the simple ceremony of Chadar Dali or throwing of the sheet, no doubt both act as a check on immoral tendencies. In their dealings with one another, the Manjha Jats often exhibit excessive greed and intemperate cruelty. In their villages they are democratic by inclination and impatient of control by those they do not fear, but to the Government officer paying them a friendly visit, they are frank and conciliatory without losing their outspokenness and customary independence of manner. Taken all around, notwithstanding his numerous faults, the Manjha Jat is a fine fellow with great capacities for good under careful guidance. Though naturally restive and resentful as individuals under injury done and always extraordinarily tenacious of their purpose, yet as a body, they are quietly disposed in the absence of disturbing elements and easily led. Whether as peasants or soldiers, they yield readily to firm discipline, provided it is accompanied with justice and fair dealing. Both in their faults and in their virtues, Sandhus are the most prominent among the Manjha Jats as they are the most striking in their external appearance, the features becoming more handsome and more decidedly marked the older the Sandhu grows.

SIDHU JATS

In the Hithar of the Sutlej Beas nearly all the Jats are Sidhus. The Sidhu Jats occupy principally the western half of the Hithar, which forms the southern portion of the Chunian Tehsil. They came here probably from the Ferozepore district on the opposite side of the river. An account of the Sidhu's migration in this direction is furnished on page 59 of the *Ferozepore Gazetteer for 1888-89*. The Sidhu is a far more peaceable, well-behaved and industrious member of society than his Sandhu brother. Having lived for many generations on the meagre profits derived from cultivation dependent on a precarious rainfall and a slow and expensive process of well irrigation by the Persian wheel (Khooh), the Sidhu Jat has gradually become accustomed to regard the cultivation of his land and constant attendance at his well as the chief, if not the same reason for his existence; he has little money and little time to spend on luxuries or on amusements. He is thrifty, hardworking peasant, cultivator, who prefers to regard farming as a pleasure as well as means of subsistence, and will not, therefore, bother himself with the more ignoble and laborious market-garden style in which the Arain delights. In enterprise, pluck and perseverance under adversity the Sidhu Jat is immeasurably superior to the Arain. He is the true "zamindar" or "husbandman" of the province, and his women and children assist him in all they can.

The Jats along the Ravi are principally Sandhus who have some large settlements along lower course of the river through this district, mostly in the Chunian Tehsil.

The above account indicates sufficiently the locality and features of such sections of the Jats as are most prominent in different parts of the district. Other principal sections are described below:

BHULLAR JATS

The Bhullar Jats occupy a few large estates in the centre of the Kasur near Lahore. They, in common with the Her and Man Jat sections, who also are found in a very few scattered villages of Lahore district, call themselves the *asl* or original Jats and are said to have sprung from the Jat or matted hair of Mahadeo, whose title is Bhola Mahadeo. In character the Bhullars resemble the Sandhu's, but are inferior in physique.

GIL JATS

There are several Gil Jat settlements near the Sutlej in Kasur Tehsil, a few in the Manjha of Lahore Tehsil, and three or four on the Ravi in the Chunian Tehsil. They are principally Sikhs, but they have not a good reputation in this district as cultivators and are said to be ill-suited for the toil and risks of cultivation by well irrigation, on which they are largely dependent in the tracts where they happen to be settled. This is possibly owing to their having long been used to the luxuries of river inundation, which now neither on the Ravi nor on the Sutlej is as good as it used to be. They give one the impression of being both querulous and quarrelsome. In physique, they are inferior to the ordinary Manjha Jat.

DHILLON JATS

The Dhillon settlements are few and scattered over the whole district, chiefly in the Manjha. Their largest village is that of Bhasin on the Amritsar border near the Ravi. There are many other miscellaneous sections of the Jats scattered about the district but further detailed mention of them does not seem required.

AMRITSAR JATS

Among the most important people of these, is the Jat, but this is a very wide term and includes classes between which there is often a strong contrast. The commonest is the Sikh Jat, the follower of Guru Gobind Singh, who has taken the Pahul at the Akal Bunga, Anandpur, or other places where the rite is administered. A Sikh Jat will not ordinarily speak of the Mohammedan Jats of a neighbouring village as Jats. If asked, he will describe himself as a "zamindar" by which he means a Hindu or Sikh Jat, but he will describe his Mohammedan Jat neighbour as a "Mussalman", even though he may be himself a Jat of the same 'got' as the Mohammedan. Not that he denies the title of the latter to be a Jat, but in common speech he restricts the term Jat' to cultivators following the Hindu or Sikh faith.

The total number of Jats returned at the Census of 1911 was 200,759. This is about 23 per cent of the total population, and 28 per cent of the rural population. Their local distribution

Amritsar Tehsil	———	81,009
Taran Taran Tehsil	———	83,175
Ajnala Tehsil	———	36,575
Total	———	200,759

The Sikh Jat of Amritsar in speaking of the Manjha refers more particularly to that part of the Taran Taran Tehsil which lies below the old road from Atari to Goindwal and to the Kasur and part of the Chunian Tehsil of Lahore. Ajnala is a Tehsil. Now that the old *badshahi* road above-mentioned has been superceded by the metalled Grand Trunk Road, the limits of the Manjha have, in common speech, been extended, and the whole of that part of the Amritsar district which lies on the right of a traveller going towards Jalandhar on the Grand Trunk Road, is spoken of as the Manjha.

SANDHU JATS

The Sikh Jats, of whom the Manjha Sikhs are the pick, are the finest of the Amritsar peasantry. In physique, they are inferior to no race of peasants in the province, and among them are men, who in any country in the world, would be deemed fine specimens of the human race. The Sikh Jat is generally tall and muscular, with well-shaped limbs, erect carriage, and strongly marked and handsome features. They are frugal and industrious; though not intellectual, they have considerable shrewdness in the ordinary affairs of life and are outspoken and possessed of unusual independence of character. They are certainly litigious, their natural stubbornness leading them to persevere in a case long after all chance of success is gone, but at the same time, they are perhaps as honest and simple a race as is to be found in India, for the false-speaking, common in the law courts, is conventional, and hardly indicative of moral depravity. They make admirable soldiers, when well led, inferior to no native troops in India, with more dogged courage than dash, steady in the field, and trustworthy in difficult circumstances, and without the fanaticism which makes the Pathan always dangerous. In private, life they are not remarkable for chastity, and they are largely addicted to the use of intoxicating drugs or spirits, but on the whole their faults are less conspicuous than their virtues.

The sub-divisions of greatest numerical strength are the Sidhu, Gil, Randhawa, Dhaun, Dhillon, Bal, Aulakh, Pannun, Chahil, Sohal, China, Mahil, Bhullar, Kang, Nijjar and Mann. Of these the first three mentioned far exceed in numbers any of the others.

The Sandhu Jats are, it will be seen, the strongest clan in the district. They are found in detached villages at different points of all three Tehsils but muster especially strong in the south-west corner of Taran Taran. The central village of this groups is Sirhali Kalan, and from this they have founded and peopled the ring of villages which lies round it. Here they hold thirty-two villages. This part of the Tehsil was formerly known as the Khara Manjha, a bleak treeless tract with deep brackish wells, as soil sometimes poor and sandy, but generally hard and unpromising, and an uncertain rainfall. Canal irrigation has now changed the appearance of the country and the system of cultivation to some extent, but still the soil yields a small return, and holdings being small, the Sandhus have always taken eagerly to military service. Hardly a family but has one or more members in the native army, the Burmah Military

Police or in Service in Hong-Kong or the Straits Settlements (Malay). Military employ is traditional among the Sandhus, and from this tribe the Sikhs drew many of their best men. They are the best specimens of the Manjha Jat which the district can show. The way they hold the land is perplexing, for most of those who own land in the later-founded hamlets round Sirhali are still recorded as owning land in three or four estates. It is difficult to cultivate each one of these separate holdings, consequently exchanges and tenancies are common, and often give rise to dispute, which as land is source, are keenly fought out. Men in service find it easy to dispose of their land by mortgage during their absence.

It is easily redeemed out of saving on their return, and in every village, there are pensioners who are only too ready to take it up, and advance money on it. The clan is found in some strength in the neighbouring corner of the Kasur Tehsil, and also across the Sutlej in Ferozepore, but there is no other collection of Sandhu villages in Amritsar. The Sandhu of the Sirhali *ilaqua* have an ancient feud with the Pannuns of Naushara and Chandiwala, which is said to have arisen out of a murder by a Sirhali man of a Pannun connection by marriage.

GIL JATS

The next strongest clan is that of the Gil Jats. They are known as excellent and hard-working cultivators. They hold about twenty-five villages in whole or part in Taran Taran, but they are scattered all through the Tehsil. They muster strongest in the Amritsar Tehsil, near Majitha, and it is to this clan that the Majitha Sardars, the descendants of Sardar Desa Singh, belong to the Sher Gil branch of the tribe. Nag and Majitha and Sohiyan Kalan (part) in the Amritsar Tehsil, and Dhotian in Taran Taran are the largest settlements of this clan. The Gils of Nag are Mohammedan, but are excellent cultivators, and get all they can out of their land, while those of Dhotian (who are Sikhs) are remarkably fine specimens of the Manjha Jat and are often found taking to service.

DHILLON JATS

The Dhillons are found most in the Manjha, in fact along with the Sindhus, the Gils, Pannuns, Aulakhs and Sidhus. They take up nearly the whole of the. Manjha proper. But the Dhillons lie further up the Tehsil, in the upper half of it, the country in which the Bhangi *misl* was once supreme. They hold twenty-eight whole villages and parts of others, and many of their villages are among the largest in the Tehsil, such as Kairon, Radri, Gaggobus, Panjwar, Chabal, Dhand, Kasel, Gandiwind. Most of them are favoured with canal irrigation and there are no better cultivated estates in the Taran Taran Tehsil than Kasel and Gandiwind. In the other Tehsils, they are more scattered, but they are fairly strong in the Amritsar Bangar, and across the Beas in Kapurthala. The Amritsar Dhillons say they came originally from the Manjha, but this is doubtful. They intermarry with all 'gots' except with the Bals. The story is that a family bard, or Mirasi, from a Dhillon village was refused help, when in difficulty in the Bal country and in revenge, he cursed the whole Bal clan. Mirasis were in those days more of a power than they are now, and the Dhillon clan took up the feud, which survives to this day in the refusal to intermarry. The Dhillons of Amritsar, who live alongside the Bals of the Sathials *ilaqua*, do not carry the feud further than this, but those of the Manjha will not eat or drink in a Bal village, or from the same dish as a Bal. Mirasis of course keep up the feud, too. Among the Dhillons, Sardar Bahadur Thakur Singh, Bhangi Zaildar of Panjwar was a leading man. His son Harnam Singh has received a grant of 10 squares in the Lyallpur district.

RANDHAWA JATS

Randhawa come next in order. They are hardly met with in Taran Taran, but are very strong all along the Batala border, and down the Sandridge in the Amritsar Tehsil, especially near Mahta and as far as Kathunangal. They are the strongest 'got' in the Amritsar Tehsil and hold thirty-nine villages. Many of them are Mohammedan, and until lately very many of them were Sultanis, but these are now fewer than they were. They rank high as cultivators and sugar cane growing is a speciality in their country. Several leading men in the time of the Sikhs belonged to this 'got' and among the best known families left in the district are those of Bhagwan Singh of Chamiari, who enjoyed a *jagir* of Rs. 600 from the villages of Dhariwal, Tehsil Ajnala, and Khushal Singh of Kathunangal.

AULAKH JATS

The Aulakh Jats are most numerous in the Ajnala Tehsil, but there is also a cluster of nine villages round Shabazpur in Taran Taran, held by this clan. Though quite a small village, Shabazpur is well known, and the corner of the Manjha in which it lies takes its name from the village and is generally known as " Shabazpur ki tarac". But it is round Kohala Ajnala that the Aulakhs are met with in strength and their chief villages are Kohala, Kohali, Lopoki, Chawinda Khurd and Kalan, Madoki, Barar and Chogawan. Their leading men are not above the yeoman class, but furnish three of the zaildars of that part of the Tehsil, *viz.* Massa Singh, Darab Khan and Bela Singh. The larger portion of their country is profusely irrigated by the Bari Doab Canal, and they are a prosperous and well-to-do clan, though with small holdings.

CHAHIL JATS

The Chahils own sixteen villages near Sheron Bagha in Amritsar. The best known member of the tribe was the late Sardar Bahadur Arjan Singh, C.I.E, who held a Jagir worth Rs. 2,800 per annum, 2,500 kanals of land in Taran Taran Tehsil, as well as 10 squares in the Lyallpur district. He was an Honorary Magistrate and Civil Judge of the first class, an Assistant Collector and Sub-Registrar, President of the Local Board of Taran Taran, a Fellow of the Panjab University, a Member of the Council of the Aitchison College and a Provincial Darbari. His estates were being managed by the court of wards during the minority of his two sons.

SIDHU JATS

The Sidhus hold, round Atari and Bhakns, fourteen villages in all. The Atariwala family belongs to this clan, and a native of the family, the present chief of which is Sardar Balwant Singh, will be found further on. They have few representatives in other parts of the district, their country being mostly in the Ferozepore district, where they hold the entire south and west of Moga, the Maharaj villages, the greater part of southern Muktsar, and numerous villages in the sandy tracts of the Ferozepore and Zira Tehsils. They trace their descent from Raja Jaisal, a Manj Rajput, from one of whose descendants, Barar, have sprung the ruling families of Patiala, Nabha, and Jind. Other details of the Sidhu clan, also known as the Barars in Ferozepore, will be found at page 494 of the first volume of Griffin's *Panjab Chiefs*, and in the *Gazetteer of the Ferozepore* district, where the clan is of the first importance. The Sidhus of Amritsar are almost entirely Sikhs and live in the Taran Taran Tehsil. Their numbers were very much underestimated in the Census of 1891, when their strength was given as 3,682, whereas by the latest census return they numbered 8,931.

BALJATS

The same remark applies to the Bal Jats, who hold the large villages of Bal Khurd, and Ralan near the city, besides Sathiala, Butala, Jodhe and Bal Serai, in the Bangar of Amritsar or twenty-three villages in all, and to the Pannun Jats, who have spread from the Jalandhar Doab, and were set down as numbering only 260, while the present Census return shows their number as 4,791. They own seven large estates in the Manjha, including Naushera and Chaudriwala, so that it is almost certain that numbers of them, owing to some mis-reading of the name, were previously classed amongst miscellaneous Jats. The principal villages of the China Jats is Har Seh China, near Raja Sansi, in Ajnala. The Sadal Jats, of whom no separate return was given in 1891, number 2,695, and all inhabit the Amritsar Tehsil. The Bhullars are a numerous clan, and with the Manns and part of the Hers, have the honour of being known as *asli* or original Jats, all others having enrolled themselves in the great tribe of Jats at a later date. No satisfactory explanation is forthcoming as to why all the Hers are not ranked as originals, nor is it clear whether any particular village or family belong to the original clan or not. The Bhangus hold the large village of Khiala (Khurd and Kalan) in the same Tehsil. They and the Sohala, inhabiting the village of that name in Tarn Taran, once enjoyed the reputation of being among the most lawless in the district. The Kangs hold a compact cluster of villages near Tarn Taran, chief among which are Kang, Kalla and Mal Chak. The Jhawara Jats of Mattewal, and the neighbourhood, and the Mahil Jats of Ajnala are not now classed separately in the census returns.

GURDASPUR

Jats as revenue-payers they are the backbone of the district, which is a great recruiting ground for the Jat regiments of the native army. It is somewhat curious, and interesting to observe how closely the general boundary between the Rajput and Jat country follows between the submontane and plains zones; the inferior race, so far as physique and energy are concerned, being confined to the tract where cultivation is carried on with less labour, and more uncertain returns, while the hardier Jats have successfully wrestled with the greater natural obstacles to agricultural development with far more satisfactory, and certain results.

The Jats are also partly Hindu, partly Muhammaden, and partly Sikh. The last are to be found chiefly in Batala, and to the south of Gurdaspur, and Shakargarh. Sikh Jat villages are, as a rule, the strongest, most active, and prosperous, and the similar Muhammaden communities are the most involved and indolent.

The chief Jat 'gots' in the different Tehsils are as under:-

Gurdaspur — Kahlon, Sidhu, Ghumman, Goraya, Gil, Randhawa, Dhariwal.

Batala — Randhawa, Sidhu, Kahlon, Riar, Gil, Sarai, Goraya.

Shakargarh — Kahlon, Malli, Goraya, Bains.

The Randhawas far exceed any other 'got' in Batala; in Gurdaspur they are found mainly in the Bangar. They are chiefly Sikhs, and once had a great reputation for drink, and illicit distillation in this respect. The Kahlons who are largely found in the Ravi valley are not far, if at all behind. The Riars are almost confined to the fertile Bangar tract called the Riarki, situated in the east of Batala, and the adjoining villages in Gurdaspur Tehsil. The Malli Jats are a strong body of cultivators in the richest part of the Shakargarh Darp, but in most cases their holdings have become deplorably subdivided, and there is greater pressure on the soil than anywhere in the district.

Here, as elsewhere, the Jats have preserved their racial characteristics. They are brave, fairly open, industrious, frugal in their personal expenditure and hardy, but are also quarrelsome, litigious, not averse to violent crime and profligate in their sex.

SIALKOT

Jats are found all over the district, and form the backbone of the agricultural community. They are found into numerous clans, and profess different religions, but a strong family likeness pervades the whole tribe. The Muhammaden is sometimes said to be less energetic than his Hindu or Sikh brother but is very doubtful whether any such distinction exists. The Sikh sometimes indulges a taste for liquor, and are patient, hard-working cultivators without much enterprise but tenacious of their right, and proud of their position as zamindars or landowners, even if their holding be but an acre or two. The Sikh Jats are freely recruited for the Army, but until the War few Mohammedans were also taken. In physique the Jat is generally of medium height with fairly regular features, and a lean but wiry frame. The principal clans are the Bajwa, Basra, Chima, Ghumman, Kahlon, Malhi, Goraya, Sahi and Sandhu.

BAJWAS

Bajwas are found in all Tehsils except Daska. In the Sialkot Tehsil they inhabit the Bhogowal zail only. In the Zafarwal Tehsil they are grouped round Chawinda, in the Rava Tehsil round Narowal, while in Pasrur they are found mainly in the north-west with headquarters at Kalawala. The Baju Rajputs of Bajwat admit their relationship with the Bajwas. The clan is almost entirely confined to this district. The Bajus and Bajwas are singularly unanimous about their origin. They claim to be descended from Ram Chandar of the Surajbansi line. Their common ancestor was one Shalip, who lived in the time of Sikandar Lodi at Uch in Jhang, which was then part of the Multan Suba. Shalip was a man of some position, as he enjoyed a large Jagir, and paid tribute to Delhi. He quarrelled with the Governor of the Suba and owing to the intrigues of the latter fell into disfavour. The imperial troops marched against him, and when his fort at Uch fell, he poisoned himself to death. He had a large number of sons, some of whom were killed with their father. Two of them Kals and Yas or Sis, however, escaped, disguised as falconers. Kals took refuge with a Sindhu Jat of Ban in the Pasrur Tehsil, and married a Jat wife. Yas took service with the Rajput chief at Jammu, and settled down at Gol, a village on the left bank of the Chenab opposite Hundal in Bajwat. Shortly afterwards, he crossed the river, and settled down in Bajwat, where his descendants, the Bajus, live to this day. He put his brother Kals out of caste, as the latter had married beneath him. But Kals was strong enough to find a flourishing family of his own, which has now grown into the powerful Bajwa clan. The words Baju and Bajwa are derived from the word "Baz" meaning falcon. The Bajus, partly owing to the unhealthy climate of Bajwat, are an inferior race, but the Bajwas, especially the Sikhs among them, are as good as any of the Jats in the district. They have three divisions. The descendants of Manak inhabit Pasrur. Those of Manga cluster round Chawinda while Narowal is the headquarters of the children of Naru. The last division is divided into two sub-divisions, which take their name from the number of villages owned by each. Tradition says that Naru, the founder of Narowal, who was a Bajwa, was unhappy enough to lose all his sons in infancy, till he was told by an astrologer that only that son would live who should be born beneath the shade of a Chhichhara (Buten frondosa) tree. Naru arranged accordingly, and his next son was born under this tree. Sometime afterwards he found, by chance, a male infant lying under another Chhichhara tree, and evidently abandoned by its parents. No trace of its belongings could be found, so Naru adopted it. The descendants of the real son of Naru live in Narowal, and own 22 villages. Those of the adopted son live on the right bank of the Jhajri nullah, and own 45 villages. The two sub-divisions are known by the terms "Baiswale" and "Paintaliswale". The latter are sometimes also called "Chhichhrial".

The Bajwa Jats are represented by two distinguished branches of the clan. The respective heads of both live in Kalaswala, a large village near Pasrur. The first member of the family, who made himself famous, was Sardar Jodh Singh, who was first the favourite of Maharaja Ranjit Singh, and then the object of his hate. After three years of an unequal struggle he submitted, and the Maharaja conferred Jagirs on him, and married his daughter to Prince Kharak Singh. On the latter's death his widow adopted Sardar Bhagwan Singh, the son of her second cousin. His grandson, Sardar Randhir Singh, who had been educated at the Aitchison College, Lahore, is the present head of the family.

The other side of the clan came into prominence at a later stage, but the authenticated history of its members presents a noble record. They were consistently distinguished by personal bravery, with one or two have displayed no small military capacity. The first member of the family of whom an accurate account is obtainable, was Sardar Khushal Singh. He was by choice a scholar, but his descendants have all been soldiers. His son, Dula Singh, was one of the most dashing cavalry leaders of the Maharaja's army. Dula Singh's eldest son, Jiwan Singh, was a remarkable character. He commanded the famous Sher Dil Paltan, and during the second Sikh War, he remained thoroughly loyal. His elder son, Sant Singh, did good service in the Mutiny, and the younger, Sardar Jagat Singh, also did much to emulate the brilliant career of his father. He was appointed Subedar of the 29th Infantry, when quite a lad, in 1857, and served in that regiment till his retirement in 1882. He saw much war service and won the Order of Merit at the Paiwar Kotal in 1878, and later received the Order of British India. On his retirement from military service, he was appointed Honorary Magistrate and Civil Judge, and Chairman of the District Board. He was also granted the order of C.I.E. His eldest surviving son, Sardar Autar Singh, is an Extra Assistant Commissioner, while a younger son, Sardar Upar Singh, who represents the family in the district is a Zaildar, and President of the Notified Area, Kalaswala. A third son, Sardar Piyar Singh, was Subedar in the 29th Panjabis, and the fourth, Datar Singh, is Jemadar in 107th Pioneers.

BASRAS

Basra Jats are found mainly near Kali or Gharial Kalan in the Pasrur and Raya Tehsils. They claim Phagwara in the Kapurthala district as their home from where they moved to village Mehli. Famine drove them with their heirs to the jungles of Sialkot, and they settled at Kali, and in the neighbourhood.

CHIMAS

Chimas are found, so far as this district is concerned, mainly in the Daska Tehsil, where they hold many of the rich estates, which, enjoy irrigation facilities from the Aik stream. They claim relationship with Chauhan Rajputs as their ancestor. Chima, belonged to that clan. They have the reputation of quarreling amongst themselves but against strangers:

"Chima aur Chatha
Khan pin nun vakh-o-vukh
Laran Bhiran nun ikhatha."

(Chimas and Chathas separate for eating and drinking. But combine for fighting).

Mohammedan Chimas still call in the Brahmin (purohit) at their weddings.

GHUMANS

The Ghuman Jats are chiefly settled in the Sialkot Tehsil to the west, and south of the city, and around Sambrial in the Daska Tehsil. They are an offshoot of the Janjua Rajputs, and so claim descent from Raja Dalip of Delhi. One of his descendants, Sanpal, married out of caste, took service in Jammu, and founded this clan, which has 21 sub-divisions, each representing an alleged son of Sanpal. They intermarry with all the leading Jats, with the exception of the Mans. They have a few peculiar wedding customs such as the worship of on idol, made of grass, tied up with red cloth, and the pouring of water on a lamb's head. They are good agriculturists.

KAHLONS

The Kahlon Jats claim descent from Raja Vikramajit through Raja Jag Deo of Daranagar, of the Lunar dynasty. The home of the clan is Batala in the Gurdaspur district. There are three divisions of the clan corresponding with the three sons of Soli, their founder. The first division inhabits Dhamthal, the part of the Raya Tehsil, and a small part of Shakargarh; the second, the remaining villages in Zafarwal; and the third, the rest of Shakargarh. Their marriage ceremonies differ somewhat from those of the western Jats, and they have special names for the various members of the marriage party. They intermarry with the other Jats. They are quiet, industrious people, and make good soldiers.

MALHIS

The Malhis of this district are found mainly around Baddomalhi in the Raya Tehsil. The interesting account of the tribe is supplied by one of its members. Ram Chandarji was of Surajbansi family, and it is through him that the Malhis trace their descent. According to Bard Chand (as Major Todd tells us) Malli, Malhi, or Mohil is one of 36 royal races of Rajasthan. Malhi was then holder of the Malwa estate, the capital of which was Udunth Kot, the ruins of which are to be found up to this day in the Multan district. From Greek history also we learn that Alexander the Great during his conquests of India met, and fought with warlike tribe of Malhi, the holder of Multan (Mohilsthan), Prithviraja, the King of Delhi (12th century A.D.), the son of Bumbi, the son of Piasal, the same tribe of Rajputs, and was one of the greatest of Malwa princes. He was conquered by Shahab-ud-din Ghori, and from that time the Malhis have been scattered all over the Panjab, founding villages wherever they settled. There is, however, even now a small state in Rajputana by the name of Srobi, the ruler of which is a Malhi.

In loyalty the Malhis are second to none. During the reign of Shahjahan, Rai Jani (being converted to Islam, called Muhammad Jani), an ancestor of the Badhomalhi family and a descendant of Badho, was granted a Jagir by that monarch. This Jagir extended from Eminaliad (Gujranwala district) to Naurangabad (Tehsil Raya). It was reduced to a few villages in Tehsil Raya by the Sikhs, and since the first settlemenr evcn out of those few villages the family has lost four or five, *viz.* Kotli Hathu Malhi, Panjgirayan Gidhian, Rathian, etc.

The Malhis have a 'Sidh' or 'Pir'. He was the great grandson of Prithviraja, and his name is Lakshman Jati Sidh Bala Korshi. From his early days he was given to the worship of God, and therefore having given up the world and its pleasures he became a Jogi, and being a prince soon came to be known as one of the greatest of the Jogis. He was so esteemed for his wonderful works that people have founded shrines in his honour all over the Panjab, and fairs are held there to commemorate the memory of Sidh Bala Korshi[51].

The customs of the Malhis are mostly those of the Hindus except for the observance of Muhammaden customs by those who have become Muhammadens, and among these too, the most important customs such as marriage are mainly Hindu, although the ceremony of Nikah is adopted from the Muhammadens the Jehaz, and many other ceremonies connected with marriage are Hindu. Brahmins attend at the marriages of Mohammedan and Christian Malhis, and the peculiar Bahi marriage customs are observed by the Hindus.

The people of this clan are also found in 12 or 13 villages round about Badiana, a village midway between Pasrur and Sialkot. One of the rising families in this tract is that of Risaldar Pal Singh of Bathe, who joined the 25th Cavalry (F.F.), served in the Afghan War, during 1878-80, and Tirah Campaign, 1897, rose to commissioned rank in 1900 and retired in 1912 after serving for 34 years. At the outbreak of the First World War he, along with his brother Ishar Singh, again joined the regiment. Two of his nephews also joined the army. One who was with the 19th Lancers, died. His son, Iqbal Singh, was an Extra Assistant Commissioner in the Panjab.

GORAYAS

The Goraya clan is found mainly in the north-east of the Pasrur Tehsil, district Sialkot and in the neighbouring villages of Daska. They were said to be descended from the Saroa family of Lunar Rajputs, and are closely connected with the Dhillon, Malhi and Saroa Jats. The ancestor of whom they trace their origin, Rana came from Sirsa to Jammu and thence to this district in the time of Emperor Akbar. They revere Pir Munda.

SANDHUS

Sandhu Jats are found round Satrah in the Pasrur Tehsil, Sialkot district and Wadhala Sandhuan in Daska. In this district they call themselves Sandhus, not Sindhus. They claim Solar Rajput origin and believe that they came here from Ghazni, but whether Ghazni in Afghanistan or in the Deccan or Bikaner is not certain. Hindu Sandhus revere their ancestor Kala Pir or Kala Mehr of whom various wonderful tales are told. There is a shrine at Satrah, district Sialkot, Pakistan, to his memory.

SIRANWALI

Sardar Shiv Deo Singh is the head of the Sandhu Jat family of Siranwali in the Pasrur Tehsil, now in Pakistan. The family rose to position and power under the early Sikh rule, and the grand aunt of the present Sardar was married into the Royal family at Lahore. Her brother, Sardar Mangal Singh, attached himself to Prince Kharak Singh, whose chief favourite he was, and received large Jagirs. On the death of the prince most of the Jagirs were resumed. After annexation of the Panjab by the British Army in 1849, he was allotted a cash pension of Rs. 1,000 a month. He died in 1864. In 1870 his only son, Rachhpal Singh, married the niece of Rani Jind Kaur, widow of Prince Kashmira Singh, and had one son, Shiv Deo Singh, who was born in 1875. In 1884 Sardar Rachhpal Singh was nominated President of the District Board of Sialkot. In the same year he was entrusted with civil and criminal powers as an Honorary Magistrate with his court at Siranwali. He died in 1907. His son has succeeded him as Honorary Magistrate at Siranwali where he lived a quite studious life, and was much respected by all who knew him. He was a Provincial Darbari.

WADHALA

The Sandhus of Wadhala in Daska, Sialkot, (Pakistan), emerged from obscurity during the Mughal ascendancy. Sardar Mahtab Singh was the first to strike out a course for himself. He threw in his lot with two of the Bhangra leaders, and became connected by marriage, soon broke with him, and a fierce quarrel ensued. After much desultory fighting the heads of the family took service in Kashmir. They returned to the Panjab in 1814, and in the two Sikh Wars some members took one side and some the other. Sardar Sahib Singh served in the Bara Ghorchara. On his death government resumed three-fourths of his service. But the second son, Baghel Singh had a distinguished career. He rendered valuable service in 1857 both in Sialkot and Oudh, and in 1873 went to the Andamans as Assistant District Superintendent of Police. He retired in 1884 on a well-earned pension, and with the title of Rai Bahadur.

Sardar Baghel Singh's son, Hakim Singh, had an honourable career, serving with the 18th Lancers in Afghanistan, and later as a Subedar in the Burma Police. After his retirement he became Honorary Magistrate, and Civil Judge at Daska. He died in 1915.

The most prominent representative of the family was Risaldar Sardar Hira Singh, son of Sardar Thakur Singh, who served in the 30th Lancers. He was a Provincial Darbari.

MANN

The Mann Jats do not properly belong to the Sialkot district, but any mention of the tribe would not be complete without a reference to this famous clan. With the Bhullar and Her clans it forms the "two-and-a-half houses" which claim to be the oldest and best of the Jat clans. The leading representative of the tribe in the Sialkot district was Sardar Harnam Singh, Honorary Magistrate of Kila, Sardar Harnam Singhwal in the Raya Tehsil. His grandfather, Sardar Budh Singh, was an exceptionally gallant and faithful adherent of the British throughout the chequered period which preceded and followed annexation. He died in 1856.

GUJRANWALA

Gujranwala district in the Lahore Division takes its name from the town where the headquarters are situated. Gujranwala literally means the abode of the Gujjars. These were nomads or cattle-grazers. They were expelled many generations ago by Sansi Jats, immigrants from Amritsar, who founded 11 villages in this vicinity. Gujranwala town, the headquarters of the district, is 42 miles from Lahore, the capital of the province and is situated on the Grand Trunk Road and main line of the North-Western Railway. The founder of Gujranwala was a Khan, who gave it the name of Khanpur, but the old name survived the change of owners.

The district lies roughly between north latitude 31° 45"and 32° 83" and east longitude 73° 12" and 74° 37". It consists of a triangular block of land running roughly east and west. The river Chenab forms the northern and north-western boundary of the district, but as the boundary is fixed small portions of the district lie on the right bank of the river. On the north the district touches the Gujrat district and the Shahpur district, on the west the Jhang district, on the south the Sheikhupura district, and on the east the Sialkot district. The area of the district is 2,302 square miles. The greatest length from east to west is 84 miles and the greatest breadth from north to south is 45 miles. The population according to the census of 1931 is 7,36,138. The district stands eighteenth in order of size and nineteenth in order of population among the districts of the Panjab. The district has three Tehsils: Gujranwala, Wazirabad and Hafizabad. Originally the district formed part of a larger district with headquarters at Wazirabad. As a separate district it was first formed of four Tehsils: Gujranwala, Ramnagar, Hafizabad and Sheikhupura, the headquarters being first fixed in the Sheikhupura Fort from which they were transferred in 1851 to Gujranwala. At the close of the regular settlement in 1855 the district was reconstructed into three Tehsils, all of Gujranwala and part of Ramnagar formed the two Tehsils of Gujranwala and Wazirabad.

RAWALPINDI

Only in Gujjar Khan Tehsil, where they cultivate nearly one fourth of the Tehsil, are the Jats of any importance or numerical strength. A few are found in Rawalpindi, fewer still in Kahuta. In Murree they are unknown. It is not clear, when or whence they came into the district. In the north-east corner of Gujjar Khan Tehsil near the Kahuta border there are a few villages of genuine Sandhu Muhammaden Jats from Gujranwala, who came here in the early days of the Sikh rule. With that exception nothing is known of a Jat immigration. All low caste agriculturists, who cannot establish a claim to be classed as Rajputs, but are of genuine zamindari descent, are known as Jats. Probably the bulk of people so classed are all converted Hindus, though the term 'Jat' may include many families from other tribes, who in the course of generations, have lost touch with their original connections, and have become merged in the great body of the cultivators.

Very probably the term covers a very heterogeneous body, including many immigrants from the east, aboriginal tribes or their descendants, and all of agricultural descent who have lost or failed to acquire Rajput status. A popular theory is that there is generally no difference of ancestry between the tribes classed as Jats and those classed as Rajputs. Social aspirations are indicated by strictness in the marriage of daughters; a daughter may be given in marriage to a tribe of equal or higher repute, but not to one of lower repute; disregard of this rule had degraded many families from Rajput to Jat, as an observance of it even now raises Jats to the dignity of being called Rajputs. This theory does not accord with the clan systems of the Jat and Rajput tribes. It proceeds from the impossibility of discerning physically and in appearance any difference between the ordinary Jats. The process of rise and fall which it describes does go on but the assertion of a common Rajput and Jat origin, which is the important part of the theory, does not accord with either the conditions or the traditions of the district. The theory of heterogeneity explains all the facts which are the basis of the common ancestry theory, and also covers these differences in clan organisation between Rajputs and Jats and within the tribe which the other theory leaves untouched. One or two of the Jat clans present an appearance of some homogeneity, but the great minority have neither a common descent nor common traditions. Classes as Jats are Aura, Bains, China, Dhanial, Kalial, Khatrel and Sadan. No detailed investigation has ever been made into the organisation of these clans in this district. The Jats are fine "thrifty" sturdy cultivators. After the Malliars they are the best in the district. They generally quiet and law-abiding, are not above daily labour, and many of them, borrowing Rajput tribal names, enlist in the native army. They have no leaders of any note.

JHELUM

Little is known of the origin and early history of the tribes inhabiting the district, of which the most important are the Gakkhars, Janjuas, Mairs, Kassars, Kahuts, Awans, Gujjars and Jats; and opinions as to the conclusions to be drawn from what we do know are conflicting. With respect to the Awans, one authority says that they are the descendants of the Rajputs who settled in the district before the time of Alexander; another group of scholars hold the view, that they may be of Greek origin, but have not been in the district more than 250 years; while the Awans themselves say that they came from Arabia with Mahmud of Ghazni, 900 years ago. There are tribal genealogies again, some of them going very far back; but our confidence in these is somewhat shaken when we find that in one of the best-kept versions of the Janjua tree, Raja Prithvi Raj, who was defeated by Muhammad-bin-Sam in 1193 A.D., is the 27th in the list, while Raja Mal, who is supposed to have been a contemporary of Mahmud, about 1000 A.D., ranks the 64th. Again it is stated that Raja Mal was the first Janjua to embrace Islam, but at least seven individuals after him have the Hindu "Deva" attached to their names. The first Mussalman name in the tree is the 71st, and the present generation is the 84th, which, at thirty years for each generation, gives 450 years only. (That this is not far wrong may be seen from the fact that Sangar Khan and Rai Purana, the 73rd generation were contemporaries of Humayun, A.D. 1554.)[52]

The Gakkhars, though not numerically important, are in other respects one of the most prominent tribes in the district, and in social position amongst the Muslims of the tract, share with the Janjuas, the honour of the first place; in popular estimation indeed they seem to rank a little higher than even the Janjuas. They are almost entirely confined in this district to the Jhelum Tehsil, where they hold the bulk of the Khuddar Circle, with a good many villages in the Maidan; elsewhere they are found only in the Rawalpindi and Hazara districts.

Of the history and origin of this tribe, much has been written; the earliest suggestion, that of General Court, that the name of the Gakkhars points to their descent from the Greeks, has not found later supporters; though it has now been adopted and improved upon by some of the present representatives of the tribe, who claim decent from Alexander himself. Mr. Brandreth *(Settlement Report,* paragraph 48) adopted the local tradition that the Gakkhars "came from Persia through Cashmere", which is still they claim of the majority of the Gakkhars themselves. The views of General Cunningham are set forth at length in his *Archaeological Survey Report*, Volume II, pages 22 to 33, to which the curious must be referred for the detailed reasons on which he based his conclusion that the Gakkhars represent the "savage Gargaridae" of Dionysius, the Geographer (who wrote probably in the 4th Century A.D.), and are descendants of the great Yuochi Scythians, who entered India from the north-west in the early centuries of the Christian Era. Mr. Ibbetson (paragraph 463 of his *Census Report)* notices with approval Mr. Thomson's comment (paragraph 57, *Jhelum Settlement Report)* on Cunningham's theory: "Though the Turanian origin of the Gakkhar is highly probable, yet the rest of the theory is merely a plausible surmise. On the whole there seems to be little use in going beyond the sober narrative of Ferishta, who represents the Gakkhars as a brave and savage race, living mostly in the hills, with little or no religion, and much given to polyandry and infanticide."

All the historians before the time of Ferishta agree that the Khokhars, not the Gakkhars, killed Shahab-ud-din Ghauri; Ferishta certainly confused these two tribes in other cases; thus he frequently refers to Shekha and Jasrat as Gakkhar chiefs; there are no such names in the Gakkhar tree, whereas Shekha and Jasrat appear as father and son in the genealogy of the Khokhars[53].

Ferishta's account of the Gakkhars as a tribe of wild barbarians without either religion or morality, practising polyandry and infanticide is a literal translation from the Arabic of Ibn Athir, an earlier historian who was there. However, writing of the wild tribes in the hills to the west of Peshawar, and not of the Gakkhars, the chapter in *Ibn Athir* immediately following deals with the murder of Shahab-ud-din by the Gakkhars, hence perhaps a mistake; or Ferishta may have borne a grudge against the Gakkhars, who are said by him to have maltreated an ancestor of his own, named Hindu Shah[54].

Gakkhar Shah alias Kaigwar Shah, is mentioned as one of the principal followers of Mahmud of Ghazni[55].

An officer who knew the Gakkhars well wrote of them: "Some of their principal men are very gentlemanly in their bearing, and show unmistakably their high origin and breeding"; another says, "They are essentially the gentlemen and aristocracy of the (Rawalpindi) district;...the Gakkhars still bear many traces of their high descent in their bearing, and in the estimation in which they are held throughout the district." Mr. Thomson wrote of them, "Physically the Gakkhars are not a large-limbed race, but they are compact, sincere and vigorous. They are self- respecting, and sometimes exceedingly well-mannered." As this does them no more than justice; and to anyone who knows them well the statement, that as late as the 13th century they were wild barbarians, without religion or morality, is in itself almost incredible. Raja Jahandad Khan seems to have succeeded in tracing the libel to its origin; he shows also that they have sometimes been confused with the Khokhars;[56] but it cannot be said that his arguments in favour of their Persian origin are very convincing; in the matter of assassination of Shahab-ud- din Ghauri, the historians who state that he was killed by the Gakkhar at Dhamiak in this district are supported by a strong local tradition; the actual spot is shown[57], and this is at a place in the heart of the Gakkhar country, never held, as far as we know, by the Khokhars.

The first settlement of the tribe in this district is generally admitted to be Abriam in Sultanpur, under the Lehri hills; thence they spread over the Khuddar, southwards towards the river, and as far as Lundi Patti to the west, being constantly opposed by the Janjuas, who were almost invariably defeated and ejected; in his first invasion of India, Babar took the side of the Janjuas, and with them defeated Hati Khan, the great Gakkhar chief of Pharwala, but in a subsequent invasion made friends with the Gakkhars and procured from them an auxiliary force. When Babar's son, Hamayun, was ousted in 1542 A.D. by Sher Shah, the principal Gakkhar chiefs took the side of the exile; to bridle the pride Sher Shah built the huge fort of Rohtas, about ten miles from Jhelum, and in the constant warfare that followed the Gakkhar country was terribly harried; but the tribe was never subdued, and on Hamayun's return to power began to grow powerful. Their subsequent history, until the rise of "Sultan" Muqarrab Khan, about 1740 A.D., chiefly concerns other districts; he was an Admal chief of the Rawalpindi district, and claimed to rule the whole of the tract from Attock to the Chenab; the Domeli Bugials, however did not acknowledge his pretentions and on his defeat by the Sikhs at Gujrat, they at once rebelled, captured Muqarrab Khan and murdered him. The usual internecine feuds then arose, and the different clans fell in turn an easy prey to the Sikhs, though the eastern hill Mandis were never thoroughly subdued, and were in constant rebellion until the beginning of the British rule: in 1849 the Gakkhars nearly all took the losing side, and therefore forfeited much of their possessions and dignities, falling on evil days, from which they have only extricated themselves by the readiness with which they have since taken employment under the Government[58].

The Gakkhars have split into many branches, of which the most important in this district are the Admal, the Iskandral and the Bugial, who occupy most of the Khuddar Circle; a smaller clan, named Firozal (not the great Firozal clan, and not thought highly by other Gakkhars), hold a few villages close to the Jhelum; and with still smaller branch, the Tulial (which is little esteemed, and with which the other clans do not intermarry), has four or five estates on the river near Dina. The clan-names are in all cases derived from those of the common ancestors: the principal seats or mother villages of each branch are called Mandis, of which there are six generally recognised in the Jhelum district, Sultanpur (Admal), Lehri and Bakrala (Iskandral), Domeli, Padhri and Baragowah (Bugial), Bheth and Sahhal, formerly flourishing Mandis of the Bugial, are now decayed.

Regarding the character of the Gakkhars, there is not much to add to what has already been said: pride of race is very strong in them, and though they make good soldiers, they are bad farmers and since they have not fallen back on Government service, they are almost always in the most unprosperous condition, being much wanting in industry and thrift: their most unpleasing characteristic is their intense jealousy of one another, which leads to bitter feuds and sometimes to murder.

The following were some of the principal Gakkhars in this district: Ata Muhammad of Pandori; Resaldar Mumara Khan of

Domeli[59], (Honorary Magistrate); Adalat Zar Khan of Domeli, Fatteh Khan of Domeli and Beli Budhar; Muhammad Khan of Lehri and his uncle Farman Ali; Muhammad Khan and Waris Khan of Bakrala; Fatteh Muhammad of Adrana; Shadiman Khan of Bheth; Muhammad Khan of Sanghoi Malhu; Muhammad Khan Sanghoi Khas; Muhammad Zaman of Baral; Resaldar Nawab of Badagran (son of the late Khan Bahadur Resaldar, Major B. Khan). A family of formerly good standing is that of Padhro Khan, late head, Fatteh Mehndi[60].

JHANG

The Nassowanas are the pure Jat tribe, though recorded as Rajputs in 1901. They inhabit the northern corner of Chiniot Tehsil and have a few villages in the Shahpur district, where 509 were enumerated as Jats. They have no connection whatever with the Sials in spite of the termination in Ana and are more nearly akin to the Tiwanas. They are a fine body of men, fearless and bold, with a great reputation for thieving, and ready for devilment of any kind. Shahu of Kandiwal was their Zaildar. Raja, one of the most prominent of them, was involved some years ago in a serious riot and was deprived of official position in the tribe. Jalla of Kandiwal is also a leading man. The large communities of Bhabhrana and Lolla have at present no very influential men. The whole of the Nassowana villages lie in the north, and all will be canal irrigated.

GILOTARS

Between the Nassowanas and the river come the Gilotars, a tribe confined entirely to this district. The cause or consequence of this is that they are great cattle owners and used to take their cattle into the Sandal Bar where they have been given land. They are expert cattle-lifters, but at the same time admirable agriculturists. All their villages are prosperous and carefully cultivated. Nothing is known of their origin, but it is said that they connect themselves with Handsi (Hissar). Nadir Gilotar of Gandhlanwali, the Zaildar and Raja of Burj Mal were their leaders.

LALIS

The Lalis occupy a group of villages in the north of Chiniot Tehsil between the Nassowanas in the north and the Bhattis in the south, and like both these clans have no river villages. About 531 Lalis were enumerated in Shahpur in 1901, where they have a few villages, but they are not found elsewhere. Nothing is known of their origin. They have several subdivisions, the Kawins and Bodhars being perhaps the most prominent. The tribe as a whole affects a somewhat sanctimonious aspect and garb. The Lalis are not a fine or spirited race of men and differ from both the Nassowanas and Bhattis in this respect. Their large villages are Lalian, Kawinwala, Walla Wanoka and Dawar, but there are many small ones, all colonies from Lalian, the original settlement. The Zaildars were Ahmadyar of Kawinwala and Samail of Kot Bahadur. Raja of Dawar and Mahmand of Walla, both ex-Zaildars, were prominent men of the tribe.

HARALS

The last of the great Jat clans of Chiniot Tehsil in 1901, were 3,491. The Harals whose villages extended along both sides of the Ghenab from Morawala to Saike. About 1,912 of the clans were enumerated in the Chenab colony. They appear to be a purely Chenab tribe, being found in numbers in Shahpur (1,849) and Gujranwala (1,007) only. Although their chief settlements were on the river, many had, before the colonisation of the Sandal Bar, settled in the desert and had obtained allotments as Janglis or Bar graziers. They owned great numbers of cattle, sheep and goats, but unlike the latter they were bad cultivators. It was always a difficult matter to appoint an unconvicted cattle thief to a vacant Haral *lambardari*, and when the original Haral Zaildar of Kharkhan died, it was found impossible to replace him by one of his tribes. Sujawala, Zaildar of Morawala, was the only Haral at that time of any importance. Tradition mentions them as a branch of the Ahir-Jats and they were said to have settled in the district during the rule of the Mughal Emperors, but it is probable that their coming was at an earlier date.

NAULS

The only Jat tribe of any importance in Jhang Tehsil are the Nauls, who hold several villages near Jhang and in the Kachhi. They have been in the past great cattle-owners, and 438 of the tribe were enumerated in the colony, where they had land. The Nauls are interesting as being one of the earlier tribes, which settled in the district; they have occupied Jhang, the lowlands round Chenab while the country was under the rule of Brahmin kings. Naul, from whom the tribe takes its name, was a son of Dhan. The Sials for some time after their first arrival were subject to the Nauls and paid tribute through them, but eventually overcame them under the leadership of Mal Khan Chuchkana. Then the Naul chief was

Todir. The principal villages of the tribe were Kot Naulan in the Kachhi and Pakkewala, Billi and Habib near Jhang. They have always been a turbulent and lawless race, and the Sikhs found it necessary to establish a post to overawe them at Kot Sahai Singh. They have at present no prominent men, like Zaildars, etc.

BHANGUS

A tribe of similar origin to the Nauls is that of the Bhangus of Shorkot. They can give no account of themselves whatever but were rulers in the Shorkot country before the arrival of the Sials. Bhangus, both Sikhs and Mohammedans, are found in the Manjha districts, but it is doubtful whether they are allied. The Dabs of Dab Kalan and some other villages on both sides of the river, south of Shorkot, have probably alike history.

JUTAS

They appear to have gravitated down the river: the leading families hold some property in Multan. Hak Nawaz Khan, Zaildar, was the leading man. The Jutas are of the same type. They are probably more numerous than the census figures show as in vernacular their name is liable to be confused with the better known Joiyas. Their two main villages are Allayar Juta and Yarewala, north of Shorkot, and Ahmad Juta is their Zaildar.

SAPRAS

The Sapras, though owning no whole village and few, if any *lambardaris*, are a numerous tribe, found associated with the Bharwana Sials in almost all their villages, whether as proprietors, tarraddadgars or tenants-at-will. Nothing is known of their origin,

TAHIMS

The Tahims of Chiniot, though numerically unimportant and owning little land, deserve mention for their connection with Chiniot where one of their members, Nawab Sadulla Khan, was Governor in the time of Shah Jahan. The clan is a strong one in Multan, where according to Mr. Maclagan, Arabic descent is claimed for them.

KATHIAS

The Kathias are one of the most important tribes of the Montgomery district. They own several villages in the uplands, east of Shorkot. They are said to have gained a footing in the Jhang district. In the days of Inayatulla Khan, the Kamlanas, being displeased with his treatment of them, left their lands at Jalalpur and went down south and settled in the country of the Multan Nawab. Inayatulla sent messengers praying them to return, but they sent word back that they would only return at the Khan's personal request. The Khan accordingly set out from Jhang. Hearing of this, the Multan Nawab, already enraged at the recent annexation of Islamabad, laid an ambush for the Sial chief. Inayatulla obtained news of the design, and calling together an army of the Kathias, Rajbanas, and other Sials, retreated northwards. The defeat of the Multan Nawab has been already noticed. The Kathias displayed the most brilliant gallantry in the battle, and the grateful Inayatulla bestowed upon them the lands that they held in this district. Previously, they lived on the Ravi and in the lower part of the Sandal Bar. Since the death of Fazil Kathia the tribe has been steadily going from bad to worse, and is now of comparatively little importance. The chief village is Kakki Kathia Nau, but since the death of Varyam Kathia, their headman, the Zail, has been absorbed.

AKERAS

The Akeras are Jats, holding a small tract of country on both sides of the Jhelam river, just above Kot Khan, the limit of the old Sial rule. Their ancestor Khizr is said to have acquired the land by grant from Walidad Khan in whose service he was for some time employed. They were thrifty and industrious zamindars, and bred very good wiry little horse, something like the Baloch in shape. Amir and Walidad were the two principal men of the tribe.

MAHNI

The Mahni clan has now almost died out. In former days they were independent, and the headquarters of their chief was at Khiwa. Mahni was the son of Sial. Khiwa was founded by the leader, who gave it his name, a descendant from Sial in the twelfth generation. Local tradition states the Chenab was then flowing east of Khiwa, but this is evidently wrong. The Chenab did no doubt once flew under the high bank of the Bar, about 16 miles south-east of Khiwa, but this must have been ages before. When Khiwa was founded, the country to the north was held by Marais and Chaddhars. At first the Mahnis remained on good terms with their neighbours; but as they increased in strength, they began to drive them back. Khanuwana was founded in their lands in the palmy days, extended from Bhawana to Chautala. The independence of the Mahnis was extinguished by Walidad. From that time the clan appears to have rapidly declined in influence and numbers. There are now no Mahnis in Khiwa. The lands of the village were granted by Sawan Mal to Bakar, a leading man among the Bharwanas whose family now holds it. Popular tradition attributes the decay of the Mahni clan to the curse of a Fakir who lived at Chautala. This Fakir had one fair daughter, who, being of somewhat weak intellect, wandered about the country in a state of nudity. In her wanderings she strayed into Khiwa, whence the Mahni chief drove her out with contempt, thinking, no doubt, that she was no better than she ought to be. This was resented by her father, who cursed the clan addressing himself to the sacred tree near his abode.

CHADDHARS

The Chaddhars, though recorded, with few exceptions, as Jats in 1901 have always been admitted to the status of Rajput descent in this district: over 8,000 were enumerated in the Chenab colony at the census: and were probably Jhang Chaddhars. They owned a block of villages in the Chiniot Tehsil from Wara Thatta Muhammad Shah nearly to Bukhari, and were divided into numerous sub-divisions, of which the Happas, Sajjankes, Rajjokes and Kangars were the more important. The claim of the Jappas to be of equal descent is, with some show of truth, denied by the Chaddhars themselves who averred that Jappas were their drovers. Nothing is known of their origin, but there appear to be numbers of them in Montogomery, Shahpur and Multan. The Chaddhars Jats were enumerated in Amritsar, but they are not probably the same tribe.

The Chaddhar tradition is that they came from Rajputana during the time of Muhammad Ghori and proceeded to Bahawalpur where they were converted to Islam by Sher Shah of Uch: and from there they came on to Jhang. However that may be, they probably followed the same line of migration as the Sials themselves and their ancestral Brahmin family is the same. At the present day, the Chaddhars themselves are not in a flourishing state, though the junior branches have obtained considerable land on the Chenab canal and many have irrigation facilities in their own villages. Their headmen were not strong, and to their late chief representative Fatah Khan of Tahli Magini, an amiable but hopeless debauchee, they owed the loss of their Zail. The chief villages of the Chaddhars are Tahli Magini and Taja Berwala; of the Jappas Bhawana and Tatta Fatah Ali and of the Kangars Kurk Mahamda (Killa Kangaran). Amir Jappa of Bhawana and Barkhurdar of Kurk were Zaildars,

and Fatah Khan Chaddhar of Taja Berwala and Shahamda of Tatta Ali were other headmen.

MONTOGOMERY

The term 'Jat' in respect of the old inhabitants of the district was of the most indefinite significance and was commonly used to include all those miscellaneous pastoral and agricultural tribes who being Mussalmans of Indian origin did not lay claim to Rajput rank. In common parlance, it was often used as almost equivalent to peasant or countryman. Thus it became almost a matter of opinion whether each tribe was to be classed as Jat or Rajput. In fact the same tribe often appeared in the censuses under both headings. There was, for instance, considerable doubt whether the Sial tribe should be classed as Rajput or Jat. In the 1921 Census the Sials of Jhang, who had previously been recorded mostly as Jats, returned themselves as Rajputs. In the Montogomery Tehsil Sials generally claimed to be Rajputs, while in the Okara Tehsil they were content to be called Jats. The Kharral is believed to be of Rajput origin, but they generally prefer themselves to be called simply Kharrals claiming to be neither Jats nor Rajputs. The Punwar tribes were recorded as Jats in 1881 and as Rajputs in 1891. The Kathias now claim to be Rajput, but they were not recorded as such either in 1881 or 1891.

In pre-colony days a more essential distinction than that between the Jat and Rajput status, was afforded by the political position of the respective tribes, and the corresponding differences in their favourite pursuits. Captain Elphinstone in his *Settlement Report* of 1858 writes as follows:

"The population is distinctly divided into marked sections — the purely agricultural inhabitants and the pastoral tribes. The former consists of the castes, both Muhammadan and Hindu, which are generally met with throughout the Eastern Panjab, *viz.*, Arains, Kambohs, Hindu Jats, etc. But the latter are almost entirely confined to the region which extends from the southern extremity of Multan district to within thirty miles of Lahore. They are all Muhammadans, and their favourite occupation is breeding and grazing of cattle. They are locally known by the name of Jats in contradistinction to the more settled inhabitants, who call themselves Ryats or subjects. The most important tribes are the Kharrals. Fattianas, Murdanas, Kathias. Wahniwals, Baghelas, Wattus and Joiyas. The latter two are chiefly confined to the Sutlej, but the others only possess land on the Ravi, and graze their herds in the two Doabs adjoining that river."

"The Ravi tribes just enumerated call themselves the 'Great Ravi' and include all the purely agricultural class residing within their own limits under the name of 'Small Ravi' or 'Nikki Ravi' a term of reproach with reference to the more settled pursuits of these people, their comparatively peaceful habits, and probably the state of subjection in which they were placed when the 'Great Ravi' had uncontrolled authority in this region. Besides the 'Small Ravi' there is another class in this tract, who unhesitatingly recognise the 'Great Ravi[5] men as their superiors. It is composed of refugees and emigrants from other parts of the Panjab, and of the Mahtams, a peculiar Hindu tribe, who resides in the swampiest parts of the alluvial lands, and rarely appears as proprietors of the soil they cultivate. These are included under the name of Wasiwans and are not unsimilar in origin to the class of that name among the Afghan tribes."

The 'Great Ravi' Jats have always been a handsome and sturdy race. Favourable comments on their appearance have been made by numerous writers from the time of Arrian (supposing the identification of Kathias with Arrian's Kathaeoi to be correct). Most of the 'Great Ravi' tribes lay claim to Rajput origin and they used one and all to look down with some contempt upon men who handled the plough. Though they possessed land, its cultivation was left to inferior castes. Those of them who have received land in the colonies, have been compelled to some extent to modify their attitude towards agricultural labour. It is to be hoped that, colonial development will not lead them to modify their aversion from early marriage which was previously recorded as the most characteristic custom attributed to them and to which it was believed to be due that their physical superiority was so long maintained. There is a good deal of similarity among the traditions of the different tribes regarding their origin. The ancestor of each tribe was, as a rule, Rajput, a Raja of the Solar or Lunar race, and resided at Hastinapur or Daranagar. He scornfully rejected the proposals of the Delhi Emperor for a matrimonial alliance between the two families, and had then to flee to Sirsa or Bhatner, or some other place in the neighbourhood.

Next he came to the Ravi, and was converted to Islam by Makhdum Bahawal Hakk or Baba Farid. Being a stout-hearted man, he joined the Kharrals in their marauding expeditions, and so his descendants became Jats. Lately, they took to agriculture and

abandoned robbery a little, and now in the Sarkari Raj, they have quite given up their evil ways, and are honest and well disposed.

Colony grants have dispersed representatives of all the old tribes of the district up and down the Ganji and Nili Bars. Before colonial days their habitat was approximately on the Ravi to the east where first came the Kharrals, then on the Montogomery and Okara borders appeared the Wattus and in order the Khaggas, Sials and Kathias. On the Sutlej on the Lahore border came the Arars followed by the Wattus, who extended to a point nearly to south of Pakpattan. Next to them came the Chishtis followed by the Hans and the Joiyas.

MULTAN

The Jats and Rajputs of the district may conveniently be considered together. The term 'Jat' is to a certain extent recognized as the name of the caste or race as in the Central Panjab, but it is also freely used to include all those whose profession is agriculture or pasturage, and to distinguish indigenous tribes of this character from the immigrant Saiyyads, Pathans, Koreishis and others of a similar social status.

Year	Jats	Rajputs
1901	140,315	91,516
1911	251,613	60,910
1921	313,355	51,836

The word is also used as a common noun to signify a cultivator, as it will be readily understood how the tribe 'Jat' does not refer to a very definite body of men, and how the number recorded as Jats in the various censuses is subject to considerable variations. The term is often found to include on the one side menial or other lowly castes which have taken to agriculture, and, on the other, clans which pretended to undoubted Rajput origin. There are no indigenous clans in the district, who call themselves in common parlance Jat or Rajput: each clan is a known by its own name, and its classification as a Jat or Rajput clan is a matter left for the Mirasi or other outsider to consider. The number of these petty clans is immense (368 such clans were returned in 1881 under the head of "Jat" alone), and attempts to classify them are almost hopeless, as by far the greater number of them are confined to one or two villages and are quite unable to give any account of themselves or of their relations with any other clan.

The chief of the Jat and Rajput clans in the district were:

Sials	:	Nuns
Thahims	:	Drigs
Traggars	:	Dangaha
Wainses	:	Joyas
Bosans	:	Mitrus
Khokhars	:	Khichis
Marrals	:	Langrials

An account of these clans is given below:

Among the less distinguished Jat and Rajput tribes, we find in Kabirwala the Sahus, Khaks, Pahors, Dahas and Pandas; in Multan, Kheras, Athangals, Metlas, Buches, Mahoias, Chhajjras, Rans, Kalrus and Hammars; in Shujabad, Khakis, Jhakkars, Rids, Langs, Ruks, Pannuhans, Shajras and Jais; in Lodhran, Channars, Ghallus, Utheras Kanjuns and Kuliars; in Mailsi, Dhudhis, Sandhals, and Wasirs.

THE SIALS

The Sials with their various sub-divisions occupied nearly all the villages on both banks of the Ravi in the Kabirwala Tehsil. The sub-divisions best known in the district are the Sargana Hiraj, Thiraj, Sanpal Daduana, Duana, Kamlana, Panjuana, Sasran, Daultana[61] and Mirali. They all take their names from various descendants of the common ancestor, Seo or Sial. Sial is said to have been a son of Rai Shankar, a Panwar Rajput. He migrated to the Panjab and was converted to Islam by Baba Farid of Pakpattan during the time of the Emperor Ala-ud-din Khalji. He married the daughter of Bahadur Khan, a local chief, and his sons established themselves in Chauntra, and then across the Chenab in Jhang, which they ruled more or less independently down to the time of Maharaja Ranjit Singh. Ahmad Khan, the then chief was the direct descendant and male representative of Sial; after repulsing one or two attacks, he was at length defeated by the Maharaja and his country was annexed. He was, however, granted a Jagir, and his descendants still reside and hold land in Jhang. During the period of the Sial supremacy and the breakdown of the Mughal power, large bands of this tribe appear to have passed down southwards, and to have settled in their present habitat along the banks of the Ravi.

THE THAHIMS

The Thahims appear from the *Ain-i-Akbari* to have been a common tribe in the district in the days of Akbar. The bulk of the present Thahims, however, are said to have immigrated from Chiniot at the time of the Sial upheaval in the 18th century; and there are still Thahims in Chiniot and its neighbourhood. The Thahims claim Arabic descent, and they say that their immediate ancestor Sambhal Shah, came to Multan eight hundred years ago, killed the local chief, and reigned in his stead for forty years. The tribe is now found mainly on the Chenab in the south-west of the Kabirwala Tehsil, where they had a bad name for crime. They are also found in other parts of the district especially in the tract between Lodhran and Kahror. The chief Thahim family in the district was that of Pir Bakhsh, of Mamdal. Among the remarkable men whom the tribe had produced were Sadullah Khan, the Prime Minister of the Emperor Shah Jahan and Shekh Halal, one of the learned men of Agra in the days of Humayun. The tribe, therefore, was not always a purely agricultural one, and there may be something true in their claims to Arabic extraction. The Bani Tamins were a large tribe in Arabia, and the Bani Tamins are a Koreishi clan to which the first Caliph belonged.

THE TRAGGARS

The Traggars held a few villages on the Chenab next to the Thahims. They say they are Bhatti Rajputs, and take their name from their ancestral home at Traggar in Bikaner. They first immigrated to Jhang, but about two hundred years ago, on account of quarrels with the Sials, they left that and settled under their leaders, Hasta, Mulah and Salabat, on the banks of the Chenab, where they hold a few villages both on the Multan and on the Muzaffargarh side of the river.

THE BAINS

The Bains clan hold two villages on the extreme north of the Multan Tehsil, and their leading man was Kadir Bakhsh, Zaildar. They were also found in the north of the Shujabad Tehsil. They say, they were Hajua Rajputs, and that their ancestor Bains came to Multan from Sakesar in the days of Firoz Shah. The Bosans held the villages south of the Bains and their ancestor was said to have come from Haidarabad, in Sindh as a disciple of Bahawal Haq, and to have received from his master some of the land which the latter obtained from the ruler of Multan.

THE KHOKHARS

The Khokhars of the district are not a very important clan except for the one family described further in this chapter. They are sometimes looked on as a distinct tribe with Awan or with Arab origin, and sometimes as a clan of the Jats or Rajputs. The Khokhars themselves generally attribute their origin to one Qutb Shah, who came from Ghazni to Sakesar with the conqueror Mahmud, and from whom the Awans also are said to be descended. Writing on the census of 1891, Maulvi Mohammed Hussain noted as follows regarding another story of their origin: 'The author of the *Jawahir Faridi*, a book written in 1016 by one of the descendants of Baba Farid, gives the Khokhars an Arab origin, but he gives us no detail. This authority cannot be relied on, because the descendants of Baba Farid took their wives out of the Khokhar families of Pakpattan: and that fact might had induced them to give an Arab origin to the Khokhars. The Khokhars, from whatever origin descended, were a considerable power in the tract between Jhelum and Multan at the time of the invasion of Tamerlane: but their history had been somewhat obscured owing to their being constantly confused in the written records with the Ghakkars.

THE NUNS

In the north of Shujabad the predominant clan is that of the Nuns, who are said to be a sub-division of the Bhatti Rajputs, and to have migrated from some place called Thanewahan, which is said to have been in the direction of Delhi. The date of the immigration appears uncertain, but they say that their ancestor Rajwaddan was converted by Makhdum Jahanian of Uchh, or as others say, by Saiyyad Jalal. They first settled at Bhangala in Shujabad, and afterwards extended over the greater part of the north of the Tehsil, and their villages benefited greatly by the opening of canals in the times of the Nawabs. They are now somewhat decaying, but still hold a good deal of land. The Nuns are said to be connected with the Jats, Jhakkars and Uteras: Jai and Utera being represented as brothers of Nun, and Jhakkar as son of Jai. The Jhakkars, who live immediately north of the Nun in the Shujabad Tehsil retain, like them, the old title of Rana. Sir Edward Maclagan saw a Manuscript genealogy in which Utera, Kanjun and Kuliar, the names of three well-known tribes in this district are represented as the brothers of Nun and the sons of Rajwaddan mentioned above.

THE DRIGS

The Drigs, who are found along the banks of the Chenab, attribute their origin to 'Kech Makran' and like other tribes, who came from the direction of Sindh, they are known by the appellation of '*Jam*'. They are thought to be Rajputs from Sindh who were driven out from that country in the end of the 15th century by the oppression of the ruler of Thatta.

THE LANGAHS

The Langahs hold villages in various parts of the Shujabad Tehsil but are in strength chiefly towards the south. The figures given for this tribe, in the various censuses differ a good deal, possibly owing to their being confused with the Langs, a smaller tribe of the same neighbourhood. The Langahs, furnished a dynasty of rulers who were supreme in Multan for about eighty years, from 1445 to 1526 A.D. The Langahs of that dynasty are said by Ferishta to have come from Sibi, and he is quoted as ascribing to them an Afghan origin. The people themselves, so far as they know about their original habitat, locate it at Delhi, and some persons express doubt on the identity of the present Langahs and those of the old reigning dynasty: but as Ferishta gives Rappri (a small village on the Chenab in the south of the Shujabad Tehsil) as the original home in this district of the Langahs whom he mentions, and as the Langahs now resident in the district own large areas of land, it seems only reasonable to suppose that the Langahs, now extant and those of Ferishta are one and the same race. In former times the Langahs owned several villages which are now in other hands. It is not unlikely that the Langahs were Rajputs from Sindh and some say that they were Panwars, and that they are allied to the Bhuttas, Kharrals, Harrals and Laks. It is also stated by Mirasis that Langah, Bhutta, Dahar, Shajra and Naich (all now represented by tribes in this district) were five sons of one Mahli, and this may reflect some original connection between those various clans. Some of them claim Arabic descent according to the fashion prevalent in this part of the Panjab (where Rajput descent is thought of little account), and say that Shujaat Khan, who founded the village of Shujaatpur, came from Arabia seven hundred years ago. The chief

Langah clans are Sanpal, Raizada, Jora, Jabuje and Jahankhania. There are also some families of Langahs at Rath Mammar in the Mailsi Bar. These men are Fakirs and do medicine work, and are said to have no connection with the other Langahs.

THE JOYAS

The Joy as hold most of the land along the Sutlej in the Mailsi Tehsil. Cunningham would identify them with the Yaudhias, who are thought to have been in the same tract of country before the Christian era. The Joyas themselves state that they came from Sindh. They are said to have been converted by Rukn-i-Alam, in the 14th century, but their own account places their conversion into Islam earlier. They say that nine hundred years ago Rai Jalal-ud-din and Rai Kamal-ud-din, two brothers, and Fatteh Khan were sent by the Delhi Emperor against Khar, a Bhatti chief, then ruling in Kahror, and that after defeating Khar they held his land in farm from the Delhi sovereign. There is reason to believe that this Khar or Kahr lived not earlier than the 14th century, and the first immigration of the Joyas probably dates from then. Jalal-ud-din remained at Kahror, while Fatteh Khan settled at Fattehpur. In the time of Akbar, the Joyas were the predominant tribe of the Mailsi and Lodhran Tehsils. Then, or soon after, probably, the four brothers—Jagan, Mangan Luddan and Lal— colonised the country round Luddan; and, as time went on fresh bands came over the Sutlej. In the later days of the Empire, the Joyas were a turbulent element in the population, but were kept somewhat in order by the Daudputras. They contain a vast number of sub-clans of which at present the Daulatanas, the Saldaras and the Lakhweras are the most prominent. Rose has a good account of the tribe in his *Glossary*, Volume II, page 410.

THE KHICHIS

The Khichis are a branch of the Chauhans, and are said to be descended from one Khichi Khan, who was ruler in Ajmer, and afterwards obtained possession of Delhi, from which he was driven out by the Muhammadens. His descendants, Sisan and Vadan, migrated to Multan during the time of the Moghal sovereigns. Sisan founded Faddah and Vadan Shergarh. They fought with the Joyas, then paramount in this direction and the names of Rai Luna Khichi of Sakhi Dalel and of Ali Khan are still remembered among them. There is a tale too, to the effect that the Bilochis of Khai having in Moghal times become rebellious, the Khichis were sent against them under two brothers. Hussain Khan and Haji Fatteh. The Khichis fought also against the Sikhs under Jhanda Singh and Ganda Singh and were discomfited. The tribe still holds several villages around Mailsi.

THE LANGRIALS

The Langrials, who inhabit the whole of the eastern Bar country, are a comparatively new tribe in the district. The tribe is found in Rawalpindi and Sialkot districts also, where they claim a Solar Rajput descent. It is sometimes stated that the Multan Langrials claim descent from a Brahman of Bikaner, but an inspection of their Kursi Nama shows, that it is only their Mirasi who claims this descent. The Langrials themselves, like many other converted tribes, say they are from Arabia and are Koreishis; and that they held power for some time in Tatta in Sindh under one Ghiyas-ud-din, who from the extent of his public kitchen (langar), obtained the clan the name of Langrial. Ghiyas-ud-din is said to have been a contemporary of Shahab-ud-din Ghori, and to have gone with him to Delhi, after which the tribe is found wandering via Kashmir to Shahpur, and then driven from Shahpur to Gariala in Jhang. From this they went to the Kamalia *ilaqua* in Montogomery, from which they removed in the time of Shuja Khan to their present habitat in the country, formerly held by the Hans tribe round Kamand. Their two chiefs were Waga and Rahman. Machhia, the descendant of Waga lived at Kamand and Bakir, the descendant of Rahman, at Sharaf. Both held Jagirs in return for services in 1857 from the British Indian Government, against the Kathias and the mutinous Multan regiments. The Langrials were by nature nomads, and by habit cattle-lifters; but they were by degrees settling down to more stable and reputable means of living. Some of them became very wealthy men since the lower Bari Doab Canal came to their lands and others were much benefited by the Sutlej Valley Project.

DERA GHAZIKHAN

The Jats are a congeries of Muhammaden tribes without any common origin; indeed the word Jat (or Jaghdal in Bilochi) may be said to be applied in this district to all Mussalman agricutural tribes other than the Biloch. The following figures, which show some of the principal Jat tribes returned at the Census of 1881, who now would be known elsewhere as distinct castes, are in this part of the Panjab classed as Jats.

SUB-DIVISIONS OF JATS IN 1881

Name	Number	Name	Number	Name	Number
Awan	1,015	Khag	888	Kurtanah	2,219
Ahir	419	Gathwal	815	Mochi	3,721
Bhatti	12,971	Khokhar	4,690	Majhar	1,076
Bhutta	3,162	Langa	2,305	Machhi	1,610
Tahim	2,220	Sumra	887	Mohana	1,318
Chhina	408	Arain	13,406	Panwar	1,919
Sial	2,536	Babbar	2,389	Jotia	1,421

TRIBES RETURNED AS JATS

1	2 Number	3
Tribe	Returned as Jats both in 1881 and 1891	Returned as Jats in 1881 but not in 1891
Awam	—	1,766
Ahir	—	37
Bhutta	1,661	—
Tahim	1,026	—
Chhina	400	—
Khokhar	—	979
Langa	2,057	—
Sumra	1,056	—
Arain	—	4,793
Mochi	—	4,767
Machhi	—	7,374

Some of these tribes in the Census of 1891 declined to allow themselves to be classified and Jats and the above table shows which of the above did so and which continued to describe themselves as Jats; those not mentioned in this table but mentioned in the first were returned and "Jats—Miscellaneous" in the Census of 1891.

Some of the Jat tribes are descendants of the original Hindu inhabitants of the district, who were converted to Islam at the time of the Muhammaden conquest. Among these may be the tribes which make use of Hindu or Sindhi titles, for example, the Sontras, who use the title Rai and the Burras and prefix the word Jam to their names. Others are immigrants from the south and from the neighbouring districts of Multan and Muzaffargarh and from the erstwhile Bahawalpur State. Some tribes are located within the country of a Biloch tribe, and have adopted their manners, customs, and dress. Examples of such are the Hanbis, of whom one branch is settled in the Gurchani and another in the Tibbi Lund country, and the Kachelas who live in the Leghari country. The Manjothas in the Sanghar Tehsil claim to have come with the Bilochis from Mekran. Biloch men marry Jat women but do not give their women in marriage to the Jats. Some of the Jat tribes are of fine physique, notably the Jamras, but the general level of their intelligence is low. They are less extravagant than their Biloch neighbours, but cannot be said to be thrifty. They are on the whole good cultivators. The name applied to these tribes in which the 't' is hard, must not be confused with the Jat, in which the 't' is soft, and which is applied to the men who tend camels.

It is to the presence of the Bilochis, in the proportion of 33 per cent of its total population, that the district owes its distinguishing characteristics. Bilochis, elsewhere scattered in occasional colonies, here form, not indeed numerically, but both politically and socially, a preponderating element in the population; so that upon them centres the whole interest both of the past history, and of the present administration of the district. They are a fine martial race, free from bigotry, and therefore disposed to view the English with more favour than can be looked for in Pathans; their history on the other hand, and social customs, offer a wide field for research.

JALANDHAR

The Jats are by far the most important section of the population in every way. They form more than one-fifth of the inhabitants of the district and own in whole or in major part half the villages. In extensive agriculture they are unsurpassed and equalled by few. In fact, here, as in other places, a man of this tribe does not call himself a Jat, but a Zamindar, or agriculturist, if he does not give the name of his clan.

The Hindu and Sikh Jat villages are found all over the district, but are comparatively very few on the Bein in Nawanshahr, and hardly in due proportion on the same stream in the Nakodar uplands. Along the Sutlej, they are scantily represented, except in the south-west of Nakodar, where the Sardars of the Kang clan of this tribe were formerly in great strength. The Muhammaden Jats were found chiefly in the alluvial plain of the Sutlej, where a large group of about 28 Mussalman Jat villages are found chiefly to the east of Rahon; again in the south-west of the Nakodar Bet, where they are hemmed in on one side by the Hindu Jat block, and on the other by Muhammaden Rajputs; and lastly, in the north of the Jalandhar Tehsil, mostly along the Kingra Choor in its neighbourhood. It thus appears that the Mussalman Jats, like Gujjars and Dogars, go after water. They undoubtedly own villages, where at present there are no traces of water, but the rule holds good generally.

The Muhammaden Jats were usually considered inferior to their Hindu and Sikh namesakes as cultivators. They ranked with Gujjars in this respect. They have not yet so completely emerged from the pastoral state as the others, as is shown by the situation of their villages; and the damp, enervating climate must tend to deteriorate the physical and, in consequence, moral vigour of the inhabitants of the river lowlands. Mr. Barkley observes "They are called Mona (Shaved) Jats in contradistinction to Sikh Jats." He also says, "Many of the Jat clans lay claim to a Rajput origin, while others have no tradition of any period when they were other than Jats. A few only of the older clans have no traditions of their first settlement in this Doab. Some came from the neighbourhood of the Ganges or Delhi, others from the Rechan or Bari Doab, and a few say that they came from Garh Ghazni, which they believe to be the city and fort of that name in Afghanistan, though the name may really be a reminiscence of the Garjni or Gajnipur, the site of which has been pointed out by Major-General Cunningham near Rawalpindi." They are sub-divided into an enormous number of clans or Gots, but very often the name of an Al, or sub-division of a Got, is taken for the name of a clan. Large tracts of country, each occupied by villages of one Got, are not found here as they are in other parts of the country. The nearest approach to such a state of things is met with in the Phillaur Tehsil, where there are a cluster of Sihota villages about Dhuleter. Barapind itself a very large estate belonging almost entirely to this clan.

The following account of the Jat clans of the district, is chiefly taken from notes left by Mr. Barkley:

Anjila

Anjila Jats hold Muthadda Kalan and Khurd near Masani, and Anjla near Bilga in Tehsil Phillaur, Nahimazara in Tehsil Nawanshahr and Kambara in Tehsil Jalandhar.

Aulakh

Aulakh Jats hold Aulakh and half Dhogar in Tehsil Nakodar.

Badaicha

Badaicha Jats hold Mundhali in Tehsil Nawanshahr, Rampur in Tehsil Phillaur, and part of Sindhanwala in the Bet of Tehsil Nakodar, in which the Jagir are of Shahkot, and Dhandowal are also of this clan.

Bagri

Bagri Jats hold Chak Kalan and Chak Waindala in Tehsil Nokodar, and part of Khusrapur near Kartarpur (where they come from Chak Waindala) in Tehsil Jalandhar.

Bains

Bains or Bains Jats hold Bains, Mazara Khurd and shares in Mazara Kalan Shahatpur, Punumazara, Chak Bilsa, Mitpur Lakha, Malah and Mahmudpur in the Nawanshahr Tehsil, and Kandhanlah, Muhaddipur and Sarowal near the N.F. border of the Jalandhar Tehsil. Muhammaden Bains Jats held portions of Sundarpur and Khojpur in the same Tehsil. The Alawalpur Sardars are Bains Jats whose ancestor left Mahilpur in the Hoshiarpur district, 10 or 12 generations ago, and settled at Jalla (near Sirhind) in the erstwhile Nabha State.

Bajwa, Bal

Bajwa Jats hold Bajwa Kalan, and Khurd in the Bet of Tehsil Nakodar. Bal Jats hold Bal Kohna and Nawa in Tehsil Nakodar, and Akalpur in that of Phillaur.

Basra

Basra Jats are found at Bangala and Umarpur in Tehsil Phillaur, and Mahili in Tehsil Nawanshahr, Bern near Jalandhar city, and Ramsinghpurs Ghassanwali and Nurpur near Kartarpur. The Chaudharis of Phagwara were of this race. In the last century one of them named Tilok Chand, married Bibi Raj Kaur, the granddaughter of Ala Singh, the founder of the erstwhile Patiala State. She succeeded on her husband's death to his property and his authority, and in 1874 A.D. went to Patiala to put an end to the distracted state into which that country had fallen under her cousin Maharaja Sahib Singh, and seems in practice to have directed the administration almost up to the date of her death 7 years afterwards. Her brother-in-law, Chuhar Mal, who is said to have been a leper eventually succeeded her at Phagwara, but, in 1803 A.D. his widow was deprived of it by Ranjit Singh, who gave it in exchange to Fatah Singh Ahluwalia. The Basra proprietors have since been ejected from Phagwara by the erstwhile Kapurthala State authorities and have settled in the village of Mehli about 3 miles, to the east of Phagwara, in Nawanshahr district.

Bassi

Bassi Jats hold Bundala, a village, paying Rs. 8,800 land revenue, and Shavampur, Bassian and Bir Bassian and part of Mithra in Phillaur; Sibewal Fazilpur Mubarakpur (resident in Kular) and Bassian in Nakodar and half Daulatpur and one Patti of Sarmastpur in Jalandhar Tehsil.

Bhullar

Bhullar Jats are found at Bhullar in the Phillaur Tehsil, Bhullar in the Nakodar Tehsil, and Maullar in that of Jalandhar.

Biring

Biring or Birin Jats hold Jandhali, Firozpur, Raipur, Lalumazara and Nyamazata in Tehsil Nawanshahr. Beling Jats, who hold part of Chak Biring. More of their villages in this area are Bhanoki, Chachoki, Bining, Mehtan, in Phagwara Tehsil.

Birk (Virk)

Birk Jats hold Birk and Jajjumazara in the Phillaur Tehsil, Birowal in that of Nawanshahr, and share in Reru in that of Jalandhar. Those of Birk settled here from Chubarkhana in Gujranwala, in which district this clan of Jats called Virk, were very numerous, 600 or 650 (?) years ago, and were afterwards divided into 4 Pattis, the proprietors of one of which emigrated and settled at Birowal near Jadala.

Bopara

Bopara Jats hold Boparai, and share in Jetowal and Bir Jetowal in Tehsil Phillaur, and hold half Pryagpur in Tehsil Jalandhar.

Chahil

Chahil Jats hold Sangwal, and part of Nizamuddinpur in Jalandhar Tehsil, Darapur in Phillaur Tehsil, Chahil near Makandpur, half Talwandi near Bahram, and part of Chahil near Musapur in Nawanshahr Tehsil.

Chhokar

Chhokar Jats hold Chhokaran Turan, two-thirds Pasla, and parts of Jetowal Bir, Jetowal and Moshampur in Phillaur Tehsil, Munder in Nawanshahr and part of Bhogpur in Jalandhar Tehsil.

Chima

Chima Jats hold Chima Kalan and part of Chima Khurd near Nurmahal, and Chima Kalan and Khurd near Nasrali, all in the Phillaur Tehsil. Chatha Jats, a clan associated with them in the Gujranwala district, hold two-thirds of Dhandowal in Nakodar Tehsil.

Didhri

Didhri Jats hold Muhaddipur, Daulatpur, and Bhikhiwal of Fattehgarh in the Bet of the Nawanshahr Tehsil.

Deo

Deo Jats hold part of Basulpur in Tehsil Nawanshahr part of Tut Sher Singh in Tehsil Nakodar, and Lorohi in Tehsil Jalandhar.

Dhadda

Dhadda Jats hold Dhadda near Laroha in Tehsil Jalandhar, and at Dhadda Daulatpur, Dhadda Haripur and Dhadda Lahna in Tehsil Nakodar.

Dhesi

Dhesi Jats hold the large villages of Kana Dhesian, and Sang Dhesian in the Phillaur Tehsil, and that of Rajput near Jamsher in Jalandhar. The villages in the Phillaur Tehsil are named after the founders, Kana and Sang, who came from the neighbourhood of Delhi about 250 years ago.

Dhaliwal

Dhaliwal Jats hold Kangniwala and Rupowal and shares in Nurmahal, Bakapur, Mansurpur, Sultanpur, and Naicha in the Phillaur Tehsil, shares in Dhaliwal, Bilechan, and Kankrah Kila in Nakodar two pattis of Kalabakra in Jalandhar, Nangal and shares in Punumazara and Malpur in Nawanshahr. They are one of the predominant castes in the Ferozepore district and the adjoining Patiala and Nabha territory.

Dhillon

Dhillon Jats hold Dingrean Sutowali and parts of Hasan Mundah Manko, and Kishangarh in Jalandhar Tehsil, Bara and parts of Jafirpur and Jalapur Kalan in Nakodar Tehsil, and Mandi and part of Moshampur in the Phillaur Tehsil.

Dhindsa

Dhindsa Jats hold Moron and Dhaindsa in Phillaur Tehsil, Rahpa near Mukandpur and part of Mahmudpur near Awar in Nawanshahr Tehsil, and part of Biaspind in Jalandhar Tehsil.

Dosanj

Dosanj Jats hold Dosanj Kalan, Khokjewal, three fourths of Pawadara in the Phillaur Tehsil, and Dosanj and a share in Khatkar Kalan in that of Nawanshahr. At Pawadara they say, they came from the Bangar towards the Ganges, but do not know the exact locality.

Dule

Dule or Dileo Jats hold Partapura, Khusrupur and one-fourth Mashmpur in Tehsil Phillaur.

Garcha

Garcha Jats hold Garcha, half Sal Kalan and part of Malka in the Nawanshahr Tehsil, and part of Jhajah in that of Phillaur.

Garhiwal

Garhiwal Jats hold parts of Jafirpur and Kankrah Kila in the Nakodar Tehsil, and Kot in that of Phillaur.

Goraya

The Goraya Jats of Goraya, Surja and Daliwal in the Phillaur Tehsil are regarded as a sub-division or family 'AP of the Dhillon Jats.

Gosal

Gosal Jats hold Ratinda, Sukar and Gosal all in the Nawanshahr Tehsil.

Gil

Gil Jats holds two out of six Pattis in Jamsher Tehsil, Jalandhar, Gil and part of Adbagil, part of Kishangarh in the same Tehsil, part of Khanpur in Nakodar Tehsil, Landra in Phillaur Tehsil and part of Mahl Khurd near Awar in Nawanshahr Tehsil. Muhammaden Gils held Kadian near Taiwan in Phillaur. That they had long been settled in this district, appears from the statement of the Sindhus of Barka Kalan that they were brought there by Gil Jats. They were also one of the principal Jat tribes in the Ferozepore district.

Her

Her Jats are found at Her and Kotla Heran in the Nakodar Tehsil, at Padi Jagir and Kala in the Phillaur Tehsil, and they share in Malpur near Awar in the Nawanshahr Tehsil. Two-thirds of Alimpur in Jalandhar Tehsil, were held by Muhammaden Her Jats. At Her in the Nakodar Tehsil a very old Jat village, they have no tradition of their first settlement, they have held the village for 1,000 years, which must be under lease, meaning simply a period of indefinite duration.

Athwal

Athwal Jats hold Pharala, and shares in Rasulpur and Musapur in the Nawanshahr Tehsil, and hold Chitti and share in Khopur in that of Jalandhar. They got their name from Uthwal or Utwal, the camel owner.

Jandher

Jandher Jats hold part of Sarmastpur in Jalandhar Tehsil. At Talwandi Jandher and Ukhara in the same Tehsil, they were Muhammadens.

Janhal

Janhal Jats hold Jandiala, a village paying Rs. 11,000 land revenue, and Janhal, and share in Shuar Kalan Adhikali in the Phillaur Tehsil, Mabalke (near Jandiala) in the Nakodar Tehsil, Salempur Masandan where they are styled Masand, as they are the agents of the Guru of Anandpur for the receipt of the offering made by his disciples, and part of Gopalpur or Bidhipur in the Jalandhar Tehsil.

Jhara

Jhara Jats hold Jhaja Kalan and part of Jhaja Khurd in Tehsil Phillaur and part of Gahlmazari in Tehsil Nawanshahr.

Jhengar

Jhengar Jats hold Mukandpur, Jagatpur, Baghaurali Jhangar and three fourths Laroka in the Nawanshahr Tehsil; Dialpur in that of Phillaur and Jaffal and Kishanpur in that of Jalandhar. The Jagirdar of Mukandpur was of this family, and was usually called Chaudhri, his family having held that position here before the Sikh conquest, when he took advantage of his position to make himself master of the surrounding country.

Kang

Kang Jats are found at Kang Shibu, and Kang in the north of the Nakodar Tehsil, Kang Chela and Kang Jassa, Kallar Kalan and Khurd, Kotak Mirajawala and Domana in the South-West of the same Tehsil, Kang Jagir in Phillaur, Kang near Rahon Kharkhuwal, and half the village of Kultham in Nawanshahr, and in Jalandhar Tehsil Kalakhera, Kotli Baghbaran and Sarmastpur are shared between them and other proprietors. Most of the Sikh Sardars of the Nakodar Tehsil, either belong to this Got, or were connected with it by marriage when they established their authority there. Tara Singh Ghaiba, who was their leader at the time of the conquest, was himself of this race and a native of Kang on the Sutlej, where it is said 18 Sardars at one time resided; but on the village being swept away by the river, they dispersed, and established themselves in their separate Jagirs on both sides of the river Sutlej. Kang Jassa was founded in the lands which remained belonging to the old town. They have a tradition that they originally came from Garh Ghazni to the Panjab. They are found in all the districts of the Jalandhar Division.

Kaler

Kaler Jats hold Kaleran, Nurpur, and two-thirds of Sirhal Kazian in the Nawanshahr Tehsil, part of Mithra in that of Phillaur, part of Khanpur in that of Nokadar and Nusi in that of Jalandhar.

Kalera

Kalera Jats hold Khankhanan and Lakhpur in Tehsil Nawanshahr.

Kalon

Kalon or Kalu Jats hold Chakrala, Musttapur, Kalwan and part of Aima, all near Kartarpur in the Jalandhar Tehsil.

Kallu

Kallu Jats (Muhammaden) were found with others at Pachhranga in the Jalandhar Tehsil, and Hindus at Mutafallu in Phillaur Tehsil. The name is perhaps a modification of the last.

Kandhaula

Kandhaula Jats hold Hapowal and parts of Kama, Musepur and Punumazari in Tehsil, Nawanshahr and Kandhaula Khurd near Bilga, and parts of Kandhaula and Phabuwan in Tehsil Phillaur.

Khangura

Khangura Jats hold Nanumazara, Ladha Ganja and parts of Samrari and Mahl in Tehsil Phillaur.

Khatkar

Khatkar Jats hold Mangowal, Khatkar Khurd and parts of Khanpur in that of Phillaur.

Khaira

Khaira Jats hold three-fourths of Adampur, and Khaira near Kartarpur in Tehsil Jalandhar, Khaira, on the Sutlej, and part of Mulawal Khaira in Tehsil Nakodar and Khaira in Tehsil Phillaur.

Khela

Khela Jats hold Mawai, Khela and Ranwen and part of Naichah in Tehsil Phillaur.

Khosa

Khosa Jats hold Khosa, Sojanwala and Kotla Suraj Mall in Tehsil Nakodar, and part of Gopalpur or Bidhipur in Tehsil Jalandhar (For this clan, see *Ferozepore Gazetteer).*

Kular

Kular Jats hold Kular, Fattahpur and Naurangpur, in the Nakodar Tehsil, and Sansarpur near Jalandhar Cantt.

Kunar

Kunar Jats hold Burki, three fourths Dhanipind, and part of Dhandowal in the Phillaur Tehsil.

Lalli

Lalli Jats hold Lallian Kalan and Lallian Khurd or Khoda Lallian, and a share in Nizamuddinpur, and hold the lands of Rampur Lallian as hereditary cultivators, and Nangal Shama all in the

Jalandhar Tehsil, in that of Phillaur they hold Lallian near Barapind, and there are also a few amongst the proprietors of Takkhar.

Lidhar

Lidhar Jats hold Lidhran and part of Ghugh in the Jalandhar Tehsil, Lidhar Kalan in that of Nawanshahr, and Lidhar Khurd and Thalia in that of Phillaur. The Jagirdars of Thalia are of this clan, Maha Singh of Lidhai; almost six miles off, where family still holds property, having established himself at Thalia, when the Sikhs conquered this Doab.

Mahal

Mahal Jats hold Mahal Gahlan, three-fifths Kama, part of Mahal Khurd near Awar in the Nawanshahr Tehsil, part of Mahal in the Phillaur Tehsil and Rajab in the Jalandhar Tehsil.

Malhi

Malhi Jats hold Malhian Kalan and Khurd and half Bilechan in Nakodar Tehsil, part of Atta in that of Phillaur, and part of Malhian in that of Jalandhar.

Man

Man Jats hold Banga and Chak Mahi Das, and shares in Mazara Kalan in Tehsil Nawanshahr, hold Katana in Phillaur, Udhowal, Bir Udhowal, and one third Baloki in the Bet of Tehsil Nakodar, and one sixth of Jamsher in Jalandhar. The proprietors of Banga settled there from Mansa in the Bhatinda country, now belonging to Patiala. The founder, Chuhar Mall, was a Sultani or Mona Jat, *i.e.* a follower of Sultan Sakhi Sarwur. He is said to have been a contemporary of Guru Gobind Singh, and to have acquired Banga and the neighbouring country by purchase. He held 60 or 70 villages, for which he paid revenue to Delhi. Sardar Dharam Singh of Amritsar took the country of Banga from him, and from the Kotgarhia Sardar.

Chak Mahi Das in Nawanshahr and Tutemazara in the Hoshiarpur Kandhi, were founded by Mahi Das and Deoraj, two brothers of the Man Got, originally from Dhada in Hoshiarpur, who got the land from Adina Beg[62]. There are said to have been originally 12 Man Jat villages near Boloka the people of whom left the neighbourhood. Some of them settled at Kishanpura across the Sutlej, and the existing village was settled by Man Jats from that place and Arains from Alowal near Nakodar.

Mander

Mander Jats hold Shujawalpur, Ramochak and Chak Mander, and part of Gahlamazari in Nawanshahr Tehsil.

Mathon

Mathon Jats hold Raswali and Sitalpur in Jalandhar Tehsil, part of Bega in Nakodar Tehsil, and part of Badapur in that of Phillaur.

Mulana

Mulana Jats (Mohammadens) held Burj Sherpur, Jodhuwal, Mithewal, and Mallikwal in the Bet of Nawanshahr Tehsil.

Nahal

Nahal Jats hold Nahalan, and Duhke in the Jalandhar Tehsil, Adhi in that of Nakodar and part of Nahal near Nurmahal in that of Phillaur.

Nagra

Nagra Jats hold Kohala in Jalandhar Tehsil, Hobowal in Nawanshahr Tehsil and Nagra, near Bilga in Phillaur Tehsil.

Nijjar

Nijjar Jats hold one Patti of Jamsher, Nijjran, Goindpur Korali, Pindori Nijjaran, Kathar, Massanian and Diyanatpur, all in Jalandhar Tehsil, the last four villages adjoining the Hoshiarpur border, and Domeli and Khajurla in Kapurthala district.

Nipal

Nipal Jats hold Lalluwal, Maliwala and Mundi Kasu in the south-west of the Nakodar Tehsil.

Pahal

Pahal Jats hold Gumtala, Gumtali, and Sagarpur, all near Bilga in Tehsil Phillaur.

Punian

Punian Jats hold Bharomazara, Bhukhri, Punian, Jindwal, Nagre and part of Musapur, all in the Nawanshahr district.

Rai

Rai Jats hold Raiwal and Nurpur in the west of Tehsil Nakodar, and Lail in Tehsil Phillaur.

Ranu

Ranu Jats hold Serhala, Bahromazara and two-thirds of Jassumazara in the north-west of Nawanshahr Tehsil.

Randhawa

Randhawa Jats hold Randhawa, Saidowal, Haripur and part of Singha Jagir in the Phillaur Tehsil, Randhawa and part of Ispur in Jalandhar Tehsil, and while Nurpur in the same Tehsil, Mohammaden Randhawas, with other Mohammaden Jats were held as tenants of the Kartarpur Guru.

Rera

Rera Jats hold Reru and three-fourths of Lasuri (from which Reru was settled) in the Bet of the Nakodar Tehsil. They came to Lasuri from Kandhaila near Delhi, and claim descent from Tunwar Rajputs.

Sara

Sara Jats hold Sara Jandu Sarai where half the property belonged to Mohammaden Jats of this race and half to Hindus, and part of Hasan Munds, near Kartarpur, also Kot Khurd, near the Jalandhar Cantonment, in the Jalandhar Tehsil; Motipur, Chak Chela and a share in Jalalpur Kalan in that of Nakodar, and part of Surapur in that of Nawanshahr.

Samra

Samra Jats hold the large village of Samrai, Machhina, one of the three Pattis of the adjoining village of Pindori, in the Phillaur Tehsil.

Sangera

Sangera Jats hold the large village of Bilga and Pharwala in the Phillaur Tehsil, and Shankar, Sirin Sadikpur and Talwandi Sangera in that of Nakodar.

Sahota

Sahota Jats hold Barapind Kulaita (one out of twelve Pattis being held by Arains) Rurka Khurd, Dhulaita, Phalpota, Chak Sahibu, Chak Indhian and one fifth of Atta and some land in Kutbiwal, all in the same neighbourhood in the Phillaur Tehsil. This is the largest group of villages of the same Jat clan to be found in the district. When the imperial authority was overthrown in this Doab, Gulab Singh of Barapind appropriated the revenues, and built a fort, and his family held possession as Jagirdars until A.D. 1806

(S. 1862 when Ahluwalia Sardar confiscated the Jagir. See further, *Hoshiarpur Gazetteer*).

Sidhu

Sidhu Jats hold Manikpur and Sindhuan in Nakodar, share in Bilocha and in Salanagar, and hold one of the Pattis of Malsian in the same Tehsil. They hold Sidhu Mutsaddi, Sidhu Hari Singh and Jaga Singh in Phillaur Tehsil, all near Nurmahal, part of Garhi Mahan Singh in the same Tehsil, half the village of Talwandi, and part of that of Punumazara in Nawanshahr Kandowal, Tajpur, Bhagwanpur and a share in Khojkipur in Jalandhar, and Mohammaden Sidhus shared in Daranwan, Khojpur and Bhogpur in the same Tehsil, and held Kamalpur in Nakodar Tehsil. Those of Manikpur say that the first settlers, an uncle and a nephew, came 500 years ago from Phul Maharaj, the original seat of the clan whence have sprung the reigning houses of Patiala, Jind and Nabha, and that the sons of the former founded Manikpur, and Sidhuan in this district, while the latter founded two villages near Dinanagar. The Sidhu Jats claim descent from the Bhatti Rajputs of Jaisalmer.

Sandhu

Sandhu Jats are found at Rurka Kalan, Atti in Phillaur, Sindhuan and Bikha in Nawanshahr, Alichak in Jalandhar, and had share in Khatkar Kalan, Sudian and Mahmudpur in Nawanshahr, Moshampur in Phillaur, and Talwandi Salem and Jalalpur Kalan in Nakodar. In Thong also, the family of Dal Singh, a Jagirdar who crossed the Sutlej, and burnt the Ludhiana Cantonment in 1845, in the absence of the British troops in the field against the Sikhs, and who was in consequence deprived of his Jagir are in possession of the lands acquired by him.

At the large village of Rurka Kalan they say that they migrated from the south to the Manjha, 300 to 400 years ago, when the Pathans had dispossessed the Manj Rajputs of the country, they settled here from Thattian in Amritsar district. The village formerly belonged to Manj Rajputs, and Gil Jats, and the latter brought in the Sandhus to take the place of the Rajputs.

Sotar

Sotar Jats hold Sotar, one-third of Pali Unchhi, and part of Chahil, Nawanshahr Tehsil and part of Mansurpur in Phillaur Tehsil.

Sunar

Sunar Jats hold Sunar Khurd, and parts of Sunar Kalan, and Sundar Tatar in Phillaur Tehsil.

Sangha

Sangha or Sanga Jats hold Jandu Singha in Tehsil Jalandhar, parts of Singha Jagir, and Singha Khurd in Phillaur Tehsil, where there are also a few families in Dosanj Kalan, and part of Shahabpur near Jadala in Nawanshahr Tehsil Kala Sangha, Rajpur Bhaian, and Langeri in Hoshiarpur district, and Daroli Bhai in Moga.

Sode

Sode Jats hold Pakhrodi near Jadala, and parts of Sodian, Malka and Nurpur Lakha, all near Awar Chakdana, in Nawanshahr Tehsil.

Sohal

Sohal Jats hold Athanlah and Sohalpur, half of Adhagil, and part of Desalpur in the Jalandhar Tehsil, Sohal in that of Nakodar, part of Atta in that of Phillaur, and part of Chak Bilga in that of Nawanshahr.

Thandi

Thandi Jats hold Daulatpur Thandian, two-third Padhana, and part of Mahal Khurd in the Nawanshahr Tehsil, and Palran in that of Phillaur.

Upal

Upal Jats hold Kat, half of Bukhara, and part of Mahmudpur in Nawanshahr Tehsil, both Upals near Nurmahal and Upal near Bilga, and part of Phabuwan in Phillaur Tehsil, and part of Biaspind in Jalandhar Tehsil.

Utal

Utal Jats hold Khurdpur, and Fattahpur near Adampur in Jalandhar Tehsil, and Utal near Jadala in Nawanshahr Tehsil.

They say that their ancestor acquired the village of Birk (Virk) by service.

Varaich

The Bharaich (known in Gujranwala as Varaich) hold Billi Bharaich in the Nakodar Tehsil. At Sarai in Phagwara, they hold one out of 4 Pattis, and say that their ancestor came from Gujranwala district, and received a Jagir for service rendered to the Kapurthala State. He afterwards acquired proprietary rights, which his descendants now hold.

The only exclusively Mussalman tribe of Jats, which is noticeable is the Kauja or Kohja, who held the five villages of Kauja, Dhurial, Nangal Fida, Alamgirpur and Kotal Kauja in the north of Jalandhar Tehsil, where the Kingra Cho enters the district, sharing the last of these with Arains. They say their ancestor was a saint, who accompanied Sultan Mahmud of Ghazni in one of his invasions, and settled down here as he liked the country. His name was Ali Muhammad, or Manju, and he was nicknamed Kochcha or 'Little Mountain', on account of his size. The change from Kochcha to Kunja or Kohja is simple[63]. That they are true Jats is shown by their intermarrying with Jats only. Marriages between members of the same Got occur, but they will not marry near relatives such as cousins, though the Mohammanden religion favours such marriages. The five villages are all said to have been settled from Khera, now a deserted site in the neighbourhood.

Six other clans (Sim, Sidhu, Arak, Sin, Dhanoe and Khunkhun) claim to be of Arab descent, and so originally Muhammadens. The other Mohammaden Jats were converted at various times since the reign of Akbar. The Mohammaden Jats of Nawanshahr say their ancestor was one Mahr Matha, who ruled at Psyi, in the Kasur Tehsil. His descendants became Mohammadens during the reigns of Akbar and Alamgir, about which time, too, they came into this part of the country, in search of pasturage for their cattle, as their old home had become too narrow for them. According to their account, they came *via* Sultanpur, Jalandhar, and Phagwara, and crossed the Bias at the Naushahra ferry, a rather circuitous route. The Nakodar men say, they came from the Ferozepore district, some in Sikh times, some previously. They can give no account of their early history.

HOSHIARPUR

The following is the distribution of the more important landholding tribes:

UNA TEHSIL

Jandbari taluka is principally occupied by Brahmins and Kanets. In Takhtgarh and Nurpur talukas Gujjars and Rajputs are found along the hills, and on the riverbank, while the greater part of the rich level tract between the hills, and the river is inhabited by miscellaneous tribes of Jats, Sainis, and Bahtis. In Babhaur taluka, again, Rajputs are found as superior proprietors; but the majority of the agriculturists are of miscellaneous castes, including Brahmins. From this northward, Rajputs and Brahmins predominate as the proprietors; Jats, Sainis, Bahtis and Gujars as tenants.

DASUYA TEHSIL

The hills are mostly occupied by Bihal Rajputs, Chahngs, and Gujjars, and the plains bordering on the Kangra district by Jarial Rajputs and Sainis. The high level plain round Mukerian is almost entirely inhabited by Awans, who owned a Barah or cluster of (nominally) 12 villages in this Pargana and the alluvial lands from Naushahra ferry southwards by Mussalman Jats, Gujjars and Pathans. A number of Dogar villages are found in the plain between the Sivaliks and Dasuya. Around Dasuya were Arains, Mussalman Jats to the north and west near the Chhamb, and Hindu Jats to the east. In the Tanda police sub-division there are several clusters of strong village communities of Sainis, Jats and Naru Rajputs, and a few villages of Pathans.

HOSHIARPUR TEHSIL

The Kandi villages are occupied by Gujjars, Dadwals Rajputs, and a few Brahmins. Next to these come several small Pathan villages in the plain in a line stretching from near Haryana to the border of the Garhshankar Tehsil, and at a distance of about five or six miles from the hills. The remainder of the plains were occupied by Hindu Jats, and Mussalman Naru Rajputs, the latter especially inhabiting some founded estates to the south. Saini and Arain villages are also found here and there.

GARHSHANKAR TEHSIL

The Kandi villages are inhabited by the same tribes as those of Hoshiarpur, *viz.* by Hindu Rajputs, Brahmins, Gujjars, Hindu and some Mussalman. The northern villages of the plain are almost entirely occupied by Hindu or Sikh Jats, with the exception of Barah of Rajput villages on the border of Kapurthala territory. The country immediately north of Garhshankar forms a Barah of Hindu Rajputs of the Banot clan; and Garhshankar itself, and the villages southward as far as Balachaur, were owned by Ghorewaha

Rajputs, who were Mussalmans near Garhshankar, and Hindus near Balachaur, the head village of the Ghorewaha Bawani, or group of 52 villages. The alluvial lands on the Sutlej were occupied by Mussalman Jats.

The Jats come first numerically. They are found almost entirely in the plains, though there is a strong village, Pubowal, in Bit Manaswal. Only in the alluvial villages of the Beas and the Sutlej, and in some Chhamb villages near Dasuya, did they profess the Muhammadan religion. The vast majority are either Hindus or Sikhs. The principal clans of good position and influence are the Bains Jats of Mahilpur, the Sahotas[64] of Garhdiwala, Barian, and the Khungas of Budhipind. The heads of the two formers are styled Chaudhri, and all three are called Dhaighar Akabari, *i.e.* the 2½ Akbari families, Mahilpur I, Garhdiwala 1; and Budhipind ½. The story is that, when Akbar took in marriage the daughter of Mahr Mitha, a Jat of the Manjha, 35 principal families of Jats, and 36 of Rajputs countenanced the marriage, and sent representatives to Delhi. Three of these Jat families reside in this district; the remainder belong to Amritsar, and other districts. They follow some of the higher castes in not allowing widow remarriage, and in having Darbaria, that is giving fees at their marriages to the Mirasis of other Akbari families. It is also the custom for Purohits to place on them at their marriages the Janeo or sacred thread, removing it a few days afterwards. Below the Akbari Jats are the Jahangir, just as the Akbaris gave daughters (according to our version) to Akbar. Thus some of the Man Jats of Tuto Mazara are Darbaris (Courtiers). Darbari Jats will only marry their daughters to Darbaris, but they will take brides for their sons from non-Darbaris, provided the dowry (dahej) is ample.

The principal Jat clans in point of numbers are the Bains who have a Bar ah of 12 villages near Mahilpur, the Gil of the Kuk Muhin, who have a Bahiya of originally 22 villages round Khararawal Bassi, Achharwal, Rajpur (a hamlet in Hukumatpur) and Lakhsian, Man Jats near Dhada, Sanghe Jats near Mugowal, and Langeri, and Pote Jats near Barian. There are many other clans, but their numbers are insignificant, and they do not own clusters of villages situated close together as in the case of those above mentioned.

Jats rank among the best agriculturists. The Sainis and Arains may be better for small plots of land and garden cultivation but taken all round as farmers and growers of cereals, sugarcane, and other crops on extensive areas, few are so industrious, and careful as the Jats, and they have the great advantage of getting the help of their women in the fields. Ploughing and reaping are carried out by the men, but the women help in weeding, in watching the crops, and in taking the food daily to the men in the fields. In some villages Jat women even do some trading on a small scale. They sell grain to other women of the village from their husbands' granaries, and so add to the family earnings.

KANGRA

So far as our records enable us to judge, the rulers of almost all the States of the eastern and central groups were Rajputs. The information at our disposal also leads to the conclusion that in few, if any, instances was the founder of the dynasty a native of the country over which he established his rule. In most cases we have a history of invasion and conquest, and in almost every State the new ruler either came directly from the plains, or was a cadet of one or other of the ruling families, which had already settled in the hills. In one or two instances, the ruling family was of Brahman origin, and was afterwards recognized as Rajput[65].

The history of these hill states is one of almost continuous warfare. When a strong ruler rose to power the larger states made tributary their smaller neighbours, but these again asserted their independence as soon as a favourable opportunity came. These wars as a rule did not lead to any great political changes, for on the whole, the hill chiefs were considerate of each other's rights. Being all of the same race and faith, and also nearly related to one another by marriage, and even closer family ties, they were content to make each other tributary or to replace a deposed chief by one of his own kinsmen. In only three instances in many hundred years, so far as known, was one state subverted by another.

That the hill states were able to maintain their political status for such a long period was also in great measure due to their isolated position, and the inaccessible character of the country. It is improbable, however, that they were entirely independent for any great length of time. In the absence of epigraphical and literary evidence we may assume that the Western Himalaya formed part, nominally at least, of the great "empires of the Mauryas, Kushanas and Guptas, which followed one another in succession in Northern India." Kashmir too, as we know, held a loose suzerainty over the hill states, between the Sutlej and the Indus, off and on for some centuries.

The Mohammaden invasions which began about A.D. 1,000 seem to have had little influence on the political condition of the hills. The early Mohmmaden rulers were too much engrossed in extending or defending their conquests on the plains to think of the hills, which were for the most part left undisturbed.

LUDHIANA

To the east of the district, and especially in the Samrala Tehsil, the multitude of Gots amongst the Hindu Jats is a very remarkable feature. Not only do adjoining villages belong to different Gots, but inside each village will generally be found two or three Pattis of distinct origin. This is accounted for by the manner in which the country was colonized. In the history of each village, it will be seen that the founders came in comparatively recent times from different parts of the country, and belonged to different Gots; and that they united merely for their own convenience, the common tie of belonging to the same tribe was sufficient. To the south and west, on the other hand, the Jats in some instances came in bodies, and villages belonging to the same Got lie either in groups or within short distances of each other. Thus the Sidhu and Gil Jats appear to have come eastward in large parties, and to have settled down in adjoining or alternate villages in the western part of Jagraon. But the rules throughout the district in variety of Gots, and the few groups of villages that there are, each belonging to one Got, are the exception. The reason for this apparently is that in the eastern parts, in the neighbourhood of Sirhind and Ludhiana, the imperial authority was always strong enough to protect its subjects, who settled down in small villages as they came; while in the west it was less felt, and people of one tribe had to collect in large villages for protection. In Samrala no attempt was made at settlement to return the land as distributed amongst the various subdivisions: but in the other Tehsils, it was possible to do this roughly, as there were a few Gots owning villages and groups of villages. And the details of area held by the leading Gots in these two Tehsils, as ascertained by the Settlement Officer, are shown below, in percentages of the total area of each Tehsil:

DISTRIBUTION OF AREA IN DIFFERENT GOTS

(in percentage)

Tehsil	Total Jats	Garewal	Gil	Sidhu	Dhaliwal	Dhillon	Sekhon	Bhandhaer
Ludhiana	58	8	3	5	3	1	1	3
Jagraon	68	1	5	9	6	2	—	—

Garewal Jats

First in rank are the Garewal Jats. This Got hold about fifty large villages near Ludhiana in a group, and members of it are also to be found scattered over the district; they number 17,471. They trace their descent to a Rajput, Raja Rikh, who came from the south, and settled in Kahlur in the Shivalik hills. Bairsi, son of Rikh, left Kahlur and settled at Naiebad Theh (mound) to the south of Ludhiana, and contracted a marriage with a Jatni, called Rupkaur, and had to start a Got. His son was Gare, whence the name of the Got; but another fanciful origin is Karewal from Karewa. The descendants of Bairsi gradually spread over the country to the southwest of Ludhiana. They are somewhat inferior as cultivators. They are also very extravagant and quarrelsome; but they take to service better than any other Got as they hold it honourable, and in all of their villages will be found men, who are either serving in army or in receipt of pensions. A great deal of money thus finds its way into their hands. When they trust to cultivation alone, they are not so successful. A widow can marry her Deuar (husband's younger brother) or Jeth (husband's elder brother) only. This is also the rule among the Gils and Sidhus. Among the endogamous subdivision of the Naibs, widow remarriage is not allowed. Among the remaining sections of the Jats, a widow is expected to marry her Deuar or Jeth, but varying degrees of laxity obtain in the observance of the custom.

The Gils

The Gils (10,289) own about forty villages, mostly in Jagraon Tehsil. They are next in rank to the Garewals, and their women are secluded. They are also fond of military service. They here claim descent from Surajbansi Rajputs, their ancestor being a king of Gharmela in the south, whose son, Akaura, took to agriculture. The son of Akaura, Gil, founded the Got which moved northwards by degrees. They came to this district from Kusla in the Jangal *ilaqua* about. The Gils are first rate agriculturists; but their habits are generally extravagant.

The Sidhus

The Sidhus (12,415) have a good many villages in Jagraon Tehsil, where there are two or three 'Sidhwans' (villages of Sidhus). They are a well-known Got throughout the Lahore, and Amritsar divisions, and much has been written of them. Those of the Ludhiana district are of the Barar subdivision; and came from the south-west from Faridkot, it is said, in the time of the Rais within the last 300 to 400 years.

The Dhariwals

The Dhariwals (12,361) have a good many villages lying about Pakhowal, and are found mostly in the Jagraon Tehsil. Their ancestor was, as usual, Rajput, who came from Jaisalmer, and settled in Kangar in Nabha territory, becoming a Jat. From Kangar his descendants came into this district, under the Rais and their Sikh successors. The Dhariwals are accounted one of the superiors Got of Jats, but do not differ much in their customs from the others.

The Bhandhers

The Bhandhers are the descendants of Bhandher, who was the offspring of the union of a Rajput and a woman of inferior caste. He settled in Bhatinda first, and thence his descendants migrated to Rao Siani in the Malaudh Ilaqa, where the tribe now holds ten or twelve villages.

The Sekhons

The Sekhons had a similar origin as the Bhandhers, and it is said that they came to this district from some place in Patiala territory, Bhadaur. Their villages are scattered all over the district.

The Dhillons

The Dhillons (6,394) say that they came from the Manjha in the reign of the Emperor Muhammad Shah.

MINOR GOTS OF THE JATS

Man	4,868
Sandhu	5,338
Mangat	3,547
Chima	3,583

It would take up too much space to detail the tradition and the origin of each of these jats. They are to be found scattered over the district, holding single villages or subdivisions of villages.

PATIALA

Nearly every caste in the Panjab is represented in Patiala, but the Jats, who comprise 30 per cent of the population (485,170), are by far the strongest element. The Jats of the Malwa, in which the main part of the erstwhile Patiala State is included, have been called the finest peasantry in India. A description of the Malwa Jat, and the points in which he differs from the Jat of the Manjha, will be found in the *Gazetteer of the Ludhiana*.

The Jats of Patiala mostly claim Rajput origin, and appear to have migrated from Jaisalmer into the Malwa, or the territory south of the Sutlej, which stretches towards Delhi and Bikaner, about the middle of the 16th century, though the Asli or original Gots Man, Bhullar and Her, which are of the Shiv Gotra, were probably settled in the Malwa before the other Jats.

Siddhu Jats

The Siddhus (42,405) are the most numerous and important subdivision of the Jats in Patiala. Besides the ruling families of the Phulkian states and Faridkot, many families of note belong to the Siddhu clan. The Siddhus are the strongest in the Anahadgarh Nizamat. They form an exogamous section, and avoid one Got only in marriage. The Jagirdars of Bhadaur are described elsewhere. Other important families in this State are the Jagirdars of Talwandi, Kotli Sabo, and Jiundan. The Siddhus are nearly all Sikhs.

Harike

Harike is one of the Siddhu septs, and is called after Chaudhri Hari, its ancestor. Chaudhri Hari and his descendants founded 14 or 15 villages on both sides of the Sutlej, whence the name 'Harike pattan', and Buddha Singh one of his descendants, settled at Sekha in Barnala Pargana. Sardar Bhag Singh, of this sept, was Bakhshi of the state, and Sardar Basawa Singh became its Bakhshi, and Adalati, and was afterwards a member of the first Council of Regency. His grandson, Sardar Bahadur Pritam Singh, was then the Bakhshi.

Mehta

Mehta is also a Munhi or sept of the Siddhu Got or clan. It is named after its ancestor Mehta, who founded the village of Mehta near Barnala. Sardars Bahali Singh, Buti Singh, Dal Singh, and Ranjit Singh of this sept all held the post of the Commander-in-Chief in the State.

Chahil Jats

The Chahil Jats claim that Chahil, their eponym, was born of a hill fairy. They are numerous in Bhikhi, in which Tehsil they own many villages, and they also hold scattered villages in Tehsils Narwana, Amargarh, Bhawanigarh, and Fatehgarh. Sardar Partap Singh Chahil, maternal uncle's son of the late Maharaja Narindar Singh, was Bakhshi to the State. He was in command of the Patiala Contingent at Delhi in 1857, and his son Ranjit Singh was then the leading representative of the tribe. To support their claim they pay special worship to Guga Pir, who was a Chauhan Rajput. They worship Baland Jogi Pir, their Jathera.

Dhaliwal Jats

The Dhaliwal Jats claim to be Chandra Bansi Rajputs by origin, through Dhaliwal, Bhatti, who migrated from Jaisalmer, and settled at Kangar in Nabha territory in the 12th or 13th century. In the time of Akbar, the chief of the Dhaliwals, Mihr Matha[66], is said to have given a daughter in marriage to that emperor, whence the Dhaliwals and the 35 Jat tribes, which concurred in the bestowal of a Jat girl on the emperor acquired the title or status of Darbari. The Darbari Jats in this State are the Tiwanas of Chinarthal, the Jhalle Gils of Dhamot, and Siawara, the Manders of Jarg, the Mangats of Rampur and Katani, the Jhij of Gidri, and Bawani, the Panders of Gahloti, and the Gandhas of Rauni. The Darbari Jats pay special fees to their Mirasis at wedding.

The tribe is chiefly represented by the family of the late Sardar Ganda Singh, C.S.I., Bakhshi of the State, and his son Sardar Hazura Singh was an officer in the state forces. A man of note among the Dinakes was Mian Mahtab Singh of Faridkot, whose daughter was married to Maharaja Mahindar Singh, and became the mother of Maharaja Rajinder Singh.

Man Jats

The Man Jats say, they migrated from the north, and claim descent from Mandhata, a Rajput, by a Karewa marriage. Mandhata settled in Ladowa in Ferozepore, and thence in Akbar's reign the Mans migrated. Their chief sub-septs in this state were Maur Sandar, Khawala and Paraga, and Mansa. They avoid only the one Got in marriages, and form no alliances with the Bhulars or Sher Gils. At weddings they give a rupee to all the Mirasis, Brahmans and Bhats of the Man villages, and their ceremony is called Tapa or

Tappa. The Mansahia Jats regard themselves as superior to another Mans. Tradition says they owe their name to the fact that the head of the family paid the revenue due to the emperor punctually. Sardar Harnam Singh Deorhiwala was the leading man among the Mansahia. Maharaja Rajindar Singh was married into this family.

Dhillon Jats

The Dhillon Jats claim descent from Raja Karn, whose descendant Thai married a Jat wife. The Dhillon are said to have migrated from Delhi under the Mughals, and are now mainly found in Govindgarh Tehsil, and in scattered villages in Bhikhi, and Fatehgarh Tehsils. Their chief sub-septs in this state were the Mahna, Bangria, Gat, Jandi, Saraya, Garah and Mutal. They only avoid the father's Got in marriage, and make no alliances with the Dhindsa and Wal (Wal is a sub-sept of the Sekhons) on account of some old dispute.

Gil Jats

The Gils trace their origin to their eponym, Gil, who fled from Rajputana, and settled in Bhatinda, where he married a Dhaliwal girl. Thence, in the time of Shah Jahan, the Gils migrated to Sahibgarh, and Sunam Tehsils, in which they are now numerous. They are found also in Tehsils Rajpura and Bhikhi. They have eleven sub-septs, Sher, Kak, Landra, Sihai, Bhadon, Hgagar, Barala, Karora, Kand, Jaji, and Jhala, the last of which is strongly represented in Sahibgarh Tehsil, where it holds eleven villages.

Marral Jats

The Marrals returned as Jats in the Censuses of 1891 and 1901, were mainly Mohammadens, but a few are Hindus. The Mohammaden Marrals of Samana laid claim to an Iranian origin, and say they were descendants of Uazdi-i-Jard, the last Sassanian King of Persia, who was conquered by the Arab Sa'd-waqas. They migrated from Kabul in the time of Prithvi Raj, Rajput King of Delhi, under Malik Salah-ud-din. On the recommendation of the Nawab of Samana, the Malik received a grant of villages in that part together with the title of Mande or lord of 100 villages (Mandal from Khanda Rao, brother of Prithvi Raj). In the time of Ala-ud-din Khilji, Qutb-ud-din Marral obtained the fiefs of Samana and Malkana, and the latter which is a Basti of Samana, is still held in Jagir by the Mandals of Karnal. Malik Suleman Yar Jang, a descendant of

Nawab Arastujah, Wazir-i-Azam of Haiderabad, Deccan, also held a Jagir in Samana itself. Malik Barkat Ali Khan of Samana was the Assistant Advocate at Patiala.

Dhindsa Jats

The Dhindsas claim descent from Raja Karn. They migrated from Sirsa in the time of the Mughal emperors, and settled in Chaumda-Manvi in Amargarh Tehsil, round which place they owned a number of villages. They are also found in scattered villages in Rajpura, Ghanaur Tehsils and Patiala and Ubhewal in Sunam Tehsil, is a village of Muhammadan Dhindsas.

Randhawa Jats

The Randhawas hold only two villages in Sahibgarh, and Mimsa village in Amargarh Tehsil, but they offer one or two points of interest. Their ancestors settled at Mimsa, near which, on their migrating thither from Tamkot, the axle of one of their carts broke, and its owners took this as an omen that, they should settle at the spot. The others went on, and failing to persuade their comrades to accompany them, they uttered a curse upon them, that they should be compelled to seek a new home every 12 years. Every 12th year on the 8th Sudi of Asarh they take a cart to the spot, and worship it, and an uncle cuts a lock of hair from his nephew's head. On their return home, it is said, the axle of the cart invariably breaks on the road.

Tiwana Jats

The Tiwana Jats claim descent from Lakkhu, seventh in descent from Tiwana, a Punwar Rajput. They migrated from Dhara Nagri in the 13th century, and now hold several villages in Sahibgarh, and two in Rajpura Tehsils. Like Rajputs, their women observe Parda and they discountenance Karewa. Their leading family is that of the Chaudharis of Chinarthal, and Sardar Sawai Singh of this family held important posts in the State under Maharaja Narindar Singh. Two Tiwana Chaudharis, Majlis Rai and Wazir Khan, were prominent chiefs of this tribe in the Mughal times. There was also Muhammadan Tiwana village in Ghanaur Tehsil.

Sarah Jats

The Sarahs or Sarais are mainly found in Nizamats Anhadgarh and Karmgarh.

Kaleke

The Kalek Sardars belong to the Sarae Got. They trace their descent from the Bhatti Rajputs of Jaisalmer, and are named after their ancestor Chaudhri Kala, who founded the village of Kalyanwali in Sirsa; his grandson Maluka founded Kaleka near Dnaula, where his descendants still hold land. Sardars Gurbakhsh Singh and Haria Singh brother-in-law of Gurbakhsh Singh, were fifth in descent from Chaudhri Kala. Sardar Gurbakhsh Singh was Maharaja Ala Singh's Diwan, and accompanied him in all his expeditions. He is best remembered for his services, when Maharaja Ranjit Singh came to Patiala to visit Maharaja Sahib Singh. Mai Fatto, wife of Maharaja Ala Singh belonged to this family, and Maharaj Karm Singh also married into it.

Pawania Jats

The Pawanias are of Shiv Gotra, like the Man, Bhular, and Her, with the two latter of whom they do not intermarry. They migrated from Hissar, and own four villages in Tehsil Sunam.

Ghuman

The Ghuman Jats also claim Rajput descent. Migrating during the time of Jahangir from Rajputana, they settled at Sajuma in the Jind State, and now hold eleven villages near Bhawanigarh, Ghumana in Rajpura, and a village in Patiala Tehsil.

The Nains

The Nains[67] claim to be, by origin, Tur Rajputs. Their ancestor Mainpal married a widow, and his son Nain is their eponym. They hold many villages in the Bangar (Tehsil Narwana), such as Dhamtan Sahib, etc., and stray villages in the Sunam and Patiala Tehsils. They are said to have migrated from Delhi, where they ruled prior to the rise of the Chauhan dynasty. Their sub-septs are Jaja, Bamir and Narain. Sardar Ude Singh Nain, was Superintendent of the Palace in the time of Mai Askaur, Diwan and Judicial Minister, Guardian to Maharaja Narinder Singh, and member of the first Council of Regency. His son, the Mashir-Ala Sardar Bahadur Sardar Gurmukh Singh, was (1904) President of the Council.

Mangat Jats

The Mangats are only found in Tehsil Sahibgarh, where they hold six villages.

Gandhes Jats

The Gandhes are descendant from Gandhu, son of Raja Gopal, Taoni Rajput, by a Jat wife, and are found in Tehsils Banur, Rajpura and Amargarh.

Sidhu Jats

The Sidhus appear to have immigrated into the State from the Manjha in the 16th century, and are found in scattered villages in Tehsils Ghanaur, Rajpura, Amargarh, Bhatinda and Barnala.

Bhular Jats

The Bhulars are said to have been driven from Mari in Ferozepore by the Sidhus, and then to have dispersed. They own nearly the whole of seven villages in Barnala, and four in Sunam Tehsils. Their sub-septs are four in number, *viz.*, Kosa, Munga, Dahr, and Bhatia.

Garewal Jats

The Garewal[68] or Girewals are well-known sept which once held rule over Raipur, and Gujaranwal in Ludhiana. Maharaja Narinder Singh married into this family, and one of its members Sardar Ghamand Singh, became Bakhshi. Sardar Mihman Singh, father-in-law, and his son Hira Singh was the brother-in-law of the Maharaja. Sardar Kishan Singh, also of this family, was Muatamad to the Panjab Government. They claim descent from Raja Mahan Chand of Chanderi in Indore, a Chander Rajput.

Sekhon Jats

The Sekhon Jats claim descent from the Punwar Rajputs. They are named after their ancestor Sekhon, who had seven sons, after whom were named seven Munhis or septs. Mai Askaur, mother of Maharaja Karm Singh, whose life sheds a lustre over Patiala history, belonged to this family, and her brother Sardar Diwan Singh was Commander-in-chief. Two daughters of the family were married in the Phulkian States, one to Raja Hira Singh of Nabha, and the other to His Highness, the Hon'ble Sir Kanwar Ranbir Singh K.C.S.I., of Patiala. Maharaja Amar Singh made Daria Singh, his Diwan. Himmat Singh and Sawai Singh were Bakhshis, Mai Singh was Adalati or Judicial Minister, and Sardar Sedha Singh was Diwan. They hold Bakhshiwala (in Sunam Tehsil), Kaulgarh (in Pail), Kishangarh and Kanhgarh (in Bhikhi), and Karmgarh (in Anahadgarh Tehsil).

Atwal Jats

Among the Atwals the family of Chaudhari Charat Ram, member of the second Council of Regency, was the most important. His grandson Sardar Sapuran Singh was Financial Minister of the State.

Mander Jats

Sardar Bhagwan Singh, Mander, was a Judge of the Patiala Chief Court. His father Sardar Basta Singh held the post of Nazim for a long time.

Mahil Jats

The Mahils trace their descent from the Tur Rajputs. They came from Delhi. The clan holds Shahpur Khurd, Shahpur Kalan, and Namol in Sunam Tehsil, and Khanpur in Dhuri. Sardar Fetah Singh of this tribe held high posts in the State, and was a member of the first Council of Regency. His son Sardar Man Singh was Nazim of Amargarh Nizamat.

Kharas

The Kharas Jats claim Chhatria descent and, say their office was at the Delhi Court, but his son Khara became a robber, and married a woman of another tribe. The Kharas believe in a Sidh whose shrine is at Khandur, where they offer Panjari, etc. They do not use milk or curd until it is offered at the shrine. On the 5th of the second half of Baisakh, special offerings are made there. The Sidh was a Khara who fell asleep while grazing his cattle. One day his head was cut off, but he pursued the cattle for some yards to the spot where the shrine stands, and though the Kharas have left Khandur the Sidh is still worshipped.

Kharoras

Uppal, the ancestor of the Kharoras, lived in Baragaon Mohammaden village, which he ruled. When he went to pay at the treasury, he got himself recorded as its owner, and the people murdered him. His wife gave birth to a son at her father's house, on a hard piece of ground (Kharara) a Kharauda or Kharora, hence the name.

Koks

The Koks derive their name from their first home. The Kokas in Mandawar Tehsil of Alwar, and are found in Bawal.

Laurs

The Laurs trace their origin to Lalhora. They are found in Bawal.

Mans

The Man's claim to be descendants of Raja Bine Pal of Jaisalmer. The Varaha or Varya claim the same descendant sank to Jat status by adopting Karewa. Panni Pal had four Sandar, Maur, and Khamala; Paraga's descendants founded Burj Agwar, Manan in the Dhanaula *ilaqua*, and Burj Mansay; Maur's descendants founded Mauran.

Nehras

The Nehras are found in Bawal. They claim to be Chhatrias, who left Gadgajni when it was the scene of conflict, picking bags of sugar. Bandeo asked the merchant what it was. They said 'salt', so when he opened them, he found only salt, but seeing Bandeo it became sugar again.

Phulsawals

The Phulsawals derive their descent from Bechal, whose four sons were sent in turn to defend the gate, hence the name Phulsawal. They ordinarily worship Bhairon, and perform the first tonsure of their children in the Dahmi *ilaqua* of Alwar.

Rahals

The Rahals also claim Rajput descent. Their ancestor was born on the way while their mother was taking her husband's food to the field. They marriage, but remove it afterwards, and reverence a Hallotali in Amloh Nizamat.

Swanches

The Swanch clan claims descent from Hari Singh, who lost status by marrying a wife of another tribe.

Sohals

The Sohals derive their name from Sohal Singh, their ancestor.

Rathis

Originally Rajputs, the Rathis in some way lost status of Jats. They revere Bandeo.

Bairwals

The Bairwals claim to be descendants of Birkhman, a Chauhan Rajput, whose son married a Jat girl as his second wife, and so lost status. The name is eponymous, and they are found in Bawal Nizamat.

Chhelars

The Chhelars, whose principal settlement is Chhelar in Narnaul Tehsil, sank to Jat status by contracting marriages with Jat women. They revere Bhagwan Das, a Hindu saint of Tikla, a village in this State, and shave their children at his shrine. They avoid tobacco.

Dhatans

The Dhatans, found in Bawal, drive their origin from Raja Dhal, a Tunwar ruler of the Lunar dynasty of Hastinapur, who lost caste by marrying a foreign wife.

Dolats

Rai Khanda, the ancestor of the Dolats, is said to have held a Jagir near Delhi. His brothers Raghbir and Jagdhir were killed in Nadir Shah's invasion, but he escaped, and fled to Sinna Gujariwala, a village now in ruins, close to Sunam, then the capital of a petty state. He sank to Jat status by marrying his brother's widows. The origin of the name Dolat is thus accounted for. Their ancestor's children did not live, so his wife made a vow at Naina Devi to visit the shrine twice for the tonsure ceremony of her son, if she had one. Her son was accordingly called Dolat (from lat hair). Dolat Jats are found in Dialgarh, Raigarh and Santokhpura in Nabha, in Longowal of Patiala, and in Dolatanwala of Ferozepor. Those of Nabha and Patiala intermarry.

Gorias

The Gorias derive their name from Goran Singh, a Rajput, who settled at Alowal in Patiala, and thus became a Jat.

Katarias

The Katarias are found in Bawal, and derive their name from Katar, a dagger.

KARNAL

There is a very extraordinary division of almost the whole countryside south of the Rajput territory, into the two factions (Khap) of Dehia and Haulania, respecting the origin of which no very satisfactory information is forthcoming. The Dehias are called after a Jat clan of that name, with its headquarters about Bhatganw in Sunpat, having originally came from Bawana near Delhi. The Haulania faction is headed by the Ghatwal Jats, whose headquarters are Dher-ka-Ahulana in Gohana, and who were, owing to their successful opposition to the Rajputs, were the accepted heads of the

Jats in these parts. Some of the Emperors called them in to assist him in coercing the Mandhar Rajputs, and thus the old enmity was strengthened. The Dehia Jats, growing powerful, became jealous of the supremacy of the Ghatwals, and joined the Mandhars against them. Thus the countryside was divided into two factions; the Gujjars and Tagas of south Karnal, the Jaglan Jats of Thapa Naultha, and the Latmar Jats of Rohtak joining the Dehias; the Huda Jats of Rohtak, and most of the Jats of southern half of the district except the Jaglans, joining the Haulanias. In the mutiny, disturbances took place in the Rohtak district, between these two factions, and the Mandhars of the Nardak ravaged the Haulanias in the south of the tract. And in framing, his Zails, the Settlement Officer had to alter his proposed division, so as to separate a Dehia village, which he had included with Haulanias, and which objected in consequence. The Dehia is also called the Jat, and occasionally the Mandhar faction. The Jats and Rajputs seem, independently of these divisions to consider each other, tribally speaking as natural enemies; and one is often assured by Jats, that they would not dare to go into a Rajput village at night.

The Jats are pre-eminently the agricultural caste of the tract, and, with the exception of the Rors, and of the Rains, Malis, and Kambohs, who are practically market gardeners, are best cultivators we have. A Jat when asked his caste, will so often answer "Zamindar" as 'Jat'. They are a fine stalwart race. Mr. Ibbetson measured one at Didwari 6 feet 7 inches high, and 42½ inches round the chest. He complained that a pair of shoes cost him Re. 1 and 8 annas. They are notorious for their independence, acknowledging to a less degree than any other caste the authority of their headmen. They hold several tribal groups of villages; but they also own parts of villages almost all over the tract save in the Gujjar, and Rajput portions. They seem to have held parts of the country about Samana in very early days, and, as already noted, that part certainly formed a part of an early Indo-Scythian kingdom. The Jats of the district seem to have come partly from the Bagar, where they were in force 800 years ago. In no case have Jats settled from across the Jamuna. The Jats are not mentioned as a prominent caste of the tract in Akbar's time, and probably gained a footing during the breaking up of the Mughal dynasty, when they became an important element in the politics of the time. Elliott and Cunningham divide the Delhi Jats into Dese and Pachade; but no trace of this division at present exists save that there is a powerful clan called Deswal in Rohtak, and that the Jats hold a Des of 84 villages in the Doab. The Jats of the tract are almost without exception Hindus. Those who had become Mussalmans were called Mule Jats, and were only found in two or three villages, and there even were only individual families, generally said to be descended from hostages taken in infancy by the Mussalman rulers, and circumcised by them. The principal clans are as follows:

Jaglan

Jaglan, sprung from Jagla, a Jat of Jaipur, to whom there is a shrine in Israna to which the whole Thapa worships. They hold the 12 villages (Barah) of Thapa Naultha, and come from Ludas, in Sirsa or Hissar.

Ghanghas

Ghanghas, sprung from an ancestor called Badkal, whom they still worship, and who has a shrine in Puthar. They hold the Thapa of Mandi, and come from Dhanana near Bhiwani, in the Bagar.

Gatwal or Malak

Gatwal or Malak, dating their origin form Garh Ghazni, and holding Bawana, whither they came from Ahulana in Gohana. They hold Ugra Kheri and the villages settled around it, and are scantily represented in this district. In the old days of Rajput ascendancy the Rajputs would not allow Jats to cover their heads with a turban, nor to wear any red clothes, nor to put a crown (nor) on the heads of their bridegrooms, nor a jewel (Nath) in their women's noses. They also used to levy signorial rights from virgin brides. Even to this day Rajputs will not allow inferior castes to wear red clothes or ample loin clothes in their villages. The Gatwals obtained some successes over the Rajputs especially over the Mandgars of the Doab, near Deoban and Manglaur, and over those of the Bagar near Kalanaur and Dadri, and removed the obnoxious prohibitions. They then acquired the title of Malak (master), and a red turban as their distinguishing mark; and to this day a Jat with a red Pagri is most probably a Ghatwal.

Deswal

Deswal, who hold Korar, Madlauda, Ataola, Mahaoti, and other villages, and came from Rohtak, where they have their headquarters in the village of Mandauthi.

Katkhar

Katkhar or Gahlaur, perhaps the most powerful Jat clan in the tract, holding the 12 villages (Bara) of Jaurasi. They came from Mot Pali in Hissar.

Sandhu

Sandhu worship Kala or Mehar or Kala Pir, their ancestor, whose chief shrine is at Thana Satra in Sialkot, the headquarters of the Sandhus. They hold Gagsina, Khotpura, and other villages; and have come here via Phul Maharaj in Patiala.

Halawat

Halawat, who hold Pabil and other villages, and came from Dighal in Rohtak. They worship a common ancestor called Sadu Deb.

Locally less important, but still holding considerable areas, are the Huda, Matyan, Mandhar, and Gotia clans from Rohtak; the Goit, Nohra, Kahral, Sumra (or Gurelia), and Dhandu clans from Jind; the Panu, Kajal, Bhakar, Gauria, Marian, Chahil, Kohar Lochab and Punia clans from the Bangar of Hissar, and Bikaner; the Phandan Bangar clans from Kaitha.

HISSAR

By far the most important group of agricultural tribes in the district, socially and economically, and even politically, are the Jats. They comprise 25 per cent of the population of the district, and may be divided roughly into these four broad classes:

- The Deswali Jat of Haryana or the Des country, a tract, which extends roughly over the eastern half of the four southern Tehsils of the district.
- The Bagri Jats who are immigrants from the Bagger country of Bikaner.
- The Sikh Jats of Sirsa who, as already stated, had come from the Malwa country in the north, and from Patiala.

The Mussalman Jats from the west who formed a small part of thc Pachhadas of the Ghaggar Valley.

This classification is not tribal or religious. The Deswali and Bagri Jats are practically all Hindus, and social intercourse, and, as a general rule, intermarriage, takes intermingle, but the Deswali, and Bagri in the tract where they markedly form the Bagri of Sirsa, and the western border of the district.

The Bagri Jat, though a thrifty, and industrious agriculturist is of slighter physique, and duller intellect than the Deswali who looks down upon him. This difference is not one, but many, due probably to the harder conditions of life which prevail in the Bagger. The Deswali Jat, on the other hand, is a lusty specimen of humanity, a thrifty and excellent agriculturist, and far superior in everything, except, perhaps, social rank, to the other agricultural tribes of the district.

There is another division of the Deswali and Bagri Jats, commonly recognised throughout the district, *viz.* Shibgotra and Kasabgotra Jats. The Shibgotras are so named after the fact that their ancestor is traditionally said to have sprung from the matted hair of Shiva. The Kasabgotra, on the other hand, claim that their forefathers were originally Rajputs, who took to agriculture, and the remarriage of widows, and so sank in the social scale. The Shibgotras, on the other hand, assert that they are Asal Jats, and do not claim Rajput origin. There are said to be 12 Gots of Shibgotra Jats. The tradition as to their origin is that one Barh, a Shibgotra, made himself master of a large portion of Bikaner; he subsequently founded a town named Jhausal, and from his 12 sons sprang the 12 Gots of the Shibgotras, of whom only three or four are to be found in this district. They do not intermarry with each other, but only with the Kasabgotra Jats. This difference of traditional origin may not improbably point to a real difference in descent, and the Shibgotras may have been originally non-Aryan aborigines whose chief deity was Siva, and with whom the less militant tribes of the Aryan invaders intermarried, adopting at the same time to some extent their social customs, and worship, thereby sinking to their social level and becoming Jats. This would also account for the prevalence of the worship of Siva among the Jats.

The principal tribes of the Deswali, and Bagri Jats to be found in the district are the following as returned in the census of 1911:

Bhainiwal	5,006
Chahil	14,247
Ghatwal	1,726
Jakhar	3,135
Man	1,302
Naln	2,344
Puniya	8,263
Sangwain	1,263
Dallal	2,492
Shoran	4,890

Bhainiwal

The Bhainiwal Jats are a Bagri tribe, but they claim to be Deswalis. They appear originally to have been Chauhan Rajputs of Sambhar in Rajputana, whence they spread into Bikaner, and Sirsa, and thence in small numbers into Tehsils Fatehbad and Hissar.

Chahil

The Chahils are one of the largest tribes in the Panjab, but comparatively few of them are to be found in this district. They are said to be descended from Raja Aggarsen Surajbansi. According to another story, their ancestor was a Punwar Rajput called Raja Rikh, who came from the Deccan. His son Birsi married a Jat woman, settled at Matti in the Malwa about the time of Akbar, and founded the tribe.

Ghatwal

The Ghatwals are a tribe of the Deswali Jats, also known as Malaks. They claim to be Siroha Rajputs, and to have come from Garh Ghazni in Afghanistan. The Ghatwals state that they settled in Mohra in the Rohtak district, where they were under the heel of the Rajputs to such a degree that their women had to wear nose rings of straw. The Jats attacked, and overcame the Kalanaur Rajputs in a dispute arising out of a marriage procession, but peace was restored, and both parties settled down. Subsequently, the Rajputs invited the Ghatwals to an entertainment, and treacherously blew them up with gunpowder; one Ghatwal woman who was not present there was the sole survivor. She happened to be in the fields at the time, and was found there by a Brahman of Depal now in Hansi Tehsil, which also was the place where the woman's family lived. The Brahman conducted her in safety to her father's home at Depal. While refusing all reward he stipulated that the child with whom the woman was pregnant should be his Jajman. The woman gave birth to two sons, who founded the villages of Sultanpur and Umra, now in the Hansi Tehsil, and the Brahmans of Depal are to this day the Purohits, or family priests, of the Ghatwal Jats of those villages.

Jakhar

The Jakhars are Deswalis, and are said to be sprung from a Rajput tribe variously stated as Chauhan, and Udha. An ancestor Jaku appears to have been settled in Rai Bagri in Bikaner, and thence moved to Jhajjar in Rohtak. It is related to him that a Raja of Dwarka had a large heavy bow, and arrow made, and promised that whoever should lift it up should be raised in rank above a Raja. Jaku attempted, but failed, and for shame left his native country, and settled in Bikaner. This story, puerile though it appears, is very possibly a mythical version of the true facts, viz. that the Jakhars became Jats by degradation from the military caste of Rajputs. They take their name from their probably mythical ancestor, Jaku. They own the large village of Kheri Gangan in Hansi.

Another story is that they have descended from a Chauhan Rajput twenty generations back. He is said to have come from Bikaner, and his four sons are said to have founded the Gakhar, Sangwan, Piru, and Kadian Jats.

Man

The Man, Dallal, and Deswali Jats are said to be descended from Man, Dille and Desal, the three sons of one Dhanna Rao of Silanthe in Rohtak by a Bargujar Rajput woman. They are evidently closely connected as they do not intermarry. The Mans are found both among the Sikh Jats of Sirsa, and the Deswali Jats of Hansi and Hissar.

The Man Sikh Jats of Sirsa give the traditional account of their origin that their ancestor Man, a Punwar Rajput, came from Garh Ghazni, and settled in Patiala during the time of a Raja Bhanipal. His descendants from the Man tribe, are connected with the Sandhu Jats, who are descendants of Sandhu, one of the twelve sons of the Man.

Nain

The Nain Jats claim to be of Tunwar Rajput origin. If so, they came probably from the south-east direction of Delhi.

Puniya

The Puniyas belong to the Shibgotra section of the Jats, being descended, as they state, from Puniya, the eldest of the sons of Barh. They claim no Rajput origin.

Sangwan

The Sangwan and Sheoran Jats are apparently closely connected, and have an identical tradition as to their origin. They say that their ancestors Sanga, and Shora were Chauhan Rajputs of Sirsa. These Chauhans immigrated, the Singwan into Dadri where, they held 40 villages, and the Sheoran into Loharu, with 75 villages. They settled down, and married Jat women, and so became Jats.

Another account connects the Sangwans with the Jakhars.

Dallal

The Dallals claim descent from a Rathor Rajput, who settled in Rohtak, and married a Bargujar woman some forty generations back. By her, he had four sons, from whom the Dallal, Deswal, Man and Sewag Jats have sprung, and these four tribes do not intermarry: but compare the account of the origin of the Man's given above.

Sahrawat

The Sahrawats claim to be descended from Sahra, a son or grandson of Raja Anangpal Tunwar.

Godara

The Godaras are a Shibgotra clan, and trace their descent from one Nimbuji, who founded a village near Bikaner. They have a tradition, that as they could not agree on one of themselves to rule over them, they asked the Raja of Jodhpur to let them have one of his younger sons to be their ruler. This request was granted, and they were given Bika in whose honour Bikaner was founded. It is said that even to this day the Tilak is placed on a new Raja of Bikaner's forehead by a Godara Jat and not by the family priest. The Godara Jats are a prosperous clan and own large areas in the Sirsa, and Fatehbad Tehsils.

In addition to some of those mentioned above, such as the Chahils and Mans, the following are the principal Sikh Jat tribes to be found in the district:

Dhariwals	759
Gils	609
Sarais	2,309
Sandhus	5,129
Sidhus	591

Dhariwals

The Dhariwals are almost entirely confined to the Sirsa, and Fatehabad Tehsils. They state that they sprang from Tunwar Rajputs, by marriage with women of inferior tribes. They are numerous in Ferozepore and Patiala, where they trace their origin to Daranagar, which was apparently somewhere in the direction of Delhi.

Gils

The Gil Jats are another Sirsa tribe; they trace their descent to a Raja Bhainipal, a Birah Rajput. They appear to have come originally from Bhatinda; whence they dispersed in the Chalisa famine of Sambat 1840. In Ferozepore the tradition appears to be confined to the Wadan section of the Gils, and it is probably this section which had settled in Sirsa.

Sidhus

The Sidhus Jats are closely connected by local tradition with the Hindu Bhatti Rajputs. It is said that the ancestor of these Rajputs, by name Bhatti, together with his brother Sunrija, came into his part of the country from the direction of Muthra. Risalu, descendant of Bhatti, had two sons, Jaisal and Dusal, the former of whom was the ancestor of the Hindu Bhatti Rajputs. Dusal had a son, Junhar or Janura, who married wives of inferior castes by whom he had sons, from whom various tribes of Jats have sprung. The whole of the Sidhu tribe including the Barars have sprung from Batera, a son of Junhar, intermediate ancestors being Sidhu and Barar.

No doubt this legendary descent expresses what is the fact that the Hindu Bhatti Rajputs, and the Sidhus, and Barar Sikh Jats are closely connected. But, as will be shown below in the case of Mussalman Bhattis, who were also connected, the common ancestor came immediately, probably not from Muthra, but from the Upper Panjab.

Most of the Sidhus of this district call themselves Barars, and insist on their close relationship with the founders of the Patiala, Nabha and Jind States.

GURGAON

The Khanzadas were interesting from their past; the Jats are important in the present, and if at any time, a native state should arise in this part of India, would probably be still more important in the future. They owned the greater portion of Palwal, and the adjoining part of Nuh, the country east and south of Bahora, and also scattered villages in other parts of Gurgaon, and in Rewari. They are almost without exception Hindus, only two small estates belonging to Mohammaden Jats; these call themselves Sheikhs, and were called by other Mulas. Many Mulas, who had been forcibly made Mohammadens by the Muslim emperors, were brought back into the caste, and were treated as Hindu Jats in all respects. They are still called Mulas, but Hindu Jats intermarry with them. The bards (Bhats) say that there are 9 lakhs of Gots in the Jat tribe. They even intermarry with the Sikh Jats of the Panjab. In Griffin's *Panjab Rajas* it is noted that the sister of the Maharaja of Patiala, a Sikh Jat, was married to the Maharaja of Bharatpur, a Hindu Jat. The chief Gots of Jats in the Gurgaon district are: (1) Sarot, who own 24 villages, including Hodal; (2) Rawat, 8 villages, including Bahin and part of 27 other villages; (3) Dagar, 12 villages, including Mandkaula; (4) Tewatiya, 2 villages, including Alawalpur (the Got of the Late Raja of Balabgarh); (5) Tanwar, 4 villages, including Pirthala; (6) Pokhwat, 5 villages, including Ghangaula; (7) Katamiya, 4 villages, including Gurgaon; (8) Raibdar, 4 villages, including Mitnaul. This last Got is famous for its bravery, and other Jats tell many amusing stories at their expense. All the Palwal Jats look to the Bharatpur Chief as their natural leader, and the fall of Bharatput made a great impression on them.

REFERENCES

1. A race related to Scythians, inhabitants of an ancient district about the Don River, 3rd century B.C.; 2nd century A.D. who spoke an Indo-Iranian language and were nomadics.
2. Born c. 63 B.C., died after A.D. 21, Greek geographer.
3. *District Gazetteer; Ferozepur*, p. 621.
4. A widow marriage.
5. Wasdev Singh Parhar-Lutera-Khurd.
6. In the 3rd story the Massegatae on the Oxus and Jaxartes, perhaps, as says Aristeas drove the Scyths farther east, out of Asia, (Encyclopaedia of Religion and Ethics. Vol. XI., p. 276).
7. *History of the Panjab,* Mohammad Latif, (Ed. 1891), p. 162.
8. *A History of the Sikhs*, J.D. Cunningham, (1840), p. 193.
9. *Ibid.*
10. *The Sikhs: An Ethnology,* Major A.E. Barstow, (1928), p. 168.
11. *The Invasion of India by Alexander as Described by Arrian, Curties Diodoros, Plutarch and Justin*, J.W. Crindle, (1896), p. 169.
12. *Glimpses of Ancient Panjab*, Dr. Budha Prakash, (1983), p. 93.
13. *History and Study of Jats,* Dr. B.S. Dhillon, (1984), p. 86.
14. *Archaeological Report 1863-64,* Major General A. Cunningham, p. 313.

15. The inhabitants of Media, an Indo-European people who expanded their rule over Persia in the reign of Sargon (705 B.C.).
16. *The Jats, Their Origin, Antiquity and Migration,* Hukum Singh Pawar, Manthan Publications, (1993), p. 168.
17. *Panjab, the Nomads and Marvericks*, p. 79.
18. Getae, an ancient people of Thracian origin inhabiting the banks of the lower Danube region who were subject of the Scythian influence and were the devotee of the deity Zalmoxis *(The Encyclopaedia of Britannica,* Vol. 5. p. 229).
19. *The Encyclopaedia of Britannica*, Vol. 5. p. 228.
20. *Census of India* (1901), Vol. I. p. 74.
21. Badden-Powell (1896), p. 99.
22. Nesfield quotejl in Crooke (1896), p. 26.
23. Miller, quoted in *District Gazetteer*, Muzaffarnagar (1920), p. 79.
24. Des Raj (1938).
25. *A History of Asia,* Harper Collins, (1996), p. 166.

    The superiority of the Chinese over the Turks caused the great Khan to turn his arms against the nomadic Getae's of Mawrul Nehr (Transoxiana), who descended from the Yuchi, and bred on the Jihoon or Oxus whence they had extended themselves along the Indus and even the Ganges, and they are yet found there. These Getae's had embraced the religion of 'Fo' *(Hist. Gen. Des Huns, Tom,* Vol. I. p. 375).
26. It must be either that the Yadus were themselves the Scythic Yuti or Yuchi, or that the branches intermarried with the Jits, and consequently became degraded as Yadus, and the mixed issue bore the name of the mother.
27. The Jiddoo Ka Dang, or 'hills of Yadu' mentioned in the sketch of this race as one of their intermediate points of halt when they were driven from India after the Mahabharata Yudh.
28. Near the spot where Alexander built his fleet, which navigated to Babylon thirteen hundred years before.
29. *Tarikh-i-Farishta*, Farishta, Vol. I. p. 30.
30. Please see for a detailed account *The Delhi Sultanate*, K.M. Munshi, pp. 116-136.
31. A river stream mostly in Panjab and in Patiala, C. 20 miles north-west of Nahan, flows C. 215 miles.
32. *Asiatic Researches*, Vol. I. p. 136.
33. *Hist Gen. des Huns, Tom. III*. p. 238.
34. A Chinese traveller.

35. *Precis de Geographic Universelle.* Malte-Brun traces a connection between the Hungarians and the Scandinavians, from similarity of language.
36. Old Persian Kureish, name of Achaemenian kings of Persia grouped among them Cyrus II the Great, 529 B.C.
37. "To my foe, Salutation I, this foe how shall I describe? Of the race of Jit Cattida, whose ancestor, the warrior Takshae, frothed the garland on the neck of Mahadeva."
38. This place existed in the 12th century A.D. as a capital; since an inscription of Komarpal, prince of Anhylawarra, declares that this monarch carried his conquests even to Salpoor. "There is Syal-Kote in Rannell's geography", and Wilford mentions Sangala, a famous city in ruins, sixty miles west north of Lahore, situated in a forest and said to be built by Porus.
39. A Rajput clan.
40. A Jat clan.
41. A Rajput clan.
42. Why should these proselytes, if originally Yadu, assume the name of Jit?
43. Kiramn (Keramam), the largest city of south-eastern Iran.
44. Elmansura or Almansura town, north-east of lower Egypt.
45. Capital of Dugahliya province, lower Egypt, the Damiotta branch of the Nile.
46. Formerly, people of ancient country of now called north-western Iran.
47. Caste No. 106, Bishnois are really a religious sect and not a true caste. Almost all the followers of this sect are either Jats or Tarkhans by caste, and come from the Bagar or Bikaner prairies. They are only found in Haryana and are all Hindus *(Punjab Castes*, Denzil Ibbetson, p. 263).
48. The Prospopies picigera is so called in the central Panjab, but in Jhelum, Pakistan the name is applied to Zizyphus nummularia and in the Jalandhar Doab to Acacia leucophlaea. Offerings are made to this tree by the relatives of Hindus suffering from smallpox.
49. A town, in Sialkot district, Pakistan, 17 miles SSE of Sialkot City.
50. This is said to be survival of an older rite in which the Hindu triad, the nine planets, the four Vedas, Fire, Water, and the Pole-Star were all invoked as witnesses of the marriage rite. The bridal pair walk four times round the Hawan, into which leaves of the Jand used to be thrown, and these had to be cut by the bridegroom and carried to the bride's house for that purpose, as the Mantra in debased Sanskrit, which is still recited, shows. The leaves are no longer thrown into the Hawan, or sacrificial, but the tree continues to be cut.

51. He is erroneously confused with Lakshman, the brother of Ram Chandarji, who indeed was not a Jogi at all.
52. *Tarikh-ul-Vakalat*, Jauhar (Stewart's Tr. p. 107).
53. 1. *Ibn Athir*—Elliot. Vol. II. p. 433.
    2. Muntakhib-ut-Tawarikh. p. 18.
    3. *Ranzat-ut-Tahrin*—Elliot. Vol. II. p. 301.
    4. See tree given in the Vernacular Settlement Report of the Gujrat District—Mirza Azim Beg, 1865.
    5. *Tabqat-i-Akbari.* pp. 18-19, 127, 147 and 600.
    6. *Tabqat-i-Nasiri.* pp. 23-24 & c.
54. *Ibn Athir*, p. 82; Ferishta, p. 159.
55. *Iqbal Nama-i-Jahangiri*, p. 109, *Akbar Nama*, p. 242.
56. Raverty (unpublished notes, pages 361 to 367) has noted the invariable confusion between the Gakkhars and the Khokhars, and says that it is a great error to ascribe to the former the attack on Mahmud's camp (which has been relied on by some as proof that the Gakkhars' own account of themselves is false); he points out that the Gakkhars are mentioned by none of the available native historian upto the time of Babar. The Janjuas, Khokhars, and others are known to have been settled in the Salt Range tract three centuries before Babar's time, for these tribes are mentioned by the author of the *Tabaqat-i-Nasiri* as the Koh-i-Jud, in his time but there is no mention whatever of the Gakkhars. Shahab-ud-din Ghauri or Muhammad-bin-Sam at Dhamizk, was the work of Khokhars.

    He comments also on the absurdity of the Gakkhar tale of their having ruled which has a history of its own showing that its rulers were Hindus at the time into this, however, it may be pointed out that the account usually given is that they ruled Kashmir proper, but that their ancestors were from some time eastern parts.
57. Local traditions are not always genuine, however, if one or two officials or historians in such matters chanced to enquire for the site of the assassination, it will be forthcoming with or without foundation in fact. The spot shown does not support the account we have that Muhammad Ghauri was killed in his tent.
58. Further information will be found in *Mr.* Brandreth's *Jhelum Settlement Report*, 1865, paras 55 to 58: Mr. Thomson's *Settlement Report*, 1883, para 57: and in *Panjab Government Selections*, New Series, No. XXIII, 1887.
59. A very important village, 10 miles from Phagwara, on Hoshiarpur Road, district Kapurthala.
60. *The Panjab, Chiefs and Families of Note,* latest edition, Volume II page 27, and Appendix.

61. To be distinguished from the Joya Daulatanas of the Luddan tract in Mailsi.
62. The Settlement Record drawn up in 1851 A.D. says that this occurred 200 years ago, which is 80 to 100 years too much. This is a fair illustration of the way in which periods of no very great duration are popularly expressed in round numbers invariably in excess of the truth. Another instance came under Mr. Barkley's notice in Taiwan. Then Kot Badal Khan was said to have been purchased by the Pathan founder from the Manj Rajputs of Shamshabad 400 years ago. Only six generations had elapsed in this interval, but the purchase deed was forthcoming, and when produced showed the purchase to have occurred in A.H. 1083 or almost exactly 200 years ago. The rule seems to be to treat three generations as equal to about 200 years, the fallacy being overlooked that it is only the interval between the mean data of the birth of one generation, and that of the next which has to be reckoned.
63. When Babar had taken Malot (in Hoshiarpur) in 1526, Dilawar Khan joined him in that neighbourhood.
64. A large body of Sahota Jats comprising representatives of all their villages, has been met in Muzaffarnagar on its way to Garh Ganga or Gurudwara near Anupshahr *(North Indian Notes and Queries* I, p. 455).
65. The ruling families in all the states between the Jhelum and the Chenab, were also originally Rajputs, except Kotali. These were Bhimbar, Rajaur, Punch and Khorishi, which became Mohammaden at a later period. Kotali was founded at a later date by a branch of the Kashmir family.
66. Also called Chaudhari, or Mihr Mitha.
67. 'Nam' is a Hindi language word meaning eye. There are said to be Nain Jats in Bikaner also.
68. The sept is so named because a Chanderi Rajput settled at Gire, a village in Rupar tehsil, and fell in love with a Jat woman, whom he kept as his mistress.

The Abhiras
(Ancestors of Ahirs)

3

ORIGIN

The origin of the Abhiras, a nomadic tribe and the stages of their migration into India are obscure. Most probably, they came into India shortly before, or along with, the Scythians. Patanjali[1] (second century B.C.) couples them with Sudras, and the same grouping is found in the Mahabharata, where the two peoples are located near the spot of the disappearance of the Sarasvati[2], in southern Panjab and northern Rajasthan. The Periplus[3] mentions Aberia with the coastal district Syrastrene (Saurastra), and Ptolemy locates Abhiria above the Indus delta. Their western association is attested to in many Puranas as well.

"In the Ramayana and the Mahabharata the Abhiras, the ancestors of Ahirs in the west are spoken of; and in ancient Hindu Geography the tract between the Tapti[4] and Devagarh[5] as named after them; they were also at one time dominant in Gujrat (Maharashtra) and Nepal. According to some, they are the descendants of a Scythian tribe who entered India from the north-west, about two thousand years[6] ago."

FOREIGN PEOPLE

The Abhiras appear to have been a foreign people who, entered India shortly before or along with the Sakas (Scythian) from some part of eastern Iran. It is tempting to connect their name with the locality called Abhiravan between Herat[7] and Kandahar[8]. The Puranas speak of the Abhiras amongst the successors of the Satavahanas. Although we have an Abhira settlement as far east as Ahirwar between Bhilsa[9] and Jhansi[10] in Central India, the Abhiras are usually associated with Aparanta, which indicated in a wider sense the western division of India and in a narrow sense only the northern part of the Konkan[11]. In one context the *Mahabharata* places the Abhiras in Aparanta; but in another, it associates the people with the Sudras, and assigns both the tribes to the land near Vinasana, where the Sarasvati lost itself in the sands of the Rajputana desert. The Abhiras are also found in association with the Sudras in Patanjali's *Mahabharata. The Periplus of the Erythrean Sea* and *The Geography* of Ptolemy locate Aberia of Abiria, *i.e.,* the Abhira country, between the lower Sindh Valley and Kathiawar, apparently in south-western Rajputana and the adjoining regions. The dominions of the Abhira kings referred to in the Puranas, however, lay in the north-west region of the Deccan and may have sometimes included the northern Konkan as far as the Broach[12] area in the north.

EPIGRAPHIC RECORDS

In early epigraphic records, the Abhiras figure as generals of Saka Mahakshatrapas of western India. The Gunda (North Kathiawar) inscription of A.D. 181 belonging to the time of Rudrasimha, records the digging of a tank by the Abhira General Rudrabhuti[13], the son of a general named Bapaka. An adventurer named Isvaradatta issued silver coins of the Satrapal style actually with the title Mahakshatrapa, and must have been in possession of the major part of the Saka territories for about a few years. The coins of this ruler, dated in the first and second years of his reign, have been assigned by Rapson to A.D. 237-40, but by Bhandarkar to A.D. 188-90. The latter view seems more reasonable, that Mahakshatrapa Isvaradatta[14] was not a Saka, is evident from his name, which does not resemble that of any of the Satrapal rulers, as well as from the independent way of the dating of his coins. He is usually regarded as an Abhira.

FOUNDER OF DYNASTY

Abhira king, who may be regarded as a successor of the Satavahanas[15] and the Sakas in the north-western Deccan, is Raja Mathariputra Isvarasena, son of Abhira Sivadatta, mentioned in the Nasik inscription of his ninth reginal year. The inscription records two investments, one of 1,000 Karshapanas, and another of 500 Karshapanas, in trade- guilds at Govardhana (old Nasik) for the purpose of providing medicines for the sick, among the monks dwelling in the monastery on the Nasik Hills. The benefactress was the lay devotee Vishnudatta, who was a Sakani, mother of Ganapaka Visavarman and daughter of Saka

Agnivarman. As the king's father Sivadatta was credited with no royal title in the inscriptions, king Isvarasena[16] may be regarded as the founder of the Abhira dynasty. There is no doubt that this dynasty flourished sometime after the death of Yajna Satakarni[17], which took place about the beginning of the third century. It is, therefore, not improbable that the so-called Kalachuri or Chedi era starting form A.D. 248-49, was counted from the accession of Isvarasena. Although the Puranas refer to ten Abhira kings ruling for 67 years, nothing is known about Isvarasena's successors.

The inscription of Isvarasena proves that his dominions comprised the Nasik region in northern Maharashtra; but the actual extent of his kingdom is uncertain. If he was really the founder of the era of A.D. 248, it may be suggested that the Abhiras extended their political influence over Aparanta and Lata where the era is found to be in use in later days.

The Kalachuris[18], originally of the Anupa region on the Narmada, probably used the era after their conquest of territories belonging formerly to the kingdom of the Abhiras.

In their early days in India, the Abhiras were a nomadic and predatory tribe, enjoyed a nomadic life— an example of which is the story of their raid on Arjuna[19] and the Yadava women escorted by him. But by the second century, we find some of them attaining high ranks and seizing political power. The Gunda (Saurastra) inscription of A.D. 181 records the digging of a tank by an Abhira General Rudrabhut, the son of a general named Bapaka.

One Abhira Isvarasena, son of Sivadatta, supposed to be the founder of the Kilachuri-Chedi[20] recording the restoration of a dam under the supervision of his provincial governor Pahlava[21] Suviskha, where Rudradaman claims, not unjustifiably mystery over Sanskrit composition, both in prose and poetry. It is noteworthy that while the inscription of the contemporary Satavahanas is in Prakrit, those of the Ksatrapas[22] are in Sanskrit.

INSCRIPTIONS

Rudradaman's own inscription is itself a landmark in the history of Sanskrit prose. He even married his daughter to Vasisthiputra Sri Satakarni of the orthodox Satavahana family. The matrimonial alliance of this family with the Ikavakus of south-eastern India is also attested by one of the Nagarjuni-Konda[23] inscriptions, where Rudradhara Bhattarika, Queen of Virapurusadatta (third century

A.D.) is said to have made a gift of a pillar in the Mahacaitya at Nagarjunikonda[24]. Other inscriptions tell the same tale about the Saka individuals. One of the Nasik[25] cave inscriptions records gift by a Saka called Vudhika son of Vishnudatta: another, belonging to the reign of the Abhira Isvarasena[26] (third century, also records a perpetual endowment for providing medicine to the sick monks by the Upasika Visnudatta, the daughter of the Saka Agnivarman. Saka Sridharavarman, son of Nanda, who was originally a Mahadandanayaka, but later on assumed independence, was a devotee of Mahasena. In his Kanakhera (Sanchi) inscription he calls himself Dharmavijayi (a religious conqueror). Like an orthodox Hindu, he aspires to attain eternal abode in heaven by doing pious works such as the digging of wells.

ABHIRA RULERS

Era beginning with A.D. 248-49, rose to the royal rank in northern Maharashtra. Towards the end of the third century A.D. the Abhiras wielded considerable power, and along with other Saka rulers of India, Abhira king sent an embassy to congratulate the Siassanian king Narseh (293-302) on his victory against Varhran III. The Puranas also recognize the rule of ten Abhira princes covering a period of sixty-seven years after the Satavahanas. In the fourth century they came into conflict with the Kadamba king Mayurasarman[27]. The Allahabad pillar inscription of Samudragupta refers to the Abhiras as paying homage to him. Stray references to the Abhiras as a political power, particularly in western India, continued in medieval literature and inscriptions.

THE BARBARIANS

The Abhiras were at first regarded as barbarians like Scythians and were despised. The Puranas brand them as Malechhas (low people) and Dasyus (robbers). According to the Amarakosa, Mahasudri[28] Abhiri, while the Nasika identifies Mahasudra with a man of the Abhira descent. According to the *Mahabharata* they were Kshatriyas degraded from their rank owing to the non-observance of Kshatriya rites. The position of the Abhiras was much improved in the estimation of Manu[29], who regards them as the offspring of Brahma by an Ambastha (descending from a Brahmana father and Vaisya mother) woman. The Abhiras made a strong impression upon the Indians. Their speech obtains distinction in the Indian drama as an Apbhramsha (low Prakrit) dialect. They also contributed to the development of Indian music. Almost all musical works recognize the Ragini (tune) Abhiri or Ahiri. But their greatest contribution is towards the growth of pastoral legend centering round Krishna, including his love affairs with Gopis (milkmaids). Today we find the Ahirs (descendants of Abhiras) scattered over the greater part of India. A number of localities in India are named after this tribe.

At the time of Alexander's[30] invasion, the Abhiras, the ancestors of Ahirs were very powerful in the Panjab. The invasion of Alexander found the Panjab, divided among a number of relatively inconsiderable tribes, a state of things which had probably always subsisted. He left it substantially unchanged, except that he recognised two of the larger states that of Takshila (Taxila[31]), which had facilitated his entrance into India, and the rival kingdom of Porus[32] (Paurava of the king Puras), whom he had conquered. The former was maintained in the region between the Indus and the Hyadaspes (The Jhelum), while the latter was made to embrace all the more easterly territory as far as the Hyphasis (the Beas). The two kings were reconciled and united by a matrimonial alliance. Alexander further confirmed, under the title of Satrap, Abhiras, rulers of the Himalayan districts of the Panjab. The mountains of the Abhiras, from which flows the river Soanus (Megasthenes), the Sohan corresponds to the Abhira reign, defined by Stein[33] as denoting the hills lying between the Jhelum and the Chenab rivers. But it may at that time had included more, extending to the Indus, as suggested by the king's relation with the Assakenoi[34] (*Supra*, p. 353). The nation occupying the large extent of country about the confluences of the five rivers were placed under Phillipus[35] as a Satrap, and Sindh under Pithon. As well as cattle owned by cultivating peasants that were large herds belonging to professional herdsmen, who led a semi-nomadic life in the wilder parts of the country. One important tribe of these people, the Abhiras, which dwelt in widely scattered localities of south Rajasthan, Malwa and Sindh around the beginning of the Christian era, was perhaps responsible for the development of the cult of Krishna in his pastoral aspect, and Abhiras chiefs set up a short lived kingdom in the northwest Deccan, on the ruins of the Satavahanas.

The Abhiras continued to rule as late as the middle of the fourth century when according to the Chandravalli[36] inscription, they came into conflict with the Kadamba king of Mayurasarman. Although the Traikutakas, who flourished in the northern Konkan in the fifth century, may have been a branch of the Abhira tribe, Mayurasarman's inscription points to the separate existence of the Abhira and Traikutaka Kingdom in the fourth century. The Allahabad pillar inscription of Samudragupta mentions the Abhiras in the list of the reference, "Here is to the Abhira kingdom in the north-western Deccan." The Abhira territories in this region appear to have later passed to the Traikutakas[37].

RELIGION

Before the advent of Abhiras into India, their religion was the worship of various objects of nature, like the other contemporary nomadic tribes of Central Asia and Russia. But they were greatly influenced by the Hindus, who, at that time, were almost all Vaishnavas. The new-comers thus became adherents of Vaishnav, the cult of Visnu.

THE DEVELOPMENT OF THE WORSHIP OF VISNU

Since the Vedic period the development of the cult of Visnu has undergone many modifications. Though he is an important deity in the mythology of the Brahmanas, Visnu occupies only a subordinate position in the *Rigveda*, his essential feature being that he takes three strides, interpreted by some authorities to mean the rising, culminating, and setting of the sun, but more probably meaning the course of the solar deity through the three divisions of the universe[38]. The later development of his personality has been fully investigated by R.G. Bhandarkar, who traces its stages as follows: in the 5th cent. B.C. a religious reform arose like that which gave birth to Buddhism and Jainism, but based on theistic principles; this soon assumed a sectarian type in the form of the Pancharatra or Bhagavata religion[39]. This, again, was combined with the cult of Narayana, 'the resting place or goal of gods'; soon after the Christian era the Abhira tribe of shepherds contributed to it their tribal hero Krishna. In the 8th century this faith, the predominant feature of which was *bhakti*, or love, came into contact with the doctrine of spiritual monism and world-illusion promulgated by Shankaracharya (q.v.); the hostility to spiritual monism gathered to a head in the 11th century, when Ramanuja (q.v.) made strenuous efforts to displace it by the religion of *bhakti* in a reinvigorated form; he was followed in the north by Nimbarka, who advocated the cow-herd element and enjoined the cult of Radha, mistress of Krishna. The same policy was continued in the 13th century by

Madhva or Anandatirtha, who established the doctrine of pluralism and brought into prominence the name of Visnu as supreme god. In the north Ramananda added the cult of Rama, and his successor Ramanuja that of Narayana. Kabir in the 15th century preached strict monotheism, the cult of Rama, and condemned idolatry; Vallabha in the 16th century founded the erotic cult of Krishna and Radha, and Chaitanya in Bengal that of the boy Krishna and Radha, a corruption which led to the degradation of Vaisnavism. In the Deccan Namdev and Tukaram discarded the worship of Krishna-Radha, cultivated a more sober type of worship, disseminated their ideas not in Sanskrit but in the vernacular languages, preached pure love of God, and laid stress on personal purification of heart and morals as necessary to salvation[40].

Visnu and his Incarnations

Vaisnavism has thus developed on several distinct lines according as the object of devotion. Visnu, varies in his manifestations, incarnations, or 'descents' *(avatara)*. This theory tends towards syncretism, the absorption of the lower animal-gods or totems of the more primitive tribes into the Brahmanical pantheon. The incarnations of Visnu are sometimes enumerated as six, ten, or twenty in number; but the most important are those of Krishna and Rama[41]. The cult of Rama goes back in the *Vayu Purana* to about the 5th century B.C.; in the *Ramayana* of Valmiki, which in its original form is based on pre-Buddhistic materials, while its kernel was probably composed before 500 B.C., and the more recent portion was probably not added till the 2nd century B.C. and later[42], Rama is depicted as a high-souled hero, and thus with his faithful wife Sita, he won the affections of the Indian people. But it was not till the 11th century of our era that his cult was fully developed. This cult is described in the *Visnu Purana*, which seems to go back to the Gupta period (A.D. 320-455)[43]. The tenth book of the *Bhagavata Purana* has exercised a more powerful influence than any other work of its class, and was translated into Hindi by Lallu Ram Kavi under the title of *Prema Sagara* ('The Ocean of Love'), and is now the most popular manual of the cult of Krishna[44]. The cult of Vasudeva-Krishna seems to be mentioned by the Greek traveller Megasthenes; and if it prevailed in the period of the first Maurya emperor, it must have originated long before that time, and probably owes its development to that stream of thought which began with the Upanishads and culminated in

Buddhism and Jainism[45]. Krishna seems to have been a local deity known as Gopala, 'cowherd', or Govinda, probably a later form of Govid, 'finder of cows', which was an epithet of Indra[46]. He was worshipped by the Abhira shepherds, who wandered with their flocks over the region from Mathura to Dwarka. With this pastoral deity, by a process of syncretism, was combined the cult of an ocean god of the western sea localised at Dwarka. How far this cult was influenced by Christianity, brought by nomad tribes like the Gurjaras from Central Asia, is still a question of controversy[47]. The imperfect combination of the cults of Mathura and Dwarka is shown by the vagueness and inconsistencies of the legends which were invented to account for the later Krishna cult.

THE SUBDIVISIONS OF THE VAISNAVAS

Influence of the Creed: Sacred Places

The subdivisions of the Vaisnavas follow the teachings of the great missionaries, of whom an account has elsewhere been given[48]. The most important is that of the Sri Vaisnavas, founded by Ramanuja, the followers of whom are more numerous in southern than in northern India. The second school is that of Madhava, or Anandatirtha, who preached the doctrine of duality (dvaita), in opposition to the non-duality of Sankaracharya. The third follows the teaching of Ramananda, whose characteristics were that no distinction was made between the Brahmans and the so-called 'untouchables', and the use of the vernacular tongues as the medium of his teaching. The fourth is the Vallabhacharya, whose worship of the *guru* has led to much scandal[49].

Vaisnavism is essentially monotheistic, while Saivism is often ultimately pantheistic or, rather, is apt to relapse into pantheism, though it, too, is monotheistic[50].

Taken as a whole, one of the chief characteristics of the United Provinces population is a real and unaffected kindliness. Vaisnavism would certainly appeal to them, and if adopted, would tend to enhance the very quality which would cause its adoption[51].

REFERENCES

1. The Sanskrit grammarian who wrote about 140 B.C. (or possibly as late as 25 A.D.), a commentary called *Mahabhashya* or Great Commentary, on the previous work of (q.v.) and especially on the criticism of Panini by Katayana. He is the reputed founder of the

Yoga system of philosophy, which proclaimed that salvation and bliss were to be attained by the union of the individual soul with the great soul, Ishvara and this can be attained by austere life and meditation (*The Encyclopaedia Americana*. Vol. 21. p. 379).

2. Flowing water (Skr.). The name at the present applied to an ancient river in the Panjab, which rises in the Sirmaur district, Himachal Pradesh and disappearing in sand, emerges once more and joins the Ghaggar in the territory of Haryana. Once it flowed through Rajasthan.
3. Pliny's *Naturalis Historia*, later half of the 1st century A.D.: a short time later the Greek document *knoen yo dvholsted sd yhr prtiplus Maris Erythraei* mentions an individual who was "king of two nations" (*The Encyclopaedia of Britannica,* Vol. 13. p. 817).
4. River in central India, rising in the Gawilgarh hills of the central Deccan Plateau in south-central Madhya Pradesh State, flows westward.
5. Deoghar, a town of north-eastern India. An ancient town, it is famous for its group of 22 temples dedicated to the Hindu god Shiva. Numerous Buddhist ruins are nearby.
6. *The Religion and Ethics of Encyclopeadia*, Vol. 3. p. 231.
7. Capital of Herat Province in western Afghanistan, lying on the Harirud river, directly south of the Safaid-Koh at an altitude of 3,026 ft.
8. Qandhar, a province, south-east of Afghanistan, bounded south and south-east-by Baluchistan, in Pakistan.
9. The Bhilsa Topes (1854) the first serious attempt to trace Buddhist history, through its architectural remains by Sir A. Cunnigham.
10. A district Headquarter, in south Uttar Pradesh, India; 130 miles south-west of Kanpur.
11. Coastal plain in west Bombay, India—Western Ghats in the east and the Arabian Sea in the west.
12. District, north of Bombay, India; a port.
13. A strong king among the Abhiras, a nomadic tribe, the ancestors of Ahirs.
14. There is no doubt that Isvaradatta and Abhira (the ancestor of Ahirs), King of Mathariputra Isvaradatta ruled over the same teritories (*The Age of Imperial Unity*, p. 222).
15. The king of Satavahana were styled "Lord of Dakshina Patha". The name Dakshinapatha, however, was not always used in the same geographical sense. Sometimes it indicated the whole of trans-Vindhyan India, but often only the present Maratha country with the adjoining eastern and western regions (*The Age of Imperial Unity, p.* 191).

16. The inscription for Isvarasena proves that his dominions comprised the Nasik region in northern Maharashtra. *(The Age of Imperial Unity*; p. 222).
17. The successors of Yajna Satkarni, according to some of the Puranas were Vijya C.A.D. pp. 203-09.
18. The dynastic name Kalachuri was Katachehuri, though in some cases we have other variants like Kalatsuri, Kalachuti, Kalachuri, Kalachurya and Kalichuri. Though it is a Sanskrit word, but it has been equated with the Turkish word Kuluchura indicating an officer of high rank. They were people who entered India in the train of the Huns and Gujjars *(The Classical Age,* p. 194).
19. The Arjunayana people claimed descent from the Pandva prince Arjuna *(The Age of Imperial Unity,* p. 222).
20. The Kalachuri or Chedi era started from A.D. 248-49 was counted from the accession of Isvarasena *(The Age of Imperial Unity,* p. 222).
21. The pahlava (from old Persian Parthava) are regarded as Parthians. But the term Pahlava possibly indicates the Sassanians or Persian general *(The Age of Imperial Unity*, p. 122).
22. *The Vedic Age,* p. 304 ff.
23. *The Age of Imperial Unity*, pp. 492-93.
24. The most important stupa *(The Age of Imperial Unity*. p. 492).
25. A district, in north Bombay, 90 miles north-east of Bombay.
26. The inscription of Isvaransena proves that his dominions comprised the Nasik region in northern Maharashtra *(The Age of Imperial Unity,* p. 222).
27. The Abhiras continued to rule as late as the middle of the 4th century A.D. when according to the Chandravalli inscription they came into conflict with Kadamba Mayurasarman *(The Age of Imperial Unity,* p. 223).
28. A contemporary historian of Alexander.
29. The inventor of Sanskrit codifications, such as the mysterious "Laws of Manu aimed at tightening of the regulations of caste for the preservation of Brahman exclusiveness." Compiled probably between 200 B.C. and 200 A.D. from diverse ancient sources *(The Concise Columbia Encyclopaedia,* p. 515).
30. Alexander, the Macedonian man of destiny, invaded India in 326 B.C. but returned in 325 B.C. with a heavy heart. Alexander the Great died on the way to Greece.
31. Takshila was a prominent centre of learning and education, to which flocked scholars from distant parts of India. It was the biggest and the richest University at that time *(The Age of Imperial Unity*, pp. 592-94).

32. When Alexander the Great crossed the Jhelum in 326 B.C., Porus, the powerful king of the Panjab, awaited the Greek invader with a formidable force of 30,000 infantry, 4,000 cavalry, 300 chariots and 200 elephants.
33. *Rajatrangini*, English Translation Stein, Vol. I. p. 180 n.
34. After conquering the city of Andaka, Alexander the Great, had still more severe resistance offered by the Assakenoi, the inhabitants of the eastern part of this region, the modern Kafarsitan *(The Age of Imperial Unity*. pp. 546).
35. In India proper, the region round the confluences of the Panjab rivers, formed the Strapy of Phillipus and Sindh, that of Pithon, the son of Agenor *(The Age of Imperial Unity,* pp. 52-53).
36. Central India on the RR. 115 miles south-east of Amaravati.
37. They derived their name from the Trikuta Hill also called Chitaldurg, town, district north Mysore, India, 120 miles northwest of Bangalore, in Aprantha, Northern Konkan. One of the Traikutaka Kings is actually described in his records as ruling over Aprantha *(The Classical Age,* pp. 192-195).
38. *Encyclopeadia of Religion and Ethics*, Vol. XII, p. 571.
39. *Vedic Mythology,* A.A. Macdonell Strasberg, 1897, p. 37 t.
40. *Vaisizmand Minor Religious Systems,* R.C. Bhandarkar, Vol. VI, p. 702 f.
41. *Ibid.* p. 361.
42. *A History of Sanskrit Literature,* A.A. Macdonell (London-1900), p. 308.
43. *The Early History of India,* V.A. Smith. (Oxford-1924), p. 23 ff.
44. *A History of Sanskrit Literature*. A.A. Macdonell, p. 302.
45. *Ancient India as Described by Megasthenese and Arrian,* J.W. Mcrindle, Calcutta, 1877, p. 201.
46. Bhandarkar. p. 35 ff.
47. *Ibid.*
48. *Art Hinduism,* Vol. VI. p. 703 ff.
49. *Ibid.*
50. *Census of India (1911) XV United Provinces*. Pt. i. p. 128 ff.
51. *Ibid.* p. 140 ff.

BIBLIOGRAPHY

Bombay Gazetteer, Vol. I. XV. Pt. Vol. XVII.

Collier's Encyclopaedia, Vol. 5.

Hassan Siraj-ul, Syad. *Ahirs, Castes and Tribes of H.E.H. The Nizam's Dominions*, Vol. I (1990).

Pliny's *Naturalis Historia*, Merced, County California Library.

Stein. *Rajatrangini.*

Risley. *Tribes and Castes*, Vol. I.

Russel, R.V. and Hira Lal. *Ahir: In the Tribes and Castes of the Central Provinces of India* (1969).

The Age of Imperial Unity.

The Classical Age.

The Concise Columbia Encyclopedia.

The Encyclopaedia Americana, Vol. 21.

The Laws of Manu.

The Religion and Ethics of Encyclopeadia, Vol. 3. p. 231.

The Ahirs
(Descendants of Abhiras)

4

AGRICULTURISTS AND CATTLE BREEDERS

Origin

Ahirs are an important tribe of agriculturists and breeders of cattle, which at the census of 1901 numbered 9,806,475, of whom a vast majority are found in Bengal, where it is by far the largest caste, in the United and General Provinces, and in smaller numbers throughout northern India. Their name connects them with the Abhiras, a people occupying the Indus Valley, and Lessen's view that the Sudras, or servile caste of the Hindu polity, along with Abhiras and Mihsadas, were a black, longhaired Indian race, occupying what is now the Valley of Sindh, is perhaps correct. Another suggestion, which would connect them with a Scythian tribe, the Abhiras, who are believed to have entered India in the 1st or 2nd century B.C., is probable. In northern India their traditions connect them with Mathura[1], the holy land of Krishana; and the Jadubansi, one of their subdivisions, claim descent from the Yadava tribe, to which Krishna is said to have belonged; while another, the Nandbansi of the United Provinces, the Nanda Ghosh[2] of Bengal, claims as its ancestor—Nanda, the foster-father of the divine child[3]. In this region besides cattle owned by cultivating peasants there were large herds belonging to professional herdsmen, who led a semi-nomadic life in the wilder parts of the country. One important tribe of these people, the Abhiras (ancestors of Ahirs), which dwelt in widely scattered localities of South, Rajasthan, Malwa and Sindh around the beginning of the Christian era, was responsible for the development of the cult of Krishna in his pastoral aspect and Abhira (ancestor of Ahirs) chief, set up a short-lived kingdom in the north-west Deccan, on the ruins of Satavahanas[4].

THEIR SOCIAL STATUS

The Ahirs are properly a pastoral caste, their name being derived from the Sanskrit *Abhira*, or "milkman". But in the Panjab they are now almost exclusively agriculturalists and stand in quite the first rank as husbandmen, being as good as the Kambohj and somewhat superior to the Jat. They are of the same social standing as the Jat and Gujjar, who will eat and smoke with them; but they do not seem ever to have been at any rate within recent times, the dominant race in any considerable tract. Perhaps their nearest approach to such a position was in Rewari and the country to the west of it still locally known as Hirwati, where they held nearly three quarters of the Parganah in 1838. A very full description of them will be found in Elliott's *Races of the North-West Provinces*, and also in Sherring, 1, 332 ff. The west coast of India and Gujarat would appear to be their ancient homes, but they are numerous in Behar and Gorakhpur, and at one time there was an Ahir dynasty in Nepal. In the erstwhile Panjab they were chiefly found in the south of Delhi, Gurgaon, and Rohtak and the Native States bordering upon these districts, and in this limited tract they formed a considerable proportion of the whole population. They are almost all Hindus, and are said to trace their origin from Mathura. They are industrious, patient, and orderly, and though they are ill-spoken of in the proverbs of the countryside, yet that is probably only because the Jat is jealous of them as being even better cultivators than himself. Thus they say in Rohtak: "Kosli (the head of the village of the Ahirs) has fifty brick houses and several thousand swaggerers." So in Delhi: "Rather be kicked by a Rajput or stumble uphill, than hope anything from a jackal, spare grass of an Ahir"; and again: "All castes are God's creatures, but three castes are ruthless. When they "get a chance they have no shame; the whore, the Banya, and the Ahir." But these stigmas are nowadays at least wholly undeserved.

"Cowherd (Caste; Ahir, Goala, etc.): Many of these large and widely distributed North Indian castes, whose members now, live far more by agriculture than by herding, are supposed to have originated from non-Aryan-speaking tribes that dwelt on the fringes of Indian civilization in ancient times. The myths of the cowherd castes stress a descent from Krishna, the divine cowherd, and a high status as Kshatriyas in the caste hierarchy. As agriculturists, Ahirs traditionally emphasize milk production and animal breeding for draft purposes, since the consumption of beef is forbidden for all but

Muslims and the lowest Hindu castes."[5] "Ahir, cattle-tending caste widespread in northern and central India. Considerable historical interest attaches to the caste because its members are thought to be identical with the Abhiras of Sanskrit literature who are mentioned repeatedly in the great epic, the *Mahabharata.* Some scholars contend that these cattlemen, scattered over southern Rajasthan and Sindh (now part of Pakistan), played a role of importance in the early development of the god Krishna as the cowherd, which has continued to be a significant aspect of the Krishna legend"[6] "Ahirs or cowherds of upper India as mentioned in the *Ramayana* and the *Mahabharata*, the Abhiras in the west are spoken of; and in ancient Hindu geography the tract between the Tapti and Devagarh is named after them; they were also at one time dominant in Gujrat and Nepal. According to some, they are the descendants of a Scythian tribe who entered India from the north-west about two thousand years ago, while others regard them as an old Indian or half Indian race who were driven south before the Scythians invasion."[7]

The Ahirs of the North-West Provinces have three great sections, the Nandbans of the central Doab, the Jadubans of the upper Doab and the Mathura country, and the Gwalbans of the lower Doab at Renaras. The Ahirs of the Panjab have returned themselves as shown in the margin. Of the Gwalbans more than 16,000 were found in Patiala. Within these tribes they have numerous clans, among which the Kossali of Rohtak and Gurgaon numbered 13322.

AHIR TRIBES

In the Census Report 1883, the Ahirs were returned as under:

1. Jadubans—63,961 2. Nandbans—44,998
3. Gwalbans—35,187.

BENGAL

Background of Bengal: Region 77,442 square miles, East India and Bangladesh, on the Bay of Bengal. Its Indian mountains slope to the fertile Ganges-Brahmaputra alluvial plains and delta. The heavy monsoon rains and warm climate makes possible two harvests a year. From the empire of Ashoka (3rd century B.C.) Bengal passed to the Buddhist Pala kings, the Hindu Sena dynasty, and then the Muslims of Turkey descent. It was during the Mughal rule that the Portuguese and the British traders arrived (16th-17th century A.D.). The latter under Robert Clive defeated the Muslims in

1757 A.D. and formed the Bengal Presidency. When India became independent in 1947, West Bengal, with population 54,845, and area 33,928 square miles, primarily Hindu, was created as a state in India, with Calcutta as its capital. It has Jute mills, steel plants, chemical industries and mineral reserves.

East Bengal, overwhelmingly Muslims, became East Pakistan in 1947 and gained independence as Bangladesh in 1971.

In Bengal this caste is known as Goala (Sanskrit Gopda, a cowherd), and in accordance with the legend of their descent, they are generally worshippers of Krishna[8], and, therefore, members of the Vaishnava[9] sect. The cult of Vaishnavism may be regarded as in direct antithesis to that of Shiv. Like the latter, it has its philosophical side. But their cult is of a much lower type than the pietistic form of Vaishnavism associated with the teaching of Chaitanya[10] in Bengal. Thus, they have a special feast, known as the Govardhan Puja, which takes its name from the holy Mathura hill associated with the cult of Krishna[11], at which they pray to a heap of boiled rice which is supposed to represent the hill, and make an offering of food, red-lead, turmeric, and flowers to every cow which they possess. In other parts the worship is paid to a mass of cow dung made to represent a human form presumably that of Krishna.

THEIR PRIMITIVE RITES

More primitive rite is that described by Buchman[12], when at the Divali, or Feast of Lamps, they tie together the feet of a pig, and drive their cattle over the wretched animal until it is killed, after which they boil and eat the flesh in the fields though on other occasions they are not permitted to taste pork. Here the pig was probably originally a sacred animal, and is sacramentally slain to promote the fertility of the fields[13]. It is a curious proof of the sympathy which even Hindus of high caste and social position exhibit towards the coarser side of Hinduism, that when, in 1895, the English officer-in-charge of the Santhal country prohibited this brutal rite, a protest was immediately made in the Legislative Council of Bengal by one of its members. It is satisfactory to find that the Lieutenant-Governor supported the action of his subordinate[14].

In West Bengal they have special reverence for the Lorik, round whom a couple of curious legend centre. Several of the caste worship deified heroes, each having its own[15]. The epic of Lerik[16], is of interminable length, and his exploits were not confined to Gaya[17]. He is also localized and sung of by Goalas in other neighbouring districts such as Shahabad, Mirzapur[18] and Balia[19], and for Kasi Baba or Kashinath, the ghost of a murdered Brahman, which is greatly feared. If he be not propitiated, he brings disease upon the cattle and Risley describes how, when the plague appears, the village cattle are massed together, and cotton seed sprinkled over them. The fattest and sleekest animal being singled out, it is severely beaten with rods. The herd, scared by the noise, scamper off to the nearest shelter, followed by the scap-bull; and thus it is thought the nurrain is stayed[20].

UNITED PROVINCES

In the United Provinces, those members of the caste who are initiated into any of the orthodox sects are either Vaishnavas or Shaivas, the former preferring the cult of Krishna, the latter that of Siva or of his consort Devi in some one of her many forms, in preference the goddess known as the Vindhyabasini Devi, who has her temple at Vindhyachal in the Mirzapur district, and is supposed to be the guardian goddess of the Vindhyan Hills. Vindya, mountain goddess had her love in the Vindhyas; she was of the savage tribe living in those hills. Her name is Vindhyabasini and she too is identified with Siva's wife. In Saharanpur[21] they have two deities who preside over marriage—Brahm Devata and Bar Devata, the former representing the great Hindu god Brahma, who has an image of God in human form; the latter the banyan tree (Hindi Bar, Sanskrit, Vata). On the night of the wedding the image of Brahm Devata[22] is brought by the goldsmith and placed upon the marriage platform. When the binding portion of the rite has been performed, the bride and bridegroom offer to the image sandalwood, rice, flowers, incense, sweetmeats, and cakes, and light lamps before it. The women of the household then bury the image in the kitchen and raise an earthen platform over it. The members of the family worship this deity by pouring water over it, and on feast days offerings of milk and rice cakes are made to it. This is done until a second marriage takes place in the family, when it is dug up and removed, and its place is taken by a new image. This is very curious survival of Brahma worship among a people where we were unlikely to suspect its existence. Except in a few temples specially dedicated to this, the head of the Hindu triad, this cult has now largely fallen into disuse. The worship of the banyan tree is closely connected with the custom of tree marriage. Among the Ahirs the bridegroom marks the trunk of the tree with vermilion at the same time as he marks the parting of the bride's hair with the same substance, a rite which is an obvious survival of the blood-covenant, marking the reception of the bride into a new kith and kin different from her own[23].

The Panchanpir

They worship the Panchanpir (see Panchpiriyas) and various minor local gods, the most popular of whom is Kasinath, a deified ghost, at whose festival pots of milk are set to boil for the refreshment of the godling: and one man, becoming possessed by the deity, pours the contents over his shoulder and is said never to be scalded. Their special cattle-God in the eastern parts of these provinces is Birnath (Sanskrit, Vira-Natha, 'hero-lord'), who is represented by a collection of five wooden images rudely carved into human form.

CENTRAL PROVINCES

A similar quintetts of gods of disease is worshipped in the Central Provinces. Here their principal deities are Dulha Deo, said to be deified bridegroom who died on his wedding day (see Dravidians) and Buddha Deo, the chief god of the Gonds. As in Bengal, their chief festival is the Diwali, when they go about bedecked with strings of *cowry* shells, singing and dancing. They also pay much respect to a deified man, Haridas Baba. He is said to have been Yogi (ascetic) , and to have possessed the power of separating his soul and his body at pleasure. One day he went to Benaras[24], and left his body in the house of one of his disciples, an Ahir. As he did not return, and the people ascertained that a dead body was lying in this house, they insisted that it should be burned. After this was done, Haridas returned and when he found that his body had been burned, he entered into another man, and through him informed the people what a terrible mistake had been made. In atonement for their error, they worship him to this day. We have here an excellent example of the worldwide belief in the separable soul. The beliefs of the Ahir in this province are of a very primitive type, and Russell points to obvious survivals of totemism in the titles of some of the sub-castes[25].

DECCAN

In the Deccan[26] the Ahirs are known as Gavli, which is the equivalent of Goala, explained above. Here they are the worshippers of the ordinary Hindu gods, in particular, of Siva, and their priests are Jangams, of the Lingayat sect. Those known as Maratha Gopals worship the mother goddess, the Devi of Tuljapur in Hyderabad[27],

Kanhoba, Khandoba of Jajur in the Poona[28] district, and Mahasoba, with offering of sandal paste, flowers and food. Each family dedicates a she buffalo to Kanhoba, or Krishna, rears her with care, and does not load her or sell her milk and butter, but presents these to a Brahman. Further south in Kanara[29], the Gollir, a kindred tribe, worship Krishna, Siva under the form of the terrible Kala Bhairava, and his consort Parvati. The rites in honour of these deities are performed after the Lingayat rule.

GADDI GHOSI

In northern India, when Ahirs were converted to Islam, they were known as Ghosi ('a shouter', Sanskrit, Qhush, 'to shout after cattle') or Gaddi, and follow the Mohammaden rule, with some admixture of Dravidian animism. In Bombay they use many Hindu rites at marriage and birth, worship an image of the goddess Devi at the Dussehra festival and of Lakhshmi, the goddess of good luck, at the Dewali, when they also adore the Tulasi or holy basil plant, as at Holi they worship the castor-oil plant. Quite distinct from these are the Gaddi of the Panjab hills, of whose beliefs Mr. Rose has given a full account. They are nominally Hindus by religion, worshipping Siva by preference, and in addition to him, Nagas or serpent gods, Siddhas or deified ascetics, Birs or heroes, and Devis or Mother goddesses.

BIRS

In some cases the stone, where the home of the deity is, is replaced by the pillars of wood, blackened by constant offering of oil and butter (ghee). Such are the representatives of Birnath, 'hero lord', worshipped by the Ahir cowherds as a protector of their cattle; a worship apparently identical with the cults of the group of deities known as Bhangar Mal, Bangrabai or in her Hinduized form, as Devi, who are worshipped in various parts of the central provinces[30].

SACRIFICES

The Nagas, as representing the earth in serpent form, receive an offering of blessings, male kids and lambs, first fruits of all crops, incense, and small cakes. The Siddhas, as befits their wandering life, are presented with a sack, stick, crutch, sandals, and thick bread cakes. The Birs receive a he-goat, a thick woollen cloak, waistband, cap, and fine bread. They and the Siddhas are thus conceived as living a life in another world, much the same as that which they enjoyed on earth. The Devies (goddesses), as female deities, receive vermillion and trinkets (ornaments) loved by women, ardent spirits, and a goat. Women have their special worship of Kali, who is a Bir and the Numen of abortion. Kali is one of the chief Nagas or serpent gods. Like Siva, she is adored under the form of a sickle, which the god always carries when grazing his flocks.

AVTARS

Besides these objects of worship, there are the autars (Sanskrit 'avatara', an incarnation of one of the greater gods), a term here applied to the ghost of a person who had died childless and who, therefore, is malignant and causes sickness. To propitiate this spirit, the sick person puts on clothes which are specially made for him, and wears an image of the spirit round his neck. Thus clad, he worships the Sutar, an image of which is always kept near a stream. The clothes and image are worn as a memorial of the dead man, to keep him in mind and conciliate him.

BATAL

Besides these, they worship a host of malignant spirits— Batal, the spirits of rivers and streams; Yoginis, or rock spirits; Rakshanis and Banasats, who are here regarded as akin to the Yoginis, but are probably in their origin female demons (Sanskrit Rakshasi): and spirits of the wood (Sanskrit Vanaspati, 'king of the wood'). This would be quite in accordance with the belief of forest tribes, who naturally worship the spirits of trees, rocks, or rivers by which they are surrounded.

THE DEMON CHUNGU

Chungu is another demon who inhabits trees. He sucks the milk of cattle and is propitiated with an offering of a coconut— a frequent form of commutation of original human victim, the coconut representing the skull,— a plough handle, almonds and grapes—the usual farmer's gifts. His effigy is made in flour, and to this incense is offered. Gunga, the demon who causes cattle disease, is propitiated by setting aside a griddle cake of bread until the final offerings can be made. Then a piece of iron, something like a hockey stick, is made, and the deity, embodied in this, is taken into the cattle shed where he is worshipped by the sacred fire on a Thursday. A he-goat is killed and a few drops of the blood sprinkled on the iron. At the same time cakes are offered and some of them eaten by one member of the household, but not by more than one, or the scourge will not abate; the rest are buried in the earth. Every fourth year the deity is worshipped in the same fashion.

KAILU

Kali[31] is a demon, worshipped by the women after childbirth, by putting up a stone under a tree, which is sanctified by magic formulae (mantra) and then worshipped. A white goat, which may have black head, is offered to the demon by making an incision in its right ear and letting the blood fall on a white cloth, a good example of the commutation of the blood sacrifice. The woman eats some coarse sugar and dons the doth, which she must wear until it is worn out, thus maintaining a sacramental communion between the demon and herself. If any other woman should happen to wear the cloth, it would cause her diverts bodily ills. These facts regarding Gaddi religion are specially interesting, as being one of the best extant accounts of Indian animism as shown in the Panjab hills.

CATTLE-BREEDERS

Ahirs, popularly known as cattle-breeders, were according to the Census 1911 numbered, 11,965,500[32]. They are the descendants of Abhiras as of Scythians. These are taken next to the agriculturists because they occupy a similar social position, and also because, with the expansion of tillage, the grazing area is getting restricted and a good many of the formerly roving castes settled down to cultivation. The prominent place assigned to cattle in the Suktas and the universal veneration of the Brahminic community for the cow bear testimony to the antiquity as to the honourable character of the calling, and in upper India the cattle-breeder ranks almost as high as the cultivator. This is not invariably the case, however. The wandering life arouses suspicions of unorthodox feeding and intercourse generally. Then, too, the use of the ox in agriculture now vies in importance with that of the cow in domestic life; but the supply of the indispensable bullock cannot be kept up without surgical operations repugnant to the conventional notions of purity and respect for animal life. Furthermore, the supply of milk for the home is, by all Vedic tradition, commendable, but the sale of dairy produce as a trade entails relegation to a lower position. In older times, however, the Abhira, or cow herding tribes, were powerful in the Satpura[33], the south Ganges valley[34] and even the lower positions of Nepal, and founded dynasties which were overthrown by the Gond in the first named tract and by the Kirata in the last. It is within living memory the Baigas (tribe) of central India had been painfully compelled by authority to abandon shifting cultivation (burning of forest strips and sowing of seeds in the fertilising ashes) and move from the axe to the plough and be traditionally known as wounder of Mother Earth. Most of the two million Gonds and Kirata (tribes retain their primitive ways, even though their tribal chiefs were assimilated many centuries ago into the feudal aristocracy (Francis Watson, *A Concise History of India* pp. 17, 21). The leading tribc seem to have been of western origin, and are supposed to have entered India long after the Vedic Arya. In upper India they go by the name of Ahir, derived from the Abhira, their ancestor just mentioned, a term which was applied by some Sanskrit authors to all tribes of the lower classes throughout the northwest. Under this name they are spread in considerable numbers all over Rajputana, Malwa, the south-eastern Panjab, the upper Gangetic Valley and Bihar. To the east, the lack of wide stretches of open pasture has prevented the formation and maintenance of a strong and well-organised pastoral community, so a number of distinct and generally not very large subdivisions are grouped under the general title of Goala, recruited from many local castes of lower origin than the pastoral bodies of the north. Many of them, too, are as much agriculturists as cattle-breeders. The same may be said, also, of the Ahir themselves, in the Panjab, where they are amongst the most successful and enterprising cultivators of the province. They have never, it is true, achieved a dominant position anywhere in modern times, but the Jat and Gujjar treat them as equals, except, of course, in regard to intermarriage. According to the Census, about half of the total number of Ahirs are found in Agra, Oudh and Bihar. They are said to have migrated to those regions from the plain of Kachchh, west Rajputana and Kathiavad. Assuming their connection with these parts, especially the last named, a basis will be found for their invariable assertion in the Gangetic region that the cradle of the Ahir is Mathura. Few legends are wider: the Gopi, or milkmaids of the Vraj[35] district; and the Jaduvansi[36] line, headed by Krishna himself, found its second home, after its expulsion from Mathura, at Dwarka[37] and in the north of Marvad[38], the very tract inhabited by the Ahirs before they entered Hindustan.

Traditional descent from the Mathura Jaduvansi is not, however, confined to the Ahir of the north, but it is claimed by the Gaura and other cowherds of Orissa, and even by some far to the south of the Arya pale. Except in the Panjab, the Ahirs enjoy but a poor reputation as a husbandman, though everywhere they are admitted being the company for the higher peasantry. This, however, may be, as in the case of the Gujjars in those parts, a question of policy with a side glance towards the village cattle, which are apt to stay into the Ahir's herd without their rightful owners' knowledge or consent.

THE GAULI AHIRS

The Gauli of the west Central Provinces and north Dakkan (Deccan) are the descendants of the tribes which, as just mentioned, once ruled the Satpura[39] from Khandesh[40] and the Sahyadri[41], to near Sauger[42], and were only expelled by the Gonds in the 16th century. As they are mentioned in the Nasik cave inscriptions, they must have been long established in their dominion. Alongside of them is the Govari (Godavari) caste, which has no trace of immigration either in nomenclature or tradition. In the Chhattisgarh[43] country to the east, comes the Ravat, another cattle-breeding caste of long standing in that region. The two last mentioned castes which in 1891 numbered about 350,000 persons, do not appear at all in the returns for 1901, so they have probably been compiled under Ahir or some other general title. Two other cattle-breeding castes of upper India may be mentioned, the Ghosi, an offshoot of the Ahir, or as some think, of the Gujjar, which has been converted to Islam. They occupy a comparatively low position, and near the large towns confine their attention to the dairy side of their occupation. The other caste is the Rabari of Rajputana and the Gujarat peninsulas. They are of Marvad origin but wandered to the coast, and now breed both cattle and camels, and some of them even became shepherds. In the north they confine their trade to camels. In the Deccan, the Gauli, and further south, the cultivator generally breeds his own cattle, and only one caste devoted to this occupation appears in the return. This is the Kannaydiyan, a small body, of apparently upland origin. The Golla of the Telugu and Kanarese tracts are thoroughly local castes, but having become Brahmanised, cast back to Mathura and the Gopi. Most of them are settled in villages, but one section in Mysore is still nomadic during the open season, and does not intermarry with the others. In Mysore it used to be the duty or privilege of the Goala State treasurer, in transit and the official now responsible for sending off the remittance was still occasionally called by that name, albeit, he may be a Brahman or Muslim.

The Ahirs are a caste of cowherds, milkers, and cattle-breeders widely dispersed across the Gangetic Plain, especially in the more easternly part (Bihar, Bengal, and eastern Madya Pradesh). The Ahirs must number well over a million today: they numbered 750,000 in the Central Provinces and Berar in 1911, ranking as the sixth largest caste in terms of numbers. In many castes there is a separate division of Ahirs, such as the Ahir Sunars, Sutars, Lohars, Shimpis, Salic, Guraos, and Kolis. The name "Ahir" is derived from "Abhira", tribe mentioned several times in inscriptions and the Hindu sacred books. "Goala", meaning a cowherd or "a protector of cows", is now used in Madhya Pradesh State to signify a dairy worker. Their ethnonyms are Gahra, Faolan, Goeli, Goala, Golkar, Mahakuland.

AHIR DIALECTS

Some dialects named after the Abhira or Ahirs are still spoken. One, known as Ahirwati, is spoken in the Rohta, Rawats and Gurgaon districts, the Panjab, and near Delhi. The Malwi dialect of Rajasthani is also known as Ahiri; there is a dialect of Gujarati called Khandeshi also known as Ahirani. These linguistic survivals are indications that the Ahirs were early settlers in the Delhi country of the Panjab, and in Malwa and Khandesh.

The Ahir were apparently one of the immigrant tribes from central Asia who entered India during the early Christian era. The Ahirs have been for centuries a purely occupational caste, mainly recruited from the indigenous tribes. As cattle must graze in the forest during hot weather, there is a close relationship between Ahirs and many of the forest tribes. Many Ahirs in Mandla, for example, are barely considered Hindus, because they live in Gond village (a forest tribe).

Only about 30 per cent of the Ahirs are still occupied in breeding cattle and dealing in milk and butter. About 4 per cent are domestic servant, and nearly all the remainder were cultivators and labourers in 1931. Formerly, the Ahirs had the exclusive right to milk cows, so that on all occasions an Ahir had to be hired for this purpose even by the lowest caste.

The caste has exogamous sections, which are of the usual low caste type, with titular or totemistic names. The marriage of persons belonging to the same section and of first cousins is prohibited. A man may marry his wife's younger sister while his wife is living. The practice of exchanging girls between families is permissible.

The Ahir have a special relation to the Hindu religion owing to their association with the sacred cow, which is itself revered as goddess. Among the special deities of the Ahirs is Kharsk Deo, who is always located at the place of assembly of the cattle. Mater Deo is the god of the pen. A favourite saint is Haridas Baba. The main festival is the Diwali, falling about the beginning of November. All Ahirs observe this feast by illuminating their houses with many small saucer-lamps and with fireworks.

GURUGAON AHIRS

Ahirs are the characteristic tribe of Rewari and are numerous also in the northern part of Gurugaon; they are found too in the following Parganahs: Bahror in Alwar, Kanaund and Narnaul in Haryana, Kanti in Nabha, Mudawar and Kot-Kasim in Jaipur; all these Parganahs are in the immediate proximity of Rewari. All the Rewari Ahirs look upon Rao Taj Singh's family, now represented by Rao Lal Singh and Rao Balbir Singh as their natural leaders. They are splendid cultivators, hard-working, frugal and orderly. It is difficult to ascertain anything very definite as to their origin and history, but their traditions state that in Rewari they supplanted Rajputs, and in two villages impoverished representatives of the old Rajput owners still linger. Ahirs are almost all Hindus.

REFERENCES

1. Muttra, city and district headquarter of the same name, west Uttar Pradesh, on the Jamuna river.
2. A great adherent of the Ahir religion.
3. *Encyclopaedia of Religion and Ethics*, Vol. I, J. Hastings, p. 232.
4. The Satvahanas faded from the scene towards the end of the third century A.D. and it was under their successors, the Vakatakas of Berar, that the closer links developed with the Gupta Empire. *(A Concise History of India,* Francis Wilson, pp. 71-76.)
5. *Collier's Encyclopedia*, Vol. 5, p. 525.
6. *The Encyclopedia of Britannica*, Vol. I, p.162.
7. *Encyclopaedia of Religion and Ethics*, Vol. 3&4, p. 231.
8. *Panjab Castes,* Denzil Abbetson, p. 202, (1883).
9. A Hindu deity, *Encyclopedia of Britannica,* Vol. 7, p. 7a.
10. On the Vaishnavite side the wide open, mystically sensuous and powerfully pervasive role of Krishna in Indian religion, can be dated from this time *(A Concise History of India)* Francis Waston, p. 94.
11. (Sanskrit Black) A very popular deity in Hinduism, the 8th *Avtar* or incarnation of Vishnu.

12. Buchanan Hamilton, *Eastern India,* Vol. I, p. 194.
13. *Golden Bough*, Frazer, Vol. 11, p. 366. ff.
14. *North Indian Notes and Queries*, p. 38.
15. *Archaeological Survey of India*, Vol. VII, p. 79. ff.
16. Delhi.
17. District Headquarters, in west Bihar.
18. District Headquarters, south-east Uttar Pradesh.
19. District Headquarters, east Uttar Pradesh.
20. *The People of India,* Sir Herbert-Risley, p. 63.
21. District Headquarters, north Uttar Pradesh.
22. A Hindu deity.
23. *Encyclopedia of Religion and Ethics*, Vol. I, J. Hastings, p. 233.
24. Formerly Benares city (population 707,772 (1981), Uttar Pradesh state, north central India on the Ganges River. The holiest Hindu city, it has c. 1500 temples, palaces and shrines. Steps lead to the sacred Ganges, where Hindus bathe. About one million pilgrims visit the city annually. Buddha is said to have begun preaching nearby. The Mosque of Aurangzeb, on the city's highest ground, is the most notable building of India's Mughal period. The city is also known for its silk brocades and brassware.
25. *Encyclopedia of Religion and Ethics*, Vol. I, J. Hastings, p. 233.
26. Deccan Plateau, triangular tableland covering most of peninsular India.
27. Hyderabad Deccan, railway station and city of India.
28. District Central Bombay, India, on west edge of Deccan Plateau.
29. Karnataka region of south Deccan Plateau.
30. *Tribe and Castes,* Vol. I, p. 63 and Vol. V, p. 12 Crook.
31. Hindi: The Black Ane, an important Hindu goddess, popular in Hinduism and Tantra, associated with destructive force.
32. This census does not cover the then whole population of the Ahirs. Many were left over.
33. A line of hills in central India, south of the Narmada River.
34. A rich alluvial tract in Uttar Pradesh, between the Ganges and the Jamuna rivers.
35. Place in Uttar Pradesh, connected with Lord Krishna.
36. The clan to which Krishna belonged.
37. A town in Jamnagar district, Gujarat state, port on the Arabian Sea.
38. North of Jodhpur.
39. Line of hills in Central India, south of the Narmada River.
40. Jalgaon district.

41. Nasik district, Bombay state, on the upper Godavari River.
42. A district, north of Madhya Pradesh, India.
43. Chhattisgarh, Eastern States agency, Headquarters at Raipur.

BIBLIOGRAPHY

Blunt, E.A.H. (1931). *The Caste System of Northern India*. London: Oxford University Press. Reprint. 1969. Delhi: S. Chand.

Buchanan, Hamilton. *Eastern India,* Vol. 1, p. 194 f.

Bombay Gazetteer, Vol. XV. Pt. Vol. 1, p. 297, Vol. XVII, pp. 151-184.

Crook. *Popular Religion and Folklore,* Vol. 11, p. 160.

Crook. *Tribes and Castes,* Vol. 1, p. 163.

Colliers's Encyclopedia, Vol. 5.

Darling, Malcolm (1947). *The Panjab Peasant in Prosperity and Debt*. 4th ed. Bombay: Oxford University Press. Reprint 1977. New Delhi.

For Bengal Dalton-Descriptive Ethnology. p. 314 f.

Galt-Bengal Census 1901. Vol. 1, p. 197.

PASB, Vol. 1, p. 42.

Risley. *Tribes and Castes,* Vol. 1, p. 197.

Rose, H.A. (1911). A *Glossary of the Tribes and Castes of the Panjab and North-West Frontier Provinces,* Vol. I, II, III, Reprint. 1970. Patiala Languages Department, Panjab.

Russell, R.V. and Hira, Lal. *Ahir in the Tribes and Castes of the Central Provinces of India*, Vol. 2, 18:38. Nagpur: Government Printing Press. Reprint. 1969. Oesterhout; Anthropological Publications.

Siraj-ul-Hassan, Syad (1920). "Ahirs", *Castes and Tribes of H.E.H. the Nizam's Dominions,* Vol. 1, pp. 1-7. Bombay: Reprint. 1990.

The Gujjars (Gurjaras)
(Descendants of Scythians and Huns)

5

ORIGIN

Gujjar (Sanskrit Gurjara), the country now known as North Gujarat and Rajputana which tell little of a tribe of the same name entering India in the train of the Huns[1]. A tribe of cultivators, herdsmen, which at the Census of 1901, numbered 2,103,023, found in the largest numbers in the Panjab, Rajputana, Uttar Pradesh, and Kashmir. The theory of Cunningham, quoted by Dr. Bhandarkar[2] that they are connected with the Yueh-chi tribe of Central Asia, afterward now as that theory, is rejected by Risley[3] on the ground that the latter are almost certainly of the brachycephalic type, while the Gujjar is dolichocephalic. He, therefore, includes them in what he calls the 'Indo Aryan Branch'. It is, however, certain that during the first five centuries A.D. hosts of the Scythian and Hun invaders of north India became absorbed in the indigenous population, and were adopted into Hinduism[4], in their purest form at present they seem to be found in Kashmir[5], where he does not regard them as 'high Arhan', found some with eyes lighter in colour than are common among other tribes of the country. There is much in the physique and customs of the Gujjars which renders it probable that they are connected with Central Asian tribes[6].

THE CONTROVERSY

The origin of the Gujjars is a subject of keen controversy. Many scholars hold the view that the Gujjars were a foreign people who came to India along with the Huns, and their gradual advance from the Panjab, through Rajputana into Gujarat, is marked by the various localities that still bear their names. This view is, however, contested by others who make Gujjars to be primarily the name of a country whose inhabitants were naturally known as Gujjars. It has been suggested that the various geographical units now called Gujarat, were originally parts of a large homogeneous country named Gujjaradesa under the political authority of its own kings, and while isolated fragments of it have retained the old name others have lost it. This view has not, however, met with the general acceptance. For a while there is no evidence that the mighty empire of the Pratiharas had a common geographical name and a homogeneous character as distinguished from the rest of India, several parts of it have retained distinct names throughout the duration of that empire and even later. The various localities clearly associated in old times with the name Gujjar and the present geographical distribution of the people called Gujjar, undoubtedly, favour the view that the term primarily denoted a people and the countries derived their names from them. The Malavas offer an exact analogy to the Gujjars in this respect. But though we can be more or less sure that the Gujjars were originally the name of a people, there is no definite evidence that they were foreigners, and came to India in Historical times in the wake of the Huns, the Kushans or other foreign hordes. Their sudden rise into prominence in the sixth century A.D., and the attempt of some of their royal dynasties to fabricate a mythical origin, no doubt lends colour to this view. But these cannot be relied upon as definite evidence, and we may cite analogous instances of the Kalachuris[7] and the Chandellas[8]. On the whole this question must be left open till more definite evidence is available.

THE GUJJARS

The Gujjars are the eighth largest caste in the Panjab, only the Jats, Rajputs, and Pathans among dominant castes, the mixed caste of Arains, the Brahmans, Chamars, and Chuhras exceeding them in point of number. They are identified by A.G. General Cunningham with the Kushan or Yuchi or Tochari, a tribe of Eastern Tartars[9]. About a century before Christ their chief conquered Kabul[10] and Peshawar country; while his son Hima Kadphises, so well-known to the Panjab numismatologist, extended his sway over the whole of Upper Panjab and the banks of the Jamuna as far down as Mathura and the Vindhyas, and his successor, the no less familiar king Kanishka, the first Buddhist Indo-Scythian Prince, annexed Kashmir to the kingdom of Kuchari. These Kuchari or Kushan are the Kespeiraei of Ptolemy; and in the middle of the second century of our era, Kaspeira, Kasyapura, or Multan, was one of their chief cities. Probably about the beginning of the 3rd century A.D., the attacks of the white Huns recalled the last king of the united Yuchi to the west, and he left his son in charge of an independent province whose capital was fixed at Peshawar; and from that time the Yuchi of Kabul are known as the Great Yuchi, and those of the Panjab as the Kate or Little Yuchi. Before the end of the 3rd century A.D. a portion of the Gujjars had begun to move southwards down the Indus and were shortly afterwards separated from their northern brethren by Indo-Scythian wave from the north. In the middle of the 5th century there was a Gujjar kingdom in south-western Rajputana, whence they were driven by the Balas into Gujarat of the Bombay Presidency; and about the end of the 9th century, Ala Khan, the Gujjar king of Jammu, coded the corresponding very nearly with the Gujarat district, to the king of Kashmir. The town of Gujarat is said to have been restored by Ali Khan, Gujjar in the time of Akbar the grounds for General Cunningham's identification will be found in full detail at pages 61 to 82 of Vol. II of the *Archaeological Reports*.

Distribution

The present distribution of the Gujjars in India is thus described by General Cunningham: "At the present day the Gujjars are found in great number in every part of the northwest of India, from the Indus to the Ganges, and from the Hazara mountain, Pakistan, to the peninsula of Gujarat. They are specially numerous along the banks of the Upper Jamuna, near Jagadri and Buriya, and in the Sahranpur district, which during the last century was actually called Gujarat. To the east they occupy the petty state of Samptar in Bundelkhand, and one of the northern districts of Gwalior, which is still called Gujjargarh. They are found only in small bodies and much scattered throughout Eastern Rajputana and Gwalior; but they are more numerous in the western states, and specially towards Gujarat, where they form a large part of the population. The Rajas of Rewari to the south of Delhi are Gujjars. In the southern Panjab, they are thinly scattered, but their numbers increase rapidly towards the north, where they have given their name to several important places, such as Gujjaranwala in the Rechana-Doab, Gujarat in the Chaj Doab, and Gujjar Khan in the Sindh Sagar Doab. They are numerous about jahlam and Hassan Abdal and throughout the Hazara districts; and they are also found in considerable numbers in the Dardu districts of Chilas, Kohli, and Palas, to the east of the Indus, and in the contiguous districts to the west of the river.

The Lower Ranges

In the Panjab, they essentially belong to the lower ranges and sub-montane tracts; and though they have spread down the Jamna in considerable numbers, they are almost confined to the riverine lowlands. In the higher mountains they are almost unknown. Gujarat is still their stronghold, and in that district they form 13% per cent of the total population. There alone have they retained their dominant position. Throughout the Salt Range Tract, and under the eastern hills also, they are the oldest inhabitants among the tribes now settled there; but in the west the Gakkhars, Janjuas, and Pathans, and in the east the Rajputs have always been too strong for them, and long ago deprived them of political importance. In the Peshawar district almost all herdsmen are called a Gujjar, and it may be that some of these, who are thus, returned are not true Gujjars by race[11]. But throughout the hill country of Jammu, Chibhal, and Hazara, and away in the independent territory lying to the north of Peshawar as far as the Swat River, true Gujjar herdsmen are found in great numbers, all possessing a common speech, which is a Hindi dialect quite distinct from the Panjabi or Pashto current in those parts. Here they are a purely pastoral and almost nomad race, taking their herds up into the higher ranges in summer and descending with them into valleys during the cold weather; and it may be said that the Gujjar is a cultivator only in the plains. Even there, he is a bad cultivator, and more given to keeping cattle than to following the plough.

The Gujjar Colonisation

It is impossible without further investigation to fix the date of the Gujjar colonisation of the lower districts. They are almost exclusively Muslims except in the Jammu districts and Hoshiarpur, and they must, therefore, have entered those districts before the conversion of the great mass of the caste. Balachaur, Garhshankar and Nurpur Bedi, Hoshiarpur district have lot of population of the Gujjars community. Few of them became Sikhs, but majority of them are Hindus. It is well-known in the area, as recently told by Dila Ram Gujjar of village Jhagrian, 6 miles west of Nurpur Bedi, that Guru Gobind Singh, visited their village and asked for some recruits for his army. But the unfortunate elders of that village refused to give any help to the Guru, who was fighting against the Muslim tyranny, saying that "we hardly make our both ends meet, by cutting grass to feed our cattle". The Guru said, "Alright!

You will remain in this condition." The villagers are of the firm view that Guru's curse is keeping them in poverty. The Jats of the adjoining area, bought land and are very successful farmers, whereas the local Gujjars either keep the cattle or work as labourers in the grain markets of the Panjab.

Conversion to Islam

The Jalandhar Gujjars date their conversion forms the time of Aurangzeb, a very probable date. The Firozpur Gujjars say that they came from Darangar in the south of India, that they moved thence to Rania in Sirsa, and again to Firozpur *via* Kasur. The Muslim Gujjars of all the eastern half of the province still retain more of their Hindu customs than do the majority of their converted neighbours, their women, for instance, wearing petticoat instead of drawers, and red instead of blue. It is noticeable that Gujarat is to the Gujjars what Bhatner and Bhattiana are to the Bhatti, a place to which there is a traditional tendency to refer their origin.

Strong People

The Gujjar is a fine stalwart fellow, of precisely the same physical type as the Jat; and the theory of aboriginal descent which has sometimes been propounded, is conclusively negatived by his caste of countenance. He is of the same social standing as the Jat, or perhaps slightly inferior; but the two eat and drink in common without any scruple and the proverb says; "The Jat, Gujjar, Ahir, and Gola are all four hail fellows well met." But he is far inferior in both personal character and repute to the Jat. He is lazy to a degree, and a wretched cultivator; his women, though not secluded, will not do field-work save of the lightest kind; while his fondness for cattle extends to those of other people. The difference between a Gujjar and a Rajput cattle thief was once explained thus by a Jat: "The Rajput will steal your buffalo. But he will not send his father to say he knows where it is and will get it back for Rs. 20, and then keep the Rs. 20 and the buffalo too. The Gujjar will." The Gujjars have been turbulent throughout the history of the Panjab; they were a constant thorn in the side of the Delhi Emperors and are still ever ready to take advantage of any loosening of the bonds of discipline to attack and plunder their neighbours. Their character as expressed in the proverbial wisdom of the countryside is not a high one: "A desert is better than a Gujjar: wherever you see a Gujjar, hit him." Again: "The dog and the cat two, the Rangar and the Gujjar two; if it were not for these four one might sleep with one's door open;" so "The dog, the monkey, and the Gujjar change their minds at every step" and "when all other castes are dead making friends with a Gujjar." As Mr. Maconachie remarks; "Though the Gujjar possesses two qualifications of a highlander, a hilly home and constant desire for other people's cattle. He never seems to have had the love of gifting and the character for manly independence which distinguishes this class elsewhere. On the contrary, he is generally a mean sneaking cowardly fellow; and I do not know that he improves much with the march of civilisation, though of course there are exceptions; men who have given up the traditions of the tribe so far as to recognize the advantage of being honest generally."

ALL ENDURING RACE

Such is the Gujjar of the Jamna districts[12]. But further west his character would seem to be higher. Major Wace describes the Gujjars of Hazara "a simple all enduring race, thrifty and industrious, with no ambition but to be left alone in peace with their cattle and fields; and many of them are fine men in every way." Mr. Thomson says that the Gujjars of Jhelam are the best farmers in the district (perhaps not excessive praise in a district held by Gakkhars, Awans, and Rajputs), though the Maliar or Arain is a better market gardener; and that they are quiet and industrious more likeable than (Salt-Ranger) Jats, but with few attractive qualities. Mr. Steedman gives a similar account of the Gujjars of Rawalpindi, calling them "excellent cultivators". So the Gujjars of Hoshiarpur are said to be "a quiet and well-behaved set". "In Jalandhar", Sir Richard Temple describes, "Here as elsewhere of pastoral habits, but more industrious and less predatory than usual;" and Mr. Barkley writes: "At present, they are as little given to crime as any other class in the agricultural population. It is still generally true that they occupy themselves more with grazing than with agriculture; but this is by no means invariably the case." But in Firozpur again Mr. Brandreth describes them as "unwilling cultivators, and greatly addicted to thieving", and gives instances of their criminal propensities. Thus it would appear that the further the Gujjar moves from his native hills, the more he deteriorates and the more unpleasant he makes himself to his neighbours. The following description of the Gujjars of Kangra by Mr. Barnes is both graphic and interesting.

Gujjars of Kangra

The Gujjars of the hills are quite unlike the caste of the same designation in the plains. There they are known as an idle, worthless and thieving race, rejoicing in waste, and enemies to cultivation and improvement; but above and below, they are both addicted to pastoral habits. In the hills, the Gujjars are exclusively a pastoral tribe, they cultivate scarcely at all. The Gaddis keep flocks of sheep and goats and the Gujjar's wealth consists of buffaloes. These people live in the skirts of the forests, and maintain their existence exclusively by the sale of the milk, ghee, and other produce of their herds. The men graze the cattle, and frequently lie out for weeks in the weeds tending their herds. The women go to the markets every morning with baskets on their heads, with little earthen pots filled with milk, buttermilk and ghee, each of these pots containing the proportion required for a day's meal. During the hot weather the Gujjars usually drive their herds to the upper range, where the buffaloes rejoice in the rich grass which the rains bring forth, and at the same time attain condition from the temperate climate and the immunity from venomous flies which torment their existence in the plains. The Gujjars are a fine, manly race, with peculiar and handsome features. They are mild and inoffensive in manner, and in these hills are not distinguished by the bad pre-eminence which attaches to their race in the plains. They are never known to thieve. Their women are supposed to be not very scrupulous. Their habits of frequenting public markets and carrying about their stock for sale unaccompanied by their husbands undoubtedly expose them to great temptations; and the imputations against their character are too well founded. They are tall, well-grown women, and may be seen every morning entering the bazaars of the hill towns, returning home about the afternoon with their baskets emptied of their treasures. The Gujjars are found all over the district. They abound particularly about Jawalamukhi, Tira, and Nadaun. There are some Hindu Gujjars especially towards Mandi but they are a small sect, compared to the Mussalmans.

THE ETHNIC STOCK

It has been suggested, and is held by many, that Jats and Gujjars, and perhaps Ahirs also, are all of one ethnic stock; and this because there is a close communion between them. It may be that they are the same in their far distant origin. They must have either entered India at different times or settled in separate parts and the reason for thinking so is precisely because they eat and smoke together. In the case of Jat and Rajput, the reason for differentiation is obvious, the latter being of higher rank than the former. But the social standing of Jats, Gujjars, and Ahirs being practically identical, why they should ever have separated if they were once the same? It is, however, possible that the Jats were the camel graziers and husbandmen, the Gujjars the cowherds of the hills, and the Ahirs, the cowherds of the plains. If this be so, they afford a classification by occupation of the yeoman class, which fills up the gap between and is absolutely continuous with the similar classification of the castes above them as Brahmans, Banyas, and Rajputs and of the castes below them as Tarkhans, Chamars and so forth. But we must know more of the early distribution of the tribes before we can have any opinion on the subject. It has been noticed by the early historians that there was a connection between the migrations and location of Gujjars and Rajputs which has struck generally as being more than accidental but the subject needs an immense deal of work upon it before can be said to be even ready for drawing conclusions.

Gujjar Tribes

The Gujjar tribes and clans appear to be very numerous, and apparently new local sub-divisions have sprung up in many places. Still the distribution of the main tribes for which figures have been given, is far more general than is the case with other castes of equal importance. The figures only include 47 per cent of the Gujjars of the Province; but they comprise 69 per cent of those of Gujarat, and include most of the great original tribes. The Khatana and Chechi far surpass the other in number.

RELIGION

In religion, the Gujjars of the Panjab have been largely converted to Islam, and not far from half of their total number now follow that faith. In the United Provinces and Rajputana they are still largely Hindu. In the western districts of the United Provinces they are usually worshippers of Siva and of the Sakti, or Mother goddesses, and in particular of Sitala Bhavani, who controls smallpox. They also worship the local village gods, such as Chamar, and two tribal deities, Pyareji and Baba Sabha Ram. The latter are deified heroes of the tribe.

The Mussalman branch of the tribe, in spite of their conversion, continue to follow many of the animistic practices of their Hindu forefathers, such as the ceremony of waving lights over a bride to scare evil spirits. They consult Brahman astrologers to fix lucky times for domestic rites; and they worship not so much Allah as a host of deified heroes and saints, such as Ghazi Miyan, the saint of Bahraich in Oudh, Madar Sahib, and other martyrs of the faith. In some parts of the Panjab, members of the tribe claim the hereditary power of wonder-working and curing disease. The head of one sept in the Jhelam district pretends to cure a skin disease which causes baldness, by pulling out a single hair from the head of the patient. He practises only on one Sunday in the month, and must accept no fee, because that condition was imposed by the Faqir who conferred the power upon his ancestor many generations ago (Rose, i.162). A branch of the tribe in the Hazara district shows that its conversion to Islam is recent and incomplete, by the retention of Hindu rules of eating, keeping strictly for personal use the vessels employed in cooking, practising purification before prayer, and praying with the hands downwards instead of upwards, as is the usual custom with Mohammaden[13]. The Gujjars in the Bharatpur State of Rajputana have a curious custom of making a cow of cow-dung, covering it with cotton, and then going through a rite of symbolical slaughter of the image. This seems to imply some form of totemistic communion, or a commutation of the actual killing of the sacred animal. The latter explanation is accepted by the neighbouring tribes, who consider that the Gujjars are degraded by the rite[14]. In western part of India many of the tribe have joined the Jain community, while others follow the Vaisnava Vallabhacharya sect[15].

SHRINE OF PYAREJI

Pyareji, whose shrine is in the Saharanpur district, flourished early in the 17th century A.D. He was one of the marvellous children of the folk tales, and when he grew up, the tribe was severely afflicted by the ghosts of certain Brahman whom they had slain by Pyareji, who had by that time acquired saintly powers exercised the evil spirits, and the reputation which he thus acquired earned for him Divine Honours. The management of his shrine still remains in the hands of his descendants, who have now joined the Vaisnavite sect. Baba Sabha Ram was another worthy of the same class who is worshipped at a shrine on the banks of the Jamna, in the Ambala District. The Panjab Gujjars are especially devoted to the cult of the Saint-Sarwar[16], whose shrine is at the Sakhi-Sarwar[17].

Some of the Gujjars of Gasrshanker Tehsil of Hoshiarpur district, Nurpur Bedi Tehsil of Ropar and Balachaur Tehsil of

Nawanshahr district became Sikhs during the period of Guru Gobind Singh and after that. The spirit of the "Khalsa" in them has wonderfully raised their social status amongst their Hindu brothers. Even the Hindu Gujjars are following the Sikh customs on the occasion of marriages and deaths, finding them to be simpler than the Hindu rites. The Gujjars of Karura village in Nurpur Bedi Tehsil still lament over the fact that Guru Gobind Singh Ji visited their village and asked for some jawans for the Khalsa Army. The cunning villagers brought forward five, half-mad youths, and some of them had broken limbs. These youths were worthless for their parents. Guruji smilingly accepted them and said, "Alright, there shall always be some jawans like them in this village." The Guru's word is still proving true and there are always some mentally sick and deformed bodied youths in this village. This story was told by the people of those days to the succeeding generations. The present day villagers feel that their ancestors should have given able-bodied jawans to the Guru and if they had become Sikhs in those days on the persuasion of the Guru, his blessings would have been showered on them.

COMING INTO PROMINENCE

The Gujjars came into prominence about the second half of the 6th century A.D. No doubt they took advantage of the downfall of the Gupta empire to establish their political authority. Their most important kingdom was founded in the heart of Rajputana near Jodhpur[18], and this region to be called after the state, now known as Gujarat[19], was not called by that name till a much later period. In addition to these two important regions called after the Gurjaras (Gujjars), there are other localities associated with the name of this people. There are, for example, place-names like Gujjaranwala[20], Gujarat and Gujjar-Khan[21] in the Panjab. The district of Saharanpur also called Gujarat in the 18th century, and one of the northern districts of Gwalior is still called Gujjargarh.

These place-names indicate that the Gujjars had quite a large number of settlements in different directions which is corroborated by the present distribution of Gujjars, who may be regarded as the modern representatives of the old Gujjars. They are fairly numerous in the western Himalayas, the Panjab, Uttar Pradesh and western Rajputana and are also found in the hilly country beyond the Indus. They constitute a large part of the population of Gujarat, but are not found to the south of the Satpura Mountains.

HARICHANDRA

The earliest Gurjara kingdom, known so far, is that founded by Harichandra in the modern Jodhpur state in Rajputana, about the middle of the 6th century A.D. Harichandra was a Brahaman, versed in the Vedas and other Shastras. He had two wives. The sons, born of his Brahman wife, became Pratihara Brahmans, while those born of his Kshatriya wife became the founder of the royal line of the Pratiharas. It is significant that the Kshatriya wife Bhadra is called queen while no such royal epithet was given to his Brahman wife. It seems that Harichandra followed peaceful Brahmanical pursuits in his early life, but when, after the fall of the Gupta empire and of the empires of Mihirakula and Yasodharman, northern India presented a favourable field for military enterprise, he gave up the Shastras (scriptures) for the Shastra (arms), as many other have done both before and after him. He proved successful and founded a kingdom.

Harichandra had four sons by queen Bhadra, *viz.* Bhogabhata, Kakka, Rajjila and Dadda. They conquered and fortified Mandavyapura (Mandor, five miles to the north of Jodhpur) which presumably became their capital. The four sons of Harichandra are described as fit to hold separate principality. But nothing is known about the first two. The third Rajjila ruled in Mandavyapura. He was succeeded by his son Narabhata and the latter by his son Bagabhata, who fixed his permanent capital at Medantaka[22]. Harichandra and his three successors mentioned above, probably ruled between c. 550 and 640 A.D. Five more generations of this family, comprising ten kings, ruled during the next two hundred years.

THE GUJJARS OF NANDIPURI[23]

In addition to the kingdom in Rajputana, there was another principality in the region round Broach[24] ruled over by Gurjara chiefs. The four earliest records of the family, dated between 629 to 641 A.D., were issued by a king named Dadda II Prasantaraga, son of Vitaraga Jayabhata I, and grandson of Dada I. It appears from this records that his principality extended from the river Mahi[25] in the north to the Kim in the south, and from the sea-coast in the west to the borders of Malwa and Khandesh in the east. As all the grants were issued from Nandipuri, that was probably the capital of the family. It has been identified by Huhiar with Broach and by Bhagwanlal Indraji with Nanded, situated on the Karjan River in the Rajpipla State.

DADA I

As Dada I is expressly said to have been born in the family of the Gurjaras Kings, and must have flourished in the last quarter of the 6th century A.D. He may be identified with Dadda, the youngest son of Harichandra, the founder of the main Gurjara family mentioned above. As noted above, all the four sons of Harichandra described as fit to bear the burdens of the earth, and it is likely that while the third son Rajjila ruled near Jodhpur, the three other sons also established separate principal Gurjara kingdom in Malwa, with its capital at Avanti, at a somewhat later date, and as the rulers called themselves Pratiharas, they might have been descended from one of the sons of Harichandra. It is, however, difficult to say whether Dada I himself advanced as far as Broach, or whether the vast intervening region was conquered by the Gurjaras. Besides, the territory over which this dynasty ruled was included in the dominions of the Kalachuri[26] kings Sankaragana and Buddharaja. If, therefore, that Dada I founded this principality in the last quarter of the 6th century A.D. It would be principality somewhere in southern Rajputana and it was only after the collapse of the Kalachuri power that he or his son occupied Broach and the district around it. It is not improbable that the Gurjaras sought the aid of Pulakesin[27] and voluntarily submitted to him in order to overpower the Kalachuris. It is probably by this means that the Gurjaras occupied their territories in Gujarat not long after 610 A.D., and eventually Malwa, or at least a large portion of it, also passed into their hands.

SAMANTAS

Dada I is said to have been overthrown by some hostile Nagas, and it is, therefore, likely that he carved out a principality by ejecting some Branch of the Naga tribe. Dada and his successors are called Samantas or feudatories, and non-royal titles are given to them in their records. On the other hand, these grants do not refer to any paramount sovereign. It may be presumed, therefore, that they owed allegiance to the main Gujjar ruling family in Rajputana or to the Chalukyas.

GURJARAS

The territory which today we call Rajputana was not known by this name in ancient times. In the 10th century A.D., the whole or at least a large part of it was called Gurjaras, an older and Sanskritised form of Gujarat. As we have seen above, the Gurjaras set up one or more principalities in Rajputana as early as the 6th century A.D., and Hiuen Tsang visited a kingdom in this area which he called Ku-che-le or Gurjara. It is probable, therefore, that the name Gurjara was applied to Rajputana as early as the 6th or 7th century A.D.

But although it cannot be traced the name of the locality as Rajputana at this early period, there already settled a number of clans or tribes who became famous as Rajputs in later days. These were the Pratiharas, the Guhilots[28], the Chapotakatas[29] and the Chahamanas[30].

GURJARAS-PRATIHARAS

The dynasty founded by Harichandra, is known as Pratihara. There was another Pratihara family which rose to power in the 8th century. These two probably belong to the same Gurjara clan and were called Gurjara-Pratihara, a name actually met with in connection with a feudatory chief of the Imperial Pratiharas[31].

The part played by the Gurjaras in the troubled politics of the first half of the 7th century A.D. has been noticed in connection with Harsha Vardhana[32] and Pulakesin[33]. It is probable that the Gurjaras in the records of this age denoted the Gurjara principality in Rajputana with its feudatory state in south Gujarat.

HIUEN TSANG

There can be hardly any doubt that the Gurjara kingdom described by Hiuen Tsang[34] refers to that ruled over by the descendants of Harichandra. The Chinese pilgrim described the young Gurjara king as a devout believer in the law of Buddha, and for distinguished wisdom and courage. He may be identified with king Tata, son of Nagabhata about whom it is said in a record of the family that considering life to be evanescent as lightning, he abdicated in favour of his younger brother Bhoja, and himself retired to a hermitage practising there the rites of true religion.

Hiuen Tsang refers to the capital of the Gurjara kingdom as Pi-le-me-le[35]. This has been identified with Bhilamala, modern Bhimal. But since he notes its distance as 300 miles north of Valabhi, we should locate for the capital furthur north, and Balmer[36] would be a more probable site. Bhilamala is associated with the name of the famous astronomer Brahmagupta who is called Bhilamalakach-Arya. Since Brahmagupta wrote his great work *Brahmasphhta*

Siddhanta under the patronage of King Vyaghramukha[37] of the Chapa dynasty, it has been held by some that this dynasty had its capital at Bhilamala. This is not, however, a legitimate conclusion, as a great scholar might write a work under the patronage of a foreign king. So even, if we identify Bhilamala with Pi-le-me-le mentioned by Hiuen Tsang, as the capital of the Gurjara kingdom, we cannot identify the Chapas with the Gurjaras, as some scholars have done.

KING TATA

King Tata[38] and his three successors ruled between 640 to 720 A.D. Nothing is known about them beyond what has been said about Tata. The next king Siluka, great-grandson of Tata, was, however, an important king. He is said to have fixed the boundary between Valla[39] and Stravani and gained supremacy by defeating Devaraja, the Bhatti king. Siluka[40] evidently achieved some success against neighbouring powers and increased the power of his family by enlarging the extent of his kingdom. If Stravani be regarded as identical with Taban of the Arab writers, which probably consisted of a part of the Panjab just to the north-west of Rajputana, Siluka's kingdom must have roughly corresponded to modern Jodhpur and Bikaner. The Bhatti king Devaraja was probably the ruler of Bhatti clan who occupied Jaisalmer and by defeating him, Siluka established his supremacy in Rajputana.

KING SILUKA

Siluka has been called Valla-Mandala-Palaka. This presumably refers to a confederacy of states of which he was recognised head. There were probably several Gurjara states founded by the several sons of Harichandra. One of these is Lata or southern Gujarat with its capital at Nandipuri. There was probably another such state in Avanti with its capital at Ujjayini, for, early in the 8th century A.D. a Pratihara chief Nagabhata was ruling in this region. His family was closely related to the Pratihara family of Jodhpur. The same wave of conquest which brought one branch of the Gurjaras to south Gujarat also established another dynasty in Malwa, and the Kalachuris had to give way to them in both these regions. The title Valla-Mandala-Palaka certainly denotes that Siluka was the head of this Gurjara confederacy which ruled over an extensive region including parts of Rajputana, Malwa and Gujarat.

ARABA

Either Siluka or his successor was on the throne when the Araba swept ever the whole of Rajputana and Gujarat, and advanced as far as Ujjayini. The Gurjara kingdom of Jodhpur was overrun, but the Pratihara king Nagabhata of Avanti withstood this terrible shock and hurled back the invaders. The credit of saving western India from the hands of the Arab invaders belongs to him, and he shares the glory with the Chalukya king Avanijanasraya-Pulakesiraja who stopped their advance into southern India.

NAGABHATA

The Arab invasion brought about great changes in the political condition in western India by destroying or weakening numerous small states. The triumphant success of the Pratiharas of Avanti offered a sad contrast to the serious reverses sustained by other states, and in particular by the Jodhpur family which had hitherto exercised the suzerain power. The prestige of Nagabhata rose very high, and it was inevitable that he should make a bold bid for the position of supremacy. It is also natural that the minor Gurjara states, and also others, should favourably entertain this claim of one who had proved himself their saviour.

An indication of the sad distracted condition of the Gurjara dominions is furnished by the claim of King Prithuvardhana, of the Saila dynasty, that he overran the Gurjara dominions.

The supremacy over the Gurjara confederacy out of the hands of Siluka's family about the middle of the 8th century A.D. The changed condition is faithfully reflected in the family record. After describing the military exploits of Siluka it states that his son and grandson, who ruled after him, were both peace-loving and spent their last days on the banks of the Ganga.

King Nagabhata had occupied the supremo position (805-833 A.D.) and his successors were destined to raise the Pratihara to the highest power and glory.

THE GURJARA KINGDOM OF NANDIPURI

The small kingdom of south Gujarat continued throughout this period under the Gurjara royal family of Dada I. The records supply the names of the following successors of Dada II to whom reference has already been made:

THE GURJARA KINGDOM OF NANDIPURI

Dada II—Prasantaraga
|
Jayabhata II
|
Dada III Bahusahaya
|
Jayabhata III
Ahirola
|
Jayabhata IV

Dada II, whose known dates are 629 and 641 A.D., gave protection to the lord of Valabhi against Harsha, but this did not save his kingdom from the greed of his powerful neighbour. As noted above, the kings of Valabhi conquered this kingdom, on at least two occasions, about 648 and 685 A.D. On the last occasion, the Valabhi king was driven out by the Chalukyas. Dada III was ruling at this time. He assumed the title of Bahusahaya means that his own arms were his support. He is said to have waged war against the great kings of the east and of the west. The western king was undoubtedly the king of Valabhi. The king of the east with whom he fought, as a feudatory of the Western Chalukyas, had been Yasovarman or the Pratihara king of Avanti.

The Gurjaras were hemmed in by great powers on all sides. The Chalukyas had gradually established an independent kingdom in south Gujarat with Navasarika[41]. The northern boundary of this kingdom extended up to the Narmada. The Gurjaras acknowledged them as their overlord and, drove away the king of Valabhi with their help.

THE ARAB INVASION

When the Arab invasion burst upon his kingdom, Jayabhata IV saved himself with the help of the Chalukya king Avani-Janasraya-Pulakesiraja who inflicted a crushing defeat upon them. Jayabhata took the credit for having defeated the Arabs of Valabhi, and here, too, he fought as a feudatory of the Chalukya overlord.

GURJARAS DEFEATED

The Rashtrakuta chief Indra I, a feudatory of the western Chalukyas, married the daughter of a Chalukya king at Khetaka by the Rakshasa form of marriage. In other words, he carried off the princess by force and married her. As Khetaka has been identified with Kaira in Gujarat, the statement indicates the occupation of this part, by the Chalukyas sometime about 725 A.D. The Gurjaras, though saved from the Arabs, thus fell a prey to the Chalukyas. Rashtrakutas shortly afterwards supplanted the Chalukyas in this region and Dantidurga, son of Indra I, conquered Lata and Sindu. But the Rashtrakuta domination too, was of short duration, and by the middle of the 8th century A.D. the Pratihara of Avanti established their supremacy over this region. For in 756 A.D., a Chahamana was ruling in Broach as a feudatory of Nagavaloka, who has been identified with Nagabhata I, the Pratihara King of Avanti. Whether the Gurjaras of Nandipuri refused to reason the suzerainty of this new family, or for other reasons incurred their displeasure, we cannot say; and for the present, no definite reasons can be assigned as to why the Pratiharas of Avanti drove out the royal family which belonged to their own clan, in favour of an outsider. Jayabhata IV is the last known king of the Gurjara family of Nandipuri and his only known date is 735 A.D.

ETHNONYMS: GUJARETA, GUJJAR, GURJARA

The Gurjaras are a historical caste who have lent their name to the Gujarat district and the town of Gujranwala in the Panjab, (now in Pakistan), the peninsula and state of Gujarat, and the area known as Gujjargarh in Gwalior. They numbered 56,000 persons in 1911, of which the majority belonged to the Hoshangabad[42] and Nimar[43] districts (in 1971, there were 20, 634 Gujjars enumerated in Himachal Pradesh alone). In those provinces the caste is principally found in the Narbada Valley[44]. The caste is broadly divided along religious and geographic lines into the Muslim Gujjaras (who also share many Hindu customs with their Hindu Gujjar brethren and are thus not fully accepted in the Muslim majority) in northern India and Pakistan.

Gujjar or Gurjara is the designation of Indian tribal groups formerly scattered in parts of Panjab, Rajasthan and Gujarat. Their ethnic origin is disputed. It was once generally believed that the Gurjaras came to India, sometimes during the 5th century A.D.; but the view now favoured is that they were indigenous to India.

The Gujjars founded a group of dynasties that controlled areas of Rajasthan, Central India, and Gujarat from 7th to 11th century A.D. The most powerful branch of the Gujjars was the Pratihara, whose power was centered in the Jodhpur region of Rajasthan.

The Pratiharas contended with the Rashtrakuta of the Deccan and the Palas of Bengal for imperial hegemony during the 9th century and controlled the great cities of Kanauj and Ujjain. The greatest Pratihara ruler was Bhoja I, reigned about 836-882 A.D., whose wealth and military might greatly impress the Arabs.

The Pratiharas were devout Hindus and acted as a barrier to the spread of Arab power south of Sind. Their administration was feudal in character, the paramount ruler receiving tributes from feudal retainers who ruled their assignments practically as independent kings. Many Pratihara rulers patronized classical Sanskrit literature and religious and literary activities of the Jains. The name of the present Indian state of Gujarat (q.v.) is derived from Gurjara (Gujjar).

Nagbhata II was succeed by his son Ramabhatra who ruled for about three years, after his death Mihira Bhoja, his illustrious son. He made a determined bid to rehabilitate the lost prestige of his family and was suitably rewarded with the establishment of his authority over Bundelkhand and in the north up to the foot of the Himalayas. The east Panjab comprising the district of Karnal of Gujjar Pratiharas Empire was annexed to his empire. He further advanced to northwest and gave the territories of Gujarat and Gujranwala to his feudal chief Alakhana.

The Arab historian Suleman, a contemporary of Mihira Bhoja visited India in 857 A.D. He denounced Mihira Bhoja as the most bitter enemy of Islam. Mihira Bhoja, the son of Mahendrapal, succeeded him in 885 A.D. and ruled till 910 A.D. He retained and successfully managed the inherited empire. His period is said to be the golden period of Gujjar Pratiharas.

About the last decade of the 10th century when Rajyapala succeeded to the Pratihara throne, the advancing tide of Mahmud's Tarkish hordes could not be stopped and it swept away not only Rajyapala but also his son Trilochanpala[45].

GURDASPUR DISTRICT

The more important minor tribes are the Mohammaden Gujjars of the northern part of Shakargarh Tehsil and the Beas Bet, the Arains of Kalanaur and Batala, the Pathans of the Shakargarh Darp and of the Ravi Bet in this Tehsil and Gurdaspur, the Sainis of the Paintla in Shakargarh and some scattered villages of Brahmans throughout the district. The Pathans and Brahmans are of course very poor farmers, while the Arains and Sainis are industrious and frugal in the extreme. They are exceedingly prolific, and the minute subdivision of holdings amongst them lends itself to the successful adoption of the system of petit culture, to which they are most inclined. The Gujjars are now ordinary agriculturists. They were originally Hindus of the country round Delhi but that in the time of the Mohammaden kings they were converted to Islam and settled in the Bharrari which was then a thickly-wooded jungle.

KARNAL DISTRICT

The Gujjars are a notorious thieving tribe; and as a rule, their cultivation is of the most slovenly description, though in many of the Khadar and canal villages they have really applied themselves in earnest to agriculture. They have a habit of breaking up far more land than their numbers and appliances can properly cultivate; and though their women will go to the well, bring food to the workers in the field, pick cotton, and do other light work, yet they will not weed or do any really hard labour in the fields like the Jat women. The difference between a Gujjar and a Rajput thief was well put by a villager as follows: "A Rajput will steal your buffalo; but he won't send his father to say he knows where it is and will get it back for Rs. 20, and then keep both the Rs. 20, and the buffalo. The Gujjar will." The local opinion of the Gujjar is embodied in the proverb—

Kutta, billi do, Yih char na ho,
Ranghar, Gujjar do; To Khule kiware so.

"The dog and the cat, two; the Ranghar and Gujjar, two. Were it not for these four you might sleep with your door open?" Again "Jitte dekhen Gujjar, itte deyie mar"; or "Wherever you see a Gujjar, hit him." This character has been enjoyed by them of old. The Gujjars are, like the Rajputs, singularly unwilling to admit strangers to property in their villages. They are closely allied with the Rajputs; and their possession of parts of the Bangar was probably contemporaneous with that of the Mandhars, parts of whose conquests, such as Kohand, were given to them. But in the Khadar they have succeeded Afghans in comparatively recent times save in a very few old villages. The principal clans are:

Rawal

This clan claims descent from a Rajput called Dhundpal from beyond Lahore, who married the daughter of a Gujjar called Ghokar. It is part of the Ghokarbansi clan, and takes its specific name from Rua Sarsa near Lahore. In one village, they say that the ancestor was a Khokhar Rajput, and this is probably the better form of the tradition. They settled in Rana Khera (Now Rajapur), but moved thence to Kabri and Kohand, where they held a Bara of 12 villages; and they also held Bapauli whence they eventually settled the 27 villages (Sataisi) of the Khojgipur Thapa in the Khadar. They still hold the Khadar villages; but have lost most of those near Kohand.

Chokar

This clan comes from Jewar Thapa, beyond Mathra via Bali Qutbpur, in Sunpat. They used to hold (24 villages) Chaubisi with Namaunda their headquarters, and are very old inhabitants. They have been to a great degree displaced by Jats.

Chamain

This clan claims descent from a Tunwar Rajput by a Gujjar mother and the real gentile's name is said to be Tunwar, Chamain being only a local appellation. They came from Delhi and settled in Nain and Sutana and the neighbouring villages; and are certainly very old inhabitants, possibly having emigrated when expelled from neighbourhood of Delhi by Sher Shah a few years after the Chauhan settlement. They have been largely dispossessed by Rors.

Kalsan

This clan claims descent from Rana Har Rai, the Chauhan of Jundla by a Gujjar wife. They had given them a part of his conquests in the Doab, where they are still in great force, and they hold a little land in the Chauhan Nardak.

Other claims are Cheharwal or Daharwal, and Puswal from the neighbourhood of Delhi; Bhodwal from Meerut; Karhawat from Jhajjar Bang and Katane from Kaithal; Bhonkal from Bagpat; Khari from Sirsa, Patan, Delhi, Chauri from Chitran in Hansi, and Gersi from Pehoa. There are none of them of any local importance.

Rors

No satisfactory information, whatever, is forthcoming as to the origin of the Rors. Most of them date their origin from the neighbourhood of Badli, near Jhajjar in Rohtak; and there are traditions of a Tunwar Rajput as ancestor. They hold a Chaurasi of 84 villages about Pehoa, and a Barah of 12 villages beyond the Ganges. They occupy many villages in the Mori Nardak, some in the east of Parangali Kaithal, and a few in the south of Kaithal Tehsil near the Jind border; but they have obtained their prosperity in the district almost exclusively by being settled as cultivators by the original owners, generally Rajputs and Gujjars, who have since abandoned their villages, or died out wholly or died in part. The Rajput say that the Rors were originally Ods who used to dig the tanks at Thaneswar. They themselves claim Rajput origin, and Rajputs have been heard to admit the origin of the Dapla Got of Rors in Amin, & c. from Rana Har Rai by a Rorni wife. Socially, they rank below Jats.

HISSAR DISTRICT

The Gujjars have been identified by A.G. Cunningham with the Lushan or Yuchi or Tochari tribe of eastern Tartars. This tribe entered India about a century before Christ and about the middle of the 5th century A.D. there was a Gujjar kingdom in southwestern Rajputana. It is to Rajputana that the Hissar Gujjars trace their origin. Most of them are Hindus. They are generally of good physique, but of poor moral character. They seem to devote most of their energies to cattle keeping and cattle stealing and they are very bad cultivators.

LUDHIANA DISTRICT

The Gujjars of this District are unable to give any distinct account of who they are or whence they came, but it appears pretty certain that they are a nomad race (Gan-Char= Gujjar) who moved from towards the hills in search of pasture, and gradually settled down along the river for the sake of grazing. They now hold a number of villages in the Bet or lowlands, mostly in Ludhiana Tehsil. Almost 100 years ago, Sardar Sudha Singh and the Kakars, who held the Bet lands under Ludhiana, located them in villages; and they have only since then taken to agriculture. The Gujjars of this district are all Mohammadens. They are of good physique, tall and well made, but are said to be lacking in courage. Intellectually, they are not strong; and they are, as a rule, much too easy-going and careless to get on in these times. As cultivators, they are not of the first class, though superior to the Rajputs. They have a hereditary liking for cattle, especially that of other people and most of the Gujjar villages contain men recognised by the police as criminal. They are, as a tribe, turbulent, discontented and lawless; and gave great deal of trouble in the Mutiny of 1857 A.D. Gujjar women help their husbands in the fields. The principal subdivisions are Gorsi and Cheehi, also Kalas and Paswal.

GURGAON DISTRICT

Gujjars are found in all five Tehsils of this district but are most numerous as proprietors in the Gurgaon Tehsil along the foot of the range, which divides the district from Delhi. In the Palwal Tehsil some of the largest Gujjar villages now belong to the Skinner estate; in the days of the heavy assessments which preceded the regular settlement, the Gujjars attempted to evade the weighty Jamas imposed on them by using their lands as grazing grounds, and throwing them out of the cultivation, and then deserting the villages, when pressed for payment, a course which led to their rights being forfeited, under a special rule issued by the Government of India to check desertion of estates in the Gurgaon district, or to their being sold by auction for the balances due.

RAWALPINDI DISTRICT

There are very few Gujjars in Kahuta Tehsil and almost none in Murree, but they are very numerous elsewhere. In Gujjar Khan they are found all over the Tehsil. Their strongest colony being in the south-west, close along the Chakwal-Mandra road. In Rawalpindi, they abound on the line of the Soan, and are found in nearly all parts of the Tehsil.

A TRADITION

Their tradition is that they migrated from Gujarat in the time of Akbar. Probably their settlement in the district dates much before that time, and it is not unlikely that they are among the oldest inhabitants of the district. Certainly in Jhelum on the one side and Hazara on the other, they are among the oldest settlers of the tribes at present inhabiting these districts. Nothing definite is known of the date of their immigration into the district, but the probabilities are against so homogenous a race of foreigners settling down in the district within historical times of Gakkhar rule, and yet leaving no trace of the wave that brought them.

A Cianish Tribe

Gujjars are a very clannish tribe, speak a separate dialect and keep very much to themselves. Socially, they do not rank high and indeed are mere peasants, without the pride of birth or dignity of bearing which mark their more blue-blooded neighbours. They own 124 villages. As cultivators they are excellent and rank among the best in the district, yet they are generally in debt and often embarrassed. Thrifty in small matters and thoughtless in large matters, they have not the same power of resistance to the moneylender and elasticity in adversity that distinguish the better tribes. Their character is only fair and they are somewhat addicted to petty crime. They are of very fair physique, and make fair soldiers, but find an increasing difficulty in getting themselves enlisted. Baz Khan, Zaildar, Raman, Tehsil Gujjar Khan, is most prominent Gujjar in the district. Nadir Ali of Mankiala in Rawalpindi Tehsil is worthy of mention. The family of Bulakhar in Tehsil Kahuta is sunk in debt, and its prestige and influence are gone.

SANGRUR DISTRICT

The Gujjars are not as numerous as the Arains, and are a pastoral rather than an agricultural tribe, bearing much the same character here as elsewhere. They hold many villages in Rajpura and Narnaul Tehsils. Some of them are Mohammadens and some Hindus. In the erstwhile Patiala state, their more important septs are the Bharwal, Lodi, Chichi, Bargat, Duchak, Katoria, Latala, Jandar, Chandija, Gorsi and Rawat, of whom the last regards itself as descended from Jagdeo Punwar, whose son Olan Palan married the fair daughter of Mor Dhaj, Katana Gujjar. Males of the Chawara sept are believed to be able to cure pneumonia by touching the sufferer with a piece of cloth.

Socially, they have 14 Chhats and 24 Makans; the Chhats in this State being Banur, Sdhron, Ajrawar, Kaulf. Ghanaur Patton Khera Gujja, Shamdo, Chamard, Manakpur and Jansla and in British territory Kharar, Khanpur and Morinda.

Table 5.1: *District-wise Distribution of Various Clans of Gujjar*

	1	2	3	4	5	6	7	8	9
	Tunwar	Chokhar	Rawal	Kalsan	Kathana	Kasanah	Kalas	Gorsi	Cherhi
Delhi	2,555	744	100	1	366	676	7	8	51
Gurgaon	324	1	...	8	1,629	797	...	...	274
Karnal	...	2,325	4,417	1,588	21	92	...	422	307
Hissar	116	34	8	20	389	508	189	10	308
Rohtak	...	19	3	1	101	128	4	41	42
Ambala	...	240	10	...	1,491	2,289	1,208	1,594	2,810
Ludhiana	...	...	...	...	749	695	1,175	3,462	3,285
Jalandhar	...	...	...	...	546	388	565	1,457	1,152
Hoshiarpur	...	...	...	...	546	2,299	1,111	3,301	3,171
Kangra	...	...	...	...	60	135	118	209	418
Amritsar	...	...	...	...	153	134	...	180	645
Gurdaspur	1,140	336	...	...	2,750	1,533	...	1,772	4,010
Sialkot	...	3	10	...	1,020	439	...	277	692
Lahore	...	1	13	...	445	82	...	290	1,020
Gujranwala	...	...	17	...	125	25	60	38	205
Firozepur	...	...	...	...	1,168	312	166	870	779
Rawalpindi	...	280	...	...	5,646	612	1,318	1,232	3,207
Jhelum	...	20	...	...	3,684	882	1,260	309	1,621
Gujarat	...	269	...	...	21,449	3,048	3,560	3,312	8,092
Peshawar	...	13	3	...	...	2	13	119	167
Hazara	...	195	...	...	8,526	11	1,314	319	7,156
States of East Plains	134	167	30	...	2,782	456	652	2,036	5,258
British Territory	4,148	4,524	4,600	1,627	51,065	15,126	12,194	19,279	39,562
Native States	134	167	67	...	3,080	1,014	1,1209	2,824	6,427
Province	4,277	4,691	4,667	1,627	54,145	16,140	13,403	22,103	45,989

(*Contd..*)

	10	11	12	13	14	15	16	17	18	19
	Dhedar	Poswal	Law	Bijar	Khaindar	Melu	Thankaria	Chauhan	Monan	Bhumla
Delhi	1	6	4	...	...	...	...	87	...	...
Gurgaon	10	782	17	...	...	...	...	155	...	3,692
Karnal	43	208	...	33	...	118	...	172	...	...
Hissar	33	79	42	70	...	602	...	86	...	...
Rohtak	2	24	1	...	...	9	...	52	...	...
Ambala	1,218	4,467	554	3,504	...	6	...	1,280	...	...
Ludhiana	1,139	1,690	613	1,584	...	109	29	518	30	...
Jalandhar	86	1,139	173	683	...	1	...	682	278	...
Hoshiarpur	...	6,910	2,825	3,230	1,172	2,357	1,200	4,530	2,585	...
Kangra	52	211	851	190	...	...	13	645	142	...
Amritsar	...	197	...	180	...	...	...	146	69	...
Gurdaspur	215	1,687	30	710	...	...	860	1,151	4,479	...
Sialkot	167	541	1	176	...	...	...	517	...	...
Lahore	54	198	40	178	...	47	4	194	91	...
Gujranwala	...	27	...	126	...	...	43	221	...	...
Firozepur	338	389	114	215	...	...	...	332	170	...
Rawalpindi	340	2,417	4	1,041	...	25	975	2,361	344	...
Jhelum	451	1,340	36	907	...	...	758	1,287	62	35
Gujarat	1,921	3,491	150	3,592	...	1,389	3,524	7,985	382	2,180
Peshawar	2	31	2	230	...	...	...	...	...	...
Hazara	899	2,684	...	2,504	...	...	2,362	5,132	221	21
States of East Plains	908	1,095	416	1,664	...	382	183	981	403	328
British Territory	7,055	28,539	5,461	19,159	1,172	4,968	9,770	27,554	9,123	4,937
Native States	1,291	1441	1,258	2,186	...	956	183	2,238	403	370
Province	8,316	29,980	6,719	21,345	1,172	5,924	9,953	29,729	9,526	5,307

REFERENCES

1. V.A. Smith, *Journal of Asiatic Society of India,* Jan-April (1909), pp. 63-69.
2. Dr. Bhandarkar. *JASB* (1909) p. 167; *Archaeological Reports,* Vol. 1. Cunningham p. 62.
3. *The People of India,* Sir Herbert Risley, p. 513.
4. V.A. Smith. *Early History of India,* 1908, p. 375.
5. Drew. *Jammu and Kashmir Territories*, 1875, p. 199.
6. James Hastings. *Encyclopaedia of Religion & Ethics,* Vol. VI, p. 453.
7. *Encyclopedia of Britannica*, Vol. 6, p. 688.
8. *Encyclopaedia of Britannica*, Vol. 3, p. 77, 3a.
9. Tatars or Tartars, Turkish speaking people being in the Soviet Union. They are largely Sunni Muslims, originally a nomadic tribe from east-central Asia, the Tartars intermixed with Mongols in the hordes of Changez Khan and the term Tatars came to mean invaders under Mongol leadership.
10. Capital of Afghanistan, a city, population is 913,764, in 1979, an economic and cultural centre, situated on the bank of Kabul River.
11. On the other hand, Mr. Steedman is of the opinion that the figures for the Gujjars of Rawalpindi are very much under the marks and that many of them must have been returned as Jats, Rajputs or even Mughals.
12. Mr. Wilson, however, writes: "The Gujjar villages in Gurgaon have on the whole stood the late bad times better than those of almost other caste—better than the Jats, and almost as well as the Ahirs. Our Gurgaon Gujjars are very little given to thieving, and I have rather a high opinion of them."
13. *PNQ*, Vol. II, p. 45.
14. *Rajputana Gazetteer,* Vol. I, (1870), p. 162.
15. *Panjab Ethnography*, D.C.J. Ibbetson, (1883), p. 262 (i).
16. Maclagan, *Panjab Census Report,* Vol. I. (1891), p. 136.
17. Maclagan, *Panjab Census Report,* Vol. I. (1891), p. 136.
18. City, Jodhpur district, Central Rajasthan, India, on the Thar Desert, 180 miles WSW of Jaipur.
19. Town, a district NE Panjab, W. Pakistan, 70 miles NNW of Lahore.
20. District NE Panjab, Pakistan, 40 miles NNW of Lahore.
21. A town in Rawalpindi district, Pakistan.
22. Probably Merta, 70 miles north-east of Jodhpur.
23. Popularly known as Chik Ballpur, a town in Kolar district E Mysore, India.
24. A district in north Bombay, India.

25. A river in west Vindhya range, west India.
26. They became powerful in the second half of the 6th century when they are found in occupation of northern Maharashtra, Gujarat and parts of Malwa *(The Classical Age,* p. 194).
27. The war between Harsha and Pulakesin has been regarded as memorable event both by the successors of Pulakesin and by modern historian (*The Classical Age,* p. 105).
28. The Guhila-Putras or Guhilots of Mewar are rightly regarded as the erst-jewel of the Rajput clans. A full genealogy of the family is given for the first time in the Atpur inscription, dated 977 A.D.
29. *The Classical Age*, p. 154.
30. *The Classical Age*, pp. 153-154.
31. Famous Rajputs, were the Pratiharas, the Guhilets and Crapotkatas and Chahamanas *(The Classical Age,* pp. 153-54).
32. *The Classical Age,* pp. 73, 96, 123.
33. *The Classical Age,* pp. 109-110.
34. A traveller and historian from China.
35. Capital of the Gurjara kingdom *(The Classical Age,* p. 152).
36. Probably the site of Bhilmala *(The Classical Age,* pp. 153-154).
37. *The Classical Age*. p. 154.
38. King Tata and his three successors ruled between 640-720 A.D.
39. Siluka was called Valla-Mandala-Palka *(The Classical Age*. p. 154).
40. The supremacy over the Gurjara confederacy passed out of the hands of Siluka's family about the middle of the 8th century A.D. *(The Classical Age*. p. 155).
41. Navsari as its capital.
42. A district, NW, Madhya Pradesh, India, on the bank of Narbada River.
43. A district in Madhya Pradesh, India, on the Deccan plateau.
44. Central India, rises near village of Amarkantak on plateau at eastern junction of Vindhya and Satpura.
45. *History of the Gujjara Pratiharas* by B.N. Puri. p. 57.

BIBLIOGRAPHY

Drew, F. *The Jammu and Kashmir Territories*, London 1875.

Goodwin, Raheja Gloria (1988). *Dominant Caste in a North Indian Village,* Ibbetson, D.C.J. *Panjab, Ethnography.* Calcutta, 1883. p. 262 f.

Ibbetson, Denzil. *Panjab Castes*, p. 131.

Munshi, Dr. K.M. *The Classical Age.*

Panjab Census Report, Vol. I, 1891.

Puri, B.N. *History of Gujjar Pratiharas.*

PNQ, Vol. II.

Risley, Sir Herbert. *The People of India.*

Rose, H.A. (1911). "Gujjar" in *A Glossary of the Tribes and Castes of the Panjab and North-West Frontier Provinces*, Vol. I. pp. 306-318.

Russell, R.V., and Lal, Hira (ed.) (1916). "Gujjar" in *The Tribes and Castes of the Central Provinces of India*, Vol. 3.

Rose, H.A. *Census Report Panjab 1901*. Vol. I, p. 324.

Rose, H.A. *A Glossary of the Tribes and Castes of Panjab and N.W. Frontier Provinces*, Vol. I.

Sharma, J.C. (1984). "Gujjar" in *Muslim Peoples: A World Ethnographic Survey*, Vol. I. pp. 298-301.

Smith, V.A. *Journal of Asiatic Society of Bengal*, Jan-April.

The Sakas

(Ancestors of Jats, Ahirs, Gujjars, Rajputs, Baloches & Pathans)

6

ORIGIN

When the Scythians advanced through Iran, as conqueror, towards India, the Persians named them 'Sakas' and henceforth they became Sakas. The Scythians had a highly developed metallurgy, and in their social structure the agriculturalists (Aroteres), who grew wheat for sale, constituted a class of their own. The quality of Scythian art, characterized by a highly sophisticated style called "animal art", remained unsurpassed in Central Asia. Although the Scythians had no script, it has been established, nevertheless, that they spoke an Iranian language, in the 1st century BC.

SEARCH FOR NEW PASTURES

The Bactrian control of Taxila was disturbed by an intrusion of the Scythians, known in Indian sources as the Sakas. They attacked the kingdom of Bactria (Balkh) and subsequently moved into India. The determination of the Han rulers of China to keep the Central Asian nomadic tribes (the Hsiung-nu, Wu-sun, and Yueh-chih) out of China forced them to search for fresh pastures to migrate southward and westward; a branch of the Yueh-chih, the Ta Yueh-chih, moved farthest west to the Aral Sea, and this displaced the existing Sakas, who poured into Bactria and Parthia. The Parthian king Mithradates II tried to hold them back, but after his death (88 B.C.) they swept through Parthia and continued into the Indus Valley. Among the early Saka kings was Maues, or Moga (1st century B.C.), who ruled over Gandhara. The Sakas moved southward under pressure from the Pahlavas (Parthians), who ruled briefly in north-western India toward the end of the 1st century B.C., the reign of Gondophernes being remembered. At Mathura, the Saka rulers of note were Rajuvala and Sodasa. Ultimately the Sakas settled in western India and Malava and came into conflict with the kingdoms of the northern Deccan and the Ganges Valley— particularly during the reigns of Nahapana, Castana, and Rudradaman—in the first two centuries A.D. Rudradaman's fame is recorded in a lengthy Sanskrit inscription at Junagadh, dating to 150 A.D. Kujula Kadphises, the Yueh-chih chief, conquered northern India in the 1st century A.D. He was succeeded by his son Vima, after whom came Kaniska, the most powerful among the Kushana kings, as the dynasty came to be called. The date of Kaniska's accession is controversial, ranging from 78 to 248 A.D. The generally accepted date of 78 is also the basis for an era presumably started by the Sakas and used in addition to the Gregorian calendar by the present Indian government; the era, possibly commemorating Kaniska's accession, was widely used in Malava, Ujjain, Nepal, and Central Asia. The Kushana kingdom was essentially oriented to the north, with its capital at Purusapura (near modern Peshawar), although it extended southward as far as Sanci and into the Ganges Valley and Varanasi. Mathura was the most important city in the southern part of the kingdom. Kaniska's ambitions included control of Central Asia, which, if not directly under the Kushanas, did come under their influence. The recently discovered inscriptions from Gilgit further attest such Central Asian connections. Kaniska's successors failed to maintain Kushana power. The southern areas were the first to break away, and, by the middle of the 3rd century A.D., the Kushanas were left virtually with only Gandhara and Kashmir. By the end of the century, they were reduced to vassalage by the Sasanian king of Persia.

Not surprisingly, administrative and political nomenclature in northern India at this time reflected that of western and Central Asia. The Persian term for the governor of a province, *Khshathrapavan*, as used by the Achaemenians, was Hellenized into *satrap* and was widely used by these dynasties. Its Sanskrit form was *ksatrapa*. The governors of higher status came to be called *maha-ksatrapa*; they frequently issued inscriptions reflecting whatever era they chose to follow, and they minted their own coins, indicating a more independent status than is generally associated with governors. Imperial titles also were taken by the Indo-Greeks, such as *basileus basileon* ("king of kings"), similar to the Persian *shahanshah*, of which the later Sanskrit form was *maharajadhiraja*. A title of Central Asian derivation was the *daivaputra* of the Kushanas, which is believed to have come originally from the Chinese "son of heaven", emphasizing the divinity of kingship.

Oligarchies and Kingdoms

Occupying the watershed between the Indus and Ganges valleys, the Panjab and Rajasthan were the nucleus of a number of oligarchies, or tribal republics whose local importance rose and fell in inverse proportion to the rise and fall of larger kingdoms. According to numismatic evidence, the most important political powers were the Audambaras, Arjunayanas, Malavas, Yaudheyas, Sibis, Kunindas, Trigartas, and Abhiras. The Arjunayanas had their base in the present Bharatpur-Alwar region. The Malavas appear to have migrated from the Panjab to the Jaipur area, perhaps after the Indo-Greek invasions; they are associated with the Malava era, which has been identified with the Vikrama era, also known as the Krta era and dating to 58 BC. It is likely that southern Rajasthan, as far as the Narmada River and the Ujjain district, was named Malwa after the Malavas. Yaudheya evidence is scattered over many parts of the Panjab and the adjoining areas of Rajasthan and Uttar Pradesh, but during this period their stronghold appears to have been the Rohtak district, north of Delhi; the frequent use of the term *gana* ("group") on Yaudheya coins indicates an adherence to the tribal tradition. References to Saivite deities, especially Karttikeya or Skanda, the legendary son of Siva, are striking. The Sibis also migrated from the Panjab to Rajasthan and settled at Madhyamika (near Chittor, modern Chittaurgarh).

Coins of the Kunindas locate them in the Shivalik hills between the Yamuna and the Beas rivers. The Trigartas have been associated with the Chamba region of the upper Ravi River, but they also may have inhabited the area of Jalandhava in the plains. The Abhiras lived in scattered settlements in various parts of western and central India as far as the Deccan. Most of these tribes claimed descent from the ancient lineages of the *Puranas,* and some of them were later connected with the rise of the Rajput dynasties.

In addition to the oligarchies, there were small monarchical states, such as Ayodhya, Kausambi, and the scattered Naga kingdoms, the most important of which was the one at Padmavati (Gwalior). Ahicchatra (the Bareilly district of Uttar Pradesh) was ruled by kings who bore names ending in the suffix *Mitra.*

SUCCESSORS TO THE MAURYA

The Sunga Kingdom

Magadha was the nucleus of the Sunga kingdom, which succeeded the Mauryan. The kingdom extended westward to include Ujjain and Vidisa. The Sungas came into conflict with Vidarbha and with the Yavanas, who probably were Bactrian Greeks attempting to move into the Ganges Valley. (The word *yavana* derives from the Prakrit *yona*, suggesting that the Ionians were the first Greeks with whom the Persians and Indians came into contact. In later centuries, the name Yavana was applied to all peoples coming from western Asia and the Mediterranean, which included the Romans, Persians, and Arabs). The Sunga dynasty lasted for about one century and was then overthrown by the Brahman minister Vasudeva, who founded the Kanva dynasty, which lasted 45 years and following which the Magadha area faded out of importance until the 4th century A.D.

Kalinga

Kalinga rose to prominence under Kharavela, dated with some controversy to the 1st century BC. Kharavela boasts, perhaps exaggeratedly for a pious Jaina, of successful campaigns in the western Deccan and against the Yavanas and Magadha and of a triumphal victory over the Pandyas of South India.

The Andhras and Their Successors

The Andhras are listed among the tribal peoples in the Mauryan empire. Possibly they rose to being local officials and then, on the disintegration of the empire, gradually became independent rulers of the north-western Deccan. It cannot be ascertained for certain whether the Andhras arose in the Andhra region (*i.e.* the Krishna-Godavari deltas) and moved up to the north-western Deccan or whether their settling in the delta gave it their name. There is also controversy as to whether the dynasty became independent at the end of the 3rd century B.C. or at the end of the 1st century B.C. Their alternative name, Satavahana, is presumed to be the family name, whereas Andhra was probably that of the tribe. It is likely that Satavahana power was established during the reign of Satakarni I, with the borders of the kingdom reaching across the northern Deccan; subsequent to this the Satavahanas suffered an eclipse in the 1st century A.D., when they were forced out of the northern Deccan by the Sakas and settled in Andhra. In the 2nd century A.D., the Satavahanas re-established their power in the north-western Deccan, as evidenced by Saka coins from this region overstruck with the name Gautamiputra Satakarni. That the Andhras did not control Malava and Ujjain is clear from the claim of the Saka king Rudradaman to these regions. The last of the important Andhra kings was Yajnasri Satakarni, who ruled at the end of the 2nd century A.D. and asserted his authority over the Sakas. The 3rd century saw the decline of Satavahana power, as the kingdom broke into small pockets of control under various branches of the family.

The Scythians appear as Sakas in the old Iranian rock inscriptions, where, three distinct groups are identified, and it is by the latter name Sakas that they appeared in the history of north-western India, which they penetrated during the 1st century B.C. On the steppes of central Asia, they were gradually succeeded into the Kushan Empire, while on the southern Russian steppes they were absorbed by the Sarmatians[1], another Iranian nomad people, whose hegemony lasted until the 4th century A.D. Saka Satrap, also called Kashatrapa either of the two dynasties of Satraps in northern India who ruled with considerable independence on behalf of the Pahlava[2] suzerains. The two families are both known to Indian history as the Sakas (from the native word for Scythians) and to the western historians as the Kshatrayas.

The shorter lived of the two families, bears the name Kshaharata and is known for two rulers, Bhumdlca and Nahapana, whose reigns were established by coinage and by a few surviving inscriptions that appear to fix A.D. 124 as a date in Nahapana's reign. These documents claim that Nahapana ruled over a large area in western India around the Gulf of Cambay[3], which he could only have won from the Ahdhras[4]. This possession Was, however, brief because, GautamipUtrk is known to have destroyed the Sakas in the latter part of the Saka years (A.D. 124-125).

The second dynasty of Satraps, founded by Chastana in 2nd century A.D., ruled western India for two or three centuries and gave its name to the Sakanripakala, or era of Saka kings, in Indian history. The rulers of this house can be dated with incomplete accuracy from their coinage. Chastana is mentioned by Ptolemy[5] as ruling into the 2nd century (A.D. 78-110) and also considerably aggrandized his holdings at the expense of the Andhras. The wars of these Sakas with the Andhras continued for several reginal generations. The; first great Saka ruler was Rudradaman I, Chastana's grandson, who reigned after A.D. 130. The direct line of Chastana became extinct in A.D. 304-305 with the death of Yisvasena, son of Bhartridamari. It is doubtful that the dynasty was important in the 4th century A.D., although one of its members probably Rudrasimha[6] III is recorded as the "Saka king" killed by Chandra Gupta II, when he sacked the Saka capital in A.D. 338.

The Sakas of Western Satraps

The principality of the Western Satraps, consisting of Malwa, Gujarat and the Kathiawar peninsula, was being ruled by the family of Chastana[7] for nearly two hundred years. But a break in the regular course of succession occurred at the beginning of the 4th century A.D., when Rudrasimha II ousted the legitimate heir and occupied the throne in A.D. 304 or 305. His father, Swami Jivadaman bears no royal title, and although it is possible the he might have belonged to a younger branch of the old royal family, his relationship to it is not definitely known.

Along with this change in succession, it is to note that two other important facts bearing upon the history of the Saka kingdom, came to light. In the first place, neither Rudrasimha II, who usurped the throne, nor his son and successor Yasodaman II assumed the title of Mahakshatrapa, and both were content with the lower title of Kashatrapa only. This is remarkable in view of the fact that since almost in the very beginning the chief political power in the kingdom was regularly exercised by a Mahakshatrapa, who associated with him the heir apparent, bearing the title of Kashatrapa. Secondly, after the reign of Rudrasimha II and his son extending from A.D. 305-332, no coins of Western Satraps are known for a period of sixteen years.

Troublesome Times

These facts indicate troublesome times though it is impossible to throw much light on the cause or nature of the troubles through which the principality must have passed. An inscription found in the village of Kanakhera near Sanchi, however, throws some light on this matter. This record refers to some pious work done by Mahadanaayaka Saka Sridharavarma[8], son of Saka Nanda, in the 13 years of his reign. Another inscription at Eran, (Saugar) dated in his 27th reginal year, calls him both Raj and Mahakshatrapa. The first inscription also contains a date, presumably in Saka era, which has been read as 241. This reading is not free from doubt, but let us accept it, we can easily conclude that Mahakshatrapa Sridharavarma refused to acknowledge Rudrasimha II as legitimate sovereign and set up an independent kingdom in A.D. 306 or 307, *i.e.* within a year or two of Rudrasimha's accession. It may be concluded, therefore, that Rudrasimha II came to throne by violent means, and it led to a civil war or internal dissension as a result of which Malwa was lost to the Western Satraps. For it is known from the Allahabad inscription of Samudra Gupta that number of tribal states flourished in Malwa about the middle of the 4th century A.D. and there is no evidence that the Saka Satraps exercised any authority in this province at the time.

There might have been similar revolts in other parts of the kingdom, and this internal dissension might have been the cause, or at least one of the causes, of the decline in power and authority of the Satraps Rudrasimha II and his son Yasodaman II, who never assumed the title of Mahakshatrapa.

The absence of coins of this dynasty between A.D. 332 and 348 A.D. shows that the political troubles, far from being over, were accentuated during this period. As a result, the family of Rudrasimha was swept away and Mahakshatrapa Swami Rudrasena III occupied the throne in or shortly after A.D. 348. He is described in his coin legends as the son of Mahakshatrapa Swami Rudradaman II, but no coins of the latter have so far been discovered whether Rudradaman was a mere pretender to the title of Mahakshatrapa. But if so, the success was very short lived. For a while we have silver coins of Rudrasena II, representing each year from 270-273 (*i.e.* A.D. 348-351). They cease altogether after that year and do not reappear till A.D. 360. Here, again, the absence of coins may be taken to indicate some political troubles, though it may not be quite safe to rely upon such negative evidence alone.

Foreign Invasions

The constant troubles of the Western "Satraps during the first half of the 4th century A.D. were due also to foreign invasions which were perhaps provoked by the internal dissensions referred to above. During the first half of the period the only two powers in this connection were the Vakatakas[9] and the Sassanians of Persia or Sassanid, the last dynasty of native rulers to reign c. 224-640 A.D., in Persia before the Arab conquest. Arda Shir I was the first king of the dynasty. The contemporary Vakataka ruler Pravarasena I was undoubtedly a powerful Saka king and was the only ruler of the family to assume the imperial title of Samrat. It is not unlikely that he helped or joined one of the contending parties in order to extend his political influence in this region, but there is no reference to any such attempt in the Vakataka records. As regards the Sassanians, there is no evidence that they played any part in Indian politics about this time, and what was known of their history makes it very unlikely. The only other power that we can think of in this connection, at least for the second quarter of the 4th century A.D. is the imperial Guptas. The Allahabad inscription of Samudra Gupta clearly refers to some sort of political control exercised by that emperor over the Sakas. It is quite possible that the Saka Satraps did not accept this position without a fight and there was a long-drawn struggle. It led to no decisive result for the time being but the Saka ruler must have been sufficiently humbled, and his discomfiture led to the weakening of his authority and internal troubles reflected in the absence of coins between A.D. 332 and 348 and again between A.D. 351 and 360. It may be recalled that according to one interpretation, the Sakas Satraps belonged to the category of subject-states which had to use the Gupta coins. This might well account for the cessation of the coins of Western Satraps, but such a conclusion can only be regarded as provisional.

The regular issue of coins from about A.D. 360 to 390 by Rudrasena[10] II shows that he had re-established his power and authority to some extent. But indications are not wanting that trouble broke out again towards the close of his reign. The coins show that in A.D. 382 (and probably also in 384) his sister's son Swami Simhasena had assumed the title of Mahakshatrapa. Either therefore, Rudrasena II was temporarily dispossessed of his authority by his nephew, or there was a civil war, involving a partition of the kingdom, at least for some years. Only a single coin attests to the rule of Swami Rudrasena IV, son of Swami Simhasena but as it contains no date we cannot say whether he ruled alone or as a rival of his granduncle Rudrasena III. In any case a new king Swami Rudrasimha III occupying the position of Mahakshatrapa in the year 369 A.D. (the unit figure of the date on the coins is lost), which may refer to any year between A.D. 388 and 398. Rudrasimha III is called in his coins the son of Mahakshatrapa Swami Satyasimha. No coins of the later period have been found and it is not known, therefore, whether he actually ruled or merely claimed the position of a Mahakshatrapa as against a rival. Nothing is also known of his relationship with the preceding rulers.

The Internal Dissensions

Thus after a brief respite of twenty years from A.D. 360 to 380 the kingdom of the western Satraps was again convulsed by internal dissensions. The accession of Chandra Gupta II in or shortly before A.D. 380 had something to do with the renewal of political troubles in the kingdom over which the new emperor had been casting covetous eyes. Whether we believe in the episode of Rama Gupta or not, the aggressive and imperialist policy of expansion sufficiently account for the determination of Chandra Gupta to put an end to this last vestige of a foreign rule on the soil of India and thereby expand his growing empire to the furthest natural limits on the west.

The Last Saka Ruler

Unfortunately we know little of the campaign which put an end to the rule of Swami Rudrasimha III, the last of a long line of Saka chiefs who had been ruling over the region for nearly three hundred years. The statement in the Harshacharita that Chandra Gupta, in the disguise of a woman, slew the Saka chief, was usually taken to refer to his final struggle with Rudrasimha III. But this simple fact has now developed into the big episode centering round Rama Gupta and Dhruvadevi[11]. If any value is to be attached to the history of the Western Satraps, it is hardly within the range of probability that they were in a position to challenge the authority of the Gupta emperor and forced him to accept the most ignoble terms which a king is ever known to have proposed to another.

Downfall of the Western Satraps

There is hardly any doubt that the downfall of the Western Satraps was hastened, if not brought about, by the internal dissensions and other troubles which marked their history almost throughout the 4th century A.D. and particularly during the last two decades. Although they disappeared from history, they left a legacy in their peculiar coins which were continued with some modifications by the Guptas and their successors for well-nigh two centuries after their fall.

The Saka or Salivahana Era

The Saka or Salivahana era (A.D. 78), now used throughout India, is the most important of all. It has been used not only in many Indian inscriptions but also in ancient Sanskrit inscriptions in Indonesia[12]. The reformed calendar promulgated by the Indian Government from 1957 is reckoned by this era. It is variously alleged to have been founded by king Kaniska or by the Hindu king Salivahana[13] or by the Satrap Nahapana. According to different practices, the recoining used to refer to elapsed years in the north or current years in the south and was either a solar or luni-solar. Months begin with full moon in the north and with new moon in the south. To reduce Saka dates (elapsed years) to dates A.D. 78 must be added for a date within the period ending with the day equivalent to December 31, and 79 for a later date. For Saka current years, the numbers to be added are 77 and 78. The official Saka year is the elapsed year, starting from the day following that of the vernal equinox. A normal year consists of 365 days, while the leap year has 366 days. The first month is Chaitra, with thirty days in a normal year and 31 in a leap year; the five following months have 31 days, the others 30 days.

Saka Language

Saka language, also called Khotanese14, middle Iranian language, is also spoken in Sinkiang, in north-western China, by the Saka tribes. Two dialectal varieties are distinguished. Khotanese, from the kingdom of Khotan, is richly attested by Buddhist and other texts dating from the 7th to the 10th century. Most of these writings remain unedited. The other dialect known from only one Buddhist fragment, is connected with Tumshuq. The texts are written in Brahmi script and contain many loanwords from the Prakrit language of India.

Satrapy Administration

Initially this system was evolved by the Persian Sakas, who after a short stay in Iran had entered India. Having some experience of Satiapy administration they patronized it in India, which ultimately became popular here.

Administrative unit of ancient Iran (Persia) which was adopted by Cyrus15 II and developed by Darius16 I, under whom the Satrapy was based on existing national or political boundaries. But there were also vassal kingdoms which were not Satrapies. The number of Satrapies varied through redistribution and occasional rebellions. Satrapies tended to become smaller in size and increase in number under the Achaemenids[17]. Each Satrapy was governed by a Satrap, a man of high birth, usually appointed for life, though in some periods the office became hereditary. The Satrap was the highest judicial authority, and was also responsible for communications and the collection of taxes. He was assisted by a secretary and a commander of the soldiers. Under the Seleucids the Satrapies appear to have been more independent of the Central Government, while under the Parthians[18] there were only a few Satrapies among many petty principalities. In the Sassanian[19] period the provinces were again divided up and governed by officials from the nobility, or later by military governors, directly responsible to the Central Government[20].

SATRAPS OF UJJAIN (C.125-400 AD)

Rulers of one of the branches of Scythians (Sakas) which invaded the Indo-Pakistani subcontinent (1st century B.C.) moved southward and finally settled down in Malwa (capital Ujjain). After few generations, they became thoroughly Indianised. The earliest rulers probably acted as governors of the Kushan emperors and so used the title of Satraps which was continued even after their successors had made themselves completely independent (c. A.D. 125). Their greatest ruler was Rudradaman, whose Girnar (Surashtra) inscription (A.D. 150) is the oldest known documents written entirely in pure Sanskrit. It deals with the repair of an ancient irrigation reservoir, the dykes of which had collapsed and caused havoc to the surrounding countryside. The power of the Satraps came to an abrupt end when the area was conquered by Chandra Gupta II (c. 400 A.D.) and incorporated into the Gupta Empire[21].

REFERENCES

1. Members of People originally of Iranian stock, who migrated from Central Asia to the Ural Mountains, between the 6th and 4th centuries B.C. and eventually settled in most of southern European-Russia and the eastern Balkans.
2. The Pahlava from old Persian Parthia are regarded as Parthians.
3. Gulf or inlet, of the Arabian Sea, India, between north Bombay and Kathiawar Peninsula (W); 15-120, miles wide.
4. The Andharas, occupied the coastal region between the Krishna and the Godavari rivers as they did in later days *(The Age of Imperial Unity,* p. 61).
5. 2nd century A.D. Greeco-Egyptian mathematician and geographer.
6. The inscription of Rudradaman I, at Junagarh shows that Saurashtra was a province of the Maurya Empire. It was ruled by Chandra

Gupta's provincial Governor Pusha Gupta *(The Age of Imperial Unify,* p. 61).

7. The authority of the new family was established in Western India by Chastaria, son of Ysamotika of Kardamake (name derived from the Kardarna river in Bactria *(The Age of Imperial Unity,* p. 182).
8. His Sanchi inscription, dated in his 13th regional year, also contains at Saka year, which is read by some as 201 corresponding to 279-80 A.D. and by others as 241 A.D. He called himself a Dharmavijayin and devotee of the god Mahasena *(The Age of Imperial Unity,* pp. 188-89).
9. They were of the most important power that held sway over parts of the Deccan (sometimes with portions of the Central India) after the fall of the Satvahanas and before the rise of the Chalukyas, about the middle of the 6th century *(The Age of Imperial Unity,* p. 217).
10. Rudrasena, son of Viradaman, the coins of Mahakshatrapa, were found between the years 177 and 198 A.D., (255-77 A.D.) (*The Age of Imperial Unity*, p. 189).
11. Samudra Gupta was succeeded by his son Rama Gupta, whose wife was called Dhruvadevi. In the course of war with the Saka king, he was closely besieged, and placed in such a difficult position, that in order to save his people he agreed to surrender his queen to the Saka king. His younger brother Chandra Gupta protested against this act of dishonour, and offered to go to the enemy's camp in the disguise of queen Dhruvadevi in order to kill the hated Saka king. The strategy succeeded and Chandra Gupta saved the empire *(The Classical Age,* p. 17).
12. Republic (less western New Guinea) Malay Archipelago. S.E. Asia. Jakarta, consists of large island, groups of volcanic origin, extending c. 3,000 miles east-west in Indian and Pacific Oceans.
13. After Allata, his son Narvahna ascended the throne and ruled till at least A.D. 971. He was succeeded by his son Salivahana, whose son and successor was Sakitumara *(The Age of Imperial Kanauj, p.* 109).
14. The Saka language.
15. It is generally held that the eastern conquest of Cyrus included the districts of Drangiana (Sistan) Satagydia, and Gandhara were held by them (*The Age of Imperial Unity*, p. 38).
16. The very word Yauna, meaning the Greeks, used for the first time in the records of Darius I, Emperor of Iran, was borrowed by the Indians without any modification (*Mahabharata* XII, 207, 43).
17. Achaemenid dynasty, the Persian 37th dynasty of Egypt (525- 400 B.C.) founded by Cambyses II of Persia and named after his family of the Achaemenids.

18. After having defeated the great king Artabanus V of Parthia in 224 A.D., Sassanian King Ardushir conquered the Western Provinces of Parthian empire and crowned himself with the title of King of Kings (Shahanshah) of Iran (*The Classical Age*, p. 51).
19. It is generally held that the eastern conquest of Cyrus including the district of Drangiana, Satagydia and Gandaritis (Gandhara which were located in the north-western regions forming the boundary between India and Iran (*The Age of Imperial Unity*, p. 39).
20. *Encyclopaedia of World Cultures*, p. 1345.
21. Indian Dynasty (c. 320 A.D.-550 A.D.) founded by Chandra Gupta. At its height, the dynasty ruled much of what is modern India.

BIBLIOGRAPHY

Encyclopaedia of Britannica, Vol. 21. p. 48.

Hucker, Charles O. *China's Imperial Past.*

Hutton, J.H. *Caste in India*, University Press, 1946.

Kaul, H.K. *Travellers India.*

Rapson, N.S. Vol. XLVII pp. 96-97.

Sarkar, Dr. D.C. PIHC, Vol. VII. p. 78.

The Concise Columbia Encyclopedia.

The Age of Imperial Unity.

Waston, Francis. *A Concise History of India.*

The Kushans

(Ancestors of Jats, Ahirs, Rajputs, Baloches & Pathans)

7

ORIGIN

The Kushans replaced the Greeks in Bactria[1], about 130 B.C. They are thought to have been of Yueh-chih stock with a strong admixture of Hephthalits, Saka, and Tocharian. One branch of this group migrated to the Tarim Basin[2] and founded a shortlived empire, while the other under the name of Kushan gained control of Central Asia. Capturing a section of the great trade route leading from India and China to the west, the Kushans derived much of their revenue from the transit dues they exacted from the caravans (Qafalas) crossing their territory, which often were carrying supplies of Chinese gold, silver and nickel from the Tarim Oasis towns to the Seleucid Persians. About 106 B.C., the first caravan to carry silk from China direct to Persia passed through the territory between the Kushans and Parthians[3].

The determination of the Han rulers[4] of China to keep the Central Asian nomadic tribes (the Haiung-nu, Wu-Sun and Yueh-chih) out of China forced these nomadic tribes to search for fresh pastures to migrate southward and westward. A branch of the Yueh-chih, (the Ta Yueh-chih), moved farthest west to the Aral Sea[5], and this displaced the existing Sakas, who poured into Bactria[6] and Parthia[7]. The Parthian king Mithradates II[8] tried to hold them back, but after his death (88 B.C.). they swept through Parthia and continued into the Indus Valley. Among the early Saka kings was Maues, or Moga[9] (1st century B.C.), who ruled over Gandhara[10]. The Sakas moved southward under pressure from the Pahlavas (Parthians), who ruled briefly in north-western India toward the end of the 1st century B.C. the reign of Gondophernes[11] being remembered. At Mathura[12], the Saka rulers of note were Rajuvala and Sodasa. Ultimately they settled in western India and Malwa and came into conflict with the kingdom of the northern Deccan and the

Ganges Valley, particularly the reigns of Nahapana[13], Castana[14] and Rudradaman[15] in the first two centuries A.D. Rudradaman's fame is recorded in a lengthy Sanskrit inscription at Junagadh[16], dating to 150 A.D.

YUEH-CHIH

Yueh-chih, Pinyin yuezhi, a branch of the Kushans, also called Indo-Scyth, ancient people, who ruled in Bactria (Balkh) and India from about 128 B.C. to about A.D. 450. The Yueh- chih are first mentioned in Chinese sources at the beginning of the 2nd century B.C. as nomads, living in the western part of Kansu province north-west of China. When Lao Shang (reigned c. 174-161), ruler of the Hsiungnu (a powerful people of North China), defeated them and killed their king, the main body of Yueh-chih moved westward into Sogdiana[17] and Bactria, putting an end to Greek rule there. They are related tribes who were the Asiani and Tocharians[18] (Tochari) of western sources. About 128 B.C. the Yueh-chih were recorded living north of the Oxus River, (Amu-Darya), ruling Bactria (Balkh) as a dependency, but little later the Great Yueh-chih kingdom was in Bactria, and Sogdiana[19] was occupied by the Ta-Yuan (Tocharians). The remnant in Kansu were called little Yueh-chih.

KUSHANS A NEW DYNASTY

A new dynasty, that of the Kushans, was subsequently founded by one of the five chieftains among whom Bactria was divided.

The Kushan kingdom extended its power southward and eastward into India and northward into Central Asia. From the 3rd century A.D. however Kushan power declined, and about A.D. 400 the Kidar, another dynasty arose in Gandhara; it survived only to about A.D. 450, overwhelmed by the Hephthalites[20].

EMPEROR KUJULA KADAPHISES

The Yueh-chih succeeded by his son Vima, after whom came Kanishka, the most powerful among the Kushan kings, as the dynasty came to power. The date of Kanishka's accession is controversial, ranging from 78 to 248. The generally accepted date of 78 is also the basis for an era started by the Saka and used in addition to the Gregorian[21] calendar by the present Indian government; the era, possibly commemorating Kanishka's accession, was widely used in Malawa, Ujjain, Nepal and Central India. The Kushan kingdom was essentially oriented to the north, with its capital at Purusapur[22] (near modern Peshawar), although it extended southward as far as

Sanci[23] and into the Ganga Valley and Varanasi. Mathura was the most important city in the southern part of the kingdom. Kanishka's ambitions included control of Central Asia, which, if not directly under the Kushans, did come under their influence. The recently discovered inscriptions from Giligit[24] further attest such Central Asian connection. Kanishka's successors failed to maintain Kushan power. The southern areas were the first to break away, and by the middle of the 3rd century, the Kushans were left virtually with only Gandhara and Kashmir. By the end of the century they were reduced to vassalage by the Sasanian king of Persia.

THE POLITICAL NOMENCLATURE

Not surprisingly, administrative and political nomenclature in northern India at this time reflected that of western and Central Asia. The Persian term for the governor of a province. Khshathrapavan, as used by the Achaemenians[25], was Hellenized into "Satrap" and widely used by these dynasties. Its Sanskrit form was Ksatrapa. The governors of higher status came to be called Mahaksatrapa. They frequently used inscriptions reflecting whatever they chose to follow, and they minted their own coins, indicating a more independent status than is generally associated with governors. Imperial titles also were taken by the Indo-Greeks, such as *basileus basileon* ("king of kings") similar to Persian Shahanshah, of which the later Sanskrit form was Maharaj adhiraj a. A title of Central Asia derivation was the Daivputra of the Kushans, which is believed to have come originally from the Chinese, "son of heaven" emphasizing the divinity of kingship.

KUSHAN DYNASTY

Kushan dynasty, also spelled Kushana, ruling line descended from the Yueh-chih (q.v.), people that ruled over most of the northern Indian-Pakistan subcontinent, Afghanistan and part of Central Asia during the first three centuries of the Christian era. The Yueh-chih conquered Bactria (Balkh) in the 2nd century B.C. and divided that of the Kushans (Kuei-shuang). A hundred years later the Kushan chief Kujula Kadphises[26] (Chiu-Chiu-Chueh) secured the political unification of the Yueh-chih kingdom under himself.

KANISHKA

The Kushan empire reached its zenith under Kanishka, who conquered the major part of northern India. He was the greatest of the Kushan emperors. His rule extended over the Madhyadesa,

Uttarapatha and Apranta divisions of ancient India. His empire seems to have stretched from Bihar in the east to Khurasan in the west, and from Khotan in the north to the Konkan in the south. Epigraphic records of the reign of Kanishka himself prove his control over U.P., the Panjab, North-western Frontier Province, and the Bahawalpur region, north of Sind. Officers like the Dandanayuka Lala and the Kashatrapas Vespasi and Liaka were serving in the north-western India, while parts of the eastern U.P. were under the joint rule of the Maha-Kshatrapa Kharapallana and the Kshatrapa Vanasphara. The discovery of a large number of Kanishka records at Mathura, with one from Suivihar, 16 miles from Bahawalpur (Pakistan), and an epigraph of 78 A.D., which is connected by its very name with foreigners and is the second popular era in the history of India[27].

In outlook, Kanishka was full-fledged Indian and took active interest in the all-around development of the country, especially in the spheres of religion, literature, and art. Celebrated as a great patron of Buddhism, he attempted to systematize the contradictory views of the various schools, and with this object summoned the fourth Buddhist Council, which marked the official recognition of the growing Mahayanism, with far-reaching results in both religion and art. The huge stupa which he built in the immediate vicinity of Peshawar[28], his capital, evoked great admiration even in later times from the Chinese and Arab travellers. From inside his stupa has been recovered an inscribed relic casket, bearing the figure of the Buddha both on its body and lid and recording a gift in Kanishka's monastery, probably in the first year of his reign. The inscription also preserves the name of the architect Agisala, which is undoubtedly a Prakrit form of Agesilaos an instance of Kushana rulers requisitioning the services of a Greek. His coins also bear the figure of the Buddha. Both the Hellenistic[29] art of Gandhara and the indigenous art of Mathura[30], which witnessed the simultaneous appearance of the Buddha-image, owe much to the active patronage of this great ruler and his successors. The extra-Indian limits of their empire helped to a very great extent the spread of the Gandhara art in Afghanistan and the neighbouring regions. Kanishka also extended his patronage to Buddhist philosophers and writers like Asvaghosa Parsva, and Vasumitra.

NUMISMATIC STUDY OF KUSHANS

Excavation and numismatic study reveal that the original religious background of the Kushans was a Mazdean[31] fire-worship of which traces remain even in the monuments they left in their new homes along the Indus. But when they reached the Indus valley they became subject to many religious influences, the first effect of which was to produce a syncretism so tolerant that its niches received deities as varied as Heracles[32], Hephaestus, Muthras, Shiv and finally the Lord Buddha. It was down this broad path of eclectic experiment that the great Kushan king, Kanishka proceeded to find in the end that Buddhist revelation which caused him to displace the other gods from their pedestals and to offer devotion to the form of worship now associated with Gandhara and the Kushan age.

KINGDOM OF GANDHARA

Kanishka having chosen Gandhara, with its capital at Peshawar as the nodal point of his empire, the state which he ruled had come to be known as the kingdom of Gandhara. And since Kanishka following in the footsteps of Ashoka, four centuries earlier, had embraced or at least greatly encouraged Buddhism, and Gandhara under his leadership became the centre of an important civilisation especially as regards art. The name has come to be used in designation of the significant art forms which spread outward from Peshawar to many other parts of Asia. It was because under Kanishka, there had developed a golden age of Buddhism that the Chinese pilgrims, Fa-Hien[33] and Hiuen-Tsang[34], later made it one of the bourns of their pilgrimage. Outside the Ganj gate of the modern Peshawar city, was discovered in 1909, the remarkable relic casket of Kanishka now deposited in the Peshawar Museum. The site of these excavations is now locally known as Shahji-Ki-Dheri, the king's mound.

The difficulty in reconstructing Kushan history arises from the fact that their main contacts extended to the inhabitants of India, the least imbued with historical sense of any ancient civilisation in the world. Relatively to the size and scope of the later empire little contemporary evidence is available and though the later Chinese Buddhist literature records defendant of Kanishka, these books do not fall in accurate historical detail and are largely repetition of Indian religious speculation. Moreover, the records which do exist throw little light on the tribes and people in the Gandhar region over whom Kanishka and his successors ruled. Coins and works of art are innumerable, and from them the dynastic overtones may be painted in. But, for the identity, or way of life, or language, of the ruled we look in vain. Only the name of the capital is known;

of the Pakkhtunes the Aparutai, the Gandarici, and their successors we have no word. We do not even know for certain of what stock the rulers themselves claimed to be. Under the Kushans Peshawar attained the dignity of an imperial capital.

CHANNELS OF TRADE WERE UNLOCKED

It was under the Kushans that the channels of trade between the Roman world and further Asia were at last unlocked. Ever since the Seleucids[35] had yielded power to the Arsacids[36] on the Iranian plateau, the state described by Sir Mortimer Wheeler as "the implacable barrier of Parthia had stood astride these routes, often at war with Rome and closing the Orient trade by extortionate levy or actual veto". But the rise of the Kushan power on her eastern flank involved Parthia in a war on two fronts; Iran, as Ghirshman observes, "had become a much reduced central state sandwiched between Rome and a new empire based on Gandhara". The Kushans and the Romans had a common interest both in politics and in commerce; the Kushans then holding merchandise to avoid Parthian territory. And it was from this time that the Parthian period of decadence set in.

THE GANDHARA ART

Gandhara art would never have been brought to birth had not Greek kings ruled in that country in the 2nd and 1st centuries B.C. But it is now more generally held that it is to this age, the age of Kanishka (A.D. 128-51), two hundred years later, that we must attribute the full flowering of the famous Gandhara art in sculpture, in stone, bronze and stucco, in coffers, plaques, bowls and objects d' art of all descriptions. This astonishing mass of material represent according to Wheeler, not a Greek influence as such but the most penetrating and enduring impact of the Roman upon the Eastern world[37]. The craftsmen may often have been Greeks but the source of this plethora of art treasures have been traced to Roman Alexandria. By the absorption of the Western modes of expression, in the representation of figure statuary and so on, the face of Buddhism was changed. The Hinayana, or lesser vehicle, expanded into the Mahayana, or greater vehicle. Under the former the Buddha was never represented; he was not a god but a sage. Under the Mahayana, a persuasion which first took shape under Kanishka and is represented by the art of Gandhara, the Buddha has become divine and is the focus of every composition. The Roman heroic and funerary art are indeed transmuted by the oriental craftsmen and given a Buddhist context, but as Wheeler points out, "both iconographically and aesthetically the change was revolutionary, and represents a synthesis of the utmost interest and importance."[38]

LINK OF INFLUENCE

As to the controversy on the point whether this new effulgence should be linked with Greece or Rome, it is possible to hold that in this region it is perhaps unreal to make a distinction between the two sources of influence. It is generally agreed that the fountainhead of inspiration was Alexandria, the centre of neo-Platonism and Hellenistic art, whether under the Graecuzed Ptlemies or the Roman who succeeded them. Admitting that Gandhara art was the outcome of Kushan commerce bringing in the craftsmanship of the Roman Empire. It is worth remembering that the time then assigned for it conceded with the reign of Emperor Hadrian (A.D. 117-138), a devotee of esoteric cults and the art, and who spoke Greek better than Latin. It is certain too that the craftsmen employed stood for an Eastern Mediterranean rather than a Latin tradition. We may follow Tarn[39] at least so far in believing that the earlier Graeco-Bactrian kingdom in Gandhara had paved the way for this development.

SHAH-KI-DHERI

In King Kanishka's later days, when he had become a fervent Buddhist, he created a great relic tower just outside the Ganjgate of Peshawar at Shahji-Ki-Dheri with a superstructure of carved wood rising in thirteen storeys to a height of some 400 feet, and surmounted by an iron pinnacle. Vincent Smith, author of *Ancient History of India* tells us how it was visited by Sung Yun[40], a Chinese pilgrim, at the beginning of the 6th century, by which time it had thrice been destroyed by fire and as often rebuilt by pious kings. A monastery of exceptional magnificence was still flourishing here as a place of Buddhist education as late as the 9th century when it was visited by Vira Deva[41], an eminent Buddhist scholar. But the Brahminical revival which began in the later Kushan period frowned on Buddhist piety, and what was left by the Brahminism have been finally destroyed by Mahmud of Ghazni[42] and his successors in the 11th century A.D.

PESHAWAR SPIRITUAL CENTER OF FAITH

It is strange reflection that Peshawar, the seat of learning which gave birth to a religion that gloried in the portrayal of life in pictorial art, later became one of the spiritual centres of the Faith which is distinguished for iconoclasm. We have collected evidence to suggest that tribes bearing names which have come down to the present day were already living in the neighbourhood of Peshawar many centuries before the Kushan renascence of Buddhism, and that the ancestor of the language now spoken in this region had already come in contact certainly no later than the Saka horsemen. The Kushans themselves, a fresh wave of Saka invaders of Iranian stock, must have spoken not so very different from that of the Sakas. In a word, there is evidence that the Pakhtu (Pashto) speakers of today, or their progenitors, were beginning to emerge when Kanishka was king. A Pathan of today would ask how could our ancestors have been followers of the image of Buddha?

It is not difficult to supply some sort of answer. A new wind may blow, and ancient fragrances grow stale. The very strength of a Pathan's reaction against the sensuous rituals of the older creeds may be indicative of his ancestors feeling for those rituals in their day. "Guftagu-yi-kufr-wa-din akhir bi-kuja mikashad? Khwab Yak Khwabast, bashad mukhtalif tabirha." This chatter of heathendom and faith, where does it lead in the end? The dream is one dream, though many and various be the interpretations.

DECLINE OF KUSHANS

The great Kushan empire broke up some time after 230 or 240 A.D., which probably represents the end of the reign of Vasudeva or one of the later kings named Kanishka or Vasudeva. Apart from other causes the growing power of the Sassanians was the most important factor that contributed to it. The first Sassanian king Ardashir (240-241) conquered the Kushana principalities to the north of the Hindu Kush[43], and although Kushan chiefs continued to rule there they had to acknowledge the supremacy of the Sassanid king. His Governor, generally the heir-apparent, assumed the proud title of 'Kushan-king' or 'King of Kushan' and issued gold coins like those of Vasudeva.

We learn from a Chinese account that Po-tiao, the king of the Great Kushans, sent an embassy to the Chinese Court in A.D. 230. This name may well represent Vasudeva and it was probably the growing power of Sassanids that induced him to seek help from the Chinese emperor. But evidently no help came, and in any case he was unable to check the aggression of the Sassanian king. But although Balkh was lost, the Kushana overlord, whose seat of authority was probably at Peshawar, still ruled over the other parts of the Kushana kingdom. His power and prestige were however, considerably weakened. Taking advantage of this Indian states now one after another asserted their independence and even the Kushana governors of the Panjab and neighbouring regions followed suit. There were probably two or more dynasties belonging to Shilada, Shaka and Gadhara clans who formed independent principalities in the Panjab. The Sassanian kings in the west grew more and more powerful. When hormanised rebelled against his brother Vahram II (A.D. 283), the Kushans and Sakas joined him probably in a desperate effort at getting rid of the Sassanian supremacy. But the rebellion was crushed and Vahram II conquered the whole of Seitstan, Makran and the lower Sindhu valley. He also tightened his hold on the Kushan principalities in Balkh.

But though shorn of his possessions in Bactria, Seistan and the Sindhu valley, the Kushan king still maintained his hold in the Kabul valley, and the Paikuli[44] inscription, refers to him as independent king (A.D. 293). His importance is indicated by the fact that the Sassanian king Hormazd (302-9) married a daughter of Kushan king of the Kabul valley. But later, about the middle of the 4th century A.D., the Kabul valley formed a part of the Sassanid empire. An inscription found at Persepolis dated A.D. 310-11, refers to Shahpur Sahanshah, an elder brother of Shahpur II (309-379 A.D.), who had the titles "King of Sakastan, minister of Sind, Sakastan and Tukharistan", and who was accompanied by the "minister of public instruction of Sakastan", by the Satrap of Seistan, (in the modern meaning of the name) and other dignitaries. Another inscription from Persepolis is probably dated in the year 47 of Shahpur II, *i.e.* A.D. 356, though the figure is doubtful. It is written by Slok, "Seleucus[45], high judge of Kabul" who, according to this record, was paying his homage to Shahpur Sahanshah as his superior, showing that even Kabul belonged to the lands governed by the Sahanshah at that time. If the date has been correctly read, Kabul must have been conquered sometime before A.D. 356.

Thus for more than a century after the death of Vasudeva, the last great Kushan emperor, the later Kushans ruled over the Kabul valley. Whether they were finally overthrown during the reign of Shahpur[46] II or they maintained a precarious existence in the lower Kabul Valley and a part of the Panjab. But the latter view seems probable and perhaps new tribal movements led to fresh Kushan migrations to this region and strengthened the kingdom.

THE EPHTHALITE HUNS

The Ephthalite Huns were a Turko-Mongol horde; in this case, it seems, more Mongol than Turk[47] and originating, according to Sung Yun, in the Kinshan hills—that is to say, in the Altai—whence they had come down to the steppes of present-day Russian Turkestan. Their name, given as Ephthalites by Byzantine historians, Hayathelites by the Persian historian Mirkhond, and Ye-tai by the historians of China, seems to be derived from the name of the royal clan Ephtha or Ye-ta.[48] Byzantine historians knew them also by the designation—here somewhat erroneous—of White Huns.

At the beginning of the 5th century A.D., the Ephthalites were no more than a secondary horde, vassal of the greater one—Mongol, likewise—of the Juan-juan, which dominated Mongolia, In the second quarter of the 5th century, these same Ephthalites acquired considerable importance by the expansion of their dominion westward. Their rule extended from the upper Yulduz in the east (northwest of Kara Shahr) across the Ili basin to Balkhash, over the Chu and Talas steppes and the Syr Darya region as far as the Aral Sea. According to some sources, one of their Khan's residences was near the town of Talas. By about 440 A.D., they had also occupied Sogdiana or Transoxiana (Samarkand) and, it seems, the country of Balkh, Bactria, or Tokharistan.

Several Orientalists, Noeldeke in particular, believe that it was during the reign of King Bahram Gor of Persia (420-438 A.D.) that the Ephthalites settled in Bactria. They are thought even to have invaded the Sassanian province of Khurasan, whence Bahram Gor drove them back in the Battle of Kusmehan near Merv. Marquart, on the other hand, believes that Bahram Gor and later his successor Yezdegerd II (438-457 A.D.) had to defend themselves not against Ephthalite aggression but against that of the Khionites, another Hunnic tribe who led a nomadic existence north of Merv[49]. However this may be, it was certainly the Ephthalites who during the reign of the Sassanid king Peroz (459-484 A.D.) attacked Khurasan family and defeated and killed that monarch. Ephthalite chief who won this victory was known by Arabo- Persian historians under the name of Akhshunwar or Akhshunwaz, apparently a corruption of the Sogdian title *Kbshevan* or king.[50]

After their victory over King Peroz, the Ephthalite Huns occupied not only the frontier district of Talekan (western Talekan, between Balkh and Merv), which until then had been the frontier town of the Sassanid Empire in the northwest, but also Merv and Herat. Furthermore, they intervened in the palace quarrels of the Persian Sassanid dynasty. It was in this way that the Sassanid Kavadh, driven from the throne of Ctesiphon, took refuge with them, married the niece of their Khan, and received from him an army, with whose aid, he regained his crown (498 or 499 A.D.). By then, the Ephthalites had become a power to be reckoned with in Middle Asia. The *Liang Shu* notes the embassy sent in 516 A.D. to the Chinese court of Nanking by their kind "Ye-tai-i-li-t'o".

Despite King Peroz's defeat, Sassanid Persia was too well defended for the Ephthalites to contemplate its conquest. They returned southeastward, in the direction of Kabul. There the first reaction to their approach seems to have been the replacement of the Kushan dynasty about the middle of the 5th century by another line of the same Yueh-chih or Tukhara extraction from Bactria. Iranian sources tell of a "Kidarite" dynasty—established apparently south of the Oxus, between Balkh and Merv—which was at war with the Sassanids. According to these same sources, the Sassanid Peroz (459-484 A.D.)—the same who was to perish under the blows of the Ephthalites—fought the Kidarite chiefs, first the eponymous hero Kidara and then his son Kungas (Kungkas). It was after his defeat by Peroz that Kungas is believed to have left Bactria, which the Ephthalites promptly occupied, crossed the Hindu Kush, and entered Kabul, where he took the place of the last Kushan rulers[51]. These events are confirmed by the Chinese, though ascribed to an earlier date and consequently to somewhat different causes. Chinese sources, in which information seems to date from as far back as the years 436-451, record that "a king of the Yueh-chih" from "Po-lo"—which here no doubt denotes the Tukhara of Balkh—had just left Bactria under Ephthalite pressure and moved to Gandhara, where he settled at Peshawar, bringing under his sway his cousin the Yueh-chih of Kabul: that is, the last of Kushans. The Chinese call this king Ki-to-lo, which corresponds exactly to our Kidara[52]. Thus it must have been the Ephthalites rather than the Sassanians who forced the Kidarites to leave Bactria and take refuge in Kabul. The Kidarites, however, were soon followed by the Ephthalites, who lost no time in crossing the Hindu Kush by the same route. Thus the whole of the old Yueh-chih territory—Bactria, Kabul, and Kandahar—passed into Ephthalite hands. In addition, from the heights of the Kabul valley the Ephthalite vanguard sprang forth as the Kushans had done before them—to the conquest of India.

The greater part of India—the whole Ganges basin, the Malwa, Gujarat, and the northern Deccan—formed at that time a huge empire under the national dynasty of the Gupta emperors, a dynasty which reached its peak during the reign of Kumara Gupta (ca. 414-455 A.D.), who was succeeded by his son Skanda Gupta (ca. 455-470 A.D.). It was either during Kumara Gupta's last years or at the beginning of Skanda Gupta's reign that the Ephthalite Huns—known to the Indians by the Sanskrit transcription *Huna*—having conquered Kabul, came down into the Panjab and were brought up short against the frontiers of the Gupta realm, near Doab or the Malwa. On that occasion they were repulsed by Skanda Gupta, either soon after his accession or just before. If before, the beginning of his reign may have coincided with a second Hun invasion, which was likewise beaten off. After this, as an inscription of 460 A.D. tells, the country was once more at peace.

Meanwhile the Ephthalites had entrenched themselves firmly on both sides of the Hindu Kush, in Bactria and Kabul. In 520 A.D., at the time of Sung Yun's pilgrimage, their Khan lived north of Hindu Kush, migrating seasonally from Bactria, where he spent the winter, to Badakhshan, his summer residence. At Kabul, in the old Greco-Buddhic provinces of Kapisa and Gandhara, a secondary Ephthalite chief had settled: a *tegin* who founded there a dynasty, of which the second sovereign was reigning in 520 A.D. Here, amid the lofty culture of Gandhara, of which Hellenism jointly with Buddhism had made a new Hellas and Buddhic Holy Land combined, the Ephthalites behaved like barbarians, massacring the inhabitants and persecuting especially the Buddhist communities, sacking monasteries and works of art, and ruining the fine Greco-Buddhic civilisation which by then was five centuries old. Persian[53] and Chinese texts agree in their descriptions of the tyranny and vandalism of this horde.

In the *Pei-Shih* and the story, related by Sung Yun—who in 520 A.D., it will be remembered, visited first their Khan at his summer residence of Badakhshan, and later the *tegin* of Ghandhara—all these Huns are described as pure nomads, "They do not live in towns; their seat of government is a moving camp. Their dwellings are of felt. They move in search of water and pasture, journeying in summer to cool places and in winter to warmer ones. A large felt tent is erected for their king, measuring forty feet a side; on the inside, the walls are made of woollen rugs. The king's clothes are of ornamented silk, and he sits on a golden bed of which the feet are in the shape of four golden phoenixes. His chief wife also wears an ornamented silk robe which trails three feet along the ground. On her head, she wears a horn eight feet long, decorated with precious stones in five colours."[54] Sung Yun also notes the Ephthalite custom of fraternal polyandry and their hostility to Buddhism, "They have no belief in the Buddhic law and they serve a great number of divinities. They kill living creatures and are eaters of bloody meat." On the testimony of Hsuan-tsang, the Ephthalites cut the throats of two-thirds of the Gandharan population, reduced the rest to slavery, and destroyed most of the Buddhist monasteries and stupas[55].

From Kabul the Ephthalites eyed the riches of India. Driven back by the Indian emperor Skanda Gupta, they bid their time. Their opportunity occurred when, after the death of that ruler (ca. 470 A.D.), the Indian Empire fell into decay. This may have been the result of the partition of the country between two branches of the Gupta dynasty, one reigning over the Malwa in the persons of Buddha Gupta (ca. 476-494 A.D.) and Buddha Gupta (ca. 499-543 A.D.), the other over Bihar and Bengal, where Puragupta and Narasimha Gupta successively held power. Profiting from this decline of Gupta power, the Huns resumed their invasions of India. The Hun chief who led them, and who is known in Indian literature by the name of Toramana (d. 502), was not the Khan of the Ephthalites, as is sometimes contended. The Khan, as we saw, lived north of the Hindu Kush, in Bactria and Badakhshan. This man was a secondary prince or *tegin;* no doubt the *tegin* of Kabul. Three inscriptions of his, found at Khewra in the Salt Range (northwest of the Panjab), at Gwalior, and at Iran, prove that he conquered not only the Indus basin but the Malwa as well. His coinage is an imitation of that of the Indian emperor Buddha Gupta, his contemporary.[56]

Mihirakula, Toramana's son and successor (known only by his laudatory Indian name "Race of the Sun" in classical Sanskrit), who seems to have ruled his horde from about 502 to 530 A.D., was indeed the Attila of India. He had taken up his residence at Sialkot in the eastern Panjab, and must have been that *tegin* of Gandhara whom the Chinese pilgrim Sung Yun met in 520 A.D. After conquering Kashmir, Mihirakula returned to Gandhara, where he perpetrated frightful massacres. Buddhist writers describe him as a terrible persecutor of their religion. Hiuan-tsang tells that the Gupta ruler of Magadha or Bihar, called Baladitya (perhaps identical with Narasimha Gupta mentioned above), was the only one who dared to oppose him. Mihirakula advanced into the Ganges region in search of his opponent. At first, Baladitya is reported to have retreated before him; then, in a surprise attack, he seems to have defeated and even captured him. The narrative ends as a moral tale. Apart from this, the inscription of Iran, in the Malwa, dated 510 A.D., which recounts the victories of Bhana Gupta—another Gupta prince—has given rise to the belief but these triumphs too were won over Ephthalite invaders. Lastly, in 533 a third Indian prince, Yasodharman, assumed to be a member of the dynasty of the rajas of Mandasur in the Malwa, boasts in his inscriptions of having conquered the Huns and forced Mihirakula to pay him homage. After these defeats, Mihirakula appears to have withdrawn to Kashmir, where for some unknown reason he took an appalling vengeance on his Gandhara subjects, as is reported by Chinese pilgrims. Buddhist texts assert that by way of punishment for his atrocities, he met with a ghastly death.

We do not know what became of the clans camped in the Panjab after Mihirakula's demise. They must have continued to be troublesome, if not dangerous neighbours, for in the second half of the 6th century the Maharaja of Thanesar[57], Prabhakara (d. 605); won honour and power by fighting them. In 605 his eldest son Rajyavardhana was still waging war on them, and later the successor to these two, the great Indian emperor Harsha (606-647), was acclaimed by the poets for his victories over these same Huns. Yet from the second half of the 7th century the Huns of India vanished from history, no doubt either exterminated or absorbed by the Panjabis. Some of their clans most likely succeeded in gaining admission to the Hindu aristocracy, in the manner of the Rajput clan of the Gurjara, which may possibly have the same origin.

REFERENCES

1. Greek kingdom in Central Asia. Its capital was Bactra present day Balkh in north Afghanistan.
2. A town (p in 1990-1380) Big Horn Co. North Wyo, on Big Horn River, just west of Big Horn mountains.
3. *The Encyclopaedia of Britannica*. Vol. 15, p. 729.
4. The Han dynasty asserted sovereignty over vast regions from Korea in the east to Central Asia in the west and Vietnam in the south. Once garrisons were established, traders were quick to follow, leading to

considerable spread of Chinese material culture (China-Cambridge University Press, 1996. p. 63).

5. One of the largest river 24,635 square miles inland seas of the world in the USSR, in Kazakh SSR and Kara-Kalpak, 175 miles east of Caspian Sea, 230 miles long.
6. Region of Central Asia, upper reaches of the Oxus (Amu-darya) and the Hindu Kush, (modern Balkh).
7. Province of ancient Persian Empire, corresponding roughly to modern Khurasan.
8. King of Parthia (d. 88 B.C.) reigned 123-88 B.C. He was the son and successor of Artabanus II. He recovered the eastern provinces that have been overrun by invading Saka nomads, during his father's reign.
9. Among the early Saka kings was Maues, or Moga (1st century B.C.), who ruled over Gandhara, ancient region of north-west India, astride the middle Indus River.
10. Ancient region of north-west Indus, Pakistan, astride middle Indus River. Main cities were Peshawar and Taxila.
11. An Indo Parthian king in the areas of Arachosia, Kabul and Gandhara (Afghanistan).
12. A district in Uttar Pradesh, in Ganges-Jamuna Doab.
13. He is known from his coins and a number of his inscriptions bearing dates ranging between the years 41 & 46 A.D. *(The Age of Imperial Unity,* pp. 180-183).
14. He was contemporary of King Nahapana.
15. The Andhra rulers known also by their dynastic name as Satavahnas, came from Telugu speaking, non-Aryan (or perhaps mixed) stock. Their line lasted for more than four centuries, but after their first conquest there was a fluctuating period in which they lost their north-western provinces to the Scythian Sakas and they did not fully recover them until the 1st century A.D. After that they still had to deal with the Aaka Prima Rudradaman who is recorded in 150 AD at Junagadh, in Sarashtra *(A Concise History of India,* Francis Watson, p. 73).
16. Sorath District, south Saurashtra, India, 55 miles SW of Rajkot near Girnar hills.
17. Transoxiana.
18. Member of a people important in the history of India and Iran during the 5th and 6th centuries-Chinese-Hoaor Hoa-tun, here they were called white Huns.
19. It is Transoxiana.

20. Missionaries from the Great Yueh-chih played an important part in the propagation of Buddhism in China. The spread of Indian culture into Central Asia as far as the borders of China also resulted from Kushan influence.
21. Pertaining to Pope Gregory I or Pope Gregory XIII.
22. Hellenistic Age (325-50 B.C.), in the eastern Mediterranean and the Middle East, the period between the death of Alexander, and the conquest of Egypt by Rome.
23. *Encyclopedia of Britannica*, Vol. 21. p. 959.
24. Seleucid Kingdom (312-64 B.C.), an ancient empire that at its greatest extent stretched from Thrace, in Europe to the border of India. It was carved out of the remains of the Empire of Alexander, the Great.
25. Achaemenids dynasty of ancient Persia. The Achaemenids rulers c. 550-330 B.C. included Cyrus.
26. Iranian name borne by the Parthian Royal House as being descended from Arsaces, son of Phriapites, a chief of the semi-nomadic tribe from the Capsian steppes.
27. The use of an era was introduced and popularized by foreign rulers. The Saka 'satraps' of western India appear to have been originally feudatories of Kanishka and his successors had naturally used the era of their lords *(The Age of Imperial Unity*, pp. 141-142).
28. Now the capital of the North-West Frontier Province, Pakistan, situated 11 miles east of the entrance to Khyber Pass, 1590 miles north-west of Calcutta.
29. Southern France. It is separated from the Mediterranean Sea.
30. Headquarters of the district of the same name, Uttar Pradesh, India, on the right bank of the Jamuna, 30 miles above Agra. For centuries it remained the centre of Buddhism.
31. Also known as Ormazed, the Parsi form of the name of the highest god of Mazdaism, the principle of good. *(Encyclopedia of Religion and Ethics,* Vol. 9. pp. 566-70).
32. One of the Greek heroes.
33. One of the main systems of Central Asia, situated largely in NE. Afghanistan, extends from the Pamir Mountain knot-at-west termination (37° N 74° E).
34. A Chinese traveller and historian, who visited India from 630 to 645 A.D., during the reign of Harsha Vardhana.
35. Seleucid Kingdom (312-64 B.C.). An ancient empire that at its greatest extent stretched from Thrace in Europe to the border of India *(Encyclopedia of Britannica,* Vol. 10. p. 617).
36. Arsacid dynasty also called Arshakuni (247 B.C. to 224 A.D.). Ancient Arsacids dynasty that founded and ruled the Parthian empire *(The Encyclopaedia of Britannica,* Vol. 1. p. 591).

37. *The Pathans,* Olaf Caroe. p. 75.
38. *The Pathans,* Olaf Caroe. p. 76.
39. The contemporary historian.
40. Sung dynasty (960-1279 A.D., Chinese dynasty that ruled the country *(Encyclopaedia of Britannica,* Vol. II. p. 395).
41. Viradeva was described as the lord of Aryadesa and the sovereign of Polandvipa was apparently an Indian adventurer. He is stated to have occupied Rajashtra for the time, but to have been soon afterwards killed *(The Struggle for Empire,* p. 262).
42. Son of Subuktigin who ruled during 998-1030 A.D., in whose reign the Ghaznavi power had reached its zenith.
43. Pashto, Hindu-Koh, one of the main mountain systems in Central Asia, situated largely in NE-Afghanistan; extends from the Pamir Mountain knot-at-west termination (37° N 74° E of the Karakoram, south-westward for 400 miles to 35° N and 68° E).
44. It is interesting to note that the Kushan Shah is referred to as an independent king in the Paikuli inscription. Evidently, the Kushan ruler of the Kabul valley and the Panjab is meant here *(The Classical Age.* pp. 52-55).
45. For a century from 305 B.C., when Seleucus, the Greek governor measured his strength with Chandra Gupta, down to c. 206 B.C., when Antiochus III, led an expedition against north-western India, the relations of India with the Seleucid emperors were very friendly *(The Age of Imperial Unity,* p. 102).
46. The Emperor of Iran.
47. *The Empire of the Steppes: A History of Central Asia*, Rene Grousset. p. 67.
48. *The Empire of the Steppes: A History of Central Asia*, Rene Grousset. p. 69.
49. *Marquart Erschar.* pp. 60-63, Christensen. L'Iran p. 289.
50. F.W.K. Muller, *Soghdische Texte* 1, 108.
51. *The Empire of the Steppes: A History of Central Asia*, Rene Grousset p. 69.
52. Also called Ki-to-lopelliot, *Tokharien et Koutcheen* JA (1934), p. 42.
53. *The Empire of the Steppes: A History of Central Asia*, Rene Grousset, p. 7.
54. *Ibid.*
55. *Ibid.*
56. On Ephthalite numismatics, see Junker.
57. *The Empire of the Steppes: A History of Central Asia,* Rene Grousset. Translator: Naomi Walford, pp. 71-72.

BIBLIOGRAPHY

Encyclopedia of China Today.

Grousset, Rene. *The Empire of the Steppes: A History of Central Asia.* (Translation from the French by Naomi Walford, Merced County Library C.A. 95340), pp. 68-69.

Hutton, J. H. *Caste in India,* University Press. 1946.

Kabul, H. K. *Travellers India.*

Rapson, S.N. Vol. XLVIL, pp. 96-97.

Sarkar, Dr. D. C. *PIHC,* Vol. VII.

The Concise Columbia Encyclopaedia.

The Age of Imperial Unity.

The Encyclopaedia of Britannica, Vol. 15, p. 729.

Waston, Francis. A *Concise History of India.*

The Huns

(Ancestors of Jats, Rajputs, Baloches & Pathans)

8

ORIGIN

A nomadic Asiatic people, probably of Turkish, Tataric, or Ugrish[1] stock, who spread from the Caspian steppes to make repeated incursions upon the Roman Empire, culminating in a series of wars under Atnla (q.v.), the most renowned of its leaders, which brought the Roman Empires of both the East and the West to the verge of destruction. At the height of their power, the Huns absorbed a number of different racial strains in their armies and assimilated the characteristics of the populations of their environment so that in their physical characteristics and of no certain ethnic or linguistic identity. All accounts, however, agree in describing them as an aggressive nomadic people of great vigour and comparatively low culture-development, who had developed much skill in the techniques of contemporary warfare particularly in military horsemanship.

The Huns were nomadic people who originated in north-central Asia. Although in customs, they resemble the Mongols[2] and Magyors[3]. They appear not to have been related ethnically to other groups. Short and somewhat Mongoloid in appearance, the Huns were organized into ravaging military hordes riding small rapid horses. In the 3rd century B.C. they invaded China, where part of the Great Wall[4] was built to exclude them. They appeared in the Volga Valley.

The Goths were pushed west, where they destroyed the Roman Empire, most of the European Russia, Poland and Germany paid tribute to Attila, the greatest Hun King, died 453, A.D., who ruled from 434 to 453. He gave a crushing defeat to the Gaul. The Huns ravaged Italy until Attila's death, after which little is known of them.

HUNS OVERRAN THE CHINESE EMPIRE

Before the beginning of their recorded European history, the Huns overran the Chinese Empire about 200 B.C. and forced the Emperor Kao-Di to capitulation. Their power in the East was weakened during the following century, and eventually they separated into two distinct camps, one of which amounting to about 50,000 families went southward, while most of the remainder, after attempting to maintain themselves to the Caspian steppes, went west and northwest in search of new homes. Of those who went northwest, a large number of them settled for a time on the banks of the Volga[5] river; then under a leader called Balamier, or Balamber, they advanced into the territories of the Alani[6] (q.v.), a powerful people dwelling between the Volga[7] and the Don river[8], and in a battle fought on the banks of the Don, completely routed the Alani army.

The Huns make their appearance in authentic history about 375 A.D. Ethnologists identify them with a Mongolian people of northern Asia, who invaded the Chinese Empire about 200 B.C. and after various migrations entered Europe. They appeared afterward to have sided with the Goths of Moesia against the Romans and sometimes in alliance with the emperors, who purchased their services, and sometimes in hostility with them, they continued to extend their dominion along the Danube until the time of Attila (434 A.D.), their greatest leader, whose reign constitutes the best-known period of their history[9].

THEIR FURTHER MOVEMENTS

With this event, which occurred in the second half of the 4th century A.D., the history of the Huns in Europe may be said to begin. Their next conquest was over the country of the Ostrogoths[10], whose retreat they followed to occupy territories abandoned by the Ostrogoths and Visigoths[11] as far west as the Danube River. A few years later the Goths revolted against the Roman authority, and the Huns crossed the Danube to join them in hostilities against the Eastern Roman Empire. In the wars that immediately followed, the Huns did not play a conspicuous role, but early in the following century they seem to have been joined by fresh hordes, and by 432 A.D., during the reign of Roman Emperor Theodosius[12] the younger, they had increased so considerably in power that the Hunnish king, Roas, or Ruilsd, took a large annual tribute from Rome.

YUEH-CHIH

Yueh-chih, Pinyin Yuezhi, also called Indo-Scyth, ancient people who ruled in Bactria and India from about 128 B.C. to about A.D. 450. The Yueh-Chih are first mentioned in Chinese sources at the beginning of the 2nd century B.C. as nomads living in the western part of Kansu province, north-west China. When Lao Shang (reigned c.174-161 B.C.), ruler of the Hsiungnu (a powerful people of north China), defeated them and killed their king, the main body of Yueh-Chih moved westward into Sogdiana and Bactria, putting an end to Greek rule there. They and related tribes are the Asi (or Asiani) and Tocharians (Tochari) of Western sources. About 128 B.C., the Yueh-chih were recorded living north of the Oxus River (Amu Darya), ruling Bactria as a dependency, but a little later the Great Yueh-chih kingdom was in Bactria, and Sogdiana was occupied by the Ta-yuan (Tocharians). The remnant in Kansu were called Little Yueh-chih.

A new dynasty, that of the Kushans (see Kushan dynasty), was subsequently founded by one of the five chieftains among whom Bactria was divided. The Kushan kingdom extended its power southward and eastward into India and northward into Central Asia. From the 3rd century A.D., however, Kushan power declined, and about A.D. 400 the Kidara dynasty arose in Gandhara; it survived only to about A.D. 450, when it was overwhelmed by the Hephthalites (originally a Yueh-chih tribe).

Missionaries from the Great Yueh-chih played an important part in the propagation of Buddhism in China. The spread of Indian culture into Central Asia as far as the borders of China probably also resulted from Kushan influence.

Yueh-ch'in, also called La Ch'in, Pinyin Yueqin, or Laqin, also called Moon Guitar, Chinese lute, one of a family of flat, round-bodied lutes found in Central and East Asia. It was invented, according to tradition, during the Chin dynasty (A.D. 265-420). It has two pairs of silk strings, tuned (in relative pitch) to c-g, which run from a fastener on the wooden belly to tuning pegs set in the sides of the pegbox. A metal plate is hung inside the body, vibrating against it when the instrument is played.

The Yueh-ch'in is frequently found in Chinese opera orchestras. Its precursor, the yacheng (yazheng) was bowed with a friction stick—a sorghum stem dusted with resin.

As early as the 2nd century B.C. the nomadic Huns were living on the borders of China. Their quarrel with Yueh-chih, a neighbouring nomadic tribe, led to the conquest of India by the Sakas and the Kushans about the 1st century of the Christian era. Later, the Huns, like the Yueh-chih, migrated towards the west, and divided into two main streams of which one advanced towards the Volga and the other to the Oxus. The activities of the former figure prominently in Roman history. The Huns in the Oxus valley threw off the yoke of the Juan-Juan tribe and became very powerful towards the middle of the 5th century A.D. From the name of their rulers' family they came to be known as Ye-tha, Hephthalites[13] or Ephthalites, and the Greek accounts refer to them as White Huns.

HUNS CONQUERED PERSIA

From the Oxus valley the White Huns advanced toward both Persia and India. Crossing the Hindu[14] Kush they occupied Gandhara[15], but their further progress was checked by Skanda-gupta[16], who inflicted a crushing defeat upon them in about A.D. 460. Persia, however was unable to stop their ravages and in A.D. 484, the Huns defeated and killed the Persian king. This success enhanced the power and prestige of the Huns, and by the end of the 5th century A.D., they ruled over a vast empire with their principal capital at Balkh[17].

According to *Concise Dictionary of the World* (pp. 377- 78), "Hun from a native name, nomadic people of Asia, notorious for the military skills and strategy, who for a time (5th century A.D.) threatened the Roman Empire. The Huns of uncertain origin, were at times identified with Hsuing-no[18], White Huns, Magyars[19], a member of the main group of people of Hungary and other skilled horsemen and archers. They appeared in Eastern Europe in 370 A.D. and fighting in roving bands (hordes), they conquered the Alani[20], Ostrogoths and Visigoths. Victorious over the latter two people, they caused great migration eastward. In the 5th century A.D. the Huns occupied eastern and central Europe and threatened Constantinople[21]. On the second they again attacked the western Empire and unsuccessfully attempted to take Gaul, a part of the Empire of ancient Rome, including mainly what is now France and some regions around it. After they were defeated by combined forces of Romans and Visigoths at the Battle of Chalons in 451 A.D., however, they invaded and briefly ravaged Italy. His fall in 453 A.D. was followed by disintegration of the kingdom and the Huns as unified people.

CONQUERED EASTERN EMPIRE

The Empire that Attila and his elder brother Bleda inherited seems to have stretched from the Alps[22] and the Baltic in the west to somewhere near the Caspian Sea, in the east. Their first known action on becoming joint rulers was the negotiation of a peace treaty with the Eastern Roman Empire, which was concluded at the city of Margus (Pozarevac). By the terms of the treaty the Romans undertook to double the subsidies they had been paying to the Huns and in future to pay 700 pounds and 300 kilograms of gold each year.

DESTROYED BULGARIA

From 435 to 439 A.D. the activities of Attila are unknown, but he seems to have been engaged in subduing barbarian peoples to the north or east of his dominions. The Eastern Romans do not appear to have paid the sums stipulated in the treaty of Margus, and so in 441 A.D., when their forces were occupied in the west and on the eastern frontier, Attila launched a heavy assault on the Danubian frontier of the Eastern Empire. He captured and razed a number of important cities, including Singidunum[23]. The Eastern Romans managed to arrange a truce for the year 441 A.D. and recalled their forces from the West. But in 443 A.D. Attila resumed his attack. He began by taking and destroying towns on the Danube and then drove into the interior of the Empire towards Naissus (Nis) and Sardica[24] (Sofia), both of which he destroyed.

He next turned toward Constantinople, took Philippopolis, defeated the main eastern Roman forces in a succession of battles, and so reached the sea both north and south of Constantinople. It was hopeless for the Hun archers to attack the Great Walls of the capital, so Attila turned on the remnants on the empire's forces, which had withdrawn into the Peninsula of Gallipoli[25], and destroyed them. In the peace treaty that followed, he obliged the Eastern Empire to pay the arrears of the tribute, which he calculated at 6000 pounds of gold, and he trebled the annual tribute, henceforth extorting 2,100 pounds of gold each year.

MURDER OF ATTILA'S BROTHER

Attila's movements after the conclusion of peace in the autumn of 443 A.D. are unknown. About 445 A.D., he murdered his brother Bleda and thenceforth ruled the Huns as an autocrat. He made his second great attack of the Eastern Roman Empire in 447 A.D., but little is known of the details of the campaign. It was planned on an even bigger scale than that of 441-443 A.D., and its main weight was directed toward the provinces of Lower Scythia[26] and Moesia[27] in south-eastern Europe, *i.e.* further to the east than the earlier assault. He engaged the Eastern Empire's forces on the Utus[28] (Vid) river and defeated them, but he himself suffered serious losses. He then devastated the Balkan provinces and drove southward into Greece, where he was only stopped at Thermopylae[29]. The three years following the invasion were filled with complicated negotiations between Attila and the diplomats of the Eastern Roman Emperor Theodosius II[30]. Much information about these diplomatic encounters had been preserved in the fragments of the *History of Prisms* of Penium, who visited Attila's headquarters in Walachia[31], in company with a Roman embassy in 449 A.D. The treaty by which the war was terminated was harsher than that of 443 A.D.; the Eastern Romans had to evacuate a wide belt of territory south of the Danube and the tribute payable by them was continued, though the rate is not known.

Attila, King of Huns (b. about 406 and d. 453 A.D.)

He became king in 433 A.D. in succession to Roas, his uncle. The Huns esteemed Attila their bravest warrior and most skillful general; and he became, as he called himself, the 'scourge' which God had chosen to chastise the human race. In a short time, he extended his dominion over all the people of Germany and Scythia, and the eastern and western emperors paid him tribute. The Vandals, the Ostrogoths, the Gepidae and a part of the Franks united under his banners. Hearing a rumour of the riches and power of Persia, he directed his march thither, but was defeated on the plains of Armenia, and drew back to satisfy his desire of plunder in the dominions of the emperor of the East.

Emperor Theodosius collected an army to oppose his progress; but in three bloody battles fortune declared herself for the barbarians. Constantinople was indebted to the strength of its walls, and to the ignorance of the enemy in the art of besieging, for its preservation. Thrace, Macedonia and Greece, all submitted to the savage robber, who destroyed 70 flourishing cities. Theodosius was at the mercy of the victor and was obliged to purchase peace.

Attila's Last Campaign

Attila now directed his eyes to Gaul. With an immense army he passed the Rhine, the Moselle and the Seine, came to the Loire, and sat down under the walls of Orleans. The inhabitants of this city, encouraged by their bishop, Agnan (Anianus), repelled the first attack of the barbarians, and the united forces of the Romans, under their general, Aetius, and of the Visigoths, under their king, Theodoric, compelled Attila to raise the siege. He retreated to Champagne and waited for the enemy in the plains of Chalons. Attila, anxious for the event of the battle, consulted the soothsayers, who assured him of a defeat. He concealed his alarm, rode through the ranks of his warriors, reminded them of their deeds, spoke of his joy at the prospect of a battle, and at the thought that their valour was to be rewarded. Inflamed by his speech, the Huns were impatient for battle. At length the ranks of the Romans and Goths were broken through, and Attila was already sure of the victory, when the Gothic prince, Thorismond, the son of Theodoric, poured down from the neighbouring height upon the Huns. Attila, pressed on all sides, escaped with difficulty to his camp. But the enemy were contented with collecting their forces during the night and having paid the last honours to the dead body of King Theodoric (Dietrich), which they discovered with difficulty, they saluted his son, Thorismond, king upon the field of battle. Thus Attila escaped, but the Franks pursued him till he had passed the Rhine.

THE TERMS FOR THE TREATY OF PEACE

He now demanded Honoria, the sister of Valentinian III, in marriage, and conquered and destroyed Aquileia, Padua, Vicenza, Verona, Bergamo, and laid waste the plains of Lombardy. The inhabitants fled to the Alps, to the Apennines and to the small islands in the shallows (lagoons) of the Adriatic Sea, where they built Venice. The emperor had no army to oppose him; the Roman people and senate had recourse to tears and supplications. Pope Leo I went with the Roman ambassadors to the enemy's camp and succeeded in obtaining a peace. Attila went back to Hungary. Not having obtained Honoria for a wife, Attila would a second time have demanded her, sword in hand, if the beautiful Ildico had not been added to his numerous wives, with whom he solemnly united himself (453 A.D.). On this occasion, he gave himself up to all the extravagance of debauchery; but on the other day after the marriage, the servants and warriors, impatient to salute their master, thronged into the tent; they found Ildico veiled, sitting by the cold corpse of her husband.

DEATH OF ATTILA

In 453 A.D. Attila was intending to attack the eastern Empire where the new emperor Marcian[32] had refused to pay the subsidies agreed upon by his predecessor, Theodosius II. But during the night following his marriage Attila died in his sleep. Those who buried him were subsequently put to death by the Huns so that his grave might never be discovered. He was succeeded by his sons, who divided his empire among them.

ATTILA'S HULIA (DESCRIPTION)

Priscus[33], who saw Attila[34] when he visited his camp in 448 A.D., described him as a short, squat man with a large head, deep set eyes, flat nose and thin beard. According to some historians, Attila was thought as a man of irritable, blustering, and turbulent disposition, a very persistent negotiator and by no means pitiless. When Priscus attended a banquet given by him, he noticed that Attila was served of wooden plates and ate only meat, whereas his chief lieutenants dined off silver platters loaded with dainties. No description of his qualities as a general survives, but his successors before the invasion of Gaul show him to have been an outstanding commander.

HUNS INDIANISED

The Huns (Ephthalities or White Huns) poured into India from the Oxus Valley in the 5th century A.D., laying waste the Buddhist establishments in Gandhara[35] and sweeping away the declining Kidara-Kusanas. The Gupta emperor Skanda Gupta (c. 455-67 A.D.) succeeded for the time being in arresting their further incursions, but within the next few decades their chief Toramana[36] was holding a substantial part of northern India, including at least a portion of the Madhya Pradesh.

TORAMANA

About the close of the 5th or the beginning of the 6th century A.D., a chief named Toramana, advancing from the Panjab, conquered large parts of western India, and even Eran[37] included them in his dominions. The conquest of Eran must have taken place not long after the reign of Budhagupta[38], for the chief who administered the districts under Toramana was the younger brother of one who held the same office under Budhagupta. His coins testify to his foreign origin and indicate his rule over parts of U.P., Rajputana, the Panjab and Kashmir. It is probable that he was connected with the Hun ruling family in Gandhara and advanced from that base to effect further conquest in India. But we possess little definite information about him. According to a Jain work he was converted to that faith and lived at Pavvaiya on the banks of the river Chandrabhaga (Chenab) in the Panjab[39].

MIHIRAKULA

Toramana was succeeded by his son Mihirakula, who probably ascended the throne about A.D. 515. According to Hiuen Tsang, his capital was Sakala or Sialkot and he ruled over India[40].

The *Rajatarangini,* chronicle of Kashmir[41] refers to Mihirakula as a powerful king who ruled over both Kashmir and Gandhara and conquered southern India and Ceylon. He is described as a king of violent disposition, and heart-rending tales of his cruelty are told at great length. The *Rajatarangini,* also refers to Toramana, but he flourished long after Mihirakula, about eighteen kings intervening between the two. The career of this Toramana hardly fits with what we know of the Huns chief of that name from other sources, though the age assigned to him fits with that of the latter. On the other hand, the stories of Mihirakula's cruelty, preserved in the *Rajatarangini,* agree with those narrated by Hiuen Tsang.

ACCOUNT OF SUNG-YUN

We get a fair idea of the power and influence of the Huns about this time from the account of Sung-Yun. After mentioning the conquest and occupation of his kingdom by the Huns, two generations before his time, he gives the following account of the kings whose court he visited.

"The disposition of the king (or dynasty) was cruel and vindictive, and he practised the most barbarous atrocities. He did not believe in the law of Buddha, but loved to worship demons. Entirely self-reliant on his own strength, he had entered on a war with the country of Ki-pin (Kashmir), disputing the boundaries of their kingdom, and his troops had been already engaged in it for three years. The king had 700 war-elephants.... The king continually abodes with his troops on the frontier and never returned to his kingdom".[42]

ACCOUNT OF COSMA5[43]

Somewhat later in date is the account given by Cosmas, surname Indicopleustee (Indian navigator), an Alexandrine Greek, in his *Christian Topography,* which was probably begun in A.D. 535; but not put in its final form till A.D. 547. In his own place, he says, "Higher up in India, that is farther to the north, are the White Huns, the ones called Gollas when going to a war takes with him, it is said, not fewer than two thousand elephants and a great force of cavalry. He is the lord of India, and oppressing the people, forces them to pay tribute."

It is generally believed that king Gollas refers to Mihirakula whose name is also written as Mihirgul. It is not also unlikely that he is the king with whom Sung-Yun met in Gandhara, somewhat earlier. It is interesting to note that both these accounts place the Huns kingdom proper to the west of the Sindhu, though according to Cosmas the Hun King exercised suzerainty over Indian kings and forced them to pay tribute.

THE DECLINE OF THE HUNS

Toramana's power suffered a decline, and after these initial successes which carried him as far as Saugar District in Madhya Pradesh he was forced to fall back, and the Hun authority was confined to the territory beyond the Indus. This might be due to a defeat inflicted upon him by Bhanu Gupta[44]. After the end of Toramana, there is no doubt that his son Mihirakula revived the ambitious project of his father. It appears from all accounts that Mihirakula was a powerful tyrant who overran a large part of Northern India. An inscription dated in the fifteenth year of his reign (c. 530 A.D.) shows that his sovereignty extended at least up to Gwalior, and probably his authority was acknowledged further beyond that territory as well[45]. As mentioned above, according to Hiuen Tsang, he subdued the whole of India. But the Huns were not destined to enjoy success for long, and Mihirakula, too, soon met his death at the hands of two Indian rulers, Yasodharman and Narsimha Gupta[46].

Respect was paid to his feet by even that (famous) king Mihirakula, whose head had never (previously) been brought to the humility of obeisance to any other save (God) Sthana (Siva), and embraced by whose arms the mountains of snow[47] falsely prides itself on being styled as inaccessible fortress. The reference to the mountain of snow probably indicates that Mihirakula was ruling over Kashmir and the adjoining regions. It may be remembered that Sung-Yun also related that the Huns chief was fighting with Kashmir. It would appear that while Mihirakula was advancing into the interior of India, he was opposed by Yasodharman, an ambitious chief of Madhya Pradesh. Mihirakula was evidently defeated but his kingdom or power was not destroyed. With the fall of Yasodharman, which probably took place not long after, Mihirakula again came to the forefront.

MAIN CAUSE OF COLLAPSE

The collapse of the Huns political power in India was due not only to the defeat of their chiefs Toramana and Mihirakula, but also, and perhaps mainly, to the crushing blow given to their central authority on the Oxus by the combined forces of the Turks and the Persians sometime between A.D. 563 and 567. That administered the fatal death blow to the Huns power in the east.

According to a Jaina tradition, Hun chiefs became a convert to that faith and lived at Pavvaiya on the Chandrabhaga[48]. Toramana's son and successor Mihirakula ruled over a large part of India, including Gwalior, up to his fifteenth reginal year. But soon afterwards he met with crushing reverses at the hands of the Central India ruler Yasodharman and probably also from the Gupta ruler Baladitya[49]. According to the *Rajatarangini,* he repaired to Kashmir where he founded a dynasty, the members of which were zealous adherents of Brahmanism. That Mihirakula himself was an exclusive worshipper of Siva is placed beyond all doubt by the Mandasor[50] inscription of Yasodharman. His coins also have on the reverse a bull and the legend Jayatu Vrsah (Victory to Sivai), represented by a Nicolo (onyx) seal depicting a Hun chief standing in a worshipful attitude before a synchronizing figure of Visnu, Siva, and Mihira. Though the Hun empire in India collapsed with the defeat of Mihirakula, small Hun principalities and communities survived even afterwards, since they are mentioned in the inscription of the medieval ruling dynasties like Paramaras[51] and Cahamanas.

NAMED RAJPUTS

Huns soon lost their individuality amid the natives of the soil and came to be regarded as one of the thirty-six Rajput clans. In the 11th century, the great Cedi[52] ruler Kama married a Hun princess named Avalladevi. The impact of this foreign people on the structure of India is palpable from the fact that the ethnic name survives even now as one of the caste surnames of Central India and the Panjab. The name of the large number of villages in these regions still preserve the memory of those people.

CONCLUSION

The foregoing brief survey made on the early invasions of the nomadic tribes such as the Scythians, Abhiras, Sakas, Kushans, Yuchchas, and Huns will amply prove, that, apart from the broad racial groups recognised by anthropologists as constituting the Indian population most of such groups having entered India in prehistoric or protohistoric times, and one or two being autochthonous, there are a number of other racial elements in the population, the contribution of which to the enrichment of Indian culture can in no way be ignored further, in addition to these peoples about whose migration there is recorded history of material evidence, there must have been many more unrecorded movements which also brought with them new races more and more complex[53]. The quick adoption of the Indian languages and faiths by the incoming peoples, due either to the compulsion of circumstances or to the comparative effects of the languages and creeds that they brought with them, hastened and completed the process of assimilation.

To refuse to take notice of the diverse and exotic elements in the Indian cultures and to regard it as wholly or even mainly the outcome of Vedism, or even of more eclectic Puranism, is to falsify history. At the same time, to isolate these elements and to emphasize them unduly is to ignore the basic homogeneity of the Indian culture—the product of absorbing forces that were in operation since the very dawn of human history in India. As Dr. Suniti Kumar Chatterjee says, "The fundamental trait of this (Indian) civilization may be described as a Harmony of Contrasts, or as a Synthesis creating a Unity out of Diversity. Perhaps more than any other system of civilisation, it is broad and expansive and all-comprehensive, like life itself, and it has created an attitude of acceptance and understanding which will not confine itself to any single type of experience only to the exclusion of all others[54]..."

We do not know what became of the Hun clans camped in the Panjab after Mihirkula's demise. They must have continued to be troublesome, if not dangerous, for in the 2nd half of the 16th century the Maharaja of Thaneswar[55] Prabhakara (d. 605 A.D.) won honour and power by fighting them. In 605, his eldest son Rajyavardhana was still waging war on them, and later the successor to these two, the great Indian emperor Harsha (606-647 A.D.) was acclaimed by the poets for his victories over these same Huns. Yet from the 2nd half of the 7th century the Huns of India vanished from history, no doubt either exterminated or absorbed by the Panjabis. Some of their clans most likely succeeded in gaining admission to the Hindu aristocracy in the manner of the "Rajput" clan of Gurjara, which may possibly have the same origin[56].

REFERENCES

1. Turkish-speaking people of the USSR, living near the Volga River region. The name once referred to Mongols. They are generally known by their popular name, the Ephthalites.
2. Asiatic people, who today live mainly in the Mongolian People's Republic, Mongolia.
3. The dominant people of Hungary, who speak a Finno-Ugric language.
4. The Great Wall of China.
5. The largest river of Europe, in central European-Russian, the principal navigable water artery of the USSR, rises in the Voldai hills.
6. Also called Alans, an ancient nomadic pastoral people that occupied the steppe region north-east of the Black Sea.
7. River c.2. 300 miles long, central and eastern European-Russia. It is the longest river of Europe.
8. One of the greatest streams, 1222 miles of Europe, in south central European Russian SFSR rises in the central Russian upland near Stalinogorsk.
9. *The Encyclopedia Americana*, Vol. 2, pp. 509-10.
10. The Goths or East Goths.
11. The Goths or West Goths, a division of the Goths, one of the chief groups of the ancient Germans separated from the Ostro-Goths or E. Goths.
12. The Odoric 455-526 A.D. king of Ostrogoths and founder of the Danube Ostrogothic monarchy.
13. *A History of Central Asia*, Rene Grousset, p. 67.
14. Hindukoh, a high mountain system, extending c. 500 miles, west from the Pamir Knot, north Pakistan into north-east Afghanistan.
15. A historic region of India, now in north-west Pakistan, situated astride the middle Indus River; the region had Taxila and Peshawar as its chief cities.
16. Skanda Gupta c. 455-467. A.D. who succeeded Kumara Gupta.
17. Province, north-central Afghanistan, borders Uzbekistan.
18. *A History of Asia*, Harper-Collin, pp. 55-60.
19. Hungarian people.
20. Also called Alans, an ancient nomadic pastoral people that occupied the steppe region north-east of the Black Sea.
21. Former capital of Byzantine Empire and of the Ottoman Empire, since 1930, officially called Istanbul.
22. A great mountain system of south-central Europe c. 500 miles long and c.100 miles wide, curving in great arc through parts of France, Italy, Switzerland, Germany and Austria.

23. Belgrade, the capital of Yugoslavia.
24. Sofia, capital of Bulgaria.
25. A town, Lecce Province, Apulia, south Italy port on Rocky Island.
26. Capital of the Scythian Empire in Ukraine, Russia.
27. In Italy.
28. Kymen province, south-east Finland, 9 miles east of Kouvola.
29. Central Greece, south-east of Lamia.
30. The Roman Emperor.
31. Historic region 29,568 square miles in South Romania.
32. Born 396 A.D., Thrace, Constantinople, Eastern Roman Emperor.
33. Priscus of Panium had seen Attila, the Hun leader, in 448 A.D.
34. History of Attila and the Huns, 1948.
35. *The Archaeological Remains of the Huns.* C. Werner.
36. *The Encyclopaedia of Britannica.* Vol. 21. p. 48.
37. Saugar district of Madhya Pradesh.
38. The Jain work of Kuvalayamala, composed in 700 Saka (778 A.D.).
39. *Encyclopaedia of Britannica.* Vol. 21 p. 48.
40. *Encyclopaedia of Britannica.* Vol. 21 p. 48.
41. *Ancient Indian History,* V.A. Smith, p. 102.
42. A Chinese ambassador to the Hun king of Gandhara in 520 A.D.
43. Also called Indicopleustes (6th A.D.), Alexandria, Egypt; merchant traveller, theologian and geographer.
44. Dr. Raychaudhari identifies Hiuen Tsang's Baladitya with Bhanugupta Phai. pp. 556-57.
45. In the first place, neither Rudrasimha II, who surrendered the throne, nor his son and successor Yasodaman II, assumed the title.
46. Mahakshatrapa *(The Classic Age,* p. 47).
47. The Himalaya.
48. The Chenab River of the Panjab.
49. He erected a temple of Vishnu at Chatsu in Jaipur, where an inscription of his reign is found.
50. It is held by competent scholars, some verses in the Mandasor inscription of A.D. 473 indicate knowledge of Kalidasa's works.
51. The Parmars of Malva had reached their height of glory and fame under Bhoja, who died in 1054 A.D., and by this time exercised little influence on affairs.
52. A branch of 36 Kul Rajputs.
53. *The Encyclopaedia of Britannica.* Vol. 21. p. 48.
54. *The Cultural Heritage of India*, p. 626.

55. North-west of Delhi, the kingdom of Thaneswar must certainly have owned its rise to the role of frontier march which it played to protect the world of Ganges against Hun invasions.
56. The Empire of the Steppes: A History of the Central Asia, Rene Grousset. pp. 71-72.

BIBLIOGRAPHY

Basham, A. L. *The Wonder That was India,* (London 1954).

Donald, P. Whitaker & Rinnhinn, Area Handbook for the People's Republic of China.

Edwardes, M.A. *History of India,* (London 1961).

Garratt, G.T. *The Legacy of India* (ed. 1937).

Hucker, Charles O. *China's Imperial Past.*

Kasombi, D.D. *The Culture and Civilization of Ancient India in Historical Outline*, (London 1965).

Majumdar, R.C. *The History and Culture of Indian People.* (ed. Bombay 1937).

Piggot, S. *Prehistoric India,* London 1950.

Tod, Sir J. *Annals and Antiquities of Rajasthan* (New ed. London 1960).

The Concise Columbia Encyclopaedia, Columbia University Press.

The Encyclopaedia of Britannica, Vol. 21, p. 48.

The Rajputs

9

Rajputana, also called Raj war, was the former group of princely states chiefly comprising what is now Rajasthan, a state of India. The name means “land of the Rajputs”. The area, 132,559 square miles (343,328 square km.), consisted of two geographic divisions; the area northwest of the Aravalli range, this being mostly sand, and unproductive and including part of the Great Indian (Thar) Desert; and the area southeast of the range, which is generally higher and more fertile. The whole area thus formed a compact block occupying the hill and plateau between the north Indian plains and the main plateau of peninsular India.

Rajputana consisted of 23 states, one chiefdom, one estate and the British district of Ahmer-Merwara. The majority of ruling princes were Rajputs, warrior rulers of the historic region of Rajputana who began to enter the area in the 7th century A.D. The larger states were Ajmer, Alwar, Bikaner, Chittaurgarh, Jaipur, Jaisalmer, Jodhpur, Kishangarh, Kota, Udaipur, Sekhawati and Marwar. In 1947 the consolidation of states began by stages, as a result of which the state of Rajasthan came into being. Some of Rajputana’s former territory in the southeast is now part of Madhya Pradesh, and some in the southwest is now part of Gujarat.

RAJPUT

Rajput (from Sanskrit Raja-Putra; “son of a king”), any of about 42,000,000, landowners organized in patrilineal clans and located mainly in central and northern India, especially in former Rajputana (“Land of the Rajputs”). The Rajputs regard themselves as descendants or members of the Kshatriya (warrior ruling) class, but they actually vary greatly in status, from princely lineages such as the Guhilot and Kachwaha, to simple cultivators. Most authorities agree that successful claims to Rajput status were frequently made by groups that attained secular power. Central Asian invaders as well as patricians' lines of indigenous tribal peoples were absorbed in this way. There are numbers of Muslim Rajputs in the northwest, and Rajputs generally have adopted the custom of Purdah (seclusion of women). Their ethics includes an intense pride in ancestry and a mettlesome regard for personal honour. They seek hypergamous marriages *(i.e.* the bride marrying into a social group higher than her own).

DESCENDANTS OF HUNS SCYTHIANS

Origin

The origin of the Rajputs may well be traced to our present problem, and Vincent Smith has much to say that is of interest. After recalling that before the Muslim invasions the three main irruptions of foreigners through the north-western passes of India include the Sakas (The Scythians), the Kushans and the White Huns. He points out that the real difference between the ancient and the medieval period of Indian history is that at some period the living tradition was broken. There is in fact no tradition concerning the ancient period; the Mauryas, the Sakas, the Kushans, belong to a dead and buried past, known only from inscriptions and coins. The tradition of the Rajput clans on the other hand is very much alive, and they still form influential sections of the people.

The break came, Vincent Smith, author of *The Early History of India* wrote that with the third irruption, the White Hun invasions of the 5th century, this incursion was so overwhelming that it destroyed all memory of descent from the first and second swarms, the Sakas and the Kushans. It was like the Anglo-Saxon invasion of Britain creating a Dark Age. He goes on:

"Who were these Rajputs, and why do they and their affairs make such a stir during the centuries before the Mohammedan conquest? Their dominance is the conspicuous fact differentiating the medieval from the ancient period in the history of North India, and the mind craves for an explanation."

Descendants of Huns

It seems to be clearly established that the Hun group of tribes and hordes made their principal settlements in Rajputana and the Panjab. The most important element in the group after the Huns themselves was that of Gurjaras whose name survives in the form of Gujjar as the designation of a widely diffused class in north-west India. The Jatts or Jats, more exclusively agricultural—the Gujjars are a pastoral people universally recognised as akin to the Jats.

THE RAJPUTS OF THE PANJAB

The distribution of the Rajputs and allied races is shown in Abstract No. 71, page No. 219 of the *Tribes and Castes of the Panjab* of Ibbetson. It will not be possible to enter into any detailed description or discussion of the Rajput. He is much the same all over northern India and more has been published about him than about any other Indian caste. The great authority is Tod's *Rajasthan,* while both Elliot and Sherring give much useful information. It has already been expressed in section 422-3, as to the identity of the Jat and Rajput stock as it stands at present, and how the Rajputs merely consist of the royal families of that stock. It might indeed have gone further, and have said that a tribe of any caste which had in ancient times possessed supreme power throughout any fairly extensive tract of country, would be classed as Rajput. It seems almost certain that some of the so-called Rajput royal families were aboriginal; and notably the Chandel. How the aborigines of the Nepal Himalayas rose to be Kshatriya is well told by Hodgson in his *Essay on the Military Tribes of Nepal.* He points out that when the Brahmans were driven up into the hills by the advancing tide of Mohammedan conquest, they wedded with the aboriginal women whom they found there. But to render this possible it was necessary to conciliate the people among whom they had come to dwell; and they called their first converts among them Kshatriya, while to their own offspring by the hill women they gave them not only Kshatriya rank and privileges, but Brahminical patronymics.

"From these two roots mainly sprang the now numerous, predominant, and extensively" ramified tribe of Khas—originally the name of a small clan of creedless barbarians, but now the proud title of the Kshatriya or military order of Nepal. Thus too the key to the anomalous nomenclature of so many stripes of these military tribes is to be sought in the nomenclature of the "sacred order". And even now in spite of the yearly increasing sway of Hinduism, and of the efforts of Brahmans in high office to abolish the custom, the Khas still insist that the fruits of commerce (for marriage is now out of the question) between their females and males of the sacred order shall be ranked as Kshatriya, wear the thread, and assume the patronymic title." So again, when the Rajput immigrants from the plains took aboriginal women in concubinage (and concubinage among the hill people is for all purposes of legitimacy and inheritance the same as marriage), they were permitted to give their children so begotten the patronymic title only, not the rank of Kshatriya. But their children again if they married for two generations with the Khas, became pure Khas, or real Kshatriyas in point of privilege and rank though no longer so in name. They were Khas not Kshatriya, and yet they bore the proud title cognominal of the martial order of the Hindus, and were in the land of their nativity entitled to every prerogative which Kshatriya birth confers in Hindustan.

A reference to description of the Kanets of our hills will show that something of the same sort has gone on in the Panjab Himalayas, though necessarily in a much lower degree, since here the Aryan and not the aborigine was predominant; and the description of the Hill Rajputs, and still more of the Thakars and Rathis, which will be found in this section under their respective heading, will show how, if the Turanian is not as in Nepal much prefer pastoral to agricultural pursuits, looking down upon all manual work as derogatory and upon the actual operating of ploughing as degrading and it is only the poorest class of Rajput who will himself follow the plough. They are in most parts of the Panjab plains, who command a great respect.

THE RAJPUT TRIBES

The Rajputs of the Panjab are fine brave men and retain the feudal instinct more strongly developed than perhaps any other non-menial caste, the tribal heads wielding extraordinary authority. They are very tenacious of the integrity of their communal property in the village lands, seldom admitting strangers to share it with them. Pride of blood is their strongest characteristic, for pride of blood is the very essence of their Rajputhood. They are lazy and poor husbandmen and much prefer pastoral to agricultural pursuits, looking upon all manual labour as derogatory and upon the actual operation of ploughing as degrading; and it is only the poorest class of Rajput who will himself follow the plough. They are, in most parts of the Panjab plains, who command a great respect.

THE RAJPUT TRIBES OF THE PANJAB

The Rajputs of the Panjab may be broadly divided into four groups, each of which will be discussed separately in the following paragraphs. First come the Rajputs of the Delhi territory and Jamna valley, for the most part belonging to the two great tribes of Chauhan and Tunwar which gave Delhi its most famous dynasties. Next come the Rajputs of the river valleys of the Western Plains, many of them hardly or not at all to be distinguished from Jats, and belonging for the most part to the Bhattis of Jaisalmer and Bikaner, and their predecessors the Punwar. The third group is the Rajputs of the western hills including the salt range tract, comprising both dominant tribes of proud position such as the Janjuas and mongrel Rajputs from the Jammu hills, and descendants either of the Yadubansi (Bhatti) dynasty of Kashmir and the mythical Raja Rasalu of Sialkot so famous in Panjab folklore, or of a group of tribes, apparently of Punwar origin, which now hold the hills on either bank of the Jhelam. Finally we have the Rajputs of the Kangra hills of whom the Katoch may be taken as the type, so ancient that their very origin and advent to their present abodes are lost in the past; and the Rajputs of the lower hills which fringe the Panjab Himalayas, with the Rajputs, the Thakars and the Rathis who also claim of the equal grades of Rajputs rather than separate castes, and the Rawats, whose position is still more difficult of definition. The Rajputs of the Sikh tract, of the central districts, and of the erstwhile Phulkian states of the Eastern Plains are not mentioned here. As a fact they are few. The Rajputs of the frontier districts are not mentioned for here again they are insignificant both in numbers and importance. The reason why the Rajput disappears before the Sikh, the Pathan, and the Biloch, have already been explained, shows the distribution of Rajputs and allied castes. The small number in the hill states is curious. There only the ruling families are Rajput, the mass of the peasantry consisting of Kanets or Ghiraths, if indeed these last can be separated at all from Rathis and Rawats. In the Delhi division and Rohtak the Jat has largely taken the place of the Rajput. In the Multan division the number of Rajputs returned is very large; but shown how large a proportion of them should more properly be classed as Jats, if indeed any distinction can be drawn between the two.

TRIBAL STATUS OF RAJPUTS

The figures for tribes will be given under the respective groups to which they belong. They are more than usually inaccurate, partly because a Rajput is so difficult of definition, but still more because the Rajputs are divided into a few great tribes or royal races as they are commonly called, the Kuls of the Rajputs annals, and each of these tribes again into innumerable local clans or Sachi or Gots. Almost every Rajput will refer himself rightly or wrongly to some one of the great Kuls, as well as state, the local clan to which he beyond all doubts belongs; and thus we have members of the same clan and descendants of the same ancestor returning themselves as belonging to different tribes, while multitudes of persons appear twice over in the Abstracts, first under their tribe or Kul and again under their clan or Got.

It must be remembered that such of the figures as are Rajput tribes in the Abstracts of the following pages under the head Jat, refer to people who have returned themselves as Jat by caste and Bhatti, Chauhan, and so forth by tribe. In the great majority of cases this latter entry represents mere traditional origin rather than that the people in question actually claim that they are Bhatti or Chauhan at the present moment. In many cases they have returned their Jat tribe as well. Hereunder is given the numbers entered for various tribes under Jat and Rajput respectively, and shows how extensively this sort of entry has been made.

Table 9.1: *Joint List of Jat and Rajput Clans*

Clans	Indian Territory		Former Native States	
	Jats	Rajputs	Jats	Rajputs
Bagri	3,519	11,141	2,251	908
Bhakral	4,863	5,144	13	3,378
Bahniwal	9,411	43	1,967	...
Bhatti	94,665	204,569	1,193	38,262
Bhutta	20,431	4,891	2,108	194
Chhadhar	26,387	16,435	17	1,311
Chauhan	27,109	145,195	3,550	18,831
Dhanial	10,026	4,388	...	...
Dhudhi	12,315	7,649	1,087	113
Gondal	47,276	43,220	325	10
Janjua	8,419	38,552	15	11
Joya	12,338	25,301	...	5,262
Kharral	18,582	14,242	237	2,042
Khichi	12,110	45,731	221	9,649
Langah	9,083	2,348	59	1
Mahal	6,598	118	1,032	721
Mandahar	1,827	14,693	15,332	2,637
Mauhas	6,570	49,424	15	216
Manj	2,654	29,309	1	2,676
Mekan	3,157	5,968	...	...

Rajput (Sanskrit Rajputra, 'A King's Son', 'a prince') is the general term applied to a group of septs which constitute the so-called 'military' class of India. At the census of 1911 they numbered 9,430,095, appearing in the greatest number in the Panjab, Uttar Pradesh and Bengal. In Rajputana, the headquarters of the tribe, they numbered 675,789.

ETHNOLOGY OF RAJPUTS

Within the last few years an important change of view regarding the origin of the Rajputs has taken place. Following the universal tradition of the Hindus, it was generally assumed that they were the direct successors of the Kshatriyas, one of the four groups (Verna 'colour') which constituted the Vedic Polity. According to Manu, "The creator commanded the *Kshatriya* to protect the people, to bestow gifts, to offer sacrifices, to study the Veda, and to abstain from attaching himself to sensual pleasures".[1] The true position of this group of septs has now been clearly ascertained.

TRUE POSITION OF THE RAJPUTS

So far back at the time when the *Dialogues of The Buddha* was composed, the Kshatriyas were recognized as an important element in the society, and in their own estimation stood high than the Brahmans. The fact probably is that from very remote days ruling clans of Kshatriyas essentially similar to the Rajputs of later days, existed and were continually forming new states, just in the same way as in the medieval period. But their records have perished and only a few exceptionally conspicuous dynasties are at all remembered, and so stand out on the page of history in a manner which it is believed always one of very vague meanings, simply denoting the Hindu ruling classes which does not fully correspond with the truth. The term Kshatriya was, it is believed, always one of very vague meanings, simply denoting the Hindu ruling classes which did not claim Brahman descent.

Occasionally a Raja might be a Brahman by caste, but the Brahman's natural place at court was that of minister rather than that of king[2].

BRIEF HISTORY OF THE RAJPUTS

The Rajputs who till the 10th century A.D., were mostly local feudal lords holding the status of revenue collectors for their Gurjara-Pratihara overlords, asserted themselves as independent rulers, after the Ghaznavid storm had blown over, and took over the earlier kingdom of the Gurjara-Pratiharas. The main Rajput kingdoms in the 11th and 12th centuries were that of the Cahamanas (Chouhans) in East Panjab, Northern Rajasthan and Delhi. The Gahadwalas (Rathods) ruled the Ganges valley, today's U.P. The Paramaras ruled Malwa in Central India and the Tomaras ruled from Gwalior. The most powerful kingdoms were those of the Chouhans and the Rathods—both of which unfortunately were incessantly at war with each other when the Muslim raiders appeared again in the 1191 A.D. The Rajputs (from Raj Putra, *i.e.* prince or literally "king's son") who were a brave and chivalrous race, held the stage of feudal rulers before the coming of the Muslims.

The Gahadwalas (Rathods)

In the 11th century A.D., *i.e.* in the post-Mahmud Ghazni era the most powerful Hindu kingdom in North India was that of the Gahadwalas or Rathods who were a Rajput clan.

The founder of the Gahadwala line was Chandradeva, whose son Govindchandra Gahadwala was the most illustrious ruler on this line. Govindchandra was an astute ruler who ruled from Kannauj. Most of North India, including the ancient university town of Nalanda was a part of his kingdom. He stoutly defended his kingdom from further Muslim's incursion. He instituted a tax for this purpose which was called Turushka Danda *(i.e.* tax to fight the Turushkas or Turks). His grandson was Jaichandra Gahadwala (Rathod) who played a tragic role in Indian history.

Prithviraj Chouhan and Mohammad Ghori

In Jaichand's days, a rival Rajput clan had established itself in Delhi (Pithoragarh). The ruler there was Prithviraj Chouhan. Prithviraj was a romantic, chivalrous and an extremely fearless person. After ceaseless military campaigns, Prithviraj extended his original kingdom of Sambhar (Shakambara) to Rajasthan, Gujarat, and Eastern Panjab. He ruled from his twin capitals at Delhi and Ajmer. His fast rise caught the envy of the then powerful ruler Jaichandra Gahadwala and there was a lot of ill-feeling between the two.

Sanyogita, Jaichandra's Daughter

The story of Prithviraj's bold exploits spread far and wide in the country and he was the centre of much discussion in the circle-of the nobility. Sanyogita, the daughter of Jaichandra Gahadwala, fell secretly in love with Prithiviraj and she started a secret poetic correspondence with him. Her father the haughty Jaichandra got wind of this and he decided to teach his daughter and her upstart lover a lesson. So he arranged a Swayamwara (a ceremony where a bride can select her husband from the assembled princes. She had the right to garland any prince and she became his queen. This was an ancient Hindu custom among Royalty). Jaichandra invited all the big and small princes of the country to Kannauj for the royal Swayamwara. But he deliberately ignored Prithiviraj. To add insult to injury, he even made a statue of Prithiviraj and kept him as a Dwarpala (doorman).

The Elopement of Sanyogita

Prithviraj got to know of this, and he confided his plans to his lover. On the said day, Sanyogita walked down the aisle where the royale had assembled and bypassed all of them only to reach the door and garland the statue of Prithviraj as a doorman. The assemblage was stunned at this brash act of hers. But what stunned them and her father Jaichandra more was the next thing that happened. Prithiviraj who was hiding behind the statue, also in the garb of a doorman, whisked Sanyogita away and put her up on his steed to make a fast getaway to his capital at Delhi.

Weakening of both Rajput Kingdoms

Jaichandra and his army gave earnest chase and in the resultant string of battles between the two kingdoms fought between 1189 and 1190, both of them suffered heavily. While this drama was being enacted, another ruler also named Mohammad who was from Ghor in Afghanistan had grown powerful and had captured Ghazni and subsequently attacked the Ghaznavid Governor of the Panjab and defeated him. The kingdom of Mohammad Ghori now stretched up to the domains of Prithiviraj Chouhan. A clash was inevitable.

The First Battle of Tarain 1191 C.E. — Victory of Prithviraj Chouhan

Mohammad Ghori threw the gauntlet by laying siege to the fortress of Bhatinda in East Panjab which was on the frontier of Prithviraj's domains. Prithviraj's appeal for help from his father-in-law was scornfully rejected by the haughty Jaichandra. But undaunted Prithviraj marched on to Bhatinda and met his enemy at a place called Tarain (also called Taraori) near the ancient town of Thaneswar. In face of the persistent Rajput attacks, the battle was won as the Muslim army broke ranks and fled leaving their general Mohammad Ghori as a prisoner in Prithviraj's hands.

Mohammad Ghori was brought in chains to Delhi, Prithviraj's capital, and he begged his victor for mercy and release. Prithviraj's ministers advised against pardoning the aggressor. But the chivalrous and valiant Prithviraj thought otherwise and respectfully released the vanquished Ghori.

The 2nd Battle of Tarain 1192 C.E.— Defeat of Prithviraj Chouhan

The very next year Prithviraj's gesture was repaid by Ghori who re-attacked Prithviraj with a stronger army and guilefully defeated him by attacking the Rajput army before day break. (The Hindus incidentally followed a hoary practice of battling only from sunrise up to sunset. Before sunrise and after sunset there was to be no fighting as per a time honoured battle code). The defeated Prithviraj was pursued up to his capital and he was taken in chains as a captive to Ghor in Afghanistan.

The Blinding of Prithviraj

The story of Prithiviraj does not end here. As a prisoner in Ghor he was presented before Mohammad, where he looked Ghori straight into the eye. Ghori ordered him to lower his eyes, whereupon a defiant Prithviraj scornfully told him how he had treated Ghori as a prisoner and said that the eyelids of a Rajput's eyes are lowered only in death. On hearing this, Ghori flew into a rage and ordered that Prithviraj's eyes be burnt with red hot iron rods. This heinous deed being done, Prithviraj was regularly brought to the court to be taunted by Ghori and his courtiers. In those days Prithviraj was joined by his former biographer Chand Bardai, who had composed a ballad-biography on Prithviraj' in the name of *Prithviraj Raso* (Songs of Prithviraj). Chand Bardai told Prithviraj that he should avenge Ghori's betrayal and daily insults.

The two got an opportunity when Ghori announced a game of archery. On the advice of Chand Bardai, Prithviraj, who was then at court said he would also like to participate. On hearing this suggestion, the courtiers guffawed at him and he was taunted by Ghori as to how he could participate when he could not see. Whereupon, Prithviraj told Mohammad Ghori to order him to shoot, and he would reach his target.

Ghori became suspicious and asked Prithviraj why he wanted Ghori himself to order and not anyone else. On behalf of Prithviraj,

Chand Bardai told Ghori that he as a king would not accept orders from anyone other than a king. His ego satisfied, Mohammad Ghori agreed.

On the said day, Ghori sitting in his royal enclosure had Prithiviraj brought to the ground and had him unchained for the event. On Ghori's ordering Prithviraj to shoot, we are told Prithviraj turned in the direction from where he heard Ghori speak and struck Ghori dead with his arrow. This event is described by Chand Bardai in the couplet, "Char bans, chaubis gaj, angul ashta praman, Ete pai Sultan hai (Taa Upar hai Sultan) Ab mat chuko Chauhan." (Ten measures ahead of you and twenty-four feet away, is seated the Sultan, do not miss him now, Chouhan).

Thus ended the story of the brave but unrealistic Prithviraj Chouhan, the last Hindu ruler of Delhi. Delhi was to remain under Muslim rule for the next 700 years till 1857 and under British rule till 1947. Those few Hindus who came close to liberating Delhi during the seven centuries of Muslim rule were Rana Sanga in 1527, Raja (Hemu) Vikramaditya in around 1556 (2nd Battle of Panipat), and Shrimant Vishwas Rao who was the Peshwa's son and was co-commander of the Maratha forces in the 3rd Battle of Panipat in 1761. Metaphorically speaking, the next Hindu ruler to actually preside over Delhi was to be Dr. Rajendra Prasad, the first President of Independent India (and Jawaharlal Nehru—who was the President's first Minister).

The Rajput Resistance to Muslim Rule

Man Singh Tomar

In spite of the establishment of Muslim rule in Delhi and UP, in the former kingdoms of Prithviraj Chauhan and Jaichand Rathod, the Muslim invaders could never overrun the entire country. The Rajput dynasties like the Tomars of Gwalior and the Ranas of Mewad still continued to rule central India. One such Rajput ruler was Man Singh Tomar, the king of Gwalior. Man Singh put up a stout resistance to the Lodis and he succeeded in halting the Muslim ruler Sikandar Lodi's southward march at Gwalior. While the Tomars of Gwalior held back the Muslims from advancing into Malwa, the Ranas of Mewad held up the banner of Indian independence from Mewad in those trying times of Muslim aggression in India. In South Rajasthan especially, the Rajputs had defiantly preserved their writ by resisting the Delhi Sultans. The centre of this Rajput resistance was the kingdom at Chittor.

The Kirti Stambha (Victory Pillar) at Chittodgad

The Rana's of Mewad had their capital at Chittor or Chittodgad. They included Rana Ratansen (Rani Padmini's husband), Rana Sanga, Udai Singh and the tallest of them all Maharana Pratap. It was these 'Lions of Mewad' who defiantly upheld the banner of Indian independence during the darkest days of Muslim rule.

Rana Kumbha

Rana Kumbha who ruled from Kumbhalgad also put up a stout resistance to Muslim incursions into Rajputana in the 14th century. His capital Kumbhalgad which is a formidable fortress in densely-forested Aravalli ranges facilitated his resistance to the Muslims. This was one of the few times when the Rajputs used guerrilla tactics against the Muslims.

Rana Sangram Singh (Rana Sanga)

The next chapter of Rajput resistance to Muslim aggression was in the year 1527 when the Timurid ruler Babar invaded India. Babar first struck at the ruler of Delhi who at that time was Ibrahim Lodi. At a battle fought at Panipat, Babar defeated and killed Ibrahim Lodi and captured Delhi. Babar next turned his attention to the most powerful Hindu kingdom in north India. This was the kingdom of Chittor ruled by Rana Sangram Singh. The clash of the Rajput and the Muslim armies took place at Sikri. The Rajputs fought bravely and many perished in the cannon fire which Babar was using. The battle of Sikri gave Babar his second victory in India and saw the establishment of the Mughal dynasty (the last Muslim dynasty to rule India).

Rana Udai Singh

Despite the defeat of Rana Sangram Singh in the Battle of Sikri, the resistance of the Ranas of Mewad to Muslim rule continued for the next 100 years. Rana Sangram Singh's son, Udai Singh was an infant when his father died after the Battle of Sikri. His uncle tried to kill the child and crown prince Udai Singh. But the supreme sacrifice of his nurse Panna Dai who misled the uncle by offering her own son for being killed, saved Udai Singh. Udai Singh was brought up secretly till he attained youth. He subsequently defeated his uncle and assumed the throne of Chittor. He continued his father's legacy of preserving the independence of Chittor from the Muslim invaders. The city of Udaipur in Mewad bears his name. A panoramic view of the city of Udaipur.

This city and the forts that dotted the hills surrounding it were the heartland of the Rajput resistance to the Muslims. Here Muslim rule could never be established for any length of time all through the 700 years when the Muslims occupied different parts of India.

Maharana Pratap

Udai Singh's son was Maharana Pratap who led the Rajputs against Akbar's armies and preserved Rajput rule in Mewad. Rana Pratap was faced with the formidable challenge of renegade Rajput princes like Raja Todar Mai and Raja Man Singh who had joined forces with the Muslim rulers.

The Battle of Haldighati

In the battle of Haldighati, fought between Maharana Pratap and the Mughals, the Rajputs were not able to overcome the combined strength of the Mughals and the renegade Rajput princes who had played the role of traitors. But Maharana Pratap who was badly hurt in the battle, was saved by his wise horse Chetak, who took him in an unconscious state away from the battle scene. Although Maharana Pratap was not able to thwart the Muslims successfully, the saga of Rajput resistance to Muslim rule continued till the 17th century when the baton of the struggle for Indian independence from Muslim tyranny was taken up by the upcoming power of the Marathas, who brought about an end to Muslim domination of India.

INVASIONS OF SAKAS AND HUNS

In the tradition, which in India ranks as history, there is a sudden gap: the old Kshatriyas disappear, until the 6th and 9th centuries A.D., when we find a group of states under Rajput rulers. But it is impossible to say whether these Rajas were merely successful adventurers, or how far they were the heads of dominant clans. The true situation has now been ascertained from a study of the epigraphic evidence in northwestern India. It is clear that the break in the tradition in other words, the disappearance of the old Kshatriyas was the result of the invasion of India by successive hordes from Central Asia. The earliest of these were the Sakas (Scythians) in the 2nd century B.C., followed by the Yuehichi or Kushans in the 1st century A.D. It is believed that the chiefs of these invading hordes rapidly succumbed to the influence of their new environment became Hindus, and assumed, as ruling princes, the old name of Kshatriya. But it is still uncertain whether the pedigrees of any of the ruling clans go back to this period. During the 5th centuries A.D. and the early part of the 6th century, the Huns (or White Huns, as the Hindus called them) made a fresh invasion, and crushed the Hindu polity. They settled principally in the Panjab and Rajputana, their most important group being that of the Gurjaras, who, in name at least, are represented by the modern Rajputs[3]. The Rajputs founded important kingdoms, and gave their name to the province of Rajasthan. These were soon admitted to the status of Hindus, and are thus enabled to interpret the strange legend of the fire sacrifice at Mount Abu[4]. Their passing through the fire was a mode of expressing the purgation which they underwent; their impurity was removed and they became fitted to enter the Hindu caste system[5].

In later times the same process of introduction into the Rajput body has continued. Many chiefs of the so-called aboriginal races, with their followers, have marked their rise to the status of rulers by assuming the title of Rajputs, which, merely implies the fact they claim to be Rajas or cadets of a ruling house. For further details of this see the most recent and important advance in our knowledge of Indian ethnography[6].

LEGENDARY PEDIGREES

The mixed body, containing perhaps some survivors of the older Kshatriyas, reinforced by foreigners and aborigines, being thus admitted to Rajput status, were naturally desirous of authenticating their descent. Complacent bards, like the heralds of modern times, were ready to provide pedigrees linking the new ruling class with the gods and ancient heroes[7]. Hence arose the mass of legend assigning to various septs their descent from the sun or moon or other gods, or from the heroes who fought in the great war described in the *Mahabharata* epic. These legendary pedigrees are recorded in great detail by J. Tod, the enthusiastic historian of the Rajputs, in his *Antiquity of Rajasthan.*

CULTS AND BELIEFS

As might be expected from what has already been said, the Rajput cult and beliefs are of a mixed type, including those taught by their bards and Brahmans who trace their pedigrees to gods or legendary heroes, and those of the foreign or aboriginal stocks from which the Rajputs are derived.

THE DEVELOPMENT OF HINDUISM

In the early Hindu period tales were told which described the antagonism between the Kshatriyas and the Brahmans. Some refractory Rajas are said to have opposed the pretensions of the Brahman[8]. Visvamitra, is said to have attained the rank of a Brahman[9]. The same feeling appears in the rise of the Bhaktimarga, or the monotheistic Bhagavata religion, which was the work of Kshatriyas. In the same way both Buddhism and Jainism were the result of a Rajput reaction against the claim of Brahmans to retain the monopoly of admission into the ascetic orders[10]. Even at the present day some Rajput septs assign a higher rank to the bard than to the Brahman, and this feeling is encouraged by the notorious laxity of practice among some classes of Brahmans in Rajputana[11]. But the Brahmans are anxious to accept the new situation, and by polite concessions to Rajput felling lose no opportunity of regaining their position in the courts of the reigning princes.

CULT OF SIVA AND THE MOTHER GODDESSES

As a martial race, many Rajputs favour the cult of Siva- Mahadeva combined with that of his consort, the latter being largely drawn from the non-Aryan races, but now freely admitted into Hinduism. If, as some believe, the cult of Siva had its origin in the Himalaya, it was introduced, or rapidly assimilated by the Scythian or Hun invaders. Vasudeva, king of the Kushans (c. 140-173 AD), figured on his coins the image of Siva with that of his bull, Nandi[12]. The chief temple of Siva in Rajputana is that known as Eklingji, (he that is worshipped under the form of a single lingam). It is also known as Kailaspuri, Mount Kailasa being the Himalayan seat of the god. It is situated 12 miles from Udaipur, the capital of Mewar[13]. The Ranas of Mewar combined the functions of prince and priest, and were known as vice-regents (Diwan) of God[14]. With the cult of Siva is combined that of his consort Durga. In another form she is known as Mama Devi, 'mother of gods,' and round her image are grouped these of the other gods[15]. Again as Gauri, the 'yellow or brilliant' goddess, probably representing the ripe corn, she is the subject of a special cult when at the Gangaur festival[16] her image is taken to the lake at Udaipur and ceremonially bathed, possibly in order to free her from the last year's pollution, or as *rair* charms as in the worship of the Bona Dea[17], no male may be present at the rite[18]. She is also worshipped as Annapurna, 'she who is possessed of food; and her mimic marriage to Siva is performed. In other forms she is worshipped as Sakambhari, 'nourisher of herbs', 'Mata Janami', 'the birth mother', and Asapurna, 'she who fulfils desire'. In Rajput belief Krishna is the deified hero of the Yadava tribe, and he has his seat at Mathura (q.v.) where he sports with the Gopis, or milkmaids. In another form, at Dwarka, he is God of the dark storm-cloud[19]. His shrine is at Nathwara[20]. His image is said to have been removed from Mathura to escape the persecution of Aurangzeb; when the cart came to this place, the god refused to go farther, and the shrine was erected for him, which is a sanctuary for criminals, receiving donations from merchants throughout the Hindu world, and his pontiff is a personage of great sanctity and authority[21]. It is strange that the gentle Krishna should be worshipped side by side with Siva. On the whole, his cult has exercised a good effect on Rajput society.

ANCESTOR-CULTS

It is the primary duty of the Rajput to visit the cenotaphs of his ancestors in the season of mourning, and to feed their hungry ghosts. Special veneration is paid to the Mahasati, or place of sacrifice of faithful wives. Tod quotes a case in which he interposed to prevent Sati (i. 423).

The Rajput never enters these places of silence but to perform stated rites, or anniversary of offering of flowers and water to the names of his ancestors[22].

TUTELARY DEITIES

Each sept worshipped its tutelary goddess; Rathasen or Rashtrasen is the embodied luck of the Sesodias of Mewar, as Nagnecha, the serpent, protects the Rathors, and Varan Mata the Chavadas, while Khatrapals, 'the field-watcher', is the patron of agriculture[23]. He also venerates the heroes of his sept, as in the remarkable court at Mandor[24], which contains images of the heroes of the Rathors[25]. The patron God or goddess of a sept used to accompany the chief to battle. On one occasion the Rathor god fell into the hands of the Kachhwahas of Jaipur. Their prince took him to his capital, wedded him to the Jaipur goddess, and returned him with his compliments to his defeated adversary. "Suvh", says Tod[26], "were the courteous usages of Rajput chivalry." The tutelary god of Kotah is Brajnath or Krishna and the chief at every battle used to carry his golden image on his saddle. He too was lost in battle, and it was many years before he was restored, to the great joy of every Hara[27].

CULT OF YOUTHFUL HEROES

The cult of youthful hero (Putra) is common among the Rajputs. Laut, the young hero of Ajmer, is worshipped by the Chauhan Rajput sept, and, as he wore at the time of his death a silver chain anklet, this ornament is taboo to the children of the sept (Tod.i.200n.). The cult is not confined to youths. The queen of Ganor, who killed by means of a poisoned robe the Mussalman who attempted to outrage her, receives no special worship, but in the spirit of sympathetic magic a visit to her tomb cures certain argue[28].

WORSHIP OF NATURAL OBJECTS

Water-spirits are honoured by throwing coconuts into the water. The spirit of the Banas river[29] used to raise her hand over the water to receive the offering, but, as in the common fairy-gift legend, "since some unhallowed hand threw a stone in lieu of a coconut, the arm has been withdrawn." There was a sun fountain at Valabhi, whence at the summons of Raja Siladitya, the seven-headed horse which bears the chariot of the sun rose to bear him to battle.

SNAKE WORSHIP

The Pushkar lake is provided with a remarkable snake legend indicating a conflict of cults[30]. The Nagpanchmi[31] festival, 'cobra's faith' is celebrated in its honour. The usual tales are told of the serpent protecting or recognizing the true heir to the throne. The worship of snake heroes, like Tejaji[32], Guga[33], and Pipa[34], is common.

SACRED ANIMALS AND TREES

Next to the cow, the boar is sacred to the Rajputs and possibly represents the corn-spirit. Birds of augury are carefully protected and the pigeon, as the bird of love, has become associated with the erotic cult of Krishna, and is still regularly fed at every courthouse and temples in Rajputana. Among trees a variety of fig is especially sacred. It was from a Pipal-tree (Ficus Religiosa) that Asapurna, the tutelary goddess of Bundi, appeared to protect the queen.

FESTIVALS

The Rajput festivals are numerous and interesting. The reader may be referred for details to Tod's classical account (i.444.ff.). But, when he compares the ritual with that of Egypt and other countries to the west of India, it must be remembered that his theories are, to a large extent, obsolete.

RAJPUT COMPARED WITH IRISH PEOPLE

In many ways the Rajput bears such a strong resemblance to the Highlanders of Scotland that one might seem to be reading one of Waltar Scott's stories, with some trifling differences of names and costumes. They had the same reckless daring the same loyalty to a chief they trusted, the same love of sport, the same readiness to take offence and quarrel among themselves when they could find no enemy to give them employment. After all these centuries the Rajput bearing remains what it was in their heroic age, something that marks him out from all other races; the poorest is by birth a gentleman, and therefore, the equal of the greatest. To see a Rajput on horseback clattering through the streets that his ancestors cleared with the sword is to realize a scene from the legends when kings go to battle.

HISTORY OF SATI

Sanskrit Sati, former Indian custom of a widow burning herself, either on the funeral pyre of her dead husband or soon after his death. Sometimes, the wife was immolated before the husband's expected death in battle and it was then called Jauhar. Some authorities feel the etymological connection between the Sanskrit term 'sat', which means "chaste wife" and which is also the name of a Hindu goddess, and the practice of widow self-immolation is erroneous. The custom possibly has links with ancient beliefs that a man needed his companion in the after-life as well as in this world. During the medieval period the hardships encountered by widows in traditional Hindu society may have contributed to its spread. Numerous Sati-stones, memorials to the widows who died in this way, are found all over India.

The first reference to this practice, in Sanskrit text is in the *Mahabharata,* in which some queens undergo Sati, but it is mentioned by the 1st century B.C. Greek author Diodows Siculus in his account of the Panjab, in the 4th century B.C. In the Muslim period the Rajput dishonoured by the enemy does so, most notably at Chittorgarh. The larger incidence of Sati among the Brahmans of Bengal, particularly dating 1680-1830 A.D. was due indirectly to the Dayabhaga system of law (c. 1100 A.D.), which prevailed in Bengal and which gave inheritance to widows. At its best, Sati was committed voluntarily, but cases of compulsion, escape, and reserve are known. Steps to prohibit it were taken by the Mughal Emperor Humayun and his son Akbar, and it was abolished in British India in 1829. Instances of it continued to occur in Indian Hindu States for more than 30 years[35] thereafter.

However this practice was patronized by the Rajputs, being need of the day. Temperamentally, the Rajputs, who were very sensitive to self-respect and lonely power of the time, had to face the foreign invaders to protect their honour. The invaders were better equipped with arms and men, superior in every field of war. Rajputs never hesitated to face the foe with might and honour but ultimately had to submit to them. They rightly thought over to save the honour of their female folk.

There are many striking examples, where Rajput women had to accept the lesser evil. Among them all the incidence of Padmini, the Maharani of Chittorgarh seems supreme.

Rajput women are quite consistent in responding to the two-fold question; who are the best exemplars of Rajput women and why are those women good? The names of Padmini and Mira Bai, in quite different ways, reject the Pativrata role and reaffirmation are vital to the admiration they inspire.

A SORCERER

In the 12th and 13th centuries, the Sultanate of Delhi, the kingdom set up by the invaders was nevertheless growing in power. The Sultans made repeated attack on Mewad on one pretext or the other. Here we may recollect the story of Rani Padmini who was the pretext for Ala-ud-din Khilji's attack on Chittor. In those days Chittor was under the rule of King Ratansen, a brave and noble warrior-king. Apart from being a loving husband and a just ruler, Ratansen was also a patron of the arts. In his court there were many talented people, one of whom was a musician named Raghav Chetan. But unknown to anybody, Raghav Chetan was also a sorcerer. He used his evil talents to run down his rivals and unfortunately for this was caught red-handed in his dirty act of arousing evil spirits.

On hearing this King Ratansen was furious and he banished Raghav Chetan from his kingdom after blackening his face and making him ride a donkey. This harsh punishment earned King Ratansen an uncompromising enemy. Sulking after his humiliation, Raghav Chetan made his way towards Delhi with the aim of trying to incite the Sultan of Delhi Ala-ud-din Khilji to attack Chittor.

On approaching Delhi, Raghav Chetan settled down in one of the forests nearby Delhi which the Sultan used to frequent for hunting deer. One day on hearing the Sultan's hunt party entering the forest, Raghav Chetan started playing a melodious tune on his flute. When the alluring notes of Raghav Chetan's flute reached the Sultan's party they were surprised as to who could be playing a flute in such a masterly way in a forlorn forest.

The Sultan dispatched his soldiers to fetch the person and when Raghav Chetan was brought before him, the Sultan Ala-ud-din Khilji asked him to come to his court at Delhi. The cunning Raghav Chetan asked the king as to why he wanted to have an ordinary musician like himself when there were many other beautiful objects to be had. Wondering what Raghav Chetan meant, Ala-ud-din asked him to clarify. Upon being told of Rani Padmini's beauty, Ala-ud-din's lust was aroused and immediately on returning to his capital he gave orders to his army to march on Chittor.

MAHARANI PADMINI

Maharani Padmini, a queen of Maharaja of Mewar, was renowned for her incomparable beauty. Ala-ud-din, the notorious Afghan invader, was determined to take Chittor and capture her. His initial charges proved unsuccessful, but lust spurred him on. Finally, frustrated, he submitted a compromise that he would withdraw his troops if he could be allowed but a glimpse of the fair lady's face. The Maharana consented but stipulated that to protect Padmini's modesty, the Muslim would only be able to see her face reflected in a mirror. The offer having been accepted, the queen was taken to a palace in the middle of a large tank. She stood next to a window with her back towards the outside. Ala-ud-din was placed in a building at the edge of the tank. From which considerable distance he was allowed to catch a fleeting glimpse of Padmini's reflection in a mirror, which was held up to the queen for a few seconds. Far from satisfying his desire, this vision inflamed it. He decided to double-cross the Maharana and make Padmini his own.

MAHARANA'S ESCORT TAKEN HOSTAGE

Because the Muslim had arrived in Chittor alone and thus demonstrated his faith in Rajput honour, the Maharana felt compelled to return the compliment by personally accompanying him back to his camp. When they arrived, however, Ala-ud-din took this escort hostage and demanded Padmini as ransom. Thc Rajput army could not contemplate such a trade. To ask the queen to compromise herself would contravene the Rajput code of honour, which protects women. Padmini herself ordered that the trade be executed but, having sized up Ala-ud-din as no man of honour, also plotted an ambush. She sent Ala-ud-din a message consenting to his terms provided that she be allowed to bring along her belonging and attendants. He agreed. Then the queen ordered many trained palanquins, which were designed to transport ladies-in-waiting, to be filled instead with soldiers. Because the soldiers who were to be concealed in this way knew they would not be able to defeat Ala-ud-din's powerful army, they prepared themselves to die in a battle of honour.

A MASS IMMOLATION

When the palanquin procession reached its destination, Padmini asked Ala-ud-din that she be permitted to bid farewell to her husband before leaving him. Having agreed, the Muslim took his bride-to-be to the place where her husband was held captive. As soon as the Maharana's location was known, the Rajput soldiers sprang upon the Muslims and liberated the captive king. In the uproar, both Padmini and her husband managed to escape. Padmini was whisked back to the palace, while the Maharana fled for the hills. Because it was clear that his forces would lose the battle, he retreated so that he might plot an assault on Ala-ud-din at a later more promising moment. Back at Chittor, seeing that the Maharana's forces were defeated, Padmini led hundreds (some say thousands) of women to the vaults under the palace, where they committed Jauhar, mass immolation.

PURITY OF RAJPUT BLOOD PROTECTED

In general, Jauhar is understood to accomplish closely related purposes. To begin with, it preserves female virtue. The noble women quoted at the very beginning of this chapter said, "Padmini had character and purity; she died by Jauhar." Rajputs have been keen to protect the purity of Rajput blood. Because conquest brought with it the likelihood of rape, they have seen conquest as a threat to family integrity and caste identity. Until now, another woman commented, the purity of Rajput blood had not been diluted. She said that with society changing, that might happen in the future, but said she was proud that "blood-mixing" really had not happened to any appreciable extent as yet.

PADMINI (THE SATI MATA)

Two matters concerning the Padmini narrative merit need immediate attention First, although Padmini is a Sati, she is not simply assimilated to the category of Sati Mata. True, Padmini is a Sati Mata to Sisodiyas. But when Sisodiyas speak of their Sati Mata, they do not single out Padmini from other Satis. Self-immolation is the basis for the worship she receives as one of the Satis whose identities merge into the integrated Sati Mata personage. What causes Padmini's name to be remembered and revered is not just the mode of her death but the manner in which she lived her life. The two women thus summarised their sentiments, "I admire Padmini because she was very clever, she showed the Muslims that" and "I like Padmini because she met danger when her husband wasn't around to protect her."

This is not to downplay the importance of Padmini's death: it is the climax of the Padmini narrative. One Rajput woman noted that when Padmini leaves the palace to attack Ala-ud-din, "her body becomes hot with Sat" which clearly foreshadows her death as a Sati. Acts that make her story something more than a Sati scenario, however, are the rescue she plots and the ambush she directs. To execute her plan she abandons her household and takes to the battlefield. For these reasons she is revered even by Rajputs and others, who do not worship her as a Sati Mata.

Second, Padmini's heroic action contrivances a cardinal rule; Padmini leaves Pardah. The story builds towards this event and dwells on its significance. The mirror incident, in which Padmini shows her face to Ala-ud-din, portends this transgression. The story of the lustful Muslim is well-known to Rajasthani history. When the villainous Ala-ud-din sees the reflection of Padmini's face, it is a foregone conclusion that desire will defeat honour and he will conspire to ravish her. The bargain he strikes is thereby transformed from an end in itself to a means of conquest. Furthermore, while the belief that Padmini does not thereby abandon her virtue, it also stresses that she deviates from custom. Her dramatic departure emphasises that the state of affairs in Chittor has become so perilously chaotic that only Padmini, a woman, can save it, Chittor must suspend its own law to re-establish the order that the law is intended to preserve.

DEFINITION OF JAUHAR

In the *Rajasthani Shabd Kosh* (Dictionary) the first definition of Jauhar is "jewel" (Ratna). The second is "proof" (Pramana) of the "character" (Swarup) of a sword as seen by fineness of the striation in its iron. The third is "quality, beauty, character" (Visheshta, Khubi, Gum). The fourth is "the mass burning of live Rajput women on a pyre when their husbands, warning saffron, are about to lose their fort to the enemy, so that the enemy cannot get the 'rite' (Kriya) of immolation of anyone (Kisi) to the motive of "revenge" (Pratikar) for injustice. (It presumably applies to immolations of others besides the Rajput women mentioned in the fourth definition. This is interesting because women sometimes perform Sat Jauhar for punishment by depriving them of the opportunity to satisfy their carnal desires). Jauhar shares basic associations of Sat. Like Sat, it refers to quality and character; like Sati it is proof of female character and goodness. The link between "gem" and character appears to be the same made in English when we refer to someone as a "real gem". In short, the primary meanings denote character; the derivative meanings refer to the rituals that demonstrate it.

JAUHAR MELA AT CHITTOR

At Chittor there is an annual celebration of heroism known as the Jauhar Mela. Rajputs parade through Chittor to honour the courage of their ancestors. Although the festival focuses Jauhar, it does not bear a specific Sati's name. It takes palace on the anniversary of another Jauhar, but most Rajputs assume it celebrates the Jauhar led by Padmini. Its organizers intended the festival to commemorate all three Satis and Jauhars at Chittor. They chose the anniversary they did because it is a time when neither students nor farmers are busy. Although the precession commemorates the bravery of Rajput ancestors, it also occasions fiery political speeches and protests against the lawmakers in Delhi for grievances related to the loss of political power.

The Rajputs emerged into political importance in the 9th and 10th centuries A.D. From c. 800 A.D. Rajput dynasties dominated northern India, and many petty Rajput kingdoms were among the main obstacles to the complete Muslim domination of Hindu India. After the Muslim conquest of the eastern Panjab and the Ganges Valley, the Rajputs maintained their independence in the fortresses of Rajasthan and the forests of Central India. Sultan Ala-ud-din Khilji of Delhi (1296-1316) took the two great Rajput forts of Chittor and Ranthambhor in east Rajasthan but could not hold them. The Rajput state of Mewar under Rana Sanga made a bid for supremacy but was defeated by the Mughal emperor Babur at Khanua in 1527. Babur's grandson Akbar took the forts of Chittor and Ranthambhor (1568-69) and then made a settlement with all the Rajasthan princes except Mewar. Accepting Mughal overlordship, the Rajput princes were admitted to the Mughal royal court and the emperor's privy council and were given governorships and commands of armies. Although damaged by emperor Aurangzeb (1658-1707).

This arrangement continued until the Mughal Empire itself collapsed in the 18th century. The Rajputs then fell victims to the Maratha chiefs until they accepted British suzerainty in 1818 at the end of the last Maratha war. After independence (1947), the Rajput states in Rajasthan were merged to form the state of Rajasthan within the Indian Union.

According to another independent and fair view, people who identify themselves as Rajputs are found across northwestern India, the Gangas Plains, Madhya Pradesh, and Himalayan valleys. Following Indian independence, the twenty-three Rajput states that formed what was called Rajputana were consolidated into modern state of Rajasthan. The great majority are Hindus, but more than one million are Muslims. In the past, Rajputs formed the fighting, landowning, and ruling castes.

Rajputs are hereditary soldiers and landowners, but the demand for soldiers is now limited and few Rajputs have any occupation except as landowners. While some Rajputs farm their land themselves, many own enough lands so that they can hire others to perform manual labour.

Their Social Organisation

The chief feature of Rajput social organisation is their division into hierarchically ranked clans and lineages. One hundred and three Rajput clans are well known. Additionally, rankings based on regional location, the degree of centralised political control within regions or Rajput states, and hypergamy were all important elements of the traditional Rajput social order. Since independence, Rajput power has been declining as other castes seek economic and political independence from Rajput control.

Still, the Rajput tradition and identity permit even poor Rajput farmers to consider themselves the equal of powerful landholders of their clan and superior to any high official of the professional classes. No people in India can boast of finer flair of arms or brighter deeds of cavalry and Rajputs still form one of the main recruiting fields for the Indian army of today.

Their Courts: Centres of Culture

The Rajput courts were centres of culture; Sanskrit literature and drama flourished and the modern vernacular languages began to prosper. The Rajput bards sang the praises of their overlords in Hindi, the earliest of these martial ballads is the *Prithviraj Raso,* which tells how prince Prithviraj carried off his bride. Rajput princes were great builders, who constructed magnificent palaces, fortresses, and stately shrines.

Rajput men and women are still much involved with elaborate ceremonies, especially weddings, for these are the rituals associated with Rajput identity. Sati is no longer performed indeed, it has long been illegal but funerals are still cause for celebration of grandeur past.

There are modern Rajputs who are followers of the Swaminarayan sect of Ramanuja, or of Vallabhacharya. These groups are all vegetarians, but other Hindu Rajputs who constitute the majority, are Shaivites. Only do these Shaivites eat meat, but many are also partial to smoking tobacco, taking opium, although most of them are non-vegetarian.

RAJPUT PAINTING

Rajput painting, art of the independent Hindu feudal states in India, is distinguished from the court art of the Mughal emperors. Whereas Mughal painting was contemporary in style, Rajput was traditional and romantic. It developed in the 16th and 17th centuries, and its late period lasted through 1825. Rajput painting is further divided into Rajasthani painting (q.v.), or the schools of the Rajasthan and Central India, or the art of the Himalayan kingdom.

SCYTHIANS & RAJPUTS

According to Rana Wasdev Singh Parhar, the life of the Scythians is paradoxical to that of the Rajputs. The Rajputs were mostly defensive and not aggressive, whereas the Scythians were always aggressive, who carried fire and sword wherever they rode. They did not like to establish forts and cities and preferred to lead a nomadic life. The luxurious Scythians made wooden houses on the four or six wheel carts. The others rode horses. Even today, among their successors in Mangolia, four-year-old children ride horses. To be brave one need to be stone hearted person; to be so cruel with captives or the enemies; to skin alive, cut to pieces, limb by limb, to bury alive, to brick alive, to drink the enemy's blood, to make a drinking bowl of enemy's skull, to boast that one has killed so many enemies in a year and disliking those who did not kill their enemy during the year. Such acts were applauded at gatherings on the annual fairs. They behaved like beasts. The Rajput traits are quite contrary to these barbarian traits of the Scythians. The traits of Scythians as described by Herodotus are much boggling and seem to be fictional. The Greek historian has described the barbarous habits of the Scythians. He has given their examples that they made scarves from the skin of their enemy; cutting their captive to pieces; their furious drinking habits. He even termed them man-eaters. For half the year they became wolves and the remaining half men. All these descriptions are mind chilling.

In Indian history there are some similarities, *e.g.* Bhim, one of the heroes of the *Mahabharata*, Hindu epic, vows to drink a cup of blood from Duryodhan's leg, as the latter had asked Dropadi to sit on his leg in the presence of all the Gurus, elders and ministers, in the open court, whereas the Rajputs never committed such barbarian acts with their enemies. Rajput king, Prithviraj Chauhan had many a time, pardoned Muslim King Muhammad Ghori who prayed for pardon. But, on the other hand when Prithviraj was defeated by the Muslim Sultan, he treated him most cowardly. He blinded the Rajput Raja, made him a prisoner and treated him most shabbily.

The heinous deed being done, Prithviraj was regularly brought to the Muslim court to be taunted by Muhammad Ghori and his courtiers. In those days Prithviraj had the company of his former biographer Chand Bardai, who composed a ballad- biography on Rajput King Prithviraj under the title *Prithviraj Raso,* the songs of Raja Prithviraj. Chand Bardai told Prithviraj, in a dramatic way, to shoot to death Mohammad Ghori when he was sitting on his throne, and thus showed his skill of archery[36].

Table 9.2: *The Hindu and Sikh Rajputs of Jalandhar Bist Doad, Panjab*

Sr. No.	Name of Village	Had Bast	Area	Gotras	Migrated From
1.	Bariana	315	685	Saroia	Chukhiara
2.	Ladhewali	220	301	Minhas Parmar Battri	Daroli Khurd Badhon Ghadial
3.	Kaki Pind			Minhas Parmar Parhar Jaswal	Daroli Kalan Panchhata Kalra Bham
4.	Rama Mandi			Minhas Parmar Parhar Jaswal	Daroli Kalan Panchhata Kalra Bham
5.	Rahimanpur			Minhas	Damunda
6.	Madar	166	303	Saroia Minhas	Chukhiara Daroli Kalan
7.	Dhogari	164	1133	Minhas	Daroli Kalan
8.	Alawalpur	139		Puar Parhar Parmar	Ghadial Kalra Panjaura Panjaura
9.	Chuharwali	167	448	Minhas Bhatti Puar	Daroli Kalan Ghadial
10.	Daroli Khurd	65	1212	Minhas	
11.	Daroli Kalan	65	1212	Minhas	
12.	Damunda	64	397	Minhas Bhatti	
13.	Padhiana	67	793	Minhas	
14.	Kalra	68	466	Parhar	
15.	Lutera Kalan	70	312	Minhas	Padhiana
16.	Lutera Khurd	69	259	Minhas Parhar Puar	Padhiana Kalara Ghadial

(Contd...)

Sr. No.	Name of Village	Had Bast	Area	Gotras	Migrated From
17.	Jalpottan	71	259	Minhas Bhatti	Daroli Khurd Ghudial
18.	Dhandhauri	72	136	Minhas	Daroli Kalan Daroli Khurd
19.	Dhandhaur	73	471	Minhas Bhatti	Padhiana Daroli Khurd Damunda
20.	Chauhan	173		Puar Parhar	Ghudial Kalra
21.	Ghudial	60	241	Bhatti Puar	
22.	Chukhiara	59	179	Saroia	
23.	Jalbhay	44	202	Saroia	Chukhiara
24.	Rampur			Bhatti	
25.	Karnana	93	520	Parhar	
26.	Kammam	187	761	Parmar Bhatti	Miopatty Sahlon
27.	Sahlon	174	257	Bhatti	
28.	Mahalon			Minhas	Daroli Kalan Padhiana
29.	Sarhal Mundi			Chauhan	
30.	Khiala	66	251	Minhas Bhatti	Padhiana Ghadial
31.	Gohawar			Minhas Puar	Daroli Kalan Ghudial
32.	Adampur			Minhas Bhatti Parhar	Daroli Khurd Damunda
33.	Ajrham	240	938		
34.	Pandori Rajputan	197	581	Rathor	
35.	Phuglana	274	791	Minhas Parmar	Padhiana Paldi, Nadalon

(Contd...)

Sr. No.	Name of Village	Had Bast	Area	Gotras	Migrated From
36.	Mehtiana	271	325	Minhas Parmar	Padhiana Jangliana
37.	Bhungarni	283	491	Parmar Saroia Parhar	
38.	Pandori Kadd	282	1921	Parmar	Binjon
39.	Ajnoha	52	563	Parmar	
40.	Thindal	4	42	Rathor	
41.	Nangal	5	1041	Parmar	
42.	Charhan	3	43	Parmar Daud	
43.	Jalwehara	2	134	Janjua	
44.	Todarpur	1	903	Janjua Parmar Dodd Jaswal	Kukawal Nadalon Jalwehara Naroor
45.	Kukawal	6	73	Janjua Parhar	
46.	Dihana	7	623	Saroia Janjua	
47.	Thakarwal	9	107	Dodd	Manjh
48.	Bham	12	772	Jaswal	
49.	Jangliana	44	218	Parmar	
50.	Baddon	51	306	Parmar	
51.	Dandian	50	124	Parmar Dodd Janjua	
52.	Dhaparhan (Thapal)	10	61	Toor (Tanwar)	
53.	Paldi	99	207	Minhas	
54.	Dohalaron	309	83	Laddoo	
55.	Chaggaran	325	219	Puar	
56.	Mahatpur	345	139	Puar	

(Contd...)

Sr. No.	Name of Village	Had Bast	Area	Gotras	Migrated From
57.	Bohan	295	732	Saroia	
58.	Reehalay	109	206	Bhatti	
59.	Binjon	107	716	Parmar	
60.	Panjorha	54	605	Parmar	
61.	Nadalon	53	675	Parmar	
62.	Saroia	243	529	Minhas	Paldi
63.	Garhshankar	143	858	Minhas	Paldi
64.	Kandhala	31	354	Minhas	Daroli Kalan
65.	Gujrattan	9	336	Parmar	Miopatty
66.	Baghana	21	1809	Parmar	Miopatty
67.	Naroor	18	1470	Jaswal	
68.	Panchhatta	25	2435	Parmar	
69.	Miopatty	24	276	Parmar	
70.	Randhirgarh (Thakarwal)	17	265	Manjh Dodd	
71.	Hargobindpur (Bhogpur)	59	638	Minhas Parmar	Paldi, Baddon
72.	Khatti	57	271	Minhas Parmar	Paldi, Baddon
73.	Khurampur	63	390	Rathaur	
74.	Meerapur	9	336	Parmar	
75.	Khalian	16	538	Manjh Dood	

Table 9.3: *Sikh Rajputs of Malwa*

Sr. No.	Name of Villages	District	Gotras	Migrated From
1.	Panjetha	Ambala	Minhas Parmar Bhatti	
2.	Sangatpura	Faridkot	Minhas Parmar Bhatti	
3.	Bahadurgarh	Fatehgarh Sahib	Minhas	Padhiana
4.	Dialpura	Patiala	Minhas	
5.	Manjari Jattan	Patiala	Janjua Saroia	
6.	Manjari Mannn Singh	Patiala	Janjua Saroia	
7.	Khanian	Patiala	Janjua	
8.	Bharhi	Patiala	Janjua Chauhan	
9.	Jasso Majjara	Patiala	Chauhan Minhas	
10.	Jeenowal	Faridkot	Chauhan Rathor	
11.	Samadh Bhai	Faridkot	Parmar Bhatti	
12.	Rania	Faridkot	Sarod Naru	Khanaura
13.	Dholan	Ludhiana	Minhas Parmar Bhatti Chauhan	
14.	Kotkapura	Faridkot	Minhas Parmar Bhatti Chauhan	

The Sikh Rajputs of Jalandhar Doab produced great leaders such as:

1. Bhai Manjh of village Kang Mai Hoshiarpur district.
2. Bhai Ude Singh Minhas, Padhiana, Jalandhar district.
3. Bhai Bachittar Singh Minhas, Padhiana.
4. Bhai Alam Singh, Sialkot, Pakistan.
5. Akali Gian Singh Chauhan (1822 A.D.), Sangrur tehsil.
5. Akali Phoola Singh, Ajnoha, Garhshanker tehsil.
7. Bhai Mani Singh Chauhan, the martyr.

The Muslim Naroo Rajputs had sprung from Mauo, near Taiwan, Phillaur tehsil, district Jalandhar. They converted to Islam much earlier and comparatively they had heavy hold in Doaba Bist, Jalandhar. They inhabited the following villages:

Lutera Kalan and Khurd, Khanaura, Mehtiana, Mona, Phuglana, Mukhaniana, Pindorian, Ahrana Kalan and Khurd, Garhshankar, Haryana, Sham Chaurasi, Machharali, Miani, Tanda Urmur, Dasuya and some more villages in Hoshiarpur district. They held Begowal and many more villages in Kapurthala district or the erstwhile Kapurthala State.

RAJPUTS
LAHORE DISTRICT

The Rajputs are the next most important agriculturist tribe in the district. They are practically all Mussalmans; no village is owned by any people who call themselves Rajputs and at the same time profess the Hindu religion. The predominant section in this district is that of Bhatti Rajputs, who number over 20,000 souls or about two-fifths of the total recorded Rajput population. Next to the Bhattis are the Khokhars, who number 8,399 according to the recent census; Chauhans 3,668, Puniar 2,009. Other clans of Rajputs in this district are very insignificant in numbers. The true Rajput agriculturists are notorious for extravagance, idleness and slack cultivation. In almost every Rajput village the mass of the people are impoverished and encumbered with debt; though on the other hand there are generally one or two leading men in prosperous circumstances. In the north-west corner of the Kasur tehsil there are a few settlements of so-called Rajputs who are as competent agriculturists as any Jats to be found in the Manjha.

One of the most important sub-divisions of the Rajputs are the Khokhars who occupy a settlement along the bank of the Ravi, a little outside Lahore city, comprising 16 estates, of which Niazbeg is the largest. These all call themselves Rajputs, ranking their section as fifth in order, and marrying women only of their own section or of the four above them. They are all luxuriously disposed and very extravagant, spending money wastefully on clothes, horses and marriages. They take no payment for their daughters nor do the parents of the girl have much expense, but the boy's parents spend anything from Rs. 500 to 2,000 on feasting the relations of either side, distribution of alms and dancing women. Also the tambol or marriage gifts to the boy's father are very extravagant among this class, and the jewellery given to the girl from the boy's people comes to a good round sum. Similarly, at funerals this section is reckless in their expenditure. Thus it comes about that the Khokhar Rajputs are generally overwhelmed with debt. They are also very inferior agriculturists, being too proud or indolent to do heavy manual work themselves. The Khokhars in the Chunian tehsil, however, are rather Jats than Rajputs and do not appear to have the idle expensive habits of the Khokhars in Lahore and Sharaqput.

AMRITSAR DISTRICT

The landowning Rajputs of the district are all Muhammedans. No village is owned by any clan calling themselves Rajputs and professing the Hindu religion. The chief clans are as follows:

Bhatti	16,608
Chauhan	2,801
Naru	1,043
Manj	816
Miscellaneous	12,871
	34,139

The above details must be accepted with caution, for it is well known that many Muhammedans call themselves Rajputs, who by birth have no claim to the name. This is probably the case mostly with the Rajput residents in the city, who number about 5,000, but these are not landowners, being for the most part labourers, or following miscellaneous occupations.

Among the landowning classes Rajputs are found most in Ajnala along the riverbank. From Dial Rajputana and Inayatpur, as far as Fatta near Bhindi Aulakh, the proprietors are almost all Rajputs, and throughout the tehsil they hold about 13 per cent of the cultivated area. They have all the faults commonly found among Muhammedan Rajputs, of which pride and indolence are the chief. They take cultivators as a low rank and are much given to employing Arains and other industrious classes to cultivate their land, with the result that many of the latter have acquired occupancy rights in Rajput villages. They are not, as a rule, prosperous, at least in Ajnala, and are often deeply in debt, but it is nearly always observable that one or two leading men, in each village are distinctly well-to-do, and make an income by lending money to their brethren.

In Amritsar they are better off and have larger holdings. Their chief villages in that tehsil are Bhorchi, Fatehpur, Malowal Khabba, Sadhar, Ajaibwali and Ibban, and in Tarn Taran, Palasaor, Bharoal, Dial, and Bhaini. Traces of the former supremacy of Rajputs are to be seen in the cases where they enjoy a Talukdari allowance exacted by them in their capacity as superior owners from neighbouring communities of Jats or Kambohs who were originally settled by the Rajputs as tenants, but who have come to be recognised as having almost full rights of ownership.

GURDASPUR DISTRICT

The following general account of the Rajputs of the district is taken from the 1892 *District Gazetteer*:

"The hilly tract is peopled almost entirely by Thakkars or spurious Rajputs, the submontane is mainly Rajput, and the plain's population is principally Jat. There are very few true Jaikaria Rajputs, as the Pathanias and Manhas, who might lay claim to this rank, have lost grade by turning personally to direct agriculture. Practically, all of these tribes come under the generic term of Salamias, and many of them hardly deserve the name of Rajput at all, and in Kangra would be called Rathis who are repudiated by the true blood Rajputs. The lowest clan of all are known as Ramrias. Leaving the classification based on the method of solution adopted, and arranging the Rajputs by the traditional races of Surajbansi and Sombansi, we have the following results:

Chandarbansi	**Surajbansi**
Guleri	Jamwal
Pathania	Jasrotia
Samrial	Janglotia
Khokhar	Manhas
Kohal	Harchand
Bhatti	Jarral
Bhamrotra	Sin
Lamin	Indauria
Kakotra	Chibh
Naru	Bagal
Ladit	Tangral
Chandar	Saroch
Makhotra	Thakkar
Rakwal	Thakial
Chohan	Bhadiar
Madar	Salehria
Kanauch	Gohotra
Awan	Malhotra
Samanch	Manj
Jhanjua	Manjrial
Dhamdial	Rial
Balim	Jhaggi
	Sanauria
	Mahotra
	Katal
	Lalotra

Some of them call themselves Jaikarias, but except the first two Chandarbansi, and the first three, Surajbansi, the other clans have really lost their claim to the salutation of Jaideya in this district. Still some others are all locally known as "Kahri" or those who only take from or give wives to a particular clan and the others as "Dohri", or those who take and give wives in the same clan. The former class are considered superior. The five true Jaikaria classes give and take in marriage amongst themselves, and take from the other Juikarias and Kahri clans. The Dohri clans intermarry, except with their own clan or that of their mothers and paternal or maternal grandfathers. Amongst the inferior Jaikaria and Kahri clans there is a regular order of precedence, and they take from a lower and give to a higher clan. Thus the Tangrals take from the Katals, Lalotras and Kohals, and give to the Jarrals, Salehrias and Indaurias; the Kohals take from the Katals and hill Thakkars, and give to the Tangrals, and the Salehrias give to the Manhas and take from the Gahotras, Katals and Lalotras. A tendency is, however observable amongst them to level away these distinctions to some extent, and if this extends it will be an excellent thing.

The Thakkars in the hills occupy the very lowest rung of the ladder, and so have not been shown in the list. They have innumerable sub-divisions amongst themselves, and practice widow remarriage. The custom of Karewa is also not uncommon amongst most of the Dohri clans. This classification into Gots or clans is not only interesting as a historical and ethnological study but is also of considerable importance from the baser points of view of the revenue assessing officer and vital statistician. A curious feature of the race is that the lower classes appear to be dying out. Their estates are undermanned, so far as the proprietors go, and badly farmed: all sorts of reasons based on poverty of soil, climate, and general impoverishment, are adduced by the people themselves to explain this, but, in my opinion, none of these are sufficient to entirely account for the results noticed. The first two affect all tribes alike, and yet amongst the higher classes there is a general tendency to increase; while the Rajputs have embraced Islam, they are just as numerous as any other race. The last result probably lends the required clue. The marriage law amongst the Hindu Rajput ordinarily requires that a higher clan should not give its daughters in marriage to a lower, though they may take from the lower class. The lower, therefore, they descend the tribal ladder, the more difficult it is for a man to obtain a suitable wife, and the climax is reached in the case of the Thakkars who are here at the bottom of the scale and amongst whom the deterioration of race and generally dwindling tendency are most marked. The daughters leave the clan, and the men must either remain unmarried or take their brides from subtribes which, though not regarded as consanguineous, have so frequently intermarried Islam in which the strict rules of the marriage law are much relaxed; and though outside marriages are preferred, there is nothing to prevent general marriages even within the clan.

The conversion to Islam is said to have occurred at a very early period during the Mughal rule, or even before that and though the converts are scattered pretty widely over the whole tract, and in many cases owners of the same stock in the same village belong to different creeds, it may generally be stated that the Hindus predominate in the hills and upper submontane, and the Muhammedans in the lower submontane and commencement of the plains. As a whole, they are very indifferent cultivators, but the pressure of population on the soil has in cases, forced them to habit of industry. In personal character they are proud of their descent and of the fact that they were original owners of the country, and so are loths to, sell, though only too ready to encumber their holdings. Simple and reasonably truthful, they are indolent and extravagant, and worst of all extremely querulous, and are probably the least satisfied with British rule of any class though the Dogra regiments and the native cavalry obtain a fair number of recruits from amongst the more promising young men. The increase in the physical standard required for recruits and the deterioration of physique noticed above are tending to cut off this avenue of employment, so that the prospects of this race are not brilliant.

The account of the Hindu Rajputs as given in the extract above requires amendment in certain points. A number of the clans enumerated in the list are not found in the district and no information about them is forthcoming. Of these shown as Jaikarias the Jarrals and Sins are now said to be Salamias only and not Jaikarias, while the Jarrals, Sins, Chibhs, Bagals, Tangrals, Thakkars, Thakials, Salehrias, Gahotras, Malhotras and Jhaggis are Chandarbansi and not Surajbansi Rajputs. Of the Chandarbansi only the Pathanias and Chibhs are Jaikarias. The terms "Kahri" and "Dohri" are apparently merely local designations of which the definition in the last Gazetteer might be made a little clearer. The "Kahris" are those who do not take wives from any of the clans to which they give them, the practice of Dohris, on the contrary, is to take wives from the same clan as that to which they give them. They are not of course restricted to this one clan, however, either in giving or taking wives. Thus, for instancc, the Jasrotias, who are Dohris, give wives to the Pathanias and also take wives from them: they also give to the Bhadwals and Hamtals, but do not take from them: similarly they take from the Sahlarias, Jhaggis, etc., but do not give to them. The Kahris, on the other hand, only take from a lower and give to a higher clan. The Salehrias have for many generations abandoned the practice of taking wives from the Gahotras who are regarded as in some sort 'bhaibands' of the Salehrias since they both give to and take from the same clans. Karewa limited to re-marriage inside the clan to which the deceased husband belongs, is practised by the Lamin, Rakwal, Chohan, Bagal, Saroch, Thakkar, Salehria, Gahptra, Malhotra, Jhaggi, Katal and Lalotra clans, no Jaikarias admit Karewa.

SIALKOT DISTRICT

The principal Rajput clans of the Sailkot district are the Bajju, Manhas, Salehria, Bhatti and Khokhar.

The Bajju clan inhabit the eastern portion of the Bajwat which is named after them. Their origin has already been noticed in connection with their relations with the Bajwa Jats. The Bajjus are all Dogras, generally of short stature and weak physique.

Owing to the dampness of the climate they suffer much from fever. Goitre is also prevalent in the Bajwat and impotence is said to be common. Like all Dogras they take a less sombre view of life than does the Jat. They revere an ancestor named Baj, a Sidh or saint, whose Samadhi exists at Chak Khoja.

According to them Baz was a holy Faquir who worshipped on the bank of the Chenab at Chak Khoja. God in the shape of Lakmanji appeared to him out of the river. So did Jal Pir, the presiding spirit of the waters. Then he became a Sidh, that is, a famous saint. When he died he was buried, not burned, and his Samadhi or tomb is at Chak Khoja. When Baz was recognized by the gods and became a Sidh, the Baj us all put on necklaces of Tulsi as a sign that they had become his followers. Bajjus are Hindus; Bajwas are Hindu, Sikh or Mussalman.

The Bajjus take girls in marriage from the Thakur castes inhabiting Jammu territory. They give daughters to Manhas, Chib and Bahu Rajputs. But towards the end of 1915 the Bajjus resolved to give up the system of hypergamy and now they say that they will give their daughters only to clans who are ready to reciprocate.

The Bajwat contains a few villages belonging to Jamwals and the western half of the tract is occupied by the Manhas clan. The Jamwals and Manhas are said to have a common solar origin. They came originally from Ajudhia. In the wars of the Mahabharata they fought on the side of the Kauravas against the Pandavas and after the battle at Kurukshetra fled to Kashmir and then to Mankot, where their ancestor Jammu Lochar defeated Chandar Hans, the ruler of the territory, now known as Jammu. The victor founded the city of that name. The Jamwals may not touch the plough, and when one of them took to agriculture he was cast off and founded the Manhas clan. The Manhas of the Bajwat claim to have fallen later than other branches of the clan and pride themselves on the fact. The Manhas gives daughters in marriage to the Chib, Bahu, Jaswal, Pathania and Guleria clans. They say that they receive daughters from those clans of Dohra Natta and also take daughters from the Charak, Salehria, Saroch, Sin, Bajju and Lange clans. Jamwals like the Bajjus are all Hindus. Some Manhas have been converted to Islam. The Hindu supply a considerable number of recruits to Dogra regiments.

The Salehria Rajput clan is found mainly in the north-east of the Zafarwal tehsil Pakistan and is mainly Muhammedan. They are of lunar origin. Two different accounts of their history are given in the *Glossary of Tribes and Castes* and they need not be repeated here. Suffice it to say, that they claim among their ancestors Raja Sal, who was, according to one story, the founder of Sialkot. The Hindu members of the clan have combined with Charaks and other Gots to refuse daughters to tribes which will not give daughters to them. Salehrias have enlisted well during the great war under the guidance of Subedar Hashim Khan, late of the 58th Rifles, a fine old native officer who was once orderly to Lord Roberts in Afghanistan.

Bhatti Rajputs are all Mussalmans. They are found in many parts of the Panjab, and are met with in different tehsils of this district. Tradition connects them with Bikaner, Jaisalmer and the old fortress of Bhatner and they claim descent from Raja Salivahan, the founder of Sialkot. The Bhattis are the most industrious of all the Rajput tribes.

Khokhars also are found here and there in different parts of the district and are not a distinctively Sialkot tribe as they inhabit various tracts along the Chenab and the Jhelum valleys of Pakistan. Their origin is very obscure and their history occupies eleven pages of the *Glossary of Tribes and Castes.* They deserve mention here mainly because the influential Mirowal family of Raya tehsil belongs to this clan.

RAWALPINDI

The Budhals and Bhakrals are two large tribes chiefly found in Gujar Khan and Kahuta. They do not, in appearance, in moral qualities or otherwise differ from the mass of agriculturists who cultivate the Pothwar plain. The claim of the Budhals to descent from the Prophet's son-in-law is utterly unfounded. They and the Bhakrals most probably came across the Jhelum from Jammu territory into this district. They have no very certain traditions as to their origin. The marriage of widows is looked upon with some disfavour among them.

None of the Rajputs have an assured position independent of Government recognition, whether as Zaildar, Inamdars or as officers in the Native Army. Chaudhri Warish Khan, Zaildar of Rawalpindi, was recently distinguished by the conferment of the title of Khan Sahib, Nawazish Ali, Takhtpari, Raja Sher Jang Khan, Traya, Allah Dad Khan, Jatal, Fazal Khan, Kotha Kalan in Rawalpindi tehsil, Jahan Khan, Devi, Faujdar Khan Ukahon, in Gujar Khan tehsil, have recently been appointed Zaildars in recognition of their prominent position among the Rajputs, but in none of the Rajput sub-tribes is there any commanding position of chieftain.

THE AWANS

The history of the Awan tribe is given in the *Gazetteers* of Shahpur and Jhelum districts, and in Griffin's *Panjab Chiefs.* Although Awans are in this district both numerically and administratively important, there is no Awankari or purely Awan tract such as exists in the adjoining districts of Jhelum and Attock.

They are to be found in every tehsil, scattered in all parts, but congregated in Rawalpindi tehsil round Golra, in Gujar Khan along the Grand Trunk Road, north of Gujar Khan, and in Kahuta tehsil on the east of the Kallar Kahuta Circle. They are a very self-contained tribe, and will not as a rule, give their daughters to any but Awans. They are not Sahu and are socially much less respected than in any of the adjoining districts. They are fairly good cultivators, especially in Gujar Khan, where they also take very readily to military service. Everywhere they are quarrelsome and much addicted to violent crime. Notorious are the Golra Awans who own all the villages around Golra, a few miles west of Rawalpindi. In the old days they levied blackmail on the road south of the Margalla pass, and were one of the most marauding tribes in the district. They are the least industrious of all Awans. At present a punitive police post is quartered upon them, a burden which their fellow tribesmen at Banda in the south of the tehsil have also to bear.

JHELUM DISTRICT
THE JANJUAS

The Janjuas are a small tribe, and they at present hold only 60 villages with an area of about 150 square miles, out of a total of nearly 4,000; but they are important as forming with the Gakkhars the aristocracy of the landed classes of the district, of the greater part of which they were at one time the rulers. Moreover, their influence still extends far beyond the limits of the country that they own, the leading yeomen of the central and eastern Salt Range, the east of the Pind Dadan Khan plain, and the south-west of tehsil Jhelum, being almost all Janjuas. They are nowhere so numerous as in this district, though there are fairly large settlements in Kashmir and in the Kahuta tehsil of Rawalpind; and they are found in small numbers in many other districts.

There seems no reason to doubt that the Janjuas are Rajput of the Lunar race, as they claim to be, a claim which no one locally thinks of questioning. General Cunningham thought that they had been settled in the district for nearly three thousand years, and derived them from Anu, the son of Yadu, a theory of which there is little real proof; and it led him to class the Awans ("Anuwans") as Rajputs and connections of the Janjuas of equally long standing in the district, a view which is almost certainly erroneous; it has found but few to support it. It is difficult for anyone who has seen much of both tribes to credit this, and in local tradition there is absolutely nothing to support the theory.

Ibbetson[37] inclines to the view that they are Rathors; and says of them and other tribes of the western that "if they are really descendants of the original Jadubansi Rajputs who fled to the Salt Range after the death of Krishna, they are probably among the Aryan inhabitants of the Panjab proper, those who have retained their original territory for the longest period, unless we except the Rajputs of the Kangra hills".

We have, however, no certain information as to their migration to the Salt Range; but there seems reason to believe that Jaipal, who opposed Mahmud at Nandana 900 years ago, was a Janjua[38], and we know from Babar's Memoirs, of which full exacts have already been given, that at the beginning of the 16th century the Janjuas held much of the country between the Jhelum and the Indus, except in the east, where the Gakkhars held possession; at least the Janjuas held all this district except the east. Malik Hast Janjua, is called "the

Hakim of the IIS and Uluses in the neighbourhood of the Sohan", and the tribes called Jud and Janja are said to have been "from old time rulers and lords" of the Salt Range hills, and of the tract between Nilab and Bhera. The Jud and Janjua are said by Babar to have been of common origin, and it seems clear that the former were merely a branch of the latter. Cunningham connects them with the Awans but the Awans are known to have conquered the western Salt Ranges at a much later date. At a later date Jahangir mentions a large predatory band of "Januwans" as far north as the Chach plain near Attock.

Mr. Thomson's account of the tribe, which follows, is contradicted on many material points by the present day Janjuas:

"At some uncertain period, then, some clans of Rathor Rajputs, emigrating from Jodhpur, occupied the uplands of the Salt Range. The leader of this movement, according to the common account, was Raja Mal, but this chieftain is a little mythical, and any large action of doubtful origin is apt to be fathered upon him. The Rajputs first seated themselves at Malot in the west Salt Range. This place, although picturesque, is so inaccessible and unfruitful, that it must have been chosen for safety more than convenience. From here the Rajputs extended their supremacy over the uplands of Jhangar and Kahun and the plain country near Girjakh and Darapur. In these regions they were rather settlers than conquerors. They not only ruled, but to a great extent occupied also. It seems very doubtful whether their real territories ever extended much further, but their traditions certainly point to a former lordship over the western upland of Vunhar, and over much of the present tehsils of Tallagang and Chakwal. If Babur's account be read with attention, it will be seen that he represents the Janjuas as confined to the hills, and ruling over various subject tribes who cultivated the plains. This account serves to explain the utter extirpation that has befallen the Janjuas in the Vunhar and elsewhere. If we conceive them as holding detached forts in the midst of a foreign population which gradually grew hostile, then this extirpation can easily we understood. This also serves to explain how one or two villages of peasant Janjuas have escaped, while all the Chiefs and Rajas roundabout have perished. The vague accounts of the people seem to point to some such history as this and not to any great racial or tribal war,"

The Janjuas were long the predominant race in the centre and west of the district. Raja Mal is said to have reigned in the days of Mahmud of Ghazni, and his authority was probably more or less recognized from Rawalpindi to the Jhelum. When Mahmud invaded India the janjuas opposed him, but were defeated, and fled to the jungles. Mahmud followed them up and succeeded in capturing Raja Mal himself. The Raja was released on condition that he and his tribe should embrace Islam. When this conversion took place, the Janju or caste-thread was broken, and the neophytes have been called Janjuas ever since[39].

The Janjuas are physically a well-looking race. Their hands and feet in particular are often much smaller and more finely shaped than those of their neighbours. They largely engage in military service where they prefer the cavalry to the infantry. They are poor farmers and bad men of business. They are careless of details and apt to be passionate when opposed. Too often they fix their hopes on impossible objects. As landlords they are not exacting with submissive tenants. They are willing to sacrifice something to retain even the poor parodies of feudal respect which time has not destroyed. Their manners are often good. They have large share of vanity, which is generally rather amusing than offensive. They are at the same time self-respecting and not without a certain kind of pride, and are eminently a people with whom slight interludes of emotional governance are likely to be useful. The even routine of our administration chafes them more than others.

The concluding remark is now scarcely correct: probably they have by now found time to adapt themselves better to the altered condition of things, and it is likely too that greater numbers of them now find scope for their energies in military service, for which they are so well fitted.

The Janjua genealogical tree has been referred to in Chapter I; it is a comprehensive document, including such celebrities as Adam, Noah, Arjan, Raja Prithviraj, Dalip (founder of Delhi) and so on: one name is that of Rai Pur, said by educated Janjuas to be Porus: it would not be profitable to enter into further details.

Leading Janjuas are: Tehsil Jhelum, Malik Talib Muhammad Khan of Darapur, Extra Assistant Commissioner, and his uncle Payanda Khan, Sakhi Muhammad of Chakri, Deputy Inspector of Police and Muhammad Ashraf of Nara, tehsil Pind Dadan Khan, Firoz Ali of Makhinl, Abdulla Khan of Dalwal, Suba Khan of Malot, Fatteh Ali of Kusak, Kasim Ali of Pindi Saidpur, Lal Khan of Sherpur, Mehr Khan of Dhariala Kahun, and Resaldar — Major

Jalal Khan of Saloi. There are few Janjuas in the other tahsils: in Chakwal, Rajmal is said to have left five sons; three of these settled in Rawalpindi or Hazara districts; two Veer and Jodha remained in Jhelum. They speedily divided their possessions. Veer took the west, and Jodh the eastern share. Ghoya Saidan Shah was the boundary between them. Veer's descendants are now represented by the Janjuas of Malot and the Kahun Ilaka. Their chief seat is at Dilwal. Jodha's descendants have split into many branches. A general supremacy was long exercised by the Sultans of Makhiala in Jhangar[40]. But the chiefs of Kusak and Baghanwala soon became practically independent, as did also those of Dilur, Karangli, and Girjkh, whose descendants are now either extinct or much decayed. The plain Ilaka of Darapur and Chakri seems to have broken off from the main stock even earlier than the others. This passion for separatism is fatal to any large authority. The feuds to which it gave rise, joined with an endless Ghakar war, and the establishment of new strenuous races beyond the mountains, brought the Janjua dominion to destruction. The Dhani country, called Maluki Dhan after the great Raja, and the forts in Tallagang and the Vunhar seem to have been all lost not long after the time of Babar; but in the centre and east Salt Range and round Darapur the Janjua supremacy remained undisputed until the advent of the Sikhs, and the rich Salt Mines at Khewra and Makrach must have always made this territory important. The Sikhs conquered the whole country piecemeal. Ranjit Singh himself besieged and captured Makhial and Kusak. Most of the influential chiefs received Jagirs, but were ousted from their old properties[41].

The lambardars of 'Dhrabi' are of fair standing, while in Tallagang the representatives of the once powerful Rajas of Kot Sarang are fast falling into insignificance.

THE PANWARS

A small number of Panwars, Chibhs, and Sohlans are found in the Jhelum tehsil: the former live at Sahsrial and Jandot in the Pabbi, their principal men being Najabat Ali and his nephew Muhammad Khan; the Chibhs and Sohlans hold a few of the river villages above Jhelum, but include no one of special note. All three claim to be Rajputs, and are so regarded by their neighbours. The claim is probably correct.

THE RHATTIS

There are a fair number of Bhattis scattered about the district who are probably of Rajput extraction, but they are here unpretentious hard-working cultivators, and little esteemed socially. The Gandals along the river are a more doubtful case, they do not always say they are Rajputs, and seem more like the ordinary Jats, they are fond of cattle lifting. There are a few Sials in the south-west corner of the district, who are generally admitted to be Punwar Rajputs. A few others, such as the Khiwas, have some pretensions to Rajput origin, and locally rank rather above the Jats, their origin is doubtful.

JHANG
(THE BHATTIS)

The Bhattis own a block of villages between the Shab Jiwana villages in Jhang and the Lali villages in Chiniot tehsil, all on the west bank of the river, only three Bhatti villages are in Jhang tehsil. The numbers of the tribe are swollen by the inclusion of menials with whom the appellation is a favourite one. The tribe seems to be the most widely distributed of the tribes in the Panjab. The Jhang Bhattis are said to be related to those of Pindi Bhattian in Guranwala, and the line of invasion was probably from the north down and not from the south up the river. Their first settlement in Jhang was at Jandmali on the right bank of the Jhelum, not far from the Shahpur boundary. With the exception of Maru Bhattian all the Bhatti villages are in the uplands and are all coming under canal irrigation. A marked feature of their villages is the absence of sales and mortgages and they seem to have been sensible enough in the past to keep their expenses within their means. The Zaildars are Bhai Kahn of Kot Sultan and Dulla of Barana. Hasta of Ghoriwala, Bhai Khan of Jhill and Bhai Khan of Thatta Umara are also prominent men. The name Bhai Khan is much affected by the present generation of Bhattis. The original settlement of the Bhattis, other than those of Barana, was at Bhurani Kanianwali where nearly all still hold shares.

THE KHOKHARS

The Khokhars are numerous in the district, but they suffer more even than the Bhattis from the frequency with which their names are adopted by menials. The origin of the tribe is by tradition ascribed to Kutb Shah, a descendant of Ali, the son-in-law of the Prophet, and they are supposed to have come to India from Ghazni with the invader Mahmud and to be distantly connected with the Awans. This origin is not by any means authenticated, and Mr. Steedman believed the Khokhars to be a branch of the Rajputs, the tribe, in which the Dhudhis are included.

MONTGOMERY DISTRICT

The Sials are divided into two principal branches, Fattianas and Tahranas. They claim to be Punwar Rajputs of Dharangar. Rai Siyal or Siu, from whom the name of the clan comes (Siyal Sruwal) was the son of Rai Shankar who settled in Jampur. Quarrels arose at Jampur, and Siyal left for the Panjab in Ala-ud-din Ghori's reign. In about 1258 AD he was converted to Muhammadanism by Baba Farid of Pakpattan. He settled at Sahiwal' and married the daughter of the chief of that place. The Siyals increased, and ultimately ousted the Nauls from the lowland of the Chenab, and founded Jhang Siyal. They afterwards became very powerful, and as we have seen, overran and held Kamalia and the neighbouring country, under Walidad Khan.

The Kharrals were Rajputs. Their ancestor was Raja Karan of Hastinapur. His descendant Bhupa left that place and came to Uch, where he and his son Kharral were converted by Makhdum Jahania Shah. From Uch the Kharrals spread over the country about the Ravi. They appear to have settled first in the Sandal Bar (Lyallpur district), no doubt with a view to having plenty of pasture for their cattle. Ranjit Singh is said to have induced or compelled them to move to villages nearer to the rivers, possibly with a view to exercising more effective control over them. Their principal Muhins or clans in the Montgomery district are:

Rabera with headquarters at Fatehpur.

Gogairah with headquarters at Gugera.

Ransinh with headquarters at Pindi Cheri and Pir Ali.

MIRZA SAHIBAN

The Kharrals are traditionally quarrelsome who quarrel among themselves, but they are supposed to have a bond of union in enmity to the Sials. There is an old story how a Kharral called Mirza fell in love with his cousin Sahiban, the daughter of the chief man of Khewa in the Jhang district. Her parents betrothed her to a youth of the Chadhar tribe, but before the marriage took place Mirza ran away with her. He was pursed and slain. Her relations strangled Sahiban. These murders were the cause of such bloody feuds between the clans that it at length was thought inauspicious to have daughters and as soon as they were born they were strangled as Sahiban had been. Colonel Hamilton as Commissioner, Multan, is said to have found female infanticide to be common among the Kharrals and to have been successful in persuading them to discontinue it. It does not appear whether Sahiban's father was a Sial or a Kharral.

The Wattus, who occupy both banks of the Sutlej for about 60 miles, and the tract about Gugera, claim descent from Raja Salvahan of Sialkot. They have probably a close racial connection with Hindu Bhattis, Mussalman Bhattis, Joiyas and with Sidhu and Barar Sikh Jats[42]. One of Salvahan's sons settled in Bhatner. Adham, the 12th in descent, came to the Sutlej near Ferozepore. There he found the Rajada Kharrals, the Dogars, and the Joiyas. They picked a quarrel with him, but he beat them. On account of venting his displeasure on them he was called Wattu, 'Wat' meaning displeasure. The next great man was Khewa, who was converted by Baba Farid. He expelled the Kharrals, Joiyas and Dogars. After him there was no famous chief till Lakha appeared. His achievements have been recorded. It does not appear when the Wattus of the Ravi settled there; but they came from the Sutlej, and were hospitably received by the Kharrals. There is very little to choose between the two tribes on the Ravi. There the Wattus rose in 1857, and are still addicted to cattle thieving. The Sutlej Wattus, however, behaved generally well during the rebellion. The tract owned by them possesses little jungle, that part of the clan therefore has taken of late years to agricultural pursuits. Some of their estates are well cultivated; their herds have diminished, and many of them now cannot be distinguished in appearance from peaceful Arains or Khokhars. The change in their habits is remarkable, they still speak of the Kardars they used to kill during the Sikh rule, and of the years in which they paid no revenues because the Sikhs were unable or afraid to collect it. The Wattus pride themselves on their politeness and hospitality. They are of only moderate industry, profuse in expenditure on special occasions, indifferent to education and exceedingly fond of cattle.

THE SIAL

About this time the Sials settled on the Ravi. They took part in the outbreak in 1857 under Bahawal, Fattiana, and Jhalla and Murad, Tahranas. Jhalla was killed in action, and the others transported. They are large in stature, of a rough disposition, fond of cattle, and care little for agriculture. They observe Hindu ceremonies like the Kharrals and Kathias, and do not keep their women in Pardah. They object to clothes of a brown (Uda) colour, and the use of brass vessels. On the whole, the Sials have made better colonists than most of the old Ravi tribes. Many of them in colony estates seem to have got over their traditional indifference to agriculture.

THE KATHIAS

The Kathias have been identified with the Kathaioi of Alexander's time. The subject is discussed at length at pages 33 to 37, Volume II of the *Archaeological Survey Reports*. It is probable that the name, as used by the Greeks, had a wider application than to one clan only. Whether the Kathias at that time enjoyed a supremacy over the great Ravi tribes, and their name on this account was applied by the Greeks to the race collectively or whether the mistake arose from the fact that Sangala, the capital town of the Kathaeans, was brought most prominently into notice by its stubborn resistance of the Macedonian army, it is impossible to decide with any confidence. The coincidences, however, which point to the identity of the race of two thousand years ago with that of the present day are too strong to be accidental. According to their own account the Kathias are descendants of Raja Karan, Surajbansi. Originally, they resided in Bikaner, whence they emigrated and founded the State of Kathiawar. From there they went to Sirsa and then to Bahawalpur. Next they crossed over to Kabul and went on to Dera Dinpanah. Here they quarrelled with the Biloches and had to leave. They then settled at Mirah Siyal in Jhang. They stole the cattle of Alawal Khan of Kamalia, who was killed pursuing them. Saadat Yar Khan obtained the release of their leaders (who were imprisoned on account of this affair), on condition of their settling on the Ravi. Thus the Kathias obtained a footing in this district. They were always held by the Kamalia Kharrals, but plundered the others whenever they could get a chance. The character given to the Kharrals applies equally to them. "They are a handsome and sturdy race. Their chief and favourite article of food is buttermilk; the consumption of wheat among them is very inconsiderable." They, of course, took part in the rebellion of 1857. Their leaders were Jalla and Muhammad Khan. The Kathias claim to be and not improbably are Punwar Rajputs. There are two main divisions, the Kathias proper and the Baghelas.

HOSHIARPUR

Next in point of numbers come the Rajputs who returned 2993,538 souls in 1941. They are mostly Hindus in the hills and Muhammedans in the plains. They are divided into many grades, the grouping of which is most complex, as it does not always follow that member of the same Got have necessarily the same status.

To make what follows at all clear it is necessary to describe in general terms the essentially Rajput system of tika, chhat and Makan villages.

The word Chhat is explained as an abbreviation of Chhatar and equivalent to Jaj or "crown". It may possibly be translated as canopy. The canopy used to be one of the insignia of sovereign power.

THE TIKA

Tika is the title of the heir-apparent to a reigning prince. Hence it is applied to villages which are the seats of a prince's rule. It would appear that a Chhat Makan was originally a Tika being a village which is the seat of a house still actually ruling or exercising authority in some way. The Chhat or Makan comes into prominence at weddings. At the wedding of a Tika, Bhaji is first distributed among the Baradari. Then a Brahm Bhoj is performed and all the Baradari feasted. In this feast all the headmen of the villages, in which the Tika has Taluqdari rights, take part, and each of them then presents a rupee as Nazr to the Tika. During the Milni, five animals, including a horse, a shawl and some money, are given to the Tika's father by the bride's father who also makes presents of cash and clothes to the near relation of the Tika, his more distant relatives getting a rupee only. The Tika's part a Saggi (Ornament) and Ghundu (a checked scarf, Harira) are given to the bride.

The Rajput residents in a Chhat or Makan have to maintain their social prestige by lavish expenditure at weddings, etc. If a leading member of the village dies, a great deal is spent in feasting for ten days all who come to condole with his family.

Mirasis, Bhats and barbers from other Chhat, Makan or Tika villages also receive heavy fees at weddings, etc., according to the status of their Chhats, *e.g.*, the Mirasi of a Chhat will get a rupee, that of a Makan eight annas, while those of ordinary villages only receive one or two annas.

THE CLASSIFICATION

The following is a tentative classification of the Rajput septs:

1st Grade — Jaswal, Dadwal, Chambial, Fathania, Guleria, Sibaya, Katoch, Kothehria, Mandial, Suketar, Kahluria, Hinduria, Sirmauria, Malkotia, and Jamwal.

2nd Grade — Luddu, Dod, Ghorewaha, Chandla, Jarial, Sonkhla, Manhas, Barihar, Bihal, Bhatti, Baria and Naru.

This is, however, by no means a final or universally accepted classification[43]. According to an account there are four grades among the Rajputs, the fourth being the Rathis who are hardly to be regarded as true Rajputs as they practice Karewa and do not marry out of their own grade thus forming a distinct sub-caste.

The other grades are:

1. The Jaikaria which comprises:
   (a) Katoch, Goleria, Jaswal, Dadwal and Sibaya.
   (b) Manhas, Sonkhla, Pathania, Jarial, Jasrotia, Malkotia and Chandla.
2. The Salamias comprising the Bariah Sat with its Als, the Mandial, Surial, Narial, Satotalie, and Ranawat and the Luddu, Dod, Patial, Bhamnauria, Ghorewaha, Jasial, Badlial and Bihal.
3. All the remaining septs.

The following statements have been recorded, which on the face of them are not altogether consistent either with each other or with what has gone before:

The Bhattis take wives from the Bhanot, Dod, Chanwal, Lalota, Gagnola, Guwal and Badalla, and are therefore superior to them; they give daughters to Dadwal, Jamwal and Janjua. They are on equal terms with Manhas, Bihal, Bariya, Luddu and Ghorewaha.

The Jarial of Budhabar give daughters to the Manhas, Kalvet, Dadwal and Jaswal, but not to the Ghorewaha.

The Badlial Janjuas of Badla say that they give daughters to the Manhas and Dadwal, and are equal to the Bhatti and Ghorewaha.

Narus are said to take wives from Ghorewaha and give to Manhas and Bhatti.

Besides Tika Ragnath Singh, its representative of the Rajas of Jaswan, there are some Jaswals owning a few villages in the northern half of tehsil Una.

The Dadwals of Zail Janauri take wives form the Narial, Pathial, Bhamnauria, Ghorewaha, Baria, Harichand, Luddu, Bihal and others (not from the Bhatti, Jarial, Janjal or Janjua) and give to the Jamwal, Kotlehria, Samial, Pathiana. They intermarry on equal terms with the Jaswal, Dod, Luddu and Jarial.

The Dadwals are found in the neighbourhood of Dalalpur, the seat of their former sovereignty and on the south-west face of the Sivaliks near Dholbaha and Janauri in Hoshiarpur tehsil where their representative is Mul Chand, Zaildar of Janauri, or Jankpuri, its ancient name, which is still used. Janak was an ancient Surajbansi ruler. There is a lithographed history of this tribe in existence. The Dadwals are a branch of the Katoch and do not intermarry with them or with the Golerias or Sibayas on the ground of a common descent. Spreading from Datarpur[44] they overran the tracts dependent on Dholbaha, Janauri and Pathial, taking the former village from the Athwal Jats by the repeated stratagem of concealing men in women's litters and getting an entrance into the place. Under Har Bhagat, surnamed Khaba, the 'left-handed', who aided a revolted Subash of Lahore and acquired the Malot and Chanaur-Ghawasan Ilakas from him, they rose to almost independent power, and Sardar Gainda, a courtier or ally of Sansar Chand Katoch, held Chanaur Ghawasan, Malot with 36 dependent villages, Dangoh with 35, and Janauri with 32. His capital was at Chauki in Patiari village and Bhatlu and Taintpal formed his own demesne. The Sardar levied revenue in kind by Kankach, a system by which the Kanoi or divider left 35 per cent as Chhot to the cultivator for expenses and divided the remaining 75 per cent into five parts, of which only two went to the Sardar. The Sikhs deprived the Dadwal of their independence and auctioned the revenue to Ijaradars, whose exactions compelled the Dadwals to leave the collection of Batai in their hands and at Settlement they only held 12 or 13 of the 32 villages, which had been founded or conquered by them, dependent on Janauri.

The Dadwals have several Als or families, whose names are derived from their settlements, such as Janaurach, Dholbahia, Datarpuria, Fatehpuria, Bhamnowalia, Khangwarah, Naruria, Rampuria, etc. Datarpur is their chief village, but they have no system of Chhats and Makans. More than one member of the family has been killed in action in service.

Of the second grade the Luddu are found in Talukas Una, Jaijon, Bhabaur, Nurpur, and Takhtgarh. The heads of their families are styled Rai, the chief being the Rai of Bhabaur.

Most of the Bet tract in Nurpur Pargana appears to have been held in former times by petty Luddu Raos under the Kangra Rajas, and their descendants still retain the customs of primogeniture and Guzara or maintenance to younger sons.

The Luddus are Surajbansi by descent. About 2,400 years ago, they say, Bhum Chand, a Surajbansi Raja in Kangra, and devotee of Durga or Shakti, had a son Sursaram Chand, the Sursaram of the *Mahabharat.* Having married Duryodhan's daughter, Sursaram Chand sided with the Kauravas on the Kurukshetra battlefield and returned daily to Kangra during the fight. One day Bhima smote Sursaram Chand's elephant with his mace and fractured its skull but Sursaram held the sides of the wound together with his feet and so rode it back to Kangra. After the war Sursaram fell to fighting with Raja Virata, an ally of the Pandavas, then ruling in Kashmir.

In the battle Sursaram was surrounded and begged for his life which Virata granted on condition that he performed a Luddi or jump. Hence the name Laddu or Luddu. The real rise of the clan, however, appears to date from Khamb Chand, 21st in descent from Bhum Chand, who attacked Nangal Kalan and its dependencies. He eventually made it his residence and married his son to the daughter of the Basdhawal Raja of Bhabaur, but seeing its prosperity he killed the Raja and made it his capital. His son Binne Chand had eight sons. Tradition says that their mother was blind, but contrived to conceal her infirmity from her husband for 22 years. But one day he discovered it, and pleased with her cleverness in concealing it, told her to ask a favour. She begged that although the custom was for the eldest son to succeed, all her sons should succeed. So they were all appointed Tikas (chief) and their villages became known as Tikas, they themselves taking the title of Rai.

LUDHIANA DISTRICT

The Rajputs are undoubtedly the oldest of the agricultural tribes that now hold the district. Mr. Walkar writes: "It might perhaps be taken as good evidence of the demoralizing effect of the Muhammadan religion that the Hindu Rajput is very little inferior to the Jat as a cultivator. In the Bet of Samra the most prosperous village belongs to them, the proprietors being free of debt and largely engaged in trade. The Muhammedan Rajput of this district possesses at least all the bad qualities generally ascribed to his tribe. He has a good physique, but this is about all that can be said in his favour. As a cultivator he is useless, being indolent and apathetic to a degree. He will never do an honest day's work if he can help it, and spends every penny he can borrow. His village is generally a picture of slovenly cultivation and he will tell one that this is because it is not his proper business to follow the plough, and because his women are secluded. If possible he will rent his land to someone else, and never fails to try to spend more than his neighbour on a marriage celebration, regardless of the fact that it is certain to ruin him. His women are said to be quite incapable of managing their household affairs, and the Hindu shopkeeper in a Rajput village makes a fortune in a very short time, at first, it is said by cheating the women, and then by getting the men into his books. If a Rajput does take to serve, it is only in a half-hearted way; and he will on the slightest excuse throw it up and return to his village. In fact the Muhammedan Rajput of this district has, as far as I know, no redeeming points in his character, and is a perfectly useless member of society. I may mention that at the Regular Settlement the Muhammedan Rajput villages were treated very leniently, and in many cases pay half or one-third less than their neighbours; but this moderative appears to have had no other effect than to encourage further extravagance. The great feature in a Rajput's character is, I think, a complete want of anything that could be so designated. He is the most vain and foolish of mortals, and can seldom give a reason for anything that he does. He is, as a matter of course, discontented; but it would require a peculiar state of society to suit him. These remarks apply to the tribe as a whole; but there is a daily increasing number of members of it in whose favour an exception should be made." The Rajputs in this district are mainly Muhammedans. At the Census of 1901 they numbered 29,473 of whom 1,331 were Hindus, and 344 Sikhs. The Hindu Rajputs inhabit two or three villages in the Samrala tehsil. The most important subdivision of the tribe are Manj, Bhatti, Ghosewaha, Punwar, Naru, Tawar, and Warya. Of these the Manj are the most numerous (5,990). They are all Muhammedans and are found chiefly in the Jagraon tehsil. They profess to be Bhatti Rajputs. The Manj Rajputs own good many villages in Jagraon, Bet and uplands. They came from the south-west, their ancestor Chachu leaving Faridkot and settling at Hatur. From Hatur the descendants of Chachu founded several large villages—Andhi, Halwarah, etc. in this district, and also crossed the Sutlej. The family of the Rais of Raikot is looked upon as the head of the Got on this side of the river. These Rais at one time held a great part of the district under their sway, and a detailed account of the family will be given elsewhere.

The Chhat system prevails among the Manj Rajputs[45]. The two ancients Chhats of Hatur and Talwandi Rai in this district date from the time of Babar, while two more, Raikot and Hatwara, have since been added as Manj Rajputs have settled in them. The Rais of Talwandi and Raikot pay a Chhat of Rs. 20. There are two Makans in the district—Raisar and Andlu. The custom appears to be losing vogue.

THE GHOREWALHAS

The Ghorewahas are another numerous section (4,562), live rather to the east of the District in the Samrala tehsil, owning a large number of villages along the Sutlej both in this district and in Jullundur. They founded the town of Rahon in the Jullundur district. They are Surajbansis and trace their descent from Hawaha, brother of Kachwaha, who came into the country in the time of Shahab-ud-din Ghori (1150 A.D.) and was allowed a grant of as much lands as he could ride round in a day. Others say he presented a Nazar of a horse and got the tract which his descendants now hold.

THE BHATTIS

The Bhattis rank highest in the tribe. They usually marry among themselves, but sometimes give their daughters to other Rajputs of good family. Their ancestor, Sheikh Chachu, was granted the state of Hatur, on his conversion to Islam.

PATIALA DISTRICT
RAJPUTS

The Rajputs in Patiala number 65,296. Though they have beaten their swords into ploughshares, they do not take comfortably to agriculture and are far inferior as cultivators to the Jats. The Taonis and Chauhans are the largest sub-divisions of them in this State, but the Bhattis rank highest.

BHATTI RAJPUTS

The Rajputs are Jadubansi and are said to have been converted to Islam by Saiyyid Jalal-ud-din, Makhdum-i-Jahanian, Jahangasht, in the time of Firoz Shah Tughlaq. They are now found in scattered groups, but still own some villages in tehsil Bhatinda.

TAONIS RAJPUTS

The Taonis claim Jadubansi descent, thus:

Raja Salvahan of Pattan in Gujrat.

Raja Tan (Grandson).

Uggar Sain (7th[46] in descent from Tan).

Migrated from Agroha in 699 Bikrami and settled in this part of the Panjab becoming king of Buras.

RAJPUT BARAH

The Barah or Varah Rajputs claim descent from Binepal of Bhatinda and emigrated at a very distant period from Udaipur. They have a proverb — "Beha Mas Na Chakhde Singh, Baz, Variah," (The lion, the hawk and the Varahs never taste stale meat') Rai Kalu of Kakra near Bhawanigarh embraced Islam in Jahangir's reign, so that their conversion is somewhat recent, and the Barahs of Bakhtri in tehsil Sunam are still Hindus. They own nearly 30 villages in tehsils Sunam, Bhawanigarh and Amargarh. Their organization is the usual Rajput one of Chhats or villages of the first rank and Makans or villages of the second rank, other villages being inferior to these in social status. The Barahs have 12 Chhats and 24 Makans, the Chhats in this state being Samana, Talwandi, Kakra, Bhumsi, Jhal, Jhondan in Nabha Baena, Bedbar, Baragraon in Jind, Bazidpur, and in British territory Budlada and Moranda. Master Muhammad Khuda Bakhsh Khan of Haryau Khurd, was the tutor of Maharaja Mohindar Singh. He also held the post of Canal Agent and that of Director of Public Instruction, Patiala State. His eldest son Muhammad Abdul Ghafur Khan was a Judge in the High Court of Patiala; his younger sons Muhammad Abdul Majid Khan was Foreign Minister, Muhammad Abdul Hamid Khan was Nazim of Anabadgarh, Muhammad Abdul Hakim Khan was State Vakil at Ambala, and Muhammad Abdul Aziz Khan was Colonel of Infantry.

MANDAHAR RAJPUTS

The Mandahars are found in tehsil Narwana, and are said to have migrated into the Bangar from Ajudhia, 2000 years ago, and to have taken the ancient town of Kalait from the Chandels. That place and Bata are now held by Hindus, Badsikri and Hittho being held by Muhammedan Mandahars. They call themselves Lachman. Socially they have 12 Tapas (as they call their Chhats) and 360 Gaons or villages, the Tapas in this state being Dhanauri, Kalait and Badsikri. The Hindus in marriage avoid only their own Got. At a funeral they give Pagris to their Mirasis.

JATUS RAJPUTS

The Jatus give their genealogy as follows:

Raja Jairath of Pattan, Tunwar.

|

Jatu

|

Assar — Harpal

Rana Amar, who migrated from his country and drove the Gujars and Khodana some 500 years ago. The Jatus of Kanaud (Mohindargarh) tehsil, in which they hold 25 villages, are his descendants. Jatu was so-called because he was born with long hair (Jatan) on his body. The Jatus do not intermarry with the Tunwars and in marriage only avoid their own Got. At a wedding, both at the Phera or circumambulation, and at the Wadai or leave-taking, the bridegrooms' barber spreads a sheet, called Chhat, over the bridegroom's head and his father puts into it as much money as he can afford. The Jatus also give Tyag and Lekh to their Mirasis. Like the other Rajputs of tehsil Kanaud, they are sun-worshippers and fast on Sundays.

KACHWAHA RAJPUTS

The Hindu Kachwahas or Kushwahas of Pargana Kanaud, in which they held seven villages, are called Shaikhawat because their ancestor was born through the benediction of Shaikh Burhan, Darvesh. On the birth of a male child they put a blue thread round its neck, and on the bathing day (the third to six days after birth) a second thread is put round its neck, a Tagra round its waist, and Kurta on its body, all three of blue colour. They worship the sun by offering water and fasting on Sundays. At a wedding they give Tyag and Lekh to a Mirasi. The Shaikhawat Kachwahas do not eat Jhatka[47].

KARNAL DISTRICT

In briefly describing the principal tribes of the district, we begin with the Rajputs. It is hardly necessary to say much about their well-known tribal characteristics. They are fine, brave men, and retain the feudal instinct more strongly developed than any other non-menial caste, the heads, of the people wielding extraordinary authority. They are very tenacious of the integrity of their communal property in the village land, and seldom admit strangers to share in it. The Nardak contributes many soldiers to the army. They are lazy and proud, and look upon manual labour as derogatory, much preferring the care of cattle, whether their own or other people's. In the canal and Khadar parts they have abandoned pastoral for agricultural pursuits; but even here they will seldom, if ever, do the actual work of ploughing with their own hands; while the fact that their women are kept strictly secluded, deprives them of an invaluable aid to agriculture. In the Nardak a great part of the actual work of cultivation is done by other castes[48].

THE MANDHARS

The Mandhars were settled in very early days in the country about Samana; for Firoz Shah chastised them, carried off their Ranas to Delhi, and made many of them Mussalmans. The Safidon branch obtained the villages now held by them in the Nardak in comparatively late times by inter marriage with the Chauhans. And though they expelled the Chandel Rajputs from Kohand and Gharaunda when they first came into these parts, the Chandels re-conquered them; and the final occupation by Mandhars coming direct from Kalayat in Patiala is probably of comparatively recent date. Tahy, with the other four clans already mentioned as connected with them by blood, are descendant from Lao, a son of Ramchandar and grandson of Raja Desarat, and said to be the founder of Lahore. Their phratry is called Lachman, after a childless son of Raja Dasarat; Ramchandar having another son Kuskumar who ruled Kashmir and founded the Kachwaha and Narban gentes. They are of Surajbansi clan. Their place of origin is Ajodhia; and Kalayat in Patiala, their headquarters are in these parts.

THE CHAUHANS

The Chauhans all sprang from the original people who settled at Jundla. They all claim descent from Rana Har Rai; but as it is improbable that he conquered the country single-handed, and as his followers probably included Rajputs whose descendants are still in possession, this cannot be true. At the same time it is probable that the eldest line, in which authority descended from Rana Har Rai, has been preserved in its integrity. According to this, 19 generations, equivalent to 475 years, have intervened since the

Chauhan conquest, which would fix it at about the time of Bahlol Lodhi, when the Chauhans of Moradabad took a new departure. They are of the Agnikula clan. Their origin is from Sambhar in Ajmer; but Rana Har Rai came from Sambhal in Moradabad, where the family bards still live. Many of them are now Mussalmans, and the change of religion dates from some generations back. They are the highest of the Rajputs clans about here, and some of the Muhammedan members will even marry with their own clans in the neighbourhood.

GURGAON DISTRICT

The figures for the principal Rajput tribes are given at the end of this chapter.

The chief Rajput settlements are those of Badgujar Rajputs round Sohna and of Chauhans round Bahora, to the north-west of the Gurgaon tehsil, and in the isolated villages to the south of Rewari. The Badgujars state that their ancestors migrated hither from Jalandhar under the following circumstances:

It appears that an ancestor of theirs was playing at dice with the goddess Devi, when he noticed that her hand was wet; he asked her the cause, and she replied that she had just rescued a ship which was sinking in the sea; this seemed to him so improbable that he somewhat rudely impugned her veracity, and was in return visited with a curse, which caused him and his progeny to wander forth, until the new seat of their race was pointed out to them by the given sign of the cart axle breaking down, and then after a series of conflicts they drove out the Khanzadas who then held the country and established themselves at Sohna and in the country round. The date given for this migration is about the middle of the 15th century. The history of the Chauhan race is given in Sir H. M. Elliott's supplemental *Glossary*. The local names which he mentions, Bighoto Rath, Dhun-dhoti and Chandain, are known by the people, but not often referred to. The great majority of the Gurgaon Rajputs are Hindus except in the north and east of Rewari. Some of these Rewari Ranghars (Muhammedan Rajputs) have but an indifferent name for honesty, but generally the Rajputs of both religions are of good repute.

Table 9.4: *Jat: Western Plains*

	1	2		3			4	5	
		Bhutta		Langah				Sumra	
	Tahim	Jat	Rajput	Jat	Rajput	Pathan	Chhina	Jat	Rajput
Ludhiana	8	36	7	...	...	...	...	847	...
Jalandhar	...	...	9	...	...	...	...	1,633	...
Hoshiarpur	...	...	691	...	...	...	...	659	...
Amritsar	...	20	241	17	91	...	2,492	388	6
Gurdaspur	...	...	...	...	936	...	...	1,240	...
Sialkot	69	555	98	169	1	...	...	52	...
Lahore	98	73	150	...	196	...	...	205	16
Gujranwala	345	311	...	234	...	...	2,310	625	7
Firozpur	38	42	57	6	25	...	...	882	1
Rawalpindi	4	5	...	479	464	...	...	1	...
Jhelum	321	1,354	11	31	284	...	...	...	...
Gujarat	5	233	...	294	2	...	...	30	...
Shahpur	93	2,570	162	401	20	...	...	...	...
Multan	2,821	4,845	169	2,190	96	2,205	25	2,214	98
Jhang	640	1,612	3,231	341	41	82	...	...	1
Montgomery	394	192	20	177	174	56	...	...	5
Muzaffargarh	1,605	4,366	3	1,144	1	207	550	1,509	5
Derah Ismail Khan	765	1,014	...	778	4	...	4,411	051	2
Derah Ghazi Khan	2,220	3,162	...	2,305	...	...	408	887	...
Bannu	72	2	...	410	...	...	...	...	...
British Territory	9,598	20,431	4,891	9,083	2,348	2,550	10,196	12,558	218
Patiala	...	663	194	...	...	...	...	...	1,564
Total East Plains	...	757	194	59	1	...	...	...	2,101
Bahawalpur	13,862	1,351	...	...	...	...	...	...	...
British Territory	9,598	20,431	4,891	9,088	2,348	2,550	10,196	12,558	218
Native States	13,862	2,108	194	59	1	...	...	...	2,101
Province	23,460	22,539	5,085	9,142	2,349	2,550	10,196	12,558	2,319

6		7	8	9	10	11	12	13	14
Chhadhar									
Jat	Rajput	Sipra	Bhatti	Sial	Punwar	Joya	Dhudhi	Khichi	Wattu
...	...	...	1,004	5	10	...	8	...	...
489	...	345	367	31	87	...	348	...	...
...	...	198	43	333	...	...	...	...	...
1,646	...	38	205	221	653	...	...	...	...
232	...	...	5	137	2,387	...	...	...	...
720	...	568	3,677	719	117	205	99	13	...
2,600	4	14	10,287	1,243	311	390	710	518	739
5,537	333	1,119	7,722	433	538	995	561	432	312
347	...	131	590	285	716	782	264	36	704
5	...	5	2,056	814	49	27	...	...	...
1,805	131	156	6,241	256	524	...	733	74	7
291	...	1,388	9,926	1,091	145	54	1,524	...	...
1,672	1,877	1,794	396	71	71	516	428	57	43
1,287	638	451	9,682	560	2,563	473	1,875	54	...
3,272	13,390	5,185	2,874	437	284	1,533	1,578	483	107
3,076	6	747	3,528	1,202	726	2,165	1,349	373	454
1,537	...	11	6,988	2,453	1,561	1,333	505	44	110
1,359	...	73	132,767	4,648	1,317	1,788	605	877	167
388	...	171	12,971	2,536	1,919	1,421	66	355	13
110	1	70	1,057	189	405	479	136	...	283
26,387	16,435	12,563	94,665	17,093	16,959	12,888	12,315	3,337	2,963
...	...	...	587	...	864	...	502	...	...
17	...	6	619	273	887	...	599	...	241
...	1,311	...	569	...	...	...	479	254	3
26,387	16,435	12,563	94,665	17,093	16,959	12,338	12,315	3,337	2,963
17	1,311	6	1,193	273	887	...	1,087	254	244
26,404	17,746	12,569	95,858	17,866	17,846	12,338	13,402	3,591	3,207

Table 9.5: *Jat Tribes of the Western Sub-Montane*

	1	2	3	4	5	6	7	8 Tribes	
	Dhanial	Janjua	Manhas	Bhakral	Mekan	Gondal	Ranjha	Jat	Rajput
Ambala	...	...	2	...	...	8	...	...	...
Ludhiana	...	12	15	...	...	...	...	...	...
Jalandhar	...	...	144	...	...	24	...	...	...
Hoshiarpur	...	60	90	...	...	203	...	...	...
Amritsar	...	11	524	...	...	65	...	1	...
Gurdaspur	...	610	67	...	...	443	230	76	...
Sialkot	...	1,110	1,156	21	67	1,791	...	960	...
Lahore	...	543	669	...	101	859	53	191	...
Gujranwala	...	1,648	1,724	...	12	3,953	1,166	2,373	2,822
Firozpur	...	44	158	...	52	161	14	...	...
Rawalpindi	6,340	92	143	1,576	...	611	8	250	...
Jhelum	3,680	232	1,711	1,253	1,125	6,354	1,601	712	5
Gujarat	6	732	48	1,965	918	24,825	6,924	13,588	...
Shahpur	...	39	...	48	160	305	258	58	1,173
Multan	...	253	74	...	19	196	143	2	...
Jhang	...	366	...	...	220	649	162	210	70
Montgomery	...	57	...	...	...	122	1	203	158
Muzaffargarh	...	966	...	...	119	155	168	...	...
British Territory	10,026	8,419	6,570	4,863	3,157	47,276	10,903	18,925	4,228
Patiala	...	...	15	13	...	...	10	...	...
Nabha	...	...	...	...	...	2	...	...	...
Kapurthala	...	...	...	...	...	...	...	17	...
Jind	...	...	...	...	...	...	...	...	...
Maler Kotla	...	...	...	...	...	...	...	...	...
Total East Plains	...	...	15	13	...	86	49	19	...
British Territory	10,026	8,419	6,570	4,363	3,157	47,276	10,935	18,925	4,383
Native States	...	15	15	13	...	325	53	18	...
Province	10,026	8,434	6,585	4,876	3,157	47,601	10,956	18,944	4,228

9	10	11	12	13	14	15	16	17	18
Varaich	Sahi	Hinjra	Chima	Bajwa	Deo	Ghumman	Kahlon	Sarai	Goraka
566	...	...	289	428	...	570	...	1,772	7
1,344	630	...	3,008	207	765	1,237	...	...	...
292	322	2,050	1,354	568	...	94	63	...	215
470	...	...	...	...	...	1,302	...	400	...
2,205	154	2,227	1,110	1,177	615	1,022	1,155	1,943	...
1,476	...	366	1,350	1,851	984	93	7,376	5,063	4,823
5,780	5,784	2,515	35,722	25,393	4,873	14,228	13,765	4,660	6,385
1,292	155	1,495	89	1,772	647	41	219	193	421
10,783	613	12,045	19,830	947	502	2,073	313	51	4,407
252	409	267	751	238	361	109	153	2,412	141
362	3	122	502	47	...	...	10	144	91
504	578	20	219	52	...	37	...	...	42
35,253	4,044	1,179	3,429	167	2	1,413	...	345	417
443	140	829	125	...	...	...	...	...	156
102	59	64	...	10	...	2	11	9	2
50	110	482	2	...	...	78	...	225	5
202	160	600	40	39	...	...	...	50	64
33	22	220	...	2	...	14	...	48	183
61,718	13,395	25,200	67,855	32,843	9,284	22,448	23,058	17,541	17,462
614	...	...	1,003	1,523	...	7,819	41	...	...
160	4	2	30	...	...	460	8	3	124
503	...	...	...	132	...	...	424	...	190
...	1	...	52	...	...	590	...	...	1
1,151	...	8	609	...	...	...	...	...	...
2,505	6	58	1,604	1,678	...	8,931	404	5	315
61,718	18,396	25,200	67,855	32,843	9,284	22,488	23,058	17,541	17,462
2,517	...	65	1,694	1,678	...	8,989	494	5	315
64,235	13,402	25,265	69,549	34,521	9,284	31,427	23,550	17,546	17,777

REFERENCES

1. *Laws of Manu,* Vol. I, p. 89.
2. *The Early History of India* (1914), V.A. Smith, p. 408.
3. "Rajputs and Marhattas", W. Crooke, *ERE*, Vol. VI., p. 453.
4. *ERE,* Vol. I., p. 51 F.
5. "Rajputs and Hindu Caste System" (1910) W. Crooke, *JRAI,* Vol. XI, p. 42.
6. *Ancient History of India*, V.A. Smith, p. 412. *Rajputs and Hindu* Caste *System*, W. Crooke, p. 41.
7. Just as livy as Virgil offoliated the New Roman Empire with the heroes of the Trojan War.
8. *Manu Laws,* Vol. VII. pp. 38-42.
9. *Origin Sanskrit Texts,* Muir, Vol. I. (1858), p. 58.
10. *ERE,* Vol. VI., p. 693.
11. *Ibid.*
12. *History of Ancient India*, V.A. Smith, p. 272.
13. *Rajputana Gazetteer* II. A. (1908). H.D. Erskine, p. 106.
14. *Annals and Antiquity of Rajasthan,* Tod. Vol. I., p. 182.
15. *Ibid.*, p. 553.
16. *Encyclopaedia of Religion and Ethics*, Vol. 5., p. 5b.
17. *Encyclopaedia of Religion and Ethics*, Vol. 7., p. 555b.
18. *Ibid.*, Vol. I. IA. XXXV (1906), p. 61.
19. *JRAS.* (1907), J. Kennedy, p. 951.
20. A town in central Rajasthan, India, 25 miles NE of Udaipur near Banas river.
21. *Annals and the Antiquity of Rajasthan*, Tod. Vol. I., 409 ff.
22. *Annals and the Antiquity of Rajasthan*, Tod. Vol. I., p. 62 & p. 573.
23. *Annals and the Antiquity of Rajasthan*, Tod. Vol. I., p. 225N.
24. A village, in west central Rajasthan.
25. *Ibid.* Vol. I., p. 573,
26. *Ibid,* Vol. II., p. 87.
27. *Annals and Antiquity of Rajasthan,* Tod. Vol. II., p. 413.
28. *Annals and Antiquity of Rajasthan,* Tod. Vol. I., pp. 479, 527, 179.
29. In Rajasthan, rises in Aravalli, Vol. I., p. 281.
30. *Rajputana Gazetteer,* C.C, Waston, Vol. I., pp. 462, 236, 580.
31. Range, south of Kumbhalgarh Fortress.
32. *Encyclopaedia of Religion and Ethics*, Vol. II., p. 413.
33. *Encyclopaedia of Religion and Ethics*. Vol. II., p. 60 and p. 412.

34. *Encyclopaedia of Religion and Ethics*. Vol. X., pp. 570-71.
35. *Encyclopaedia of Britannica.* Vol. 2., p. 397.
36. Rana Wasdev Singh Parhar of Kalra, Distt. Jalandhar.
37. Para 452, *Census Report,* 1881.
38. He appears on their pedigree table.
39. The Janjuas themselves now reject his story, which is not in itself very plausible. They say the name of the tribe is derived from that of one of their forefathers. Janjuha in most of the genealogies comes eight or nine generation before Raja Mal. It is like improbable that the general conversion of the Janjuas took place 900 years ago, it is like enough that Mahmud made them converts, and that these reverted as soon as his back was turned but the Janua village pedigree tables nearly all agree in introducing Muhammedan names only about 15 generation back which would point to their general conversion about the middle of the 15th century.
40. The formalities at the accession of a new "Sultan" of Makhiala are cyruiys; seven, eleven or thirteen days after the death of his predecessor, the prinicipal people of the around collect and are feasted. In the afternoon they proceeded to a certain rock behind and house, and the family Brahman puts the Tika mark on his forehead: those present congratulate him, and present small offerings as Peshkash, being given pagras in return: then appoints Wazir and four Diwans, who swear fidelity, and are supposed to assist him when required; at evening another feast is given, eastern and then all disperse: representatives of practically all the villages of the eastern Salt Range attend to these occasions. The Malik Hast, mentioned frequently by Babar, was an ancestor of the Makhiala Vatli Sultans.
41. For an account of company of the Janjua power, see Mr. Brandreth's *Settlements Report,* paragraphs 51-53.
42. Vide pages 76 and 91 of the *Hissar Gazetteer.*
43. The social groupings of the Rajput septs are of some practical importance in connection with the subject of female infanticide, and the following list of Rajput dynasties, which purports to be the classification attested in 1877 by Major G. Gordon Young as Deputy Commissioner, has come to hand. It is given here for what it is worth:

    List of Rajput dynasties in the Hoshiarpur district classified and confirmed by Rai Rattan Chand, Rais of Bhabaur, Mian Hardas Singh of Chauki and Mian Lehna Singh, Rana of Manaswal.

    (Attested in presence of Major G. Gordon Young, Deputy Commissioner.)

    1st Class: Rajputs, Katoch, Goleria, Jaswal, Sibaya, Dadwal, Pathania, Kahluria, Hinduria, Sirmauria, Mankotia, Mandial, Bhadwal Kotlehria.

2nd Class: Manhas, Luddu, Dod, Ghorewaha, Chandla, Bhabauria, Jarial, Sonkhla, Bhanot.

3rd Class: Taunfa, Chauhan, Dehra, Raghubansi, Jasril, Ranot Kothlehria, Patial, Bhadiartakhi, Harchand, Baria, Badlial, Narial, Datial, Surial, Dhurial, Sandhwal Chamnaurfa, Bihal, Kopahtia, Dasohta, Samkaria, Pahria, Khanaur, Gori.

4th Class: Dhontial, Patrial, Ladol, Rajan, Bangwain, Lauria, Kharohia, Katial, Dogra, Dangohar, Chaungran, Malpota, Sindhe, Mahatta, Bedial, Garal, Bachhohar, Kharial, Bhadmania, Salohar, Kharohar, Charnota.

5th Class: Barangwal, Sahotra, Chahotra, Lahuhia, Badhan, Tareru, Chareru, Dharru, Oghatha, Sahotha, Gari Panjota, Chammrreta, Rakhwal, Khudyali, Gorni, Nadaunta, Kali, Pathwal, Damol, Mandahar, Garota, Pandial Anawat, Changra, Aneri, Sedi, Wadhal, Barial, Maloys, Chaftauria, Laharu, Dauru, Atri, Naloch, Gangait, Tatwan, Dharwal, Jabra, Harwal.

44. Raja Makhwal Chand, a descendant of Phuman Chand, settled in Dada and thus founded the Dadwal sept. His descendant Datar Chand, wrested the tract round Daterpur and 12 dependent village from a Chahag Rani, founding Datarpur. The next Raja Karn Chand made Kamairo Jos capital and the third, Ghagi Chandi chose Dholbaha.

45. *Panjab Census Report,* 1901, p. 323.

46. Dhirpal, or Nawab Abu'l Karim, embraced Islam under Shahab-ud-din of Ghor after his victory over Prithviraj at Tarain (Tarawari) in Karnal district in 1193. His tomb is said to be at Banur, which is a great Taoni centre, for Taonis are numerous in that tehsil and in Patiala, Rajpura and Ghanaur. The Hindu Taonis hold Bular (in tehsil Patiala), Lalru, Nagla and Khelan in tehsil Banur, and Dhakansu, Tepla, Banwari, Pabra and Dhamoli in Rajpura. They have 12 seats, said to be named after the sons of Raja Gopal, *viz,* Dhirpali, Ambpali, Bhatian, Motian, Rai Ghazi, Jaisi, Sarohd, Ajemal, Jhagal and lagai, the last six being Rais.

47. Animal or a bird killed with one stroke.

48. It is said that the Balian and Sakilan Jats of the Doab joined the Dehias; and that the Tagas of the Doab joined the Haulanias.

BIBLIOGRAPHY

Basham, A.L. The Wonder that was India, 1954.

Cunningham, Sir A. The Ancient Geography of India.

Encyclopaedia of Britannica. 1 to 26 Vols.

Enthovan, Reginald E. "Rajputs", in the *Tribes and Castes of Bombay,* Vol. 3.

Hiralal and Russel, R.V. Rajputs in the Tribes and Castes of the Central Provinces of India.

James, H. Encyclopaedia of Ethics and Religions. I to XII Vols.

James, Tod. The Annals & Antiquities of Rajasthan. 3 Vols.

Minturn, Leigh 6c Hitchcoolk, John T. *The Rajputs of Khalapur,* 1966.

Majumdar, R. C. *The Vedic Age.* Bombay, 1951.

Majumdar, R.C. *The Age of Imperial Unity.* Bombay, 1951.

McRindle, J. W. Ancient India as Described in Classical Literature, 1901.

The Baloches

(Descendants of Scythians)

10

BALUCHISTAN

The country of Baluchistan, in the widest sense of the word, comprises all the territory occupied by the Baloch and Bruhi races and some minor tribes subordinate to or mixed up with them, and must be understood as including not only the Baluchistan in Pakistan that is the Khanat of Kalat[1], Makran[2], and Las Bela[3], but also the southern part of the province of Pakistani Baluchistan, parts of the districts of Dera Ghazi Khan[4] in the Punjab, Jacobabad[5] in Sind, and the province of Persian Baluchistan.

Meaning of Baloch

The word Baloch is variously used in the Punjab to denote the following people:

(1) The Baloch proper, a nation which traces its origin from the direction of Makran, and now holds the lower Sulemans.

(2) A criminal which had tribe settled in the great jungles below Thaneswar, Haryana.

(3) Any Mussalman camelman except in the extreme east and west of the Punjab.

(4) A small Pathan tribe of Derah Ismail Khan, more properly called Baluch.

It is almost certainly of true Baloch stock. It also is in all probability a small body of truc Baloches who have become affiliated to the Pathans. Our figures for the most part refer to the true Baloch of the lower frontier and to their representatives who are scattered throughout the Punjab. But in the upper grazing grounds of the Western Plains the Baloch settlers have taken to the grazing and breeding of camels rather than to husbandry; and thus the word Baloch has become associated with the care of camels, insomuch that throughout the Peshawar, Rawalpindi, Lahore,

Amritsar, and Jalandhar divisions the word Baloch was used for any Mussalman camelman whatever be his caste, every Baloch being supposed to be a camelman and every Mohammedan camelman to be a Baloch. In Sirsa there are Punwar Rajputs from Multan who are known as Baloch because they keep camels, and several Deputy Commissioners recommended that Untwal, Sarban and Baloch should be taken together as one caste. The headmen of these people are called Malik, chiefly in the Lahore division, as Baloch. It is impossible to say how many of them returned as Baloch because they keep camels are of true Baloch origin. Settlements of Baloches proper are, excluding Multan and Deraj at divisions, and Shahpur, reported in Delhi, Gurgaon, Karnal, Hissar, Rohtak, Ludhiana, Amritsar, Gujranwala, Firozpur and Rawalpindi. But in all these districts except the first five the word is used for camelmen also, and the figures cannot be separated.

GEOGRAPHY AND TOPOGRAPHY OF BALUCHISTAN

Baluchistan, by contrast, is very thinly inhabited indeed. A large tract of high and arid country to the north and west of Karachi[6], about equal in area to Italy, its population is only about 1,384,000, that is to say, less than two-thirds of Karachi's, the density per square mile being only about ten. Except for the narrow Makran[7] coastal strip, and the small and in summer atrociously hot Sibi[8] plain—which in logic ought to be reckoned part not of Baluchistan at all but of Sind—it consists of poorly watered, stony plateau at an average elevation of about 5,000 feet, traversed by complex mountain systems which, here and there, rise to peaks of 11,000 feet or so. It is, in fact, the easternmost finale of the high tablelands of Persia. Impressive barriers separate most of it from the great Indus Valley below: towards the north, curving like a scimitar round its shoulder, is the Sulaiman range; farther down, against its flank, rests the arrow-straight precipitous limestone Kirthar range. Between them, however, the Sibi-Bolan gap lies open, up which road and railway wind deviously to Quetta[9], its only sizable town; a place famous for its Army Staff College, and for earthquakes (In 1935, about 30,000 people died in one).

The distance from the head of the gap at Bolan[10], on over high country to Chaman close to the Afghan frontier, is only seventy miles. Thus the plateau narrows markedly at this one point; and the constriction, in effect, almost cuts Baluchistan into two: in the south, a large rectangle; in the north-east, a smaller triangle or wedge. These segments differ considerably from one another, both in scenery, and in inhabitants. Though both consist of lofty flattish country, crumpled by a confusion of large, bare, often strongly coloured hills—olive-green, slate-black, russet-red, ochreous—the confusion becomes increasingly wilder and more devoid of semblance of meaning in the south, until, as you near the rectangle's base, what you see verges on the impossible, and might be a creation of dream. "Gigantic cap-crowned pillars and pedestals", writes Holdich, "are balanced in fantastic array about the mountain slopes, with successive strata so well defined that they possess all the appearance of massive masonry construction, standing stiff, jagged, naked and uncompromising", and beyond them, "that brazen coast washed by a molten sea."

The highest ground of the rectangle is however near Kalat[11], farther north, the pivot perhaps of such coherent mountain structure as exists. And between the great crests and spurs, from there to the coast, you may find hidden in deep defiles occasional pleasant fertile strips, green with date-groves, and cereal crops, laid out in little terraced fields. Of the main riverbeds—which often go dry—only one, the Mula[12], drains into the Indus. This thrusts through the Kirthar range by a spectacular gorge: in ancient times it was an important route for trade, and for marching armies. The others run either direct into the Arabian Sea, or wander vaguely off north-west to sink into the futile sun-scorched pools and marshes, perpetually evaporating, of the Mushkel depression against the Persian frontier. In that far-off tract may also be seen the strange, extinct volcanoes of the Chagai hills, and the wind-rippled sands of the Kharan[13] desert.

Almost throughout, despite southern Baluchistan's nearness to the sea, its climate remains 'continental', alternative fiercely between cold and extreme heat. And winds can be very strong, for—unlike the Indo-Gangetic plain—Baluchistan as a whole is shielded by no Himalayan rampart from air-drift circulating from the immense open steppes or snows of Asiatic Russia, and Tibet, and inner China. In its wedge-shaped north-eastern segment particularly, the cold in winter—despite bright sunshine—has a piercing, bone-searching quality difficult to believe by those unacquainted with it; and temperatures before dawn may fall far below zero.

Although there are some higher mountains in that segment than in the southern one—among them the conspicuous Takht-i-Sulaiman, and Zarghun, which reaches nearly 12,000 feet high, its geophysical layout is less improbably extravagant. A typical landscape of the Zhobits best-known tract because traversed by a strategic road, and (as far as Fort Sandeman) also by railway—would be a wide stony level, dotted with small sparse bushes and dried grass, and slightly uptilted from the horizontal towards the nearest mountain wall; a wall which, above its short talus screen stands up immense and brown and almost bald, its abrupt lower surface perhaps weirdly sculptured by wind-erosion, but with upper slopes and clefts enriched by scattered clumps of dark green juniper, wild olive, and the chilgoza or 'edible' pine. Beyond and behind, you would glimpse remoter ranges, huge hogsbacks, most of them snow-topped in winter and spring—the whole conveying an impression of vast vacant windy space.

AFGHAN FRONTIER

But as you motor on north from Fort Sandeman via Sambaza probably under escort, for the Afghan frontier lies near, and there might be ambushes—that impression dissolves. Soon after you cross the stream of the Gomal[14], which flows in from the left, the landscape begins to contract. It becomes an intense confined affair of crag and scree and precipice; Baluchistan's broadly horizontal theme has been abandoned for a vertical one. Of course, from the higher points, grand distant views can be got; but they lack curved surfaces, nearly everything seems jagged. You are in Waziristan here, the most notorious tract of tribal territory; in the heartland of the Pathan or Pakhtoon people, the speakers of Pashto or Pakhtu; and it has none of that withdrawn, not quite credible, dreamlike quality of southern Baluchistan. It is hard, practical, cruel as a knife.

This same vertical type of terrain stretches north ahead. In detail, it can be very varied; and sometimes, in an unexpected way and despite the harshness when all of a sudden it discloses a breathtaking beauty, cupped between arid tawny steeps, delicious little green hollows, blessed with tinkling streams, tiny well-tended fields, good orchards, perhaps a few shade giving cedars; or reveals, far-off, glimpses of snowy Sikaram in the Safed Koh, nearly 16,000 feet high. But even at moments of enchantment such as these, it retains that first, special feeling of sharp-edged immediacy. All the way ahead, about 250 miles it stretches, to the Pathan tribal principalities of Dir[15] and Swat[16], first mentioned in the start of this description of Pakistan's West wing; stretches through tracts of gory historical renown such as the Tochi, Kurram, Tirah, Khyber, Bajaur, and Malakand; spills over on the left, beyond the international frontier or Durand Line, into Afghanistan; drops down on the right to include the wide, richly fertile, populous vales of Bannu, Kohat, and Peshawar, each gripped within its half-circle of fine bold hills; and actually, though you may not have noticed it, lies for miles behind you as well, because the north-east triangle of Baluchistan, almost as far back as Quetta, if inhabited at all, is inhabited mainly by Pathans; that being the second factor, ethnic instead of scenic—which distinguishes it from the larger southern rectangle, whose people are altogether non-Pathan in speech and race.

THE BALOCHES AND THE PATHANS

The Baloch presents in many respects a very strong contrast with his neighbour the Pathan. The political organization of each is tribal; but while the one yields a very large measure of obedience to a chief who is a sort of limited monarch, the other recognizes no authority save that of a council of the tribe. Both have most of the virtues and many of the vices peculiar to a wild and semi-civilised life. To both hospitality is a sacred duty and the safety of the guest inviolable. Both look upon the exaction of "blood for blood" as the first duty of man; both follow strictly a code of honour of their own, though one very different from that of modern world; both believe in one God whose name is Allah, and whose prophet is Muhammad. But the one attacks his enemy from front, the other from behind; the one is bound by his promises, the other by his interest. In short the Baloch is less turbulent, less treacherous, less bloodthirsty, and less fanatical than the Pathan, who has less of God in his creed and less of the devil in his nature[17].

THE TRAITS OF A BALOCH

His frame is shorter and more spare and wiry than that of his neighbour to the north; though generations of independence have given to him too a bold and manly bearing. Frank and open in his manners and without servility, fairly truthful when not corrupted, faithful to his word, temperate and enduring, and looking upon courage as the highest virtue, the true Baloch of the Deraj at frontier[18] is one of the pleasantest men to deal with in the Punjab. As a revenue payer he is not so satisfactory, his want of industry, and the pride which looks upon manual labour as degrading, making him but a poor husbandman. He is an expert rider; horse-racing is his national amusement, and the Baloch breed of horses is celebrated throughout the northern India. Till quite lately he killed his colts as soon as they were born and his preference for mares is expressed in the proverb— "A man with his saddle on a mare has his saddle on a horse; a man with his saddle on a horse has his saddle on his head." If he cannot afford a whole mare he will own as many legs of one as he can manage, and the Baloch mare having four legs will keep her a quarter of each year for remaining legs. He is a thief by tradition and descent, for he says, "God will not favour a Baloch who does not steal and rob" and "the Baloch who steals secures heaven to seven generations of his ancestors." But lately he has become much more honest.

His face is long and oval, his features finely cut, and his nose aquiline; he wears his hair long and usually in oily curls and lets his beard and whiskers grow, and he is very filthy in person, considering cleanliness as a mark of effeminacy. He usually carries a sword, knife and shield; he wears a smock frock reaching to his heels and pleated about the waist, loose drawers and a long cotton scarf; and all these must be white. His wife wears a sheet over her head, a long sort of nightgown reaching to her ankles, and wide drawers; her clothes may be red or white; and she plaits her hair in a long queue.

THEIR CUSTOMS

As the true Baloch is nomad in his habits he does not seclude his women; but he is extremely jealous of female honour. In cases of detected adultery the man is killed, and the woman hangs herself by order. Even when on the war-trail, the women and children of his enemy are safe from him. The Baloch of the hills lives in huts or temporary camps, and wanders with his herds from place to place. In the plains he has settled in small villages; but the houses are of the poorest possible description. When male child is born to him, ass's dung in water symbolical of pertinacity, is dropped into his mouth from the point of a sword before he is given the breast. A tally of lives due is kept between the various tribes of families; but when the account grows complicated it can be settled by betrothals, or even by payment of cattle. The rules of inheritance do not follow the Islamic law, but tend to keep property in the family by confining succession to agnates; though some of the leading and more educated men are said to be trying to introduce the share into their tribes.

The Baloches are lavish in their hospitality. Even among the poorest of them, all who turn up during a meal are welcomed to a share of whatever is going on, and the chiefs spend a great part of their income in entertaining guests. All Baloches who come to a chief's village on business or on the occasion of a great ceremonial are fed from the chief's kitchen.

The tribes on both sides of the Suleman hills being under British control, blood feuds and reprisals were much less common than they were, but an occasional outbreak shows that in ferocity the Baloches are no whit superior to the Pathans. In fighting the Baloch tactics may be summed up in the simple principle that an attack is never to be made unless the enemy can be surprised, or is in inferior numbers. Battle once given, however, the fight is carried on hand to hand with sword and shield, and not, as in the case of the Pathans, by a desultory matchlock fire at long ranges.

The Baloches are nominally Mussalmans, but singularly ignorant of their religion and neglectful of its rites and observances; and though they once called themselves and were called by old historians "friends of Ali", and though if account of their ejection from Arabia be true, they must have originally been Shiah, they now belong almost without exception to the Sunni sect. Like many other Muslim races of the frontier they claim to be Qureishi Arabs by origin, while some hold them to be of Turkoman stock, their customs are said to support the latter theory: their features certainly favour the former.

Their language is a branch of the old Persian, and apparently contains many archaic forms which throw light upon other modern developments from the same source. It is now hardly spoken, so far as the Punjab is concerned, beyond the tribal organisation of the Derah Ghazi Baloches; and even, among them it is being gradually superseded by Multani or Jatxi, the language of the plains, and a Baloch chief has been known to learn the English language. They have no written character, and no literature; but they are passionately fond of poetry, chiefly consisting of ballads, describing the events of national or tribal history, and of love-songs; and local poets are still common among them.

EARLY HISTORY OF THE BALOCH

The account of their origin is that they are descendant from Mir Hamzah, a Qureishi Arab and an uncle of the Prophet, and were settled at Halab or Aleppo[19] it is believed, till, siding with

Husen, they were expelled by Yazid, the second of the Umeyid Caliphs. This would be about 680 A.D. They fled to the hill country of Kirman[20] in Persia, where they lived quietly for some time, and so increased in numbers that the king became desirous of binding them to himself by ties of marriage. He accordingly demanded a wife from each of the forty-four Balaks or tribes into which they are said to have been divided; though all traces of them have long since been lost. But their fathers had never given their daughters in wedlock to a stranger, and they therefore sent forty-four boys dressed up in girls' clothes, and fled before the deception could be discovered. They moved south-eastwards into Kech Makran or the tract between Afghanistan and the coast of the Arabian Sea, then partially inhabited, but they finally settled in the country which is now known as Baluchistan.

JALAL KHAN

From Jalal Khan, the chief under whose leadership they made their last migration, sprang four sons, Rind, Hote, Lashari and Korai, and a daughter Jatoi. Five of their tribes still bear these names, but the Rind and Lashari appear to have been preeminent; and the Baloches, or at least that portion of the nation which later on moved northwards to the Indian border, were divided into two great sections under those names, and it is believed that all Baloch tribes still consider themselves as belonging to one or other of these sections. Thus the Mazari and Drishak who trace their descent from Hote[21] claim to belong to the Rind section. Some five hundred years after their settlement in Kech Makran, the Rind, Lashari, and Jatoi moved northwards into the country about Kelat, to the west of the lower Sulemans, "the Rind settling in Shoran, the Lashari in Gandava, and the Jatoi in Sevi and Dhadon, while the Khosa remained in Kech and the Hote in Makran". They are said to have dispossessed and driven into Sindh a Jat people, ruled over by a Hindu prince with the Sindhi title of Jam and the name of Nindaya, whose capital was at Kelat. After a time the charms of a woman led to jealousy between the nephews of Mir Chakar and Mir Gwahram Khan, the chiefs of the Rind and Lashari sections. Their claims were to be decided by a horserace held in Rind territory, in which the hosts loosened the girth of their rival's saddle. A fight resulted, and the Rind, who were at first worsted, called to their aid Sultan Husain, the king of Khorasan and drove the Lashari out into Haiderabad[22] and Tatta[23] in Sindh, where they no longer exist as an individual tribe. From this event the Baloches date the growth of their present tribal organization; and as there is now no localized tribe bearing the name of Rind, and as almost all the great tribes of the frontier claim to be of Rind extraction, it is probable that the Rind, left sole possessors of the hill country of Kelat (for the Jatoi also consider themselves as belonging to the Rind section of the nation), gradually split up into the tribes which now are found on the Derah Ghazi Khan border. Several of these tribes have taken their names from the localities which they now hold, which shows that their names are not older than the occupation of their present territories.

ADVANCE OF THE BALOCHES INTO THE PUNJAB

The Baloches had thus spread as far north as the Bolan; but apparently they had not yet encroached upon the Suleman range which lay to the east of them, and which was held by Pathans, while a Jat population occupied the valley of the Indus and the country between the Sulemans and the river. But about the middle of the 15th century, the Turks or Mughals under their Arghun leader invaded Kachhi and Sindh, and twice took Sibi[24], in 1479 and in 1511 A.D. About the same time the Brahoi, a tribe believed to be of Dravidian origin, and who appear to have followed in their tracks, drove the Baloch out of the fertile valley of Kelat and established supremacy over their northern tribes. Yielding to the pressure thus put upon them, the Kelat tribes moved eastwards into the lower Sulemans driving the Pathans before them along the range, while the Baloches from Sindh began to spread up the Indus. Many of these later took service with the Langah rulers of Multan and were granted lands along the river; and in about 1480 A.D. Ismail Khan and Fatah Khan, the two sons of Malik Sohrab Khan and Ghazi Khan, son of Haji Khan, all Dodai Baloches and of Rind extraction, founded the three Derahs which still bear their names, overcame the Lodis of Sitpur, and established themselves as independent rulers of the lower Deraj at and Muzaffargarh, the position they and their descendants maintained for nearly 300 years. Thus the southern Baloches gradually spread up to the valleys of the Indus, the Chenab, and the Sutlej; while the Derah Ghazi tribes came down from their hills into the Pachhad or sub-montane tract, displacing a Jat population and driving them down to the river, where they still form an important element of the population even in tracts owned by

Baloches. In 1555 a large body of Baloches accompanied Humayun, whom they had previously harassed in his retreat, and victorious re-entry into India, under the leadership of Mir Chakar, the great Rind hero of Baloch history. They are said to have consisted chiefly of Laghari, Drishak, Gopang, and Jatoi, Mir Chakar eventually settled in Montgomery, where a considerable tract, still partly held by Baloches, was granted to him by the grateful sovereign. He died and was buried at Satgarh in that district. It is probable that many of the Baloch settlements in the eastern districts of the province sprang from Humayun's attendants.

THE TRIBAL ORGANISATION

The tribal organization of the Baloches now covers the whole southern frontier as far north as the boundary between the two Derahs, being confined for the most part to the hills and the land immediately under them, but stretching east to the Indus in the neighbourhood of Rajanpur. There is also a large Baloch element throughout the river lands of the Indus in both the Derahs, more especially in the southern and northern portion of Derah Ghazi and just above the Derah Ismail border; while in Bahawalpur[25] and Muzaffargarh[26] they form a large proportion of the whole population, and they hold considerable areas on the Sutlej in Multan, to the north of the Ravi in Montgomery, on the right bank of the Chenab and along the Jhelam in Jhang, and on the latter river in Shahpur[27]. But outside the Derah Ghazi Khan district, and indeed along the greater part of the river border of that district, the Baloch settlers own no allegiance to any tribal chief, are altogether external to the political organization of the nation, and do not hold that dominant position among their neighbours which is enjoyed by the organized tribes of Derah Ghazi Khan. Many of them have been settled in their present holdings within comparatively recent times or, to use the words of Mr. Tucker have acquired them "as cultivating proprietors, rather than as a military caste which ruled the country but left the occupation of the land to the Jats".

BALOCHES, A CONGLOMERATION OF CLANS

Sohrab Khan, the chief of the Dumki, a Rind tribe, was the nominal head of the Baloches, or at any rate of those on Pakistan frontier; while all the northern tribes beyond our border acknowledge the supremacy of the Brahoi Khan of Kelat[28], a supremacy, the reality of which has always varied with the personal character of the Khan, and which it is probable that Pakistan's own frontier policy has lately saved them from total extinction. But for all practical purposes, the frontier tribes are independent both of foreigners and of one another, and are held together by a common nationality against outsiders only. The tribe, at least in its present form, is a political and not an ethnic unit, and consists of a conglomeration of clans, bound together by allegiance to a common chief. Probably every tribe contains a nucleus of two, three, or more clans descended from a single ancestor. But round these have collected a number of affiliated sections; for the cohesion between the various parts of a tribe or clan is not always of the strongest, and it is not very uncommon for a clan or a portion of a clan to quarrel with its brethren, and leaving its tribe to claim the protection of a neighbouring chief. They then become his Hamsayas or dwellers beneath the same shade, and he is bound to protect them and they to obey him. In this manner, a small section formerly belonging to the Laghari tribe, and still bearing its name, has attached itself to the Qasrani; while there is a Jiskani section in both the Drishak and the Gurchani tribes. Thus too, Rind tribes are sometimes found to include Laghari clans. So when Nasir Khan, the great Khan of Kelat who assisted Ahmad Shah in his invasion of Delhi, reduced the Hasanni tribe and drove them from their territory, they took refuge with the Khetran, of which tribe they now form a clan. Even strangers are often affiliated in this manner. Thus the Laghari tribe includes a section of Nahar Pathans[29], who are not Baloch but who are Khetran. And the Gurchani tribe includes section which, though bearing a Baloch name and talking the Balochi language, are not allowed to be of Baloch race and are almost certainly Jat.

TUMANDAR

The tribe (Tuman) under its chief[30] is sub-divided into a small number of clans (Para) with their Muqaddams[31], and each clan into numerous septs (Phalli). Below the Phalli come the families, of which it will sometimes contain as few or a dozen. The clans are passed upon common descent; and identity of clan name, even in two different tribes, almost certainly indicates a common ancestor. The sept is of course only an extended family. The tribal names are often patronymics ending in the Balochi termination 'ani', such as Gurchani, Balachani; or in some few cases in the Pashto, Zai. An individual is commonly known by the name of his clan, the sept being comparatively unimportant. Marriage within the sept is forbidden, and this appears to be the only restriction. The Baloches freely marry Jat women, though the first wife of a chief will always be a Balochni. They say that they never give their daughters to Jats; but this assertion, though probably true of the frontier, is most certainly not so beyond the tribal limits.

THE BOUNDARIES OR ADMINISTRATIVE UNITS

The tract occupied by each division of a Baloch tribe is sufficiently well defined; but within this area the people are either wholly nomad or, as is the case within the frontier live in small hamlets, each inhabited by only a few families, having property in their cultivated lands and irrigation works, but without any actual demarcation of the surrounding pasture lands. Thus the large and compact village community of the Eastern Punjab is unknown, and the village or Mauzah in these parts, is merely a collection of hamlets included within a common boundary for administrative purposes.

THE BALOCH TERRITORY & THEIR ORIGIN

A line drawn from Dera Ghazi Khan through the Suleiman range due west to Quetta demarcates approximately, the Pathan on the north from the Baloch on the south, but the latter have advanced considerably to the north of this limit in the Indus valley, and have also established large colonies in upper and middle Sindh. The Baloch statement of their origin is to the effect that they belong to Aleppo[32], and were expelled from Syria on sectarian grounds. They found their way through Baghdad and Kirman to Makran, where they lived for many generations before they occupied Kalat and the south Suleman hills, which they took from the Pathans. A large section of their community was expelled from Baluchistan in a tribal dispute, and settled in Sindh. Members of these exiled clans joined with their kinsfolk of the plains in rendering assistance to the Mughal Emperor Hamayun, when regaining India after his expulsion. They were rewarded with grants of land along the Indus, and had spread well up to the Chenab and the Sutlej valleys. The result of this movement was that there were more Baloch in Sindh and the Panjab than were enumerated in their native country, where they were outnumbered by the Brahis[33].

THE RIND BALOCH

There are many Baloch tribes, but the predominant section is the Rind, from which most of the rest claim to be descended. The Lashari stands next in rank, but according to the tradition of the others, it was treated as the Khsatriyas were treated by Parasurama, and swept off the face of the country, thereafter, being known only in middle Sindh, and there in a disjointed condition which has never been repaired. The Rind, too, colonised a part of upper Sindh, but are not found to any great extent elsewhere in Pakistan territory, outside Pakistan, Baluchistan. The tribes best represented on the frontier and along the rivers are the Marri, with their hereditary foe the Bughti, of the hills, and the Mazari, Gurchani, Laghari, Lund, Bozdar, and of course, the Rind itself. Except in upper Sindh and the Dera Ghazi Khan district, the Baloch of erstwhile Pakistan domicile do not keep up in particular the characteristic tribal organisation so strictly observed in their own country. As they get higher up the rivers, they tend to amalgamate with Jats and Pathans. In the south-west Punjab, indeed, every camel driver is called Baloch owing to the marked engagement of the race to that occupation. In spite of this dilution of the original stock, the independence of the artificial restrictions of caste and the strongly-marked character of the Baloch and Pathan alike, different as these peoples are in other respects, have had many considerable effects upon the customs and general tone of the population in the midst of which these races have settled. This influence, competent historian observes, has been greater than that of the political supremacy of Islam in producing that laxity in religious matters which is generally attributed to the latter cause alone. It should not be forgotten, however, that people of the west enjoyed, many centuries before a single Muslim was in existence, a unique reputation in the eyes of the singers, on the Sarasvati, for religious indifference and "neglect of rites", which justified their inclusion amongst the Maleshas.

BRAHUIS

Last among the more definite communities acknowledging Islam is that of the Brahuis, inhabiting Baluchistan and upper Sindh, of whom only 148,000 were enumerated within the scope of the survey. For centuries the Brahui have been Muslims, and have entertained with Jat and Baloch and have even admitted adult recruits from the races into their tribes, Nevertheless, they have preserved their distinct physical features, being shorter and more swarthy than their neighbours.

THEIR LANGUAGE

Their language has been overlaid with Sindhi and Balochi, for they keep, for domestic use at all events, a tongue, undoubtedly Dravidian in its main characteristics. In common with their neighbours, from whom they have perhaps borrowed it, they hold the tradition of Arab descent, Aleppo or Alepo being their chosen seat of origin. On the other hand, they are equally certain that they have never lived in any other country but that which they occupy. Setting on one side the conjecture that the Brahui are of Scythian race, for which there is little corroborative evidence, it is known that there was hope of a considerable Indian population settled along the hill-country west of Sindh, with its own customs and temples. It is possible, therefore, that the Brahui may denote the high watermark of the Dravidian extension northwards, left derelict and isolated under the protection of desert, after the Indus had changed its course and the tide of Aryan occupation had absorbed the bulk of the darker race. In the present day, the Brahui are specially engaged in the rearing and tending of camels. They enjoy a good social position in Baluchistan, but are rarely found far from their wide pastures, except for purposes connected with their occupation.

With these tribes ends the list of the communities which have been selected as representative of the different elements of which the vast and complicated society of India is compounded. That the review of their leading characteristics is imperfect has been fully admitted throughout, and the certainty of error will not be denied by anyone who has attacked even the outworks of a task of this nature. It needs but little experience of Indian life to bring home to the student of ethnography the vanity of thinking that the whole field can be adequately surveyed in the light of such knowledge as can possibly be acquired by a single individual. Here, indeed if anywhere, a little knowledge is dangerous, because, as has been abundantly shown in the course of this review. Indian society differs from tract to an extent which inevitably involves the looming danger of being led astray by analogy or similarities of nomenclature, rites or customs, into the assumption that what is true of a community in one part is equally applicable to a body of perhaps the same name elsewhere. Information upon such distinctions must be obtained, as a rule, at second-hand, and fortunately, the supply, thereof, has greatly increased of late years both in amount and quality and had received valuable additions ever since the body of this review was written. It is on such material that reliance has been mainly placed in the attempt here made, perhaps rashly, to give a word-picture of society as it exists today in India, not merely geographically, but as a whole.

RELIGION OF THE BALOCHES

The two main races, the Baloch and Brahui, although differing from one another in origin, appearance, and language, are yet bound together as members of one social organization. The tribes of both races live in close contact, and their religious beliefs and practices cannot easily be discriminated. The universal religion among them is Muhammadanism. The few Hindu traders found scattered through the country are either themselves immigrants from India or the descendants of recent settlers. The Baloches and Brahuis all profess to be Sunnis, or followers of the orthodox creed; but in practice they show great laxity, and follow many customs rather resembling those of the Shi'ahs and other, which no doubt go back to the days of Paganism. They show the greatest respect to Ali Hasan and Husain, and observe fast during the full ten days of the Muharram, like the Shi'ahs, and not the last day only, as observed among the strict Sunnis. The observance of the five times of prayer[34] prescribed for all Mussalmans has till lately not been at all prevalent among the hill tribes. It was considered sufficient for the chief of a tribe to say prayers for the whole body of tribesmen.

TOLERANT PEOPLE

The Baloches all wear their hair long, and cut neither hair nor beard, except to clip the ends of their moustache in the Sunni fashion, to show that they are not Shi'ahs. Many of their more civilised or orthodox neighbours say that Baloch's orthodoxy consists of little else, and indeed deny them the possession of any religion except one of a negative kind. They are fond of repeating a Persian verse to the effect that a Baloch earns heaven for seven generations of his ancestors by committing robbery and murder. This is unjust; for although the tribesmen are addicted to raiding and the blood feud, yet many of them have a keen sense of right and wrong, and their defeats are those common to all races in the same stage of civilization. Their laxity has its good side; for it is accompanied by a tolerant spirit and an absence of the fanaticism so prevalent among their Afghan neighbours. As Sir D. Ibbetson has described if the Baloch has less of God in his creed he has less of the devil in his nature[35]. His faithfulness to his code of honour, and the respect shown to women and children (who are never injured in Baloch raids), are points in his favour which should not be forgotten. There are few Mullahs and Saiyyids among the Baloches, who do not have great influence; on the other hand, great respect is shown to the shrines of saints. Mosques are not common, and, where found, often consist only of a pattern of stones roughly marked out on the hillside, sufficient to indicate the Qibla[36].

CONVERSION TO ISLAM

The conversion of the Baloches and Brahuis to the Muhammedan faith had taken place before their settlement in the country now known as Baluchistan, and may be assigned to the period following the first Arab conquest of south-east Persia. The Baloches occupied the mountains and deserts of Kirman[37], and were associated with another race known to the Arabs as Qufs and to the Persians as Koch, who may possibly be identical with the Brahuis, but the origin of this race is obscure. In any case, there is no historical information regarding their presence in Baluchistan until after the Baloch settlement there. The conversion of these races is ascribed by the historian Istakhri, who wrote in the 10th century, to the period of the Abbasid Khalifs, Yaquit, who on the authority of er-Rohini speaks of the Qufs as savages without religion of any sort; but er-Rohini added that they did show some respect for 'Ali out of imitation of their neighbours. The hatred of a Sunni writer for Shi'ahs is clearly perceptible here, and his language is very like that used today regarding the Baloch and Brahui mountaineers.

THEIR SETTLEMENT

The settlement of the Baloches in the country they now occupy was during a period extending from the 13th to the 16th century. They gradually spread over Makran, and in the beginning of the 16th century a great migration took place in the Indus valley, the Brahuis taking the place of the Baloches on the plateau of Kalat. The invasion of India was led by Mir Chakur and his son Shahzad. It is probable that the Shi'ah sect was still prevalent among the Baloches, for Pershia relates that Shahzad was the first person to bring the Shi'ah creed into vogue at Multan[38]. Baloch legend represents Shahzad as a man of mysterious origin. A shadow (that of Ali) fell upon his mother while she was bathing, during Mir Chakur's absence at the stage of Delhi with the emperor Hamayun. She conceived and gave birth to a son shortly before her husband's return. When he returned, the child, who was then three months old addressed him and told him to fear nothing, as he had been begotten by the influence of the saint. A mystical poem, half in Balochi and half in corrupt Persian, which is attributed to Shahzad has been verbally handed down to the present day.

A MYSTICAL POEM

The following extract will give an idea of its nature: "I gaze upon the brightness of the King: he created the golden throne of Heaven; his speech was sweet and hearten trancing; he was like upon the Lord of Light. Day and night he created, day and night are of small account to him. The dry earth he created, and the smoke that went upwards. There was neither sky nor firmament; there was neither existence nor speech; there was neither Grandmother Eve nor Grandfather Adam. There was no Ibrahim the Friend of God, not the throne of Suleman. He himself was 'He is', Hamid 'Ali".

After this period the Baloches seem gradually to have adopted the Sunni faith, in name at least, although the change has made little practical difference.

STORIES

Ali figures largely in Baloch legend, and in some of the stories about him it is impossible not to suspect a Buddhist origin. Such is the legend of the hawk and the pigeon. A pigeon was struck down by a hawk at Ali's feet and appealed to him for protection. The hawk, on the other hand, represented that he had left his young one's starving, and could find no other food for them but the pigeon. Ali in order to satisfy the hawk cut off a piece of his own flesh. Whereupon both the pigeon and hawk revealed themselves as angels sent by God to try him.

On another occasion Ali had sold himself as a slave in order to pay the marriage portion of the daughter of a petitioner. Again he is said to have given a whole caravel of money to bring a beggar by the roadside, who afterwards rose to eminence as the celebrated saint Sakhi Sarwar[39], whose shrine at Nigaha, near Dera Ghazi Khan, is one of the chief places of pilgrimage, not only for Baloches but equally for Hindus and Mussalmans from all parts of the Punjab.

SHRINES OF SAINTS

The shrines of saints, or Pirs, are centres of worship and pilgrimage throughout the country and form the most important feature in the actual religion of the Baloches. In many cases there can be no doubt that these shrines have been in existence from times preceding the introduction of Islam, and that most of them were found already established by the Baloches and Brahuis when they settled in the country. Some are of great importance, and attract visitors from far and wide, while others are known only locally. Pieces of cloth, bells, horns, fossils, and other objects are left at the shrine by pilgrims in fulfillment of their vows[40].

THE TRIBAL CODE

A strict adhesion to the tribal code of honour is regarded by all Baloches as of supreme importance, and this code has greater influence than the tenets of their nominal religion. Liberality to all petitioners and hospitality to all comers first, and all people are judged by this standard, which plays a large part in the legends of the saints. The legendary hero most admired is Nodhbandagh, who gave away all his possessions and his verses in praise of giving are often quoted.

SUPPORT AND PROTECTION TO REFUGEES

Next comes the duty of supporting and protecting refugees and refusing to surrender them to their pursuer or to the law. The maintenance of family honour by the punishment for infidelity in wives is also considered of the greatest importance, and death is the penalty both for her and her paramour, although in modern times under British influence compensation was accepted. This was fixed in money, but in practice the debt is generally discharged by the marriage or betrothal of a woman belonging to the family of the aggressor to a man of the family of the 'injured' husband.

CODE OF SUPERSTITIOUS NATURE

These are the principal articles of the tribal code, and in addition to these customs there are others of a superstitious nature. Signs and omens are observed and augury is carried out by examining the blood-vessels on the surface of the shoulder-blade of newly killed sheep. To see a shrine on the left hand when starting on a journey is an inauspicious omen, and is sufficient to make a whole band of horsemen turn back. The flesh of swine is of course, forbidden, as to all Mussalmans but the Baloches add certain national or tribal prohibitions. Fish is universally avoided by them, the reason assigned being that they cannot be killed in the orthodox fashion or are 'unclean'. The Sardar Khels among the Rinds of Kachhi will not eat camel's flesh, and the Lashari clan of the same tract avoid the Alro or Launsh, a small milky juiced plant much eaten by the hillmen generally. It is possible that some of these prohibitions have a totemistic origin.

NAMES DERIVED FROM THE NAMES OF PLANTS OR ANIMALS

A few tribal or clan names are derived from the names of plants or animals, which give some countenance to this idea. There is, however, no instance of an actual survival of totemistic practice among either Baloches or Brahuis. The wearing of the hair and beard long is a national custom almost possessing the force of a religious precept, as among the Sikhs. It is considered most disgraceful for a Baloch to cut either hair or beard, although the moustache is trimmed in the Sunni fashion.

ORDEALS

The ordeal by fire and water is still occasionally met with. A case of the ordeal by fire occurred among the Bozdars in 1889[41], which is described by Mr. Hughes Bhullar in a slightly differing form, as also the ordeal by water.

LEVITICAL FUNCTIONS

There are certain tribes or sections of tribes which have special Levitical functions, and whose members are believed to have the power of curing the sick by breathing on them. Such are the Nothani clan among the Bughtis, the Kahiri tribe and the Kalmati tribe. The last named are probably not Baloch by origin, although now assimilated. There seems to be a probability that they are the descendants of the Karmati or Karmathian[42] heretics who were expelled from Multan by Mahmud of Ghazni at the commencement of the 11th century.

HERETICAL SECT

The only heretical sect which now has any influence in Baluchistan is that known as the Zikri, which is powerful in Makran and Las Bela. Its members appear not to be Baloches but Jats and other tribes of Indian or indigenous origin, and some Brahuis, especially the Bizanjo tribe. The Zikris believe that their founder, Dost Muhammad, was the twelfth Mahdi, and his abode, Koh-i-Murad, near Turbat takes the place of Mecca as the object of their pilgrimages. Their Mullahs have great power[43].

TOKENS OF HEAVEN

And these are the tokens of heaven. A tree stands by the gate to shade the city. The fruit of the garden ripens at all seasons; by His might there are figs and olives, grapes pomegranates, and mangoes, and the scent of musk and Attar. There the Peris'[44] may not enter.

There is the place of the great assembly where He himself sits with martyrs, the king Kasim sits by him, and royal Husain with his followers. Beds and couches are spread, 'hur's'[45] are their attendants standing in their service. There dwell the men of Paradise and they eat the fruit of the garden.

Listen, Oh young men! I have seen the greatness of God, of the Lord the breaker-down of stronghold. I have seen, and am terrified, how hundreds of thousands are born and if he does not give them breath their bodies are dust and their souls go to meet their fates. Some are lords of the land, some are poor and hungry. I am not a great man, I fear none; I shall speak, I ask of the Mullahs.

Save me from Doomsday[46], from the fury flames of hell; make my passage over 'Sirat'[47] like the crossing of a bridge. May I pass over at once by the order of God, the Creator, and enter into Paradise!

LOCATION

Baluchistan is the name of the westernmost province of Pakistan as well as of the transnational territory of the traditional Baluchi home. This larger region was carved up by the imperial powers concerned more with administration than with recognition of the territorial limits of the inhabitants. The traditional Baluchi territory extends from the south-eastern portion of the Iranian plateau across the Kirman desert to the western borders of Sindh and the Punjab and from the Gomal river[48] in the north-east to the Arabian Sea in the south. This is a largely inhospitable land, much of it is barren desert or harsh mountainous terrain. Baluchi territory lies outside the monsoon belt, and annual rainfall is very low, not exceeding 16 centimeters. Throughout the region, winters are harsh and cold, and summers are very hot. In the mountains, the rains come in October and March, while in the lowlands they come in July and August.

DEMOGRAPHY

Population figures for the Baluchi are somewhat suspect, in part because of the unreliability of census-taking procedures across the three major political units that now control Balochi territory, and partly because the criteria for ascribing Balochi identity are not tightly defined. On the strength of linguistic criteria, there are an estimated million or so Balochi speakers living in eastern Iran, southern Afghanistan and in Pakistan. However, Balochi have in some areas become linguistically assimilated to neighbouring people while retaining a specifically Balochi cultural identity; this means that if social cultural rather than purely linguistic criteria were used, the population count could easily exceed two millions. Many Baloches have migrated to Pakistan's Sind and the Punjab provinces, and to the emirates of the Persian Gulf.

LINGUISTIC AFFILIATION

The Balochi language is a member of the Indo-Iranic language family, having some affinity with Kurdish. There are three distinct divisions: Eastern, Western and Southern Balochis; until the 19th century the language had no written form, because Persian was the language of official use. Illiteracy is extremely high among the Baloches.

HISTORY AND CULTURAL RELATIONS

Legend has it that the Balochi people are direct descendant of Amir Hamza, one of Mohammad's uncles, and migrated into the transnational region of Baluchistan from somewhere in the vicinity of Aleppo[49], and Suria. The migrations that brought them to their current territory began as long ago as the 5th century and were more or less complete by the end of the 7th century. Prior to the 12th century, there was a society of independent, more or less autonomous semi-nomadic groups, organized along principles of clan affiliation rather than territorial association. As the population of the region increased, access to land assumed greater and greater importance giving rise to a system of tribes, each with a territorial base.

MIR JALAL HAN

The first successful attempt to unite several Balochi tribal units was accomplished by Mir Jalal Han, who set up the first Balochi confederacy, in the 12th century, but this unity did not long survive his rule. Warfare between various Balochi tribes and tribal confederacies was frequent during the 15th century, largely owing to economic causes. By the 16th century the Balochis were roughly divided up into three separate political entities; the Makran State, the Dodai Confederacy, and the Khanate of Baluchistan (the Kalat Confederacy). In the 18th century, Mir Abdullah Khan of the Kalat Confederacy succeeded in reuniting all of Baluchistan, providing a centralized government based on Rawaj[50]. The arrival of the British in the region had profound effects on the future trajectory of Balochi development. Uninterested in the region economically, the British were solely concerned with establishing buffer zone that could forestall the encroachment of the Russians upon the rich prize of India. To further this end, the British relied on the manipulation of Balochi tribal leaders, cash handouts, and the establishment of garrisons, but they paid no attention to the economic development of the region itself.

SETTLEMENTS

The Balochi have two types of settlements, consistent with their semi-nomadic way of life. Village settlements are clusters of mud houses, loosely oriented around the house of the local chief. These permanent settlements are found in the mountains and valleys, and they are occupied chiefly in the summer. In winter the people migrate to the plains and the coastal areas, seeking pasturage for the livestock that are central to the traditional Balochi economy. During this time the Balochi live in tents, moving freely across the landscape as conditions favour the care of their herds, and settlements are smaller, consisting of closely related kin.

ECONOMY

Subsistence and Commercial Activities

The traditional Balochi economy is based on a combination of subsistence farming and semi-nomadic pastoralism, rearing cattle, sheep, and goat. Because of the harshness of the environment agriculture is somewhat limited, but it nonetheless constitutes a significant part of the economy. The principal crop is wheat. Wild fruits and vegetables also form a part of the household economy, and chickens may be raised as well. When the local economy cannot provide adequate opportunities, young men may migrate out in search of paid labour.

Industrial Arts

The Balochis are a self-sufficient lot, as a whole, and they rely on their own skills to construct their houses and many of the tools necessary in their day-to-day life. Rugs are woven for household use and as items of trade also.

Division of Labour

The entire household participates in the work of tending the family's herd, but in other aspects of the economy there is a division of labour by sex; women work in groups to thresh and winnow the grain harvest, while plowing and planting are men's work. The gathering of wild foods, water and firewood is done by groups of women.

Land Tenure

By tradition, land is not privately owned but rather is vested in the subsection of the tribe to which one belongs. It, therefore, is inalienable by the individual. However, during the British period, tribal leaders often managed to have title to some property conveyed in their own names.

KINSHIP

Balochi kinship is patrilineal, tracing descent through one of several lineages, ultimately back to the putative apical ancestor Amir Hamza. Clan membership is based on familiarities, while tribal membership has a more specifically territorial referent. For both males and females, one remains a member of one's patrilineal group for life even after marriage.

MARRIAGE AND FAMILY

Baluohi marriages are arranged between the bride's father and the prospective groom upon the payment of a bride-price consisting of livestock and cash. On marriage, a woman passes from the control of her father to that of her husband. Marriage is monogamous and is expected to be for life. Adultery was traditionally punishable by the death of both parties involved. Marriage to a non-Balochi is rigidly proscribed. Postmarital residence is patrilocal.

INHERITANCE

All inheritable property passes from father to sons.

SOCIALISATION

Balochmayar, or "the Balochi Way" is the guiding principle of proper conduct for the Balochi people. It is a sort of honour code, entailing the extension of hospitality, mercy, refuge, and honesty to one's fellows, and it is reaffirmed in the oral traditions of Balochi song and poetry. Children learn proper behaviour through observing their elders and through being subject to taunt and gossip should they behave badly.

SOCIO-POLITICAL ORGANIZATION

Baloch society is organized both into kin-based clans and territorially defined tribes. One could claim a rough correspondence between the clan and the social hierarchy as distinct from the tribe and the more specifically political sphere, but this correspondence is not absolute. The Balochi people are an amalgam of many large units, or chieftaincies, each one of which is itself composed of a nested set of small units. These constituent units can best be understood as clans, clan sections, and subsections, with smaller segments of this last division being the level that most closely corresponds to actual settlement units. At each level of this hierarchy, leadership is in the hands of a male elder. At the least comprehensive level, such leadership is as likely to be achieved as inherited, but over time authority at the more inclusive levels has devolved to the elders of what have become hereditary "chiefly clans" (Sardarkel). By the 15th century, the Sardarkel formed the organizational units of a loosely understood feudal system, which had developed into a set of semi-autonomous sovereign principalities by the 18th century. During the Imperial period, the Sardarkel served as mediators between the British and the local interests losing a great deal of their original autonomy in the process. However, as a result of their participation in securing the interests of the ruling power, much land and wealth accrued to these groups establishing a new and more purely economic basis for their leadership role, as well as allowing them to develop something of a monopoly over access to the larger political systems within which the Balochi people now found themselves. As a "stateless" people, the Balochi political presence is today somewhat attenuated. In the 1970s and 1980s, a number of groups sprang up in the name of Balochi nationalism, but their activities have been largely of a guerrilla nature and as yet, they have been unable to secure international support for their cause.

SOCIAL CONTROL

Although Muslim, the Balochi do not invoke Sharia (Islamic law) to deal with social transgression. Rather, secular authority is vested in the traditional tribal leaders (Sardars) and conducted according to Rewaj (practice) which is based on the principles of Balochmayar. The ultimate traditional sanction was provided by the mechanism of the blood feud, invoked by the clan to avenge the wrongful death of one of its members. Capital punishment was also traditionally applied in cases of adultery or the theft of clan property. Refusal to comply with the socially prescribed norms of hospitality is punishable by fines imposed by the local elders. Pardon for many social infractions can be obtained by the intercession of female representations of the offender's family. In the case of all offences except that of adultery the offender may seek refuge in the household of a non-related clan, which obligated the household providing sanctuary to fight to the death to defend the refugee. Petitions for such sanctuary must be granted, according to the code of Balochmayar. Formal public taunting, in verse as well as in direct speech, provides a further mechanism by which compliance with Balochi code of behaviour is enforced.

CONFLICT

The warrior tradition of the Balochis extends back throughout their history, reaching its fullest flowering in the 11th to 14th centuries, as a time coincident with their need to establish a settlement base from which to conduct their semi-nomadic way of life. During the Imperial period the British imposed a policy of pacification upon the region and enforced it by maintaining a substantial garrison presence. The Balochi reputation for producing fierce warriors is today recalled primarily in the activities of the free 'fighters' of the Balochi Nationalist Movement.

THE ART

Although the Balochi are largely an illiterate people and their language was until quite recently unwritten, they have a long tradition of poetic composition, and poets and professional minstrels have been held in high esteem. Their oral literature consists of epic poetry, ballads of war and romance, religious compositions and folktales. Much composition is given over to genealogical recitals as well. This poetic creativity traditionally had a practical as well as aesthetic aspect. Professional minstrels long held the responsibility of carrying information from one to another of the scattered Balochi settlements and during the time of the first Balochi Confederacy these travelling singers provided an important means by which the individual leaders of each tribe within the confederacy could be linked to the central leadership. The earliest securely dated Balochi poem known today, dates to the late 12th century, although the tradition of such composition is no doubt of much greater antiquity.

BALOCHES SHAHPUR DISTRICT[51]

The Baloch, who form more than two per cent of the total population, have increased from 10,583 to 13,661 or by 29 per cent in this district. They are a fairly distinct tribe, and the term is seldom applied to camelmen, who are not true Baloch, except in the Bhera[52] tehsil, where the tribe owns little land. In this district they are found chiefly in the Shahpur (4,536) and Khushab[53] (4487) tehsils; in Shahpur and Khushab[54] 15 estates with an area of 65,669 acres, they are found chiefly; (1) round Khushab where before Ranjit Singh's time they held independent sway, and again (2) on both sides of the Jhelum about Sahiwal[55] which was the seat of another ruling family of this tribe. Its leaders are now Sardar Dahadur Khan of Khushab and Sardar Mohammad Chiragh Khan of Sahiwal, both Divisional Darbaries. The Baloches are only fair agriculturists, and some of them are extravagant. They furnish many good cavalry recruits, especially from the village of Jamali in the Thai. The principal clans are the Laghari, Lashari and Rind, but these account for a very small proportion of the whole. Only one man in the district is returned as speaking Balochi.

MULTAN DISTRICT

The Balochis first obtained a footing in the district during 1901 when they were enumerated 24,488 and in 1911 they numbered 29,594 when the Dodais[55] and afterwards the Rinds in 1921 made incursions into the district, they rose to 30,583, in some cases enlisting as mercenaries under the Langahs, and in others, settling down as agriculturists. They are now found for the most part in the Lodhran[56] tehsil and its. immediate neighbourhood; and though they own no very prominent men, they include several sturdy agricultural families of a good stamp in villages, such as Wahi Jagguwal, Haveli Nasir Khan, Chauki Sobha Khan, etc. The Baloch villages in the east of Lodhran are mostly called Chaukis, the story being that the Balochis were settled there as outposts in former days to protect the boundary of the neighbouring desert, which is still known as the Chit Dain or the Desert of Terror. The Balochis of the district are chiefly Rind and Korais. They have long been, for practical purposes, ordinary Jatts, having forgotten their old language, disused their old costumes and intermarried freely with the neighbouring population. They not uncommonly, however, still wear their hair long and among the Rinds the married women wear white clothes only.

THE DADUPUTRAS

The Daduputras, though claiming a separate origin, are commonly looked on as Balochis. This is of the same family as the Nawab of Bahawalpur, and those found in this district are mainly descendants of men who obtained a footing in the Sutlej tehsils during the days of Bahawalpur supremacy. In appearance they resemble the Balochis. They are mainly tenants and labourers, and own very little land.

MOGHALS

Of the so-called Moghals of the district but few are real 1911— 8,038 Moghals: the assumption of Moghal clan 1911— 1,651 names, 1921—2,250. The census figures regarding this tribe are, therefore, especially untrustworthy. Considering the enormous number of Moghal invasions from which the district had suffered, there are remarkably few families in Multan which can show Moghal or Turkish descent. There is a tribe called Kaum, near Mitra, which is said to have come from Central Asia.

JHANG DISTRICT

There are a considerable number of Baloches in the district, but with one or two exceptions all their villages (in 1901— 12,966) lie to the west of the Chenab. Above Kot Khan, the old limit of the Sial country, the Baloch villages are numerous. They are said to have settled in the district before the Sials. Babar in his memoirs mentions that there was colony of Baloches in the countries of Bhera and Khushab. This was in 1519 A.D., and it must have taken the Baloches sometime to spread east as far as Bhera. The tribal tradition is that the Baloches first came into this part of the Punjab in the reign of Shah Husain, the Langah ruler of Multan. This was early in the 15th century, and after the arrival of the Sials. But on the other hand, there is undoubted evidence that the Sandal Bar east and south of Jhang was held by Rind Baloches before the Bharwana Sials, and the Baloches were only driven out after severe fighting. The Baloch headquarters were at Mirpur near the Ravi. Again, west of the lower Chenab, the country along the banks of the river was certainly occupied by Baloches before the Rajbana Sials pushed their way down to Ahmadpur. In fact the Baloches seem to have been in force and to have strenuously resisted the Sial advance. Possibly, however, the date generally accepted of the arrival of the Sials may be wrong, or it may have taken the Sials longer to spread over the country than is generally supposed, but at all events it seems to be satisfactorily established that the Baloches were holding the southern portion of the Sandal Bar and the country west of the Chenab before the Sials. The Baloches in this district never attained any importance. They have furnished no chief. Among them are to be found representatives of almost every clan and tribe. They possess no distinctive moral or physical features distinguishing them from other tribes, they are good agriculturists and especially in the Kachhi cultivate their own holdings. They are inclined to be quarrelsome, and the Baloches of Kadirpur Baksha are notorious in this respect. Several of the sections of the tribe are incorrigible cattle thieves and Nur Mahram and Akil Hyata Baloches, in the colony police station of Mochiwala, have been gazetted a criminal tribe. The most numerous clans are the Rinds who numbered in old villages of the district, 2,229 in 1901. The Baloches have numerous conspicuous villages; among them Mari Shah Sakhira, Kot Shakar, Chhatta and Kadirpur Baksha in Jhang tehsil and Bulla in Shorkot. The Zaildars were Alladad Khan, Gadi, of Chhatta; Ahmad Yar Khan of Mari and Lal Khan of Kot Shakar. Muhammad Khan, Gadi, of Jhok Daya, father of Alladad Khan who has recently died, was in the past one of the strongest men in the district who enjoyed great authority. Other leading men were Haidar Khan of Kiran and Lal Khan of Bulla.

ATTOCK DISTRICT

Ownership is less simple in Fatehjang than in Pindigheb, and indeed in the extreme east of the Gheb circle and throughout the Sil Soan circle the ownership is a good deal mixed. The principal tribes together with the percentages of the cultivated area owned, and of the land revenue paid, are shown in the table below:

Table 10.1: *Percentage of Cultivated Areal and Land Revenue Owned by Different Tribes*

Tribes	Percentage of area cultivated		Percentage of land revenue	
Gheba	36	(31)	21	(19)
Khattar	20	(21)	18	(17)
Miscellaneous Rajputs	12	(12)	16	(14)
Awan	8	(10)	11	(15)
Alpial	6	(10)	10	(17)
Gujjar	4	(4)	5	(6)
Saiyyad	1	(2)	2	(3)
Khatri		(3)		(4)
Other Mussalmans	8	(3)	10	(4)
Other Hindus	5	(1)	7	(1)
Total	100	(100)	100	(100)

The Khattars hold the whole of the Nata circle on the north and the east of the Gheb circle in the centre of the tehsil, forming part of the old Khattar Ilaqa which extends from Fatehjang to Hassan Abdal in Attock and along the Kala Chitta from the Indus river to the Margalla pass in Rawalpindi. The Ghebas own the whole of the west and south of the Gheb circle up to the Pindigheb border which marks the separation of the Ghebas and the Jodhras. The Alpials are in the Sil Soan circle alone, and though mixed with Awans and other tribes, are far the largest owners in the circle. The extreme east of the Gheb circle on the Rawalpindi boundary is held by miscellaneous Rajput tribes who belong ethnologically to the Rawalpindi tehsil. It will be noticed that the Ghebas and Khattars, who own large Barani tracts, pay much less revenue in proportion to their holdings than any other tribes.

OWNERSHIP COMPLICATED

Ownership is more complicated still in Attock tehsil. The Chhachh is almost wholly Pathan, though Awans own a good deal of land and pay 9 per cent of the revenue. The Sarwala circle is divided between Awans, who own a third of it, Khattars owning a fourth, and Gujjars, Shaikhs and Pathans preponderate in the Nala circle, followed in order of importance by Gujjars, Khattars and Awans. Roughly, Khattars lie all along the Kala Chitta. Pathans hold the Chhachh and the Nala estates along the Haro. Awans inhabit the centre of the Sarwala, the west of the Nala circle, the neighbourhood of Shamsabad in the Chhachh, and are scattered through the rest of the tehsil. Gujjars and Shaikhs are settled along the boundary of the Chhachh and Sarwala circles and the former are strong in the centre and east of the Nala circle.

Such is the tribal picture of each tehsil.

RELATIVE IMPORTANCE OF PRINCIPAL TRIBES

Before proceeding to discuss the tribes individually, it will be convenient to focus the tribal picture of the district as a whole, with reference to their importance as agriculturists.

Awans are by far the most important tribe in the district and predominate in Tallagang. They are also found in the greater part of Jandal as well as in the south of Makhad and in the west of the Sil circle of Pindigheb. In Attock we find them in both the assessment circles of Sarwala and Nala. The premier Awaii in Tallagang is Khan Sahib Mohammad Khan of Tamman, but the leadership of the tribe is ascribed to Khan Bahadur Malik Muhammad Amin Khan of Shamasabad in the Attock tehsil.

Rajputs follow Awans, and include the Rajput Jodhras of Pindigheb, Dandi, Kamrial and the Maliks of Khunda who hold lands in the Sil circle of the Pindigheb tehsil, as well as the Alpial Rajputs of the Soan circle of Fatehjang. The chief family of the Alpial are the descendants of Chowdhari Sher Khan of Chakri. The head of the Rajput Jodhras, and of the Rajputs generally, is Khan Bahadur Nawab Malik Ghulam Muhammad Khan of Pindigheb, a noble gentleman of the old school.

The Khattar tribe comes next. Tribally, the senior branch is that of the late Sardar Dost Muhammad Khan of the Fatehjang tehsil. Politically, the most important family at present is the branch at Wah in the Attock tehsil. The tribe lies along and across the Kala Chitta hills in the tehsils of Attock, Fatehjang and Pindigheb.

The percentage of the total population and of the cultivated area, held by the various tribes will appear from the following table:

Table 10.2: *Percentage of Population and Cultivated Area by Tribes*

Tribes	Percentage of area cultivated	Percentage of land revenue
Awan	37	34
Rajput	15	6
Khattar	11	1
Pathan	9	8
Mughal	9	1
Gujjar	3	2
Other Agriculturists	8	13
Non-Agriculturists	4	35
Shamilat, etc.	3	103

No attempt has been made at comparison of these figures with those recorded in the *Gazetteer* of 1947. In the latter there were clearly grave misprints, *e.g.* Pathans were shown as owning 1.7 per cent of the cultivated area, and paying 49 per cent of the land revenue.

TRIBES GAZETTED UNDER LAND ALIENATION ACT

The tribes gazetted under the Land Alienation Act are Awan Baloch, Gakhar, Gujjar, Jat, Jodhra, Khattar, Qureishi, Maliar, Mughal, Pathan. Saiyyad, Bhatti, Janjua, Jodh, Kahut, Maar and Manhas, Bhatti Shaikh, Sadiqi Shaikh, and Mohial Brahmins. Besides these, various Rajput clans gazetted under this Act are given below:

Rajput	Hun	Rajput	Johad
Rajput	Janjua	Rajput	Chib
Rajput	Tuh	Rajput	Mangeal
Rajput	Bhatti	Rajput	Bhohan
Rajput	Hattar	Rajput	Adhial
Rajput	Chanial	Rajput	Kurar
Rajput	Dhamial	Rajput	Jhottial
Rajput	Mitwal	Rajput	Jodhara
Rajput	Bhakral	Rajput	Bhatti Mehra
Rajput	Alpial	Rajput	Bhatti Kanjal
Rajput	Kahut	Rajput	Bhatti Jangle
Rajput	Khingar	Rajput	Bhatti Badhuer

PRINCIPAL TRIBES IN ORDER OF STANDING

Social standard in the district is a somewhat complicated matter. A certain halo invests a Saiyyad: as also saint of any caste who has established a reputation for holiness. Qureishis command respect though less than that accorded to a Saiyyad. The Jodhra Rajputs in Pindighe command special respect as do the leading Khattar and Awan families. Among the peasants the Awan has the better name. An Awan will accept a Khattar bride but will not give his daughter to a Khattar family. A Khattar may think himself better than an Alpial but the Alpial would not agree. Ghebas and Khattars are of similar position. Pathans are recognized as well-born, and marry only with Pathans or Saiyyads.

Jats, Gujjars and Miliars occupy the lower strata in agricultural society, and rank in the order in which they are given. After them come the Kamins[57]. Sunaras[58] are socially the highest and Lohars[59] are slightly superior to the Tarkhans[60], but the names are often used alternatively, the same man being both a carpenter and a blacksmith. Kumhars[61], Julahas[62], Nais[63], Telis[64], Machhis[65], Mallahs, Dhobis[66], Marasis[67], Mochis[68], Mussalies[69] are given in the order of their social importance.

Hindus are principally Brahmans, Muhials, Khatris and Aroras and rank in that order.

DERA GHAZI KHAN

It is to the presence of the Balochis, in the proportion of 33 per cent, of its total population, that the district owes its distinguishing characteristics. Balochis, elsewhere scattered in occasional colonies, here form, not indeed numerically but both politically and socially, a prepondering element in the population; that upon them centres the whole interest both of the past history and of the present administration of the district, hands of the woman's relatives. The Balochis are lavish of their hospitality. Even among the poorest of them, all who turn up during a meal are welcome to a share of whatever is going on, and the chiefs spend a great part of their income in entertaining guests. All Balochis who come to a chief's village on business or on the occasion of a great ceremonial are fed from the chief's kitchen.

Now that the tribes on both sides of the Suleman hills who were under direct British control, blood feuds and reprisals are much less common than they were, but an occasional outbreak shows that in ferocity the Balochis are no whit superior to the Pathans.

THE FIGHTING TACTICS

In fighting the Baloch tactics may be summed up in the simple principle that an attack is never to be made unless the enemy can be surprised, or is in inferior numbers. Battle once given, however, the fight is carried on hand to hand with sword and shield, and not, as in the case of Pathans. The following interesting description of the Balochis of 1871 is quoted from Sir F. Fryer's *Settlement Report:*

"It is not often that the Balochis meet each other in fight tribe to tribe. The ordinary rule is that small parties of a tribe go out on a marauding expedition. These parties are called 'Chapaos', and object is to murder and plunder only those enemies whom they can surprise."

"The wild hill men see the Balochis from within border sleek and well-to-do, and they contract their own condition with that of the people. The hillman is lean, hungry, unkempt, clad in filthy rags and sheepskin, in constant fear of his life, never able to call the cattle which form his only wealth, his own. The plain Baloch from within the border has cotton, cloth, a good mare to ride, and is prosperous and free from anxiety. The element of danger has a charm of its own to the Baloch as to all wild tribes, but it is a charm which the stern realities of hunger and privation are fast dissipating. The hill Balochis live from hand to mouth, and are often reduced to great straits. Most of them grow no crops, but live by herds of cattle, which they graze in the numerous plains of their country. When grass is scarce and the graziers are scattered comes the season for Chapaos. Of course the victims of a Chapao, if they escape with their lives, can join a return Chapao; but a Chapao must, it should be said very profitable to repay those who join one for the trouble and fatigue they undergo. The members of a Chapao have to travel long distances by night, lying concealed by day, and they have no food but what flour they can carry with them, which they dare not light a fire to bake. They often end by falling into an ambuscade themselves, or by finding their intended victims too much on the alert for an attack to be ventured.

The Baloch tradition of their origin is that they came from Aleppo in the 12th century via Baghdad, the banks of the Euphrates, and the northern border of the Persian Gulf to Mekran from where they spread north, intermixing with the Pathan tribes.

Elphinstone says in his *History of India* that in the 7th century of the Christian era, the mountains of Mekran were inhabited by Balochis and those of Suleman by Afghans. The Afghans were certainly at one time in possession of part of the Suleman Range, as remains of their tanks and tombs are still to be seen on the Mari Mountain, which now belongs to the Gurchani tribe of Baloches, but Elphinstone's authority for saying that the Baloch nation reached Mekran so early is not clear. Another theory advanced by Pottinger and adopted to some extent by Dr. Latham is that the Balochis belonged to the horde of Seljuk[70] Tartars which in the 5th century of the Christian era overran Persia and, forming two branches, wrested on the east under the house of Ghor, the sovereignty of Khorasan and India from the house of Ghazni, and on the west under the lead of Toghral[71] Beg conquered Western Persia, captured Baghdad and invaded the Roman Empire. This theory agrees with the statement advanced by Elphinstone. The religion, manners and customs of the Baloch tribes in their fondness for horses, their nomadic habits, their mode of life and their dress present a strong resemblance to those of the Turkomans[72]. At the same time Dr. Latham thought that the outline of their physiognomy is very similar to that of the Arabs of Egypt and Syria; and if a Baloch was dressed in the Arabic dress, it would be exceedingly difficult to detect his nationality. Others, he considered, were Sindhis, who fled to the invasion of their country by the Muhammadans. This modified theory that the Balochis are partly of Turkoman origin but have a by-no-means homogenous descent from anyone source, met with the approval of Sir Frederick Fryer. The Balochis, who are almost certainly Tartar mountaineers by origin are represented in this district only by a sub-section of the Mazari tribe, the Kirds, a name which, by the well-established rule that the Balochi 'i' corresponds to the Persian 'u', is identical with Kurd. The Dast-i-Bedaulat in Balochistan is inhabited by Kurds who probably came from Kurdistan, and perhaps, laden with spoil, preferring on their return to stay where they now are rather than continue their march to their own country, made a choice of the Dast-i-Bedaulat.

THEIR CONSTITUTION

The Constitution of a Baloch tribe may be best described as a species of limited monarchy. At the head of the tribe, or Tuman, is the Tumandar[73], hereditary referee who settles all matters of dispute in time of peace, and is a leader in the war. The tribe is divided into sections (Phalli); each Baloch has its own headman, called Mukaddam, whose office, as that of the Tumandar, is hereditary. No business of importance can be transacted by the Tumandar without consultation with the Mukaddams, and a system of responsibility is maintained which runs through the tribe, and it ensures the harmonious working of the whole. Practically, the power of the Tumandar, if he is a man of common ability and energy, is unlimited; for the Baloch is docile, and from long custom has acquired the habit of implicit obedience to his chief. Still, when the common interests of the tribe are at stake, he cannot with impunity act contrary to the wishes of the tribes as expressed by its Mukaddams. Before the tribes came under British control, the Tumandar was within the tribal country a sort of limited monarch. He could not declare peace or war without the advice of his council of Mukaddams, but when war was declared he was charged with the conduct of it. Every member of when the tribe was bound to render military service to the chief; the chief also received a one-fifth share in all plunder of the tribe, and in the produce of its fields. When the tribes were under British rule plunder ceased to form an item of the chief's income, and it was only as an assignee of Government revenue that he was permitted to take a share of the produce of the land.

Still for all matters of administration the power of the Tumandar for good or evil in his tribe is immense, and is through him that an alien Government can best rule his tribesman.

PRESERVATION OF THEIR ORGANISATION

All the Tumandars are invested with Magisterial powers.

One of the chief causes which preserved the tribal organisation amongst the Balochis who were subject to the British may be referred to the manner of their original settlement in the district. When the Balochis came down from the hills and settled in the plains, they parcelled out the lands they acquired according to their sections, and the sections divided the lands amongst their own members. The Tumandar retained a considerable private estate for himself and his family; and where the Tumandar is influential, he still retains the right to provide for the cultivation of waste lands and of lands deserted by their occupants. The Tumandar also usually receive some payment in kind from all the members of their Tuman as an acknowledgement of their position. All but two Tumandars retained up to the time of the regular Settlement of the district the right to collect in kind from all or part of their Tumans. The Tumandars received the Mahsul or authorised Government share of the produce, and in return paid the cash assessment. It was this right to collect in kind which most served to preserve the hold of the Tumandars over their Tumans; and by giving the Tumandars full granaries, it enabled them to exercise that liberal hospitability which is regarded by the Baloch as the greatest of all virtues. Hospitality alone would not give a Baloch influence if he had none of the other qualities of a chief, but no qualities of mind or body would secure a chief power with his tribes if his doors were closed to the members of it. Every Baloch, when attending his chief, is entertained at the expense of the latter.

Pottinger, who travelled in Balochistan in A.D. 1838, wrote that the Balochis were divided into three branches, the Narboi, the Rind and the Mughal and gave a list of the Rind tribes, in which all the tribes located in this district were mentioned. He described the Drishaks and Mazaris, who are now almost wholly resident in the plains, as living in the hills. Sections of them, however, had settled in the plains long before that time. All the tribes were then at continual war with one another and kept no engagements.

The detail of religions and tribes according to the Census of 1891 was as follows:

Table 10.3: *Population of Different Communities*

Community	Population
Hindus	52,903
Sikhs	1,424
Muhammedans	3,49,587
Christians	117
Total	4,04,031
Percentage of total population	100

Table 10.4: *Population of Different Tribes*

Religion and Tribe	District
Baloch	
Natkani	6,305
Kasrani	3,841
Khosa	24,286
Lashari	6,469
Laghari	20,410
Lund	11,087
Gurchani	3,259
Pitafi	2,186
Mazari	5,514
Dishak	4,649
Gopang	4,610
Jatoi	2,372
Ahmdani	3,849
Chandia	4,303
Other	28,992
Total	1,32,192
Percentage of total population	33
Religion and Tribe	**District**
Jat	116,740
Saiyyad	6,774
Pathan	8,808
Rajput	13,909
Sheikh	4,641
Arain	4,793
Mughal	859
Machi	7,741
Other agriculturists	8,270
Total	55,804
Percentage of total population	14

Table 10.5: *District-wise Distribution of Different Tribes*

	1	2	3	4	5	6	7	8	9
	Rind	Laghari	Jatoi	Gurchani	Lashari	Khosa	Koral	Tibbi-Lund	Chandia
Lahore	351	...	1,045	...	86	...	36	...	...
Gujranwala	...	...	147	...	78	...	...	...	...
Firozpur	36	...	595	...	80	...	30	...	...
Rawalpindi	48	...	...	...	16	...	102	...	...
Jhelum	87	...	400	...	148	...	916	...	49
Gujarat	...	...	13	...	14	...	71	...	...
Shahpur	1,350	...	2,229	...	1,053	...	402	...	35
Multan	6,008	35	506	...	1,865	...	2,695	...	872
Jhang	5,223	167	1,849	...	696	...	197	...	167
Montgomery	1,460	...	4,106	...	754	...	805	...	4
Muzaffargarh	4,536	1,159	4,574	...	2,629	106	3,385	...	7,290
Derah Ismail Khan	2,233	2,195	1,232	42	4,270	32	1,234	...	1,612
Derah Ghazi Khan	6,136	22,980	2,829	17,099	1,354	11,308	727	10,000	412
Bannu	237	75	1	...	325	...	70	...	124
Delhi Division	158	...	...	...	...	...	15	...	...
Hissar Division	108	...	504	...	467	...	59	...	...
Ambala Division	...	...	65	...	18	...	23	...	...
Jalandhar	1	...	48	...	...	...	...	...	...
Amritsar Division	...	...	9	...	46	...	29	...	...
Peshwar Division	16	25	7	...	3	...	179	...	...
British Territory	27,988	26,636	20,159	17,141	13,902	11,446	10,995	10,888	10,785
Nabha and Faridkot	68	...	163	...	98	...	30	...	...
Bhawalpur	8,287	97	4,272	...	3,295	1,011	4,435	...	1,263
Total Province	36,343	26,788	24,598	17,141	17,295	12,457	15,481	10,888	12,048

(Contd...)

10	11	12	13	14	15	16	17	18
Gopang	Mazari	Hot	Nutkani	Gurmani	Kulachi	Qasranl	Jiskani	Drishak
...	...	78	...	...	...	...	...	...
...	...	148	...	...	...	...	...	...
...	...	59	...	...	...	...	...	...
...	...	21	...	...	...	...	13	...
...	...	121	...	...	...	...	...	...
...	...	1	...	...	...	...	...	...
...	...	176	...	...	...	...	...	...
992	2	842	...	62	157	4	78	...
17	...	774	21	...	53	59	270	...
1	...	654	...	...	1	...	...	...
8,400	7	1,105	257	2,522	977	...	317	374
21	5	1,072	597	1,078	3,724	1,675	3,705	...
1,230	3,649	282	4,671	1,666	...	2,615	13	3,796
...	...	66	...	1	14	...	2	...
...	...	11	...	...	2	7	...	...
14	...	317	...	...	...	55	...	...
...	...	7	...	...	...	...	...	...
...	...	4	...	...	...	...	...	...
...	...	10	...	...	...	...	...	...
...	...	36	...	...	...	...	...	...
10,733	8,663	5,783	5,546	5,837	5,268	4,418	4,395	4,170
...	...	11	...	...	...	...	...	...
5,497	548	3,311	...	...	371	...	333	74
16,175	9,211	9,188	5,546	5,827	5,688	4,418	4,781	4,244

REFERENCES

1. Former princely state, now part of Balochistan province, southwest Pakistan *(The Columbo Gazetteer of the World*, p. 1482).
2. A district in Kalat division, Balochistan.
3. A district in Kalat division, Balochistan.
4. A district in Punjab province, Pakistan.
5. A district in Sindh, Pakistan.
6. A large city and former capital of Pakistan, in Sindh province.
7. A district, 23196 square miles, in Kalat division, Balochistan.
8. A district HQ, 11,457 square miles in north-east Balochistan.
9. Capital of Balochistan, 30° 12 N, 6° 700 East.
10. Region, 407 square miles, a former division of Baluchistan, southwest of Pakistan, includes the Bolan Pass.
11. A former princely state, now part of Balochistan province.
12. A pass, at the south end of central Bruhi Range.
13. A district 18,508 square miles, in Kalat division, Balochistan, southwest Pakistan.
14. A Pass in Afghanistan, elevation c. 5000 ft, 31° 56 N, 69° 20 East.
15. A district HQ in Malkand Agency, Balochistan.
16. A district in Malkand Agency, Balochistan.
17. *Panjab Castes,* Denzil Ibbetson, (1883), pp. 41-42.
18. The alluvial plain in Derah, Ghazi Khan district, south-west Punjab, Pakistan.
19. Aleppo or Alep, city NW Syria, located in a semi-desert region where grain, cotton, fruits and other goods are grown, got independence in 1941, also called Halah.
20. Situated in Sindh province, Pakistan.
21. A clan.
22. Also spelt as Hyderabad, a district in Sindh, Pakistan.
23. A district in Pakistan, Punjab province.
24. North-East Balochistan, Pakistan.
25. A district in Punjab province, Pakistan.
26. In Sindh Sagar Doab, Punjab province, central Pakistan.
27. A town, District Headquarters in Punjab province, Pakistan.
28. An erstwhile Princely State of Balochistan.
29. The family from which sprang the Lodi dynasty of Delhi.
30. Tumandar.
31. The headmen.
32. Allepo or Alep, city, in 1978, population 878000, NW Syria, located in semi-desert region. It was settled as early as 6th millennium B.C.

and passed to the Assyrians *(The Concise Columbia Encyclopaedia,* p.18).

33. A clan of Afghanistan.
34. Namaz.
35. *Outlines of Punjab Ethnography,* D. Ibbetson, (1883). p. 112.
36. Direction of Mecca.
37. Also written as Kirman, a city in the province, south-east of Iran.
38. District in Bari Doab, rounded south by the Sutlej river west by Chenab river, north by Ravi, Pakistan.
39. A popular Muslim saint, worshipped by Hindus also.
40. *Balochi Folklore*, (1902). pp. 159-163.
41. *JRAS* 1890-1930. A.D.
42. Also Carmathians. *Encyclopaedia of Religion and Ethics,* Vol. 3, pp. 222-225.
43. A full account of this sect is given by Mr. Hughes Bhuller in the *Baluchistan Census Report,* 1902.
44. Beautiful ladies of Heaven.
45. Most beautiful and virgin girl inhabitants.
46. The *Qiamat.*
47. Sarat-ul-Mustqeem—A bridge to be crossed after death.
48. Which rises in east Afghanistan, west of Urgun, flows SE to Pakistan border.
49. A district in south-west Syria.
50. The customary law of the Balochi people.
51. 16 miles from south-west of Sargodha, Pakistan,
52. In Pakistan.
53. In Pakistan.
54. In Pakistan, a district.
55. A clan of Balochistan.
56. *A* town in Multan district, Pakistan.
57. The menial and artisan class.
58. The goldsmith.
59. The ironsmith.
60. The carpenter.
61. The potter.
62. The weaver.
63. The barber.
64. The oil maker.
65. The shoe mender.
66. The washerman.

67. The joker.
68. The shoemaker.
69. The torch-bearer.
70. Or Seljugs, the name of a nomadic family of Ghuzz Turk who founded several Turkish dynasties in Asia *(Collier's Encyclopaedia.* Vol. 20, p. 58).
71. Born c. 990 A.D., died September 4, 1063 A.D., founder of the Seljuk dynasty, which ruled over Iran, Iraq, Syria and Anatolia.
72. Or Turk men, people who speak a language belonging to the southwestern branch of the Turkic languages. The majority live in Turkminstan, neighbouring parts of Central Asia *(Britannica,* Vol. 11. p. 819).
73. Alam-bardar—the headman.

BIBLIOGRAPHY

Balochi Folklore, (1902).

Bhuller, Hughes. *The Balochistan Census Report*, (1902).

Collier's Encyclopedia.

Encyclopaedia of Britannica.

Encyclopaedia of Religion and Ethics, Vol. 3, pp. 222-225.

Ibbetson, Denzil. *Punjab Castes,* (1883).

Ibbetson, D. *Outline of Panjab Ethnoghraphy*, (1883).

JRAS. 1890-1930.

The Columbia World Gazetteer, 3 Vols.

The Pathans

(Descendants of Scythians and Huns)

11

AFGHANISTAN

Geography And Topography

Officially Islamic Republic of Afghanistan, Persian Jamhuri-e-Islami, Afghanistan is a landlocked country of south-central Asia. The country extends about 600 miles (970 km) from north to south and about 800 miles (1,300 km) from east to west, including the narrow Vakhan (Wakhan), a corridor of 150 miles (241 km) long connecting Afghanistan with China to the northeast. Afghanistan is also bordered on the south and south-east by Pakistan, on the west by Iran, and on the north by Turkmenistan, Uzbekistan, and Tajikistan. A description of the country is as follows:

Capital	—	Kabul
Population (2003 est.)	—	27,717,000
Density	—	71/sq. mile
Distribution	—	Urban 20%, Rural 80%
Area	—	251,826 square miles
Elevation	—	Highest point 24,557 feet
Principal Languages	—	Pashto, Dari and Persian
Principal Religion	—	Islam
Political Division	—	27 Provinces
Currency Unit	—	1 Afghani-100 puls
National Holiday	—	April 27. Day of the Great April Revolution
National Anthem	—	Sorud-i-Melli in Urbu

The Land

Afghanistan has three distinctive regions. The northern plains are the major agricultural area. The south-western plateau consists primarily of desert and semi-desert landscape and includes the Rigestan desert. These regions are separated by the central highlands, an extension of the Himalayan Mountain chain, which includes the Hindu Kush Mountain range.

The Amu Darya (ancient Oxus river) forms a major portion of Afghanistan's northern border. The 715 mile-long (1,150-kilometre) Helmand river provides most of the agricultural water needs of the south-western plateau region. The central highlands have a subarctic climate (winters below freezing and cool, short summers), while most of the remainder is semi-arid steppe (cold winters and hot summers) or desert. Annual precipitation varies from less than 3 inches (75 mm) in the south-western desert to more than 50 inches (1,270 mm) in the Hindu Kush mountains.

Much of Afghanistan has thin, infertile mountain and desert soils, but the northern plains region has some of the best agricultural land in Asia. About one-eighth of the country's land area is arable, and approximately one-third of that area is irrigated. More than 80 per cent of the country's crops are regularly produced on this irrigated area. Afghanistan has significant mineral resources, including huge deposits of high-grade iron ore, which remained virtually unexploited in the early 21st century. There are significant reserves of natural gas in the northern plains.

There are many fertile valleys and plains within the mountain ranges and on their edges. In the south, and particularly in the south-west, are great stretches of desert, including the regions of Seistan and Registan. To the north, between the central mountain chains (notably the Band-i-Turkestan, the Koh-i-baba, and the Paropamisus) and the Amu Darya (the Oxus river) which forms the entire Uzbekistan Afghanistan border and marks part of the boundary with Turkmenistan, are the highlands of Badakhshan (with the finest lapis lazuli in the world), Afghan Turkistan, the Amu Darya plain, and the rich valley of Herat on the Hari Rud river in the north-west corner of the country (the heart of ancient Ariana). The country has a dry continental climate, with precipitation (largely winter and spring) varying from 10 in/25 cm annually in the central highlands to 2 in/5cm in the southern marginal deserts. Strong winds ("Wind of 120 Days") in the western plains recall the climate of the adjacent Iranian plateau. The humid subtropical Jalalabad basin constitutes a special climatic area. Vegetation is differentiated vertically and ranges from true desert lowlands, through steppes in the foothills of the Hindu Kush, to alpine mountain meadows.

True forests are found only in Nuristan (Asmar Forest) and Khost in east. The rivers are mostly unnaviagable; the longest is the Helmand, which flows generally southward from the Hindu Kush to the Iranian border. Its water has been used since remote times for irrigation, as have the waters of the Hari Rud and of the Amu Darya. The Kabul river, on which the capital stands, is particularly famous because it leads to the Khyber Pass and thus south to Pakistan. Irrigation is carried out by rivers in the north and east, by karez or kariz (subterranean aqueducts) in the south lowlands, and by natural springs in the hilly areas.

The People

About half of the population are Pashtuns, and the rest are Tajiks, Uzbeks, and Hazaras. The Pashtuns mainly inhabit the southern and eastern parts of the country. Most Pashtuns are sedentary, though some remain nomadic. The Tajiks, mostly farmers and artisans, live predominantly in the north-east and in the west around Herat. The Uzbeks are mainly farmers living north of the Hindu Kush. The Hazaras are nomads who inhabit the central mountains.

The Official Languages

The official languages of the country are Pashto (Pushtu) and Persian(Dari), both Indo-European languages. Pashto is spoken by about half of the population. Dari is spoken by about a third of the population mainly the Tajik, Hazara, Chahar Aimak, and Kizilbash peoples. Uzbek and Turkmen both belong to the Altaic language family and are spoken in the north. Some three-fourths of the people are Sunnite Muslims, and about one-fourth are Shiite Muslims.

History

Variations on the word Afghan may be as old as a 3rd century A.D. Sasanian reference to "Abgan". The earliest Muslim reference to the Afghans probably dates back to 982 A.D., but tribes related to the modern Afghans have lived in the region for many generations. For millennia the land now called Afghanistan has been the meeting place of four cultural and ecological areas: the Middle East, Central Asia, South Asia, and East Asia.

Prehistory

Paleolithic (Old Stone Age) people probably roamed Afghanistan as early as 100,000 years ago. The earliest definite evidence of human occupation was found in the cave of Darra-i-Kur in Badakhshan, where a transitional Neanderthal skull fragment in association with Mousterian type tools was discovered; the remains are of the Middle Paleolithic Period, dating to about 30,000 years ago. Caves near Aq Kupruk yielded evidence of an early Neolithic culture (c. 9000-6000 B.C.) based on domesticated animals. Archaeological research since World War II has revealed Bronze Age sites, dating both before and after the Indus Civilization of the 3rd to the 2nd millennium B.C. There was trade with Bronze Age Mesopotamia and Egypt. In addition, a site with links to the Indus Civilisation has been excavated at Shortughai, northeast of Konduz.

Historical Beginnings (7th century A.D.)

The Achaemenids and the Greeks. In the 6th century B.C., the Achaemenian ruler Cyrus II (the Great) established his authority over the area. Darius I (the Great) consolidated Achaemenian rule of the region through the provinces, or satrapies, of Aria (in the region of modern Herat), Bactria (Balkh), Sattagydia (modern Ghazni to the Indus river), Arachosia (Kandahar), and Drangiana (Sistan).

Alexander the Great overthrew the Achaemenids and conquered most of the Afghan satrapies before he left for India in 327 B.C. After Alexander's death in 323 B.C, the eastern satrapies passed to the Seleucid dynasty. About 304 B.C. the territory south of the Hindu Kush was ceded to the Maurya dynasty of northern India. Bilingual rock inscriptions in Greek and Aramaic found at Kandahar and Laghman date from the reign of Ashoka (Asoka; c. 265-238 B.C., or c. 273-232 B.C.), the Maurya dynasty's most renowned emperor. Diodotus, a local Greco-Bactrain governor, declared the Afghan plain of the Amu Darya independent in about 250 B.C.; Greco-Bactrian conquerors moved south in about 180 B.C. and established their rule at Kabul and in the Panjab. The Parthians of eastern Iran also broke away from the Seleucids, establishing control over Sistan and Kandahar in the south.

THE KUSHANS

About 135 B.C. a loose confederation of five Central Asian nomadic tribes known as the Yueh-chih conquered Bactria. These tribes united under the banner of the Kushan (Kusana), one of the five tribes, and conquered the Afghan area. The zenith of Kushan power was reached in the 2nd century A.D. under King Kanishka

(c. 78-144 A.D.), whose empire stretched from Mathura in north-central India beyond Bactria as far as the frontiers of China.

A major branch of the Silk Road passed through Afghanistan, where a trans-shipment centre existed at Balkh. Indian pilgrims travelling the Silk Road introduced Buddhism to China during the early centuries A.D., and Buddhist Gandhara art flourished during this period. The world's two largest Buddha figures (175 feet and 120 feet tall, respectively) were carved into a cliff at Bamiyan in the central mountains during the 4th and 5th centuries A.D.

THE SASANIDS AND HEPHTHALITES

The Kushan empire did not long survive Kaniska, though for centuries Kushan princes continued to rule in various provinces. Persian Sasanids established control over parts of Afghanistan in 241 A.D. In 400 A.D., a new wave of central Asian nomads under the Hephthalites took control, only to be defeated in 565 A.D. by a coalition of Sasanids and Western Turks. From the 5th century B.C. through the 7th century A.D. many Chinese Buddhist pilgrims continued to travel through Afghanistan. One such pilgrim, Hieun Tsang, wrote an important account of his travels, and several of the religious centres he visited, including Hadda, Ghazna (Ghazni), Konduz, Bamian, Shotorak, and Bagram, have been excavated.

PLACE OF VARIETY OF CULTURES

Afghanistan is a meeting place of a variety of cultures. The area was part of the Persian Achaemenian Empire of Cyrus II, the Great during the 6th century B.C. and was conquered in the 4th century B.C. by Alexander III, the Great. After Alexander's death, part of the area came under Seleucid control and part under the Maurya empire of northern India. The Seleucid satrapy of Bactria (Balkh) forged its own kingdom and created a unique fusion of Greek and Indian cultures.

During the 2nd century B.C., Afghanistan became part of the empire of the Kushan king Kanishka (c. 78-144 A.D.). Hindu influence entered Afghanistan by way of the Hephthalites and the Sasanians; during the rule of the Saffarids, in about 870 A.D., Islam became firmly entrenched. The Mongols under Genghis Khan invaded Afghanistan in 1219 A.D. The dissolution of his empire resulted in the rise of independent principalities, and until the 18th century, Afghanistan existed partly within the Mughal Empire of

India and the Safavid Empire of Persia. In the early 18th century, the Persian leader Nadir Shah took control of Afghanistan from the Mughal and was succeeded by his chief bodyguard, Ahmad Khan Abdali, who assumed the name Ahmad Shah Durrani and is considered the founder of the country.

After Durrani's death (1772), the empire foundered because of recurring tribal and family loyalties and the imperialist designs of Russia and Great Britain. The British sought to extend control over Afghanistan in a series of wars (1839-42; 1878-80; 1919), but they were unable to subdue the population, and Afghanistan retained its independence. From the 1930s, a series of cautious and moderate governments under the Afghan monarchy brought political stability. Party politics became less stable in the 1970s, and a 1973 coup supported by the leftist Banner (Parcham) Party ended the monarchy and made Afghanistan a republic. The Banner and the People's (Khalq) Party joined to form the People's Democratic Party of Afghanistan (PDPA) in 1977, and together they seized control of the government in 1978. But friction arose between the two factions, and their Marxist reform programs sparked major rebellions in the countryside by 1979. Soviet troops invaded Afghanistan in 1979 to prevent their Afghan clients from being overthrown, but, in the war that followed, groups of Afghan rebels (Mujahideen) seeking to overthrow the PDPA and expel the Soviets from their country were able to mount a successful guerrilla resistance. Millions of Afghan civilians fled into Pakistan and Iran to escape the destructive Soviet military campaigns against the Mujahideen, who controlled most of the countryside, while the Soviet troops held the cities and those areas near local garrisons. After years of futile effort, the Soviet Union withdrew its troops from Afghanistan by 1989. In April 1992, several rebel factions succeeded in capturing Kabul, overthrowing the communist government, and establishing a provisional Islamic republic. Rival rebel groups fell out among themselves, however, and the country slowly slid into chaos. The Taliban seized power in 1996 and instituted a strict interpretation of Islamic law. The Taliban was overthrown in the aftermath of the September 11 attacks (2001) by a coalition of Afghan and foreign forces led by the United States.

Political Divisions

The country is divided into 30 administrative divisions provinces): Badakhshan, Badghis, Baghlan, Balkh, Bamian, Farah, Faryab,

Ghazni, Ghor, Helmand, Herat, Jozian, Kabul, Kandahar, Kapisa, Kunar, Kunduz, Laghman, Logar, Nan Garhar, Nimruz, Oruzgan, Paktia, Paktika, Parwan, Samangan, Sar-i-Pul, Takhar, Wardak and Zabul.

DESCRIPTION OF THE PATHANS

The true Pathan is the most barbaric of all the races with which they are brought into contact in the Punjab. His life is not so primitive as that of the gipsy tribes. But he is bloodthirsty, cruel, and vindictive in the highest degree; he does not know what truth of faith is, in so much that the saying Afghan-Beiman[1], has passed into a proverb among his neighbours; and though he is not without courage of a sort and is often curiously reckless of his life, he would scorn to face an enemy whom he could stab from behind, or to meet him on equal terms, if it were possible to take advantage of him, however meanly. It is easy to convict him out of his own mouth; here are some of his proverbs, "A Pathan's enmity smoulders like a dung-fire." "A cousin's tooth breaks upon a cousin." "Keep a cousin poor, but use him." "When he is little, play with him, when he is grown-up, he is a cousin; fight him." "Speak good words to an enemy very softly: gradually destroy his root and branch."

PAKHTUNWALI

At the same time, he has his code of honour which he observes strictly, and which he quotes with pride under the name of Pakhtunwali. It imposes upon him three chief obligations, Nanawatai[2], which compels him to shelter and protect even an enemy who comes as a suppliant; Badal[3] and Melmastia[4]. And of these three, perhaps, the last is the greatest. And there is a sort of charm about him, especially, about the leading men, which almost makes one forget his treacherous nature. As the proverb says, "The Pathan is one moment a saint, and the next a devil." For centuries, he has been on the frontier at least, subject to no man. He leads a wild, free, active life in the rugged fastnesses of his mountains; and there is an air of masculine independence about him which is refreshing in a country like India. He is a bigot of the most fanatical type, exceedingly proud, and extraordinarily superstitious. He is of stalwart make, and his features are often of a markedly Semitic type. His hair, plentifully oiled, hangs long and straight to his shoulders, he wears a loose tunic, baggy drawers, a sheet or blanket, sandals and a sheep skin coat with its wool inside; his favourite colour is dark-blue and his national arms the long heavy Afghan knife and the matchlock[5]. His women wear loose shirt, wide wrinkled drawers down to their ankles, and a wrap over the head and are as a rule jealously secluded. Both sexes are filthy in their persons. Such is the Pathan in his home among the fastnesses of the frontier ranges.

CIVILIZED PATHANS

But some of the Pathans have been much softened and by the agricultural life of the plains, so they look down upon the Pathans of the hills, and their proverbs have it, "A hill man is no man" and again, "Don't class burrs as grass or a hill man as a human being." The nearer he is to the frontier the more closely the Pathan assimilates to the original type; while on this side of the Indus, even in the river rain itself, there is little or nothing, not even language, to distinguish him from his neighbours of the same religion as himself. The Pathans are extraordinarily jealous of female honour, and most of the blood feuds for which they are so famous originate in quarrels about women.

PATHAN WOMAN

As a race they strictly seclude their females, but the poorer tribes and the poorer members of all tribes are prevented from doing so by their poverty. Among the tribes of their territory a woman's nose is cut off if she be detected in adultery: and it is a favourite joke to induce a Pathan woman to unveil by saying to her suddenly "You have no nose!" The Pathan pretends to be purely endogamous and beyond the border he probably is so; while even in their territory the first wife will generally be a Pathan, except among the poorest classes. At the same time Pathan women beyond the Indus, seldom if ever married to any but Pathans. They intermarry very closely, avoiding only the prohibited degrees of Islam. Their rules of inheritance are tribal and not Mohammedan, tend to keep property within the agnatic society, though some of the more educated families have lately begun to follow the Mussalman law. Their social customs differ much from tribe to tribe, or rather perhaps from the wilder to the more civilized sections of the nation. The Pathans lived beyond and upon the frontier positions which serve as watch- towers and places of refuge for the inhabitants. Small raids from the hills into the plains below are still common; and beyond the Indus the people, even in those of the British territory, seldom sleep far from the walls of the village.

A DOMINANT RACE

Pathans are the dominant race throughout the whole tract, west of the Indus as far south as the southern border of the tehsil of Derah Ismail Khan[6], which roughly divides the Pathan from the Baloch. On this side of the Indus they hold much of the Chach country of Hazara[7] and Rawalpindi. They have considerable colonies along the left bank of the Indus till, it finally leaves the Salt range, and they hold the northern, portion of the Bhakkar[8]. Besides those tracts which are territorially held by Pathans, there are numerous Pathan colonies scattered about the province, most of them descendants of men who rose to power during the Pathan dynasties of Delhi, and received grants of land-revenue which their children often increased at the expense of their neighbours during the turmoil of the 18th century.

ORIGIN OF THE PATHANS

The Afghans proper claim descent from Saul[9], the first Jewish King, and there is a formidable array of weighty authority in favour of their Semitic origin. Mr. Thorburn quotes in support of their Jewish extraction, "Some peculiar customs obtaining among the tribes of the purest blood, for instance the Passover-like practice of sacrificing an animal and smearing the doorway with its blood in order to avert calamity, the offering up of sacrifices, the stoning to death of blasphemers, the periodical distribution of land, and so forth." And he points out that most of the learned men who reject the tradition of Jewish descent have no personal acquaintance with the Afghan people. The Afghan proper is said still to call himself indifferently Ban-i-Afghan or Ban-i-Israil to distinguish himself from the Pathan proper who is of Indian origin, and the Ghilzai who is probably of mixed Turkish or the Persian extraction. Pashto, the common language of all three, is distinctly Aryan, being a branch of the old Persian stock.

GREAT CONFLICT OF OPINION

There is great conflict of opinion concerning both the origin and constitution of the Pathan nation. Not a few deny that there is any distinction whatsoever between the original Afghan and Pathan stocks, though these are for the most part officers of the frontier who are not brought into contact with the original Afghans. I have however been obliged to adopt some one theory of the constitution of the nation as a basis for my classification of tribes; and I have, therefore, adopted that of Dr. Bellow, who probably has a greater knowledge of the Afghans of Afghanistan as distinct from the Panjab frontier, and especially of the old histories of the nation, than any other of the authorities who have treated the matter. But whatever the origin of Afghans and Pathans proper may be, the nation to which the two names are now applied indifferently in Persian and Pashto respectively, occupying as it does the mountain country lying between the Persian empire on the west, the Indian on the east, the Mongol on the north, and the Baloch on the south, includes as at present constituted of many tribes of very diverse origin. They are without exception Mussalmans and for the most part bigoted followers of the Sunni sect, hating and persecuting Shiahs, or as they call them Rafazis[10].

TRIBAL ORGANISATION OF THE PATHANS

The tribe is probably far more homogeneous in its constitution among the Pathans than among the Baloches. Saiyad, Turk, and other clans have occasionally been affiliated to it; but as a rule people of foreign descent preserve their tribal individuality, being merely associated, and not intermingled with the tribes among whom they have settled. Even then they generally claim Pathan origin of the female side, and the tribe usually descended in theory at least from a common ancestor. The Hamsayah[11] custom, by which strangers are protected by the tribe with which they dwell, is in full force among the Pathans as among the Baloches. But with the former though, it does protect in many cases families of one tribe who have settled with another, it seldom accounts for any considerable portion of the tribe; and its action is chiefly confined to traders, menials, and other dependents of foreign extraction, who are protected by but riot received into the tribe. Thus a blacksmith living in a Utmanzai village will give his clan as Utmanzai; but his caste will of course remain Lohar.[12] The nation is divided genealogically into a few great sections which have no corporate existence, and the tribe is now the practical unit. Though the common name and tradition of common descent are still carefully preserved in the memory of the people. Each section of tribe, however small, has its leading man who is known as Malik, a specially Pathan title. In many, but by no means in all tribes, there is a Khan Khel or Chief House, usually the oldest branch of the tribe, whose Malik is known as Khan and acts as chief of the whole tribe. But he is seldom more than their leader in war and their agent in dealing with others; he possesses influence rather than power; and the real authority rests with the Jirgah[13].

The tribe is split up into numerous clans, and these again into septs. The tribe, clan and sept are alike distinguished by patronymics formed from the name of the common ancestor by the addition of the word Zai or Khel. Zai being the corruption of the Pashto Zoe meaning "son" while Khel is an Arabic word meaning an association or company. Both terms are used indifferently for both the larger and smaller divisions. The stock of names being limited, the nomenclature is exceedingly puzzling, certain names recurring in very different tribes in the most maddening manner. Moreover, the title with genealogical accuracy would allot to a tribe or clan is often very different from that by which it is known for practical purposes, the people having preferred to be called by the name of the junior ancestor who had acquired local renown. The frontier tribe whether within or beyond the border has almost without exception a very distinct corporate existence, each tribe and within the tribe each clan occupying a clearly defined tract or country, though they are in the Indus valley often the owners merely rather than the occupiers of the country, the land and smaller villages being largely in the hands of a mixed population of Hindu origin who cultivate subject to the superior rights of the Pathans. These people are included by the Pathans under the generic and semi-contemptuous name of Hindki; a term very analogous to the Jat of the Baloch frontier, and which includes all Mohammedans who, being of Hindu origin, have been converted to Islam in comparatively recent times.[14]

CONSTITUTION OF THE PATHAN NATION

The words Pathan and Afghan are used indifferently by the natives of India to designate the nation under discussion. But the two words are not used as synonyms by the people themselves. The original Afghans are a race of probably Jewish or Arab extraction; and they, together with a tribe of Indian origin with which they have long been blended, still distinguish themselves as the true Afghans, or since the rise of Ahmad Shah Durrani[15] as Durranis, and class all non-Durrani Pashto-speakers as Opra[16]. But they have lately given their name to Afghanistan, the country formerly known as Khorasan, over which they have held sway for more than a century, and which is bounded on the north by the Oxus, on the south by Balochistan, on the east by the middle course of the Indus, and on the west by the Persian desert; and just as the English and Scotch who early in the 17th century settled among and intermarried with the Irish are now called Irish, though still a very distinct section of the population, so all inhabitants of Afghanistan are now in common parlance known as Afghan, the races thus included being the Afghan proper, the Pathan proper, the Gilzai, the Tajim, and the Hazara, besides tribes of less importance living on the confines of the country.

PATHANS OF INDIAN ORIGIN

The true Pathans are apparently of Indian origin. Their language is called Pashto or Pakhto and they call themselves Pukhtana[17], or Pakhto-speakers; and it is this word of which Pathan is the Indian corruption. They held in the early centuries of the Christian era the whole of the Safed Koh and Northern Suleman system from the Indus to the Helmand and from the sources of the Swat river and Jalalabad to Peshin and Quetta. The Afghans and Gilzais spread into their country and adopted their language and customs; and just as Irish. Scotch, and Welsh speaking the English language are commonly called Englishmen, so all who speak the Pakhto tongue came to be included under the name Pathan. Thus the Afghans and Gilzais are Pathans by virtue, who have retained their Persian speech, are not Pathans; while all five are Afghans by virtue of location, though only one of them is of Afghan race.

EARLY HISTORY OF THE AFGHANS

The origin and early history of the various tribes which compose the Afghan nation are much disputed by authorities of weight who hold very different views. Here the account given by Dr. Bellow has been followed, as it affords a convenient framework on which to base a description of those tribes. But it is said to be doubtful whether the distinction which he so strongly insists upon between Pathan proper and Afghan proper really exists or is recognised by the people; while the Jewish origin of any portion of the nation is most uncertain. But the division of the nation into tribes, the internal affinities of those tribes, and the general account of their wanderings are all beyond question; and the theories which account for them are only accepted generally to serve as connecting links which shall bind them into a consecutive story. The traditions of the true Afghans who trace their name and descent from Afghana, the son of Jeremiah, the son of Saul, and Solomon's commander-in-chief and the builder of his temple, say that they were carried away from Syria by Nebuchadnezzar[18] and planted as colonists in Media[19] and Persia. Thence they emigrated eastwards into the mountains of Ghor[20] and the modern Hazara country. The Afghans early embraced the creed of Islam, to which they were converted by a small body of their tribe on their return from Arabia, where they had fought for Mohammed under their leader Kais. It is from this Kais or Kish, namesake of Saul's father, who married a daughter of Khalid-ibn-Walid, a Qureishi Arab and Mohammad's first apostle to the Afghans, that the modern genealogists trace the descent alike of Pathans, Afghans and Gilzai, or at any rate of such tribes of these races as we have here to deal with and to him they say that the Prophet, pleased with his eminent services, gave the title of Pathan, the Syrian word for rudder, and bade him direct his people in the true path. Meanwhile, about the 5th and 6th century A.D., an eruption of Scythic tribes from beyond the Hindu Kush into the Indus valley drove a colony of the Buddhist Gandhari, the Gandarii of Herodotus and one of the four great divisions of that Pactyan nation which is now represented by the Pathans proper, from their homes in the Peshawar valley north of the Kabul river and in the hills circling it to the north; and they emigrated enmasse to a kindred people on the banks of the Helmand where they established themselves and founded the city which they named Gandhar after their native capital, and which is now called Kandahar.

It is not certain when the Afghan of Ghor moved down into the Kandahar country where the Gandhari colony was settled; but they probably came as conquerors with the Arab invaders of the 1st century of the Mohammedan era. They soon settled as dominant race in their new homes, intermarried and converted the Gandhari, and adopted their language; and in course of time the two races became fused into one nation under the name of Afghans, as distinguished from their neighbouring Pathans.

ZOROASTER'S INFLUENCE

In the first chapter of *Avesta*[21] (Vol. I, p.7), the ancient northern capital Balkh[22] (Bakhdhi) is referred to as a beautiful city with banners floating from its high walls, and there is a persistent tradition that the city was a strong religious centre, the abode of Lohrasp, the father of Vishtasp, patron of Zoroaster, and that Zoroaster himself was slain there when the Turanians stormed Balkh during the Holy War, which Iran had started against Turan. The modern capital Kabul appears in the *Avesta* (Vol. I. p. 9) as Vaekarata, and the region of Helmand[23], the Etymandros of the Greeks, is called

Haetumant in the same Zoroastrian law-book. The modern low-land district of Seistan in south-western Afghanistan was the home of the Zoroastrian dynasty of the Kaianians and the place of the holy lake Kansaoy[24] of the Avesta, from whose waters the savior was to arise at the Millennium. Zoroastrianism appears also to have prevailed in the land during the Parthian and Sasanian eras, from 250 B.C. to 650 A.D although some Greek religious influence may have followed in the wake of Alexander's invasion. Buddhism made some progress in Afghanistan, being traceable chiefly to the Indians, who emigrated from the Indus to the Helmand region after Scythian invasion, and who carried with them, among their sacred treasures, the water-pot of the blessed Buddha himself. This relic was preserved in a shrine near the ancient site of Kandahar, and is described by Bellow, who saw it as a huge bowl carved out of a solid block of dark green serpentine[25].

HISTORY OF AFGHANISTAN

Afghanistan was traversed by Alexander the Great in his march to India, and it is alluded to by Strabo (p. 699) as Lavoaples. This latter term is of particular interest, in that it represents the Sanskrit Gandhara, which lay on both sides of the Kabul river immediately above its junction with the Indus[26]. After Alexander, this region came under the sway of his successors, and Indo-Scythian dynasties. With the latter line of kings, a new religious influence was introduced into Afghanistan, particularly by Kanishka (1st century A.D.)—the faith of the Buddha. By this time nearly all traces of Zoroastrianism had almost disappeared though even in the middle of the 19th century local tradition at Herat told of the destruction of a fire temple there by Mohammedans in the reign of the Tahirid Abdallah[27] (d. 844), while Zoroastrians seem to have flourished in the Pamirs as late as the 13th century. Ruins of three forts ascribed to them still exist in Wakhan[28], where the natives even now treat fire with reverence, being reluctant to blow out a light[29]. Buddhism, however has left not only many small figures at Hidda and Kabul[30], but also some sixty topes, dating mostly from the 4th to 5th century A.D. and found chiefly at Darunta, Chahar Bagh, Hidda, Kabul, Koh Daman, and Kohwat; as well as ruins of elaborate monasteries at Jamalgiri, Takht-i-Bahi, and Sahris Bhalol, which show distinct influence of Greek art. Sculptures of the Buddha have also been found at Bamian[31] both describe Kanishka's magnificent Pagoda at Peshawar.

MOST SENSITIVE AND EXPLOSIVE AREA

One must not give the impression that any problem on the Frontier is clear-cut; here geography jostles with ethnology, strategy with history. Although India stops at the Indus, the plain continues for another fifty miles, and inevitably the rulers of the Panjab had extended their domain to the very edge of it, taking in the Peshawar Valley. The plain has, therefore, come to mark the edge of the Administered Area. But between this boundary and the frontier of Afghanistan (the land of the Hindu Kush) lies a strip what is called tribal territory. Starting from the Little Pamir in the north this runs through Chitral, Kohistan, Bahaur, Khyber, Tirah, Waziristan (the Frontier territory), comprising some 40,000 square miles, once belonged to Afghanistan, and is still largely inhabited by Pathans, the principal race of that country constituting some 3,900,000 of them. The political frontier, therefore, does not constitute an ethnic boundary; though the Pathans inside Afghanistan are usually called Afghans, they are the same race as those living on the Frontier, and recognize themselves as such. If nature had made them a docile, peace-loving people this fact might not have complicated the situation on the Frontier[32].

PATHANS MOST FEROCIOUS

The Pathans are the most ferocious, independent, and warlike race ever known. They may be hated or loved but never can they be ignored. The Pathans, in fact, form an ethnic factor, which allied to the geographical and political factors already outlined, have through the centuries made the North-West Frontier of Pakistan, one of the most sensitive and explosive areas on the earth's surface.

THEIR DIVISIONS

Their own name for themselves is 'Pukhtunwala', or the men who speak Pashtu, their native tongue. They are divided into some dozens of tribes, varying in strength from thousands to hundreds of thousands, and the tribes in turn are divided into 'Khels' which are roughly comparable with clans.

But modern science is somewhat sceptical, pointing out that there is only a facial likeness and the prevalence of Biblical names which in any way can be considered as evidence[33]. So far as anyone can tell, the Pathan is of the Turko-Iranian type, and usually has some Indian and other blood in him. The Red Kafirs and northern Pathans, for example, have undoubtedly intermingled with the

Dinaric[34] race which was thrown out of Russian Turkestan during the Mongol invasions. They are undoubtedly an ancient race. The Greek historian Herodotus speaks of the most warlike of all the Indians, who live around the city of Kaspaturos in the country of Paktuike, and Sir Olaf Caroe had identified Kaspaturos at Peshawar, the unchallenged queen of the Pathan cities, some twelve miles from the mouth of the Khyber[35]. By the tenth century Pathans were already converted to Islam, and by the fifteenth were powerful enough to invade Delhi under Bahlol Lodi and establish a dynasty which lasted seventy-five years.

THEIR APPEARANCE

In appearance, they vary considerably. Some men are light of skin, eye, and hair: many have a long head, aquiline nose, rosy-white complexion, and nut-brown eyes and hair. Other tribes are short in stature, with medium noses, broad faces, and brown complexion. But whatever their strain, the Pathans always, have a remote, proud, independent air about them. They are no one's lackey. For many people they hold a strange fascination; an American State Department official like James Spain having read of them in Kipling, could throw up his career to go in quest of the people, Sir Olaf Caroe, the British administrator could write after many years in the Frontier, 'for the stranger who had eyes to see and ears to hear, always as he drove through the Margalla[36] Pass just north of Rawalpindi[37] and went on to cross the great bridge at Attock[38], there was lifting of heart and knowledge that however hard the task and beset with danger, here was people who looked him in the face and made him feel, he had come home.

APPREHENSION AND FEAR

Not everyone feels this fascination; and for many the excitement of crossing from India to Central Asia has always been mixed with apprehension and fear. This feeling has been beautifully caught by John Masters, as he describes the passage of his heroine, Anne Hildreth at the outbreak of the Second Afghan War in 1899:

"Across the scrub-covered plain approached men with camels. The men had the faces of eagles and walked with a long, slow lifting stride. One of them looked up as he passed by, and smiled at him, expecting the 'salaam' and the answering smile of an ordinary Indian wayfarer. But this was not India. The man stared her down, from pale green Kohl-rimmed eyes. He carried a long rifle slung across his shoulders; a woman; shapelessly swathed in red and black cotton, swayed on top of the camel that he led; a lad of fourthen walked behind the camel; the lad had no beard, but his stride was an exact imitation of his father's lilt, and he too carried a rifle."

SOCIAL LAWS OF THE PATHANS

Revenge

Whether fascinated by the rifle carrying Pathans or not, one must never forget that one of the basic facts about the Pathans is their taste for violence. Thinking of themselves as Afridis, Wazirs, Mahsuds or Mohmands, their absolute allegiance goes to the clan, and they live according to their own law, Pukhtunwali[39]. The first commandment of this law is Badal[40] or Badala. A Pathan is bound to take revenge for any wrong, whether actual or fancied, and whether he has suffered it personally, or his family or 'Khel', most of their grievances stem from "Zar[41], Zan[42], or Zamin[43].' Vendettas may have their origins in trivial, even negative actions, such as a failure to show proper respect, but once begun, they grow in size and violence; because a man has been slighted in a remote village by the Helmand river another may be murdered in Bombay or London or Paris many years later. Some vendettas are ended only after one of the families concerned has been wiped out, or has submitted to the ultimate humiliation of 'nanawatai' and throws itself at the feet of its enemy to ask for mercy.

THE MELMASTIA (HOSPITALITY)

The second law of the Pathans is Melmastia or Mehmannwazi or hospitality, and this is so strong that it takes precedence over Badal on certain occasions; even an enemy who seeks refuge must be granted it, and if necessary protected against his pursuers. The clan leader is called 'Malik', the Arabic title for living; but the Malik has no regal powers and only maintains his positions through constant exertions. He is intensely democratic and the 'Jirga' or council is one of their oldest institutions. Its decisions are ruthlessly enforced. Within the family, however, the husband is a law up to himself. He can, if he wishes, put his wife to death for infidelity, and can deal with a daughter who has disgraced the family just as severely. Pathan women, in fact, outside the small circle of noble families, are little more than chattels.

THE GHILZAS PATHANS

Though the Pathans are the principal people of Afghanistan and the Frontier area, there are other considerable groups, notably the Ghilzais, who claim to be descended from Noah[44]. The probability is, however, that they are of Turkish origin, and come from the Khalaj tribes, who originated to the north of the Tien Shan mountains[45]. Like the Pathans, the Ghilzais are subdivided into clans the Tokhi and Hotak, the Andar, and Taraki. For centuries, the Ghilzais have come down into the Deraj at[46] in the northern Panjab for period of the years with the whole of their families and their animals, and some have stayed. Other tribes of Turkish origin are the Turkmen, who live along the southern bank of the Oxus, and smaller groups like the Kazaks and Chagatia Turks of Northern Afghanistan. To complicate the ethnological picture even further there are Mongol tribes such as the Hazaras, descendants of the Mongal Tartar regiments of Genghis Khan[47]. These inhabit the narrow valleys and rugged passes of central Afghanistan, and are courageous, good-natured people. In the summer, they tend their sheep, and in winter, when their lands are entirely covered with snow, they occupy themselves in spinning and weaving and working in cloth and leather. The Tajiks, a tribe settled chiefly around Kabul and in Kohistan, are of Persian origin, a shrewd, avaricious, but hard-working race, apart from the races and tribes to be introduced as the narrative demands. But even this cursory glance at the people of Afghanistan and the Frontier region should serve to show that it is an ethnological jigsaw of frightening complexity, the relic of a dozen or more lost empires. Along the Frontier alone, there are Kafirs, Chitralis, Mohamands, Shinwaris, Afridis (who guard the Khyber), Orakzais, Darwesh Khels, Bannuchis, Waziris, Dawaris, Marwats, Mahsuds, Bhittinis, Baluchis and in Kalat and Mekhran, the Brahuis and even this list is by no means comprehensive.

THE PATHAN AND BALOCH

If the hypothesis of the identity of the Pathan with Paktyes of Herodotus be true, as is now generally believed these tribes must have been from time immemorial neighbours of India, and even occupants of some part of the territory which is now included in that country, some of them again, were people amongst whom Brahmanism found a favourable reception, and then, Buddhism, the latter especially lingering long in these secluded valleys and on the high road to India which passes near them. The Pathan, however, accepted with equal zeal and devotion the exceedingly narrow and superstitious form of Islam now current amongst them, and anything less like the mild and tolerant character of the Indian Buddhist then. The present temperament and habits of the Frontier men of nowadays can hardly be imagined. At the same time, the Pathan like all highlanders in the tribal stage, has his virile independence and his strict observance of the national code of hospitality and asylum, even towards an enemy — the great solace of his life. It cannot be denied, however, that the epithet of "faithless", universally appended to his name by those who have to deal with him is like most of the proverbial sayings of the countryside, very well deserved, by at all events the hillman. Those who have settled in the plains of the Panjab even though within easy reach of their fellow tribesmen of the highlands, are soon softened by their circumstances, and the more they prosper the less respect they show for the hard life they have left behind. In the interior of India, there is no Province without its quota of this race, and no doubt, looking at the extent to which soldiers of fortune were settled by their victorious employers disseminated amongst them, but not to anything like amount indicated on the face of the returns for regions like Bengal or the peninsula. In the former, indeed, the title of Pathan is regarded as the right of a converted member of a Brahmanic military caste, and further detail of selecting a tribe or clan presents no more difficulty to him than that of a Rajput clan does to an aspiring skill.

THE ETHNOLOGY OF PATHANS (AFGHANS)

The name 'Afghan', first appearing in literature in *Al-Birani India* (tr. *Sachau,* Vol. I. 208), is of uncertain signification; and the Afghans themselves prefer the designation Pashtun or Pukhtun, older form Pashtun, Pakhtun (where their original name Pathan)— a term which Lassen[48] connected with the Paktyas[49] of Herodotus; while Darmesterer *(Chants Populaires des Afghans*[50], has suggested that the Afghans may also be implied by the *liapovittai* of Ptolemy[51]. At all events, the native appellation Pushtun signifies 'mountaineers', and may be implied by the passage in Arrian's *Anabasis*[52], Vol. III, 8.4. Several other names are given by Dorn[53] most interesting being Sulaimani (doubtless from their residence in the Koh-i-Sulaiman, Bani Asif (Asif being the cousin of Afghana), Bani Israil, and of course, Rohillas (mountaineers).

PATHAN LEGENDS (MYTHS)

Though pre-Islamic Afghanistan has no real history, it is rich in legends of its origin. The best known of these traditions, is preserved in a Persian history of the Afghans by Ni'amat Allah, an author of the 16th century[54]. According to his account, the eponymous hero of the Afghans was Afghana-ibn-Irmia-ibn-Talut (Saul). Afghana himself was the commander-in-chief of Solomon's[55] army, and through his executive ability he was enabled to complete the Temple at Jerusalem. When, however, the Israelites were scattered abroad by Nebuched[56] Razzar, Afghana and his children (numbering forty) were also dispersed; and some settled around Ghor and other near Mecca, where they remained for fifteen hundred years, obeying the Torah[57] in all things. With the advent of Muhammad, the contemporary head of the Afghans or 'Israelites', Khalid-ibn-Valid, embraced Islam, and after a long and victorious career, which included exploits in Persia, sent letters to the Afghans at Ghor concerning the coming of Muhammad, where upon several of their chiefs, headed by Kais, went to Medina and there accepted the new faith, spreading it in Afghanistan on their return. The historic worthlessness of this legend is beyond question; and equally absurd is the tradition recounted by Frishta[58], tracing the Afghans to descendants of Pharaoh's nobles, who, after his fall, emigrated to India and settled in the Sulaiman Mountains[59]. Many joined Abraha in his attack on Mecca, but were converted, and later returned to neighbourhood of their early home.

SAINT-SHRINES

Modern Afghanistan, is wholly Muhammadan. Besides official Sunnite orthodoxy however, there exists a mixture of Semitic and Indian belief. To this category belongs the vast number of saint-shrines (Ziarat), which consist either of the domed tomb of some saint or of a heap of stones, enclosed by and usually surrounded by traces of busses[60], a religious phenomenon common amongst both the modern Semites and Hindus.

LEVITATE MARRIAGE

Again, levitate marriage is practised, and it is a grievous affront not to ask for the brother's consent if the widow be again married, though, if she has children, it is considered more honourable for her to remain unwedded[61]. Amongst some tribes, moreover, it is customary for the suitor to serve the father of his would-be bride for many years, as Jacob served Laban for Rachel's sake. The blood feud, as amongst the Semitics, as a sacred duty; and blasphemers, as amongst the Hebrews, are stoned to death[62]. In time of pestilence a buffalo or cow is led through or around the village or camp. The sins of the community are then ceremonially transferred to the victim's head, after which it is either slaughtered and its flesh divided between the priests and the poor, or it is driven into wilderness. This practice, familiar from the Hebrew scapegoat, is also found extensively in Northern India.

DREAMS

Dreams, the evil eye, exorcism, ordeals, and omens are attentively regarded by the Afghans; so that a high wind for three days is a sign that a murder has been committed since, when Cain slew Abel, there was a similar commotion of the elements[63]. The popular demons of Afghan folk-belief are Jinns, Peris, Als, and Parrias. The Jinns and Peris are common to all popular Muhammedan mythology, but the Als and Parrais (the latter word a semasiologic variation of Pari, 'peri') are plainly Indian in origin. The Al, described as a woman, about twenty years of age, with long teeth and nails, eyes curving down the side of the nose, feet turned, heel foremost, and feeding on corpses[64], is manifestly the Churel (female ghost) of northern India, who though she may assume a beautiful form, is in reality Very ugly and black, breastless, protruding in stomach and navel, and feet turned, back[65]. In Armenian folklore the Al is also found, though differing materially from the Indo-Afghan concept[66]. The Parrai, huge monster, with flabby breasts thrown back over the shoulders stretching out her hairy arms to any length and devouring those who answer her plaintive cry for help, is clearly the Indian Rakshasi, the female demon, who plays an important part in Hindu folktales. Though the Afghans are essentially an Iranian people, they thus exhibit a total loss of Iranian concepts, for which they have substituted an amalgam of Semitic and Indian beliefs.

IMPORTANT TOWNS

Kabul: The capital and the largest city, it is in northeastern Afghanistan; near the Pakistan border. It lies at an altitude of 6,000 feet, along both banks of the Kabul river, a very old and historic city.

Kandahar: Capital of Kandahar province, in the south, it is Afghanistan's second largest city. It is rapidly growing centre of farming area. This area is irrigated by water impounded by dams on the Helmand river and its tributary, the Araghndali. An international airport is located just east of Kandahar.

Herat: In eastern Afghanistan, Herat is situated in the heart of the valley of the Hari Rud, an area that produces fruit and grain.

Jalalabad: On the highway between Kabul and Khyber Pass into Pakistan, enjoys a semi-tropical climate and is known for the citrus fruits cultivated in the surrounding areas.

Mazar-i-Sharif: Lies on a well-watered plain, 13 miles south-east of the Soviet Frontier. West of the city are the ruins of the ancient Balkh. Mazar-i-Sharif is situated on a region where vast flocks of sheep are raised.

Ghazni: 75 miles, south-west of the capital, Ghazni is an important commercial city in an area noted for its fine fruits. The city contains the ruins of the great 11th century capital of Mahmud of Ghazni. His mausoleum and two towering minarets still stand.

THEIR OCCUPATIONS

Pashtun tradition asserts that they are descendants of Afghana, grandson of King Saul of Israel though most scholars believe it more likely that they arose from an intermingling of ancient Aryans from the north or west with subsequent invaders, like Scythians and Huns. Several Pakhtun tribes are known to have moved from Afghanistan to Pakistan between the 13th and 16th century, each tribe, consisting of Kinsmen who trace descent in the male bloodline from a common tribal ancestor, is divided into clans, subclans, and patriarchal families. Tribal genealogies establish rights of succession and inheritance and the right to use tribal lands and to speak in tribal council. Disputes over property, women and personal injury often result in blood feuds between families and whole clans; these may be inherited unless settled by the intervention of clan chiefs or by tribal council.

AGRICULTURIST

The Pashtuns are farmers, herdsmen, and warriors. Most tribesmen are sedentary farmers, combining cultivation with animal husbandry; some are migratory herdsmen and caravanners. Large numbers of them have always been attracted to military service.

There are estimated to be about 75,00,000 Pashtun in Afghanistan and 1,40,00,000 in Pakistan. They comprise about 60 tribes of varying size and importance, each of which occupies a particular territory. In Afghanistan, where Pashtuns are the predominant ethnic group, the main tribes — or, more accurately, federation of tribes — are the Durrani in south of Kabul and the Ghilzai in east of Kabul.

MAIN TRIBES

In Pakistan, the Pashtuns predominate north of Quetta between the Sulaiman Range and the Indus River. In the hill areas, the main tribes are, from south to north; the Kakar, Sherani, and Ustarana, south of the Gumal river; the Mashud, Darwesh Khel, Waziri, and Bitani between the Gumal river and Thai; the Turi, Bangash, Orakzai, Afridi, and Shinwari from Thai to the Khyber Pass; and the Mahmand Utman Khel, Tarklani, and Yusufzai north and northeast of the Khyber.

The settled area includes lowland tribes subject to direct administration by the provincial government. The main tribes there are from south to north; the Panuchi and Khatak from the Kurram river to Nowshera, and the Khalil and Mandan in the valley of Peshawar.

THE PATHAN LANGUAGE

Pashto Language

Pashto language, also called Pushtu, Pakhto, or Afghan, Eastern Iranian language spoken by the Pashtun in eastern Afghanistan and northern Pakistan. Its dialects fall into two main divisions; the southern, which preserves the ancient 'sh' (as in Pashto) and 'zh' sounds, and the northern, which has 'kh' (as in Pakhto) and 'gh' sounds instead. Written in a modified Arabic alphabet, Pashto shows strong Indian influence, many Arabic and Persian loanwords, and numerous archaic Persian features. It has been attested from the beginning of the 16th century and became prominent after the creation of the Afghan state in the 18th century. In 1936, Pashto was declared the national language of Afghanistan and instruction in it is now compulsory. Dari is the other official language.

Pashto literature exists certainly from the 17th century, less certainly from the 11th. The national poet of Afghanistan Khushhal Khan (1613-94), chief to the Khatak tribe, wrote spontaneous and forceful poetry of great charm. His grandson Afdal Khan was the author of a history of the Pashtun. Popular mystical poets were Abd-ar-Rahman and Abdal-Hamid, in late 17th or early 18th century, and Ahmad Shah Durrani, founder of the Afghan nation, was himself a poet. The Pashto Academy published a variety of literary works.

PATHANS
SHAHPUR DISTRICT

Before the partition of the Panjab, in 1947, the Pathans numbered 6,747 at the last Settlement. Of these the 2,914 Pashtu-speakers were probably coolies and merchants only temporarily resident in the district. There were one or two Pathan villages in the Bhera (853) and Shahpur (1,746) tehsils but the Pathans were chiefly found in the north-west corner of Khushab tehsil (2,200) in which they owned 23,312 acres of land. Here, we are just on the border of the territory occupied by the cis-Indus Pathans of the Bannu district. They were fairly good agriculturists, but somewhat extravagant and hot-tempered. This tribe owned altogether some 58,000 acres land in the district.

MULTAN DISTRICT

They were mainly agriculturists. During the British rule, they alone of all Muhammedan tribes in the district showed any taste for Government service, and a certain number were recruited in Cureton's Multani Horse, the old XVth Bengal Lancers. They were, as a rule, men of gentlemanly manners, even if in a lowly position in life, but many of them were reckless and extravagant, and they made, as a rule, poor managers of property. The people have a proverb: "Pathan da put, Kadahin Jinn Kadahin Bhut" (A Pathan's son is sometimes a devil, sometimes a demon), that is to say, he is never anything but bad though some are worse than others. This saying is probably a reminiscence of the oppressions practised in the palmy days of Pathan supremacy; for the Pathan as he now is, it seems a bit hard.

Besides the indigenous Pathans, there are a certain number of immigrants, chiefly from Ghazni who come every year in winter and wander about the district, either as builders of walls or as peddlers of fruit, cloth and indigo. They are looked on as excellent workmen, but are a bit turbulent in exacting their dues. They live on the proceeds of begging, and take away with them in the spring the whole of their earnings for the winter. They almost always leave their women behind them in "kirris" in the Deraj at, and this accounts for the small proportion of Pathan women returned in the census.

The Pathans in the district, even those of the ragged wall building species, are commonly addressed by the people as 'Khan' or 'Khan Sahib'. Of the settled Pathan families very few have any knowledge of Pashto, and they maintain little or no connection with their fellow tribesmen on or beyond the border, having in most cases intermarried freely with the native races of the district.

The first settlement of Pathans in the district was in 1901, when they were 8,251 in numbers. Their number rose to 10,106 in 1911. Princes Aurangzeb and Dara Shikoh tried to recover Kandahar from Persia (A.D. 1649-53). The Pathan adherents of the empire, then flocked in large numbers into India, and many of them were located by royal grants in this and the neighbouring districts. The position of the refugees was subsequently much improved by the accession of one of their members, Zahid Khan, to the post of Naib Nazim of Multan. From this time for more than a century and a half of Afghan influence was predominant throughout the Multan province, and the members of the tribe largely profited by its political predominance. But when Multan fell before Ranjit Singh in 1818, their position became much altered. Naturally, Muzaffar Khan had found his most devoted adherents among his own tribe, and these equally naturally, were objects of special dislike to the Sikh agents who took over charge of the province. During the first two years, accordingly, of Sikh rule many Pathans left the district finding their claims lightly regarded by the new rulers. Under Sawan Mal, however, their position again improved. He enlisted them in large numbers into his army, and many who had left their estates after the fall of the city were encouraged to return. During the revolt of Diwan Mulraj they sided for the most part with the British power, and after annexation in 1849 great efforts were made by them to become reinstated in their former position. The Multani Pathans, as might be expected from their history, belong mostly to clans of the Abdali or Durrani stock which, coming from the country round Kandahar and Herat, are little known in the northern frontier districts.

The Pathans of this district live very largely in Multan city or as fairly large landowners in the villages; they are seldom found.

LUDHIANA DISTRICT

The following Pathan tribes are represented in this district: Balozai, Tarban, Barakzai, Daudzai, Ghilzai, Gore, Taman, Khel, Yusafzai, Jangzai. Besides their own women, they will marry among the

Chohans, Mujis and Behues, but will not give their daughters in marriage to them. Pathans number 3,939. They are mostly refugees from Kabul living in Ludhiana town but in an ancient colony of them hold lands in Bahlolpur.

SANGRUR DISTRICT

Pathans live chiefly in the towns, and though they own land, rarely handle the plough. Khiljis, Lodis, Mullagoris, Adilzais, Mamuzais and Umarazais are found in the erstwhile state. Muhammad Namdar Khan Umarzai, was a member of the last Council of Regency, and his elder son Muhammad Ashraf Khan was then Nazim of Karmgarh. His younger son Muhammad Sarif Khan, was a barrister-at-law. The Pathans generally married among themselves and did not practise Karewa.

REFERENCES

1. Dishonest, undependable.
2. The right of asylum.
3. The necessity to revenge by retaliation.
4. Open-handed hospitality to all who demand it.
5. Jazali.
6. A district, 4,216 square miles at the south tip of North-West Frontier Province, west central Pakistan.
7. Division HQ, north Pakistan.
8. A town in Mianwali district Pakistan.
9. First king of Israel (c. 1021-1000 B.C.).
10. Unbelievers, faithless (Kafirs).
11. The neighbour.
12. The blacksmith.
13. A democratic council composed of all the Maliks.
14. Afghan, the races thus included being the Afghan proper, the Pathan proper, the Gilzai, the Tajik and the Bazars, besides tribes of less importance living on the confines of the country.
15. Born 1722, founder of the state of Afghanistan and ruler of an empire that extended from the Amu Darya to the Indian Ocean.
16. A foreigner, an alien.
17. Dr. Bellow and Major James identify them with the Pactiyans of Herodotus, and seem half inclined to connect them with Pacts of Britain, as also the Scythes with the Scots, and certain Pathan and Brahoi tribes with Cambrians and Ligurians.
18. A king of Babylonia (605-552 B.C.) who died in 552 B.C.

19. Ancient of west Asia in a region now in West Iran, South Azerbaijan.
20. A province in the west-central Afghanistan.
21. Also called *Zend, Avesta:* sacred book of the Zoroastrians, containing its cosmogony, law and liturgy, the teachings of the prophet Zoroaster.
22. A town, north-central Afghanistan on the Balkhali river.
23. The chief river of Afghanistan.
24. Kansaoya — modern human.
25. *Races of Afghanistan,* Bellow, p. 22.
26. Ancient India as described in *Classical Literature,* Mc-Crindle Westminster (1901), p. 31n4.
27. *Caraven Journeying and Wanderings,* Ferrier, London, 1857, p. 181.
28. *Roof of the World,* Gordon-Edenburgh, 1876, p. 141.
29. Journey to the *Sources* of River Oxus, New Ed. London, 1872, p. 333.
30. Personal Narrative of a Visit to Ghazni, Kabul and Afghanistan, Vigne, London, 1840, p. 207.
31. In Vigne, *op. cit.,* Wilson, pp. 187-192.
32. Chinese travellers Fa Hsien (Tr. Legge-Oxford. 1886. pp. 33-40).
33. *Encyclopaedia of Britannica*, Vol. 10., p. 475.
34. Dinaric Alaps Serbo-Oroation, south-eastern stern division of the eastern Alps running paralled to the Daimation (Adriatic coast from Trieste and Slovenia South to Alliance).
35. A tribal region, centrally administered.
36. *The Pathans* (550 B.C. — 1957 A.D.), Olat Caroe. p. 79.
37. The capital of Pakistan.
38. On the river Indus, Pakistan.
39. The Pathan code of life.
40. Revenge.
41. Money, gold.
42. Women.
43. Land or property.
44. Also Noe, in the *Bible,* the builder of the ARK at divine direction, that saved human and animal life from the Deluge.
45. One of the greatest mountain systems of Asia, in China and USSR, includes Pobeda. Victory peak 24,406 ft.
46. Alluvial plain in south-west Panjab and SE North-West Frontier Province, west Pakistan, in Dera Ghazi Khan and Dera Ismael Khan.
47. *Encyclopaedia of Britannica*, Vol. I., p. 129.
48. *Ind-Altertumskunde,* Leipzig, 1867, Vol. I., p. 513.
49. Vol. III., pp. 93-102; Vol. II., p. 44; Vol. VII., p. 68.

50. Paris, 1888. Vol. I., Intred p. 182.
51. Book VI., pp. 18-20.
52. Book III.
53. Book II, pp. 62-64.
54. English Translation by Dorn, *History of the Afghans,* 2 Vols. London, 1829-36.
55. A king of Israel in 10th century B.C. famous for his wisdom.
56. King of Babylon from about 604 to 562 B.C. He conquered Jerusalem.
57. Law or Mosaic law or Pentateuch (Judism).
58. Hindu Beg Farishta, the author of *Twarikh-i-Frishta,* in Persian and translated into English by Briggs.
59. Range, central Pakistan, extending C. 250 miles north-south along the west edge of the Indus river valley in east Balochistan province.
60. Journal of a Political Mission of Afghanistan, Bellew, London, 1862. pp. 70-71, 107-109, 386.
61. *Account of the Kingdom of Kabul,* Elphinstone, London, (1015), Vol. I. p. 236.
62. Journal.... Bellow. p. 68.
63. Crooke, *op. cit.* Vol. I. pp. 142, 166-167, 169-170.
65. Vigne, *op. cit.* pp. 211-212.
66. *Wide-Awake Stories,* Steel and Temple, Bombay 1884. p. 318.

BIBLOGRAPHY

Allagh, Ni'mat. *History of the Afghans,* Vol. 2 Tr. Dorn, London 1829-36.

Baluchi Folklore, Vol. II. 1902. pp. 339-41, Vol. 6. pp. 715-396, Vol. XI. pp. 412 a.

Bellow. *Journal of a Political Mission of Afghanistan,* pp. 46-77, London, 1862.

Bhuller, Hughes. "The Chapter on Religions", *Baluchistan Census Report,* 1902.

Fergusson. *History of Indian and Eastern Architecture,* pp. 72-79, 169-84, London, 1876.

Het, Ra. *Baluchi-Nama* (1885), Doui's Translation.

Ibbetson. *Panjab Census Report,* Calcutta, 1882.

Journey to the North of India, Vol. 2., pp. 136-150. London 1838.

Lassen. *Ind. Altertumskunde,* Vol. I., pp. 503-515; Vol. II., pp. 289-360. Leipzig 1867-74.

Melleson. *History of Afghanistan,* 1879.

The Baluchi Race. Royal Asiatic Society of Bengal, 1904.

Willson. *Topes and Sepulchral Monuments of Afghanistan.*

PANJAB CASTES

Principal Divisions of the Pathan Nation

Abstract No. 69, p. 204

Serial No.	Origin and Natural Division and Affinities						Tribal Divisions						Serial No.
1	A Turk stock (Khilchi or Ghizai) combined with Persian blood; the two fused together under a traditional descent from a Persian father and an Afghan mother.		GHILZAI NATION	The Ghilzai proper, combined with tribes of Persian origin, in the male line at least, all claiming descent from the Pathan progenitor Kais.	Baitani Pathans, descended from Baitan, son of Kais.	Mattitribe, descended from Shah Husain, a Persian prince.	By Musa mmat Mahiya		Sarwini			Sarwini	1
2		Doubtful					By Bibi Matto, daughter of Baitan.	Lodi	Khasor			Khasor	2
3									Siani	Prangi		Prangi	3
4										Ismail	Sur	Sur	4
5											Lohani	Tator	5
6		Doubtful										Baluch	6
7												Daulat Khel	7
8												Mian Khel	8
9		Saiyad										Bakhtiar	9
10												Marwat	10
11									Niazi			Nikzi (proper)	11
12												Kundi	12
13									Dutanni			Dutanni	13
14								Ghilzai (proper)	Turan			Hotak	14
15												Tokhi	15
16												Nasar	16
17		Doubtful										Kharoti	17
18									Ibrahimzai			Sulemankhel	18
19												All Khel	19
20												Aka Khel	20
21												Ishaq	21
22												Andar	22
23												Tarakki	23

BILOCH, PATHAN, AND ALLIED RACES

Principal Divisions of the Pathan Nation

Notes	Present Holdings	Country, district, of forntier to which each tribe appertains.	Sections of the report in which each tribe is described.	Serial No.
No longer found in Afghanistan, Maler Kotla family belongs to the Saripal clan.	Scattered through Hindustan	Hindustan	398-9	1
A small tribe of doubtful origin.	Trans-Indus Salt Range of Derah Ismail Khan	D.I. Khan	399-402	2
Gave Lodi dynasty to Delhi } Migrated to Hindustan	Scattered through Hindustan	Hindustan	399	3
Gave Sur dynasty to Delhi.			398-9	4
Insignificant, since crushed by Nadir Shah.	Tank in Derah Ismail Khan	Derah Ismail Khan District	401	5
Small and uncertain origin. Affiliated to No. 7.	Derah Ismail Khan Salt Range and cis-Indus plain		399-402	6
A sect of the Mamu Khel, to the would of which it has given its name. Rulers of Tank are the Katti Khel sept.	Part of Tank in Derah Ismail Khan		401	7
Often held to include No. 9.	The central part of trans-Indus Derah Ismail Khan		401-2	8
A Saiyad tribe from Persia, affiliated to No. 8. See also No. 29.			401	9
Known as Spin Lohani, Nos. 5 to 9 being called Tur Lohani.	South-west portion of Bannu district	Bannu	404	10
Chief clans, Isakhel, Sarhang, Mushani.	Both banks of Indus in north of Bannu		403	11
The Niazi descent not always admitted.	Part of Tank in Derah Ismail Khan		402	12

Notes	Present Holdings	Country, district, or frontier which each tribe appertains.	Sections of the report in which each tribe is described.	Serial No.
Unimportant...	Pawindah tribes with home in the Ghilzai country, between Jalalabad and Kelat-Ghilzai. Their families spend to winter there, and the summer in the Derah Ismail Khan plains. For a description of the Pawindah traffic, see Section 398.	Derah Ismail Khan District.	402	13
Gave the Ghilzai kings to Kandahar. Crushed by Nadir Shah			402	14
Once the principal Ghilzai tribe			402	15
Their Ghilzai origin is doubtful			402	16
Their Ghilzai origin is doubtful			402	17
Not the principal Ghilzai tribe			402	18
Unimportant				19
Unimportant				20
Chief clan is Yusuf Khel				21
The Musa Khel Kakar are affiliated to this tribe			402	22